ETHNIC RELATIONS IN THE UNITED STATES

APPLETON-CENTURY-CROFTS SOCIOLOGY SERIES

John F. Cuber, editor
The Ohio State University

Sociology: A Synopsis of Principles, 2nd edition
> by JOHN F. CUBER

The Crime Problem
> by WALTER C. RECKLESS

Social Movements: An Introduction to Political Sociology
> by RUDOLF HEBERLE

Ethnic Relations in the United States
> by EDWARD C. MCDONAGH and EUGENE S. RICHARDS

Ethnic Relations
IN THE UNITED STATES

Edward C. McDonagh

Associate Professor of Sociology
University of Southern California

and

Eugene S. Richards

Chairman, Division of Social Sciences
Texas Southern University

New York

APPLETON-CENTURY-CROFTS, INC.

Foreword

AN OUTSTANDING POINT of this analysis of ethnic relations is its biracial authorship. One member of this team, having received his early
training in the North concerning ethnic relations in the United
States and having taught in a university in the South and studied
ethnic attitudes there as a resident, brings a well-seasoned and objective viewpoint to bear upon this complicated field of human
relations. The other member, having been born and reared in the
South, having made racial adjustments according to the prevailing
mores in the South, and having received his advanced sociological
training in a university located in a city essentially Northern in its
ethnic outlook, also contributes a remarkably well-balanced and sane
viewpoint to the analysis of ethnic materials. Moreover, these two
disciplined and balanced points of view are so well integrated that
the book appears to have been written by one author, not by two.

The most original aspect of this treatise is its status approach. No
other book dealing with ethnic and race relations has attempted
this unique presentation. The analysis of ethnic relations in terms
of four aspects of status offers a rewarding frame of reference and
brings to light explanations of ethnic discriminations not hitherto
made clear. This special sociological approach is an exceptionally
fruitful one for all students of ethnic relations.

The part of the book on understanding ethnic relations carries
many implications regarding methods of possible removal and even
of prevention of ethnic prejudice. In placing emphasis upon the
formation and functioning of attitudes the authors point to the
heart of racial discrimination.

It will be a great day for the reputation of the United States in
many countries when the discriminations due to differences in ethnic
status in this country are largely overcome. When the struggle to
even up ethnic status is won throughout the world, one of the major
causes of world conflicts will be eliminated. To the achievement of
such a far-off goal this book points the way.

Emory S. Bogardus

University of Southern California

v

Preface

THIS BOOK is designed to present a factual picture of the statuses of selected ethnic groups in the United States in terms of a definite frame of reference. While intensive studies have been made of each of these ethnic groups or minorities, no effort has been made to integrate this information into a definite pattern. It is our opinion that a common frame of reference will reveal many of the same problems for each of the ethnic minorities discussed. Also, it will be observed that a common frame of reference may disclose the comparative position each of these ethnic groups occupies in the status system of the United States. We have selected four aspects of status for analysis: social or interpersonal, educational, legal, and economic. The above selection was made after a careful consideration of the many possible areas of life that might be utilized. Objective data and empirical findings have been relied upon to depict the status of each ethnic minority.

In order to present a better understanding of the ethnic minorities under consideration a number of readings have been included. These readings have been selected to give the reader the "feel" for the problem at hand, and so arranged as to become an organic part of the work. Further, it is our intention to present readings that will reflect the major problem, or problems, confronting each of the ethnic minorities discussed.

The book is organized into three major parts: *understanding* ethnic relations, *analyzing* ethnic relations, and *improving* ethnic relations. In the first part of the book the nature of ethnic groups and some of the major considerations growing out of ethnic relations are examined. Seven ethnic minorities are analyzed in the second part of the book in reference to four aspects or facets of status. The findings of research and programs for improving ethnic relations are presented in part three.

It has been the goal of the authors to present the major ethnic minorities in the United States with fairness and objectivity. In some instances writers in this field have permitted their personal feelings and prejudices to enter unduly into the discussion of ethnic relations. We have attempted to avoid bias by (1) having a definite frame of reference, (2) utilizing objective data, and (3) having a biracial authorship wherein each author freely questioned the ideas and points of view of the other.

E.C.M.

E.S.R.

Contents

Part Two

ANALYZING ETHNIC RELATIONS

CONTENTS

Part Three

IMPROVING ETHNIC RELATIONS

Tables

I

UNDERSTANDING ETHNIC RELATIONS

I

Race and Ethnic Minorities

Introduction

BASIC TO AN understanding of race and ethnic relations are four central terms: *nationality, cultural group, race,* and *ethnic minority.* Many Americans use these terms as though they refer to groups that are differentiated by the same standards. Thus, it is not unusual to hear people refer to the French race, the German race, or the Italian race without realizing that these are nationality groups and that all three are members of the Caucasoid subgroup of the human race. In the thinking of some people two nationality groups that are members of the same racial group, the Chinese and Japanese, are considered as different racial groups. The Mexican, a nationality group consisting of several "races" and various mixtures of these, is commonly considered as a specific racial group. Also, the Jew, a cultural group, is referred to as a racial group by many Americans.

Still more baffling are the ways by which one ethnic minority, the Negro, is legally defined in the United States as a racial group. Mangum [1] shows this confusion in his attempt to answer the question: Who is a Negro? A Negro might be a person with one-eighth or more of Negro blood; he might be one with any quantum of Negro blood; he might be anyone of mixed blood who descended from Negro ancestry; or he might be any person of African descent.[2] Surely, these uses and definitions are not accurate and cannot be defended as contributing anything to a scientific understanding of ethnic relations. Inasmuch as a common understanding of the con-

[1] Charles S. Mangum, Jr., *The Legal Status of the Negro* (Chapel Hill, N. C.: University of North Carolina Press, 1940), pp. 1-17.

[2] Mangum is using the term "blood" synonymously with the term ancestry. For a logical but exaggerated statement of this problem see the novel by the late Sinclair Lewis, *Kingsblood Royal* (New York: Random House, Inc., 1947). See also the fascinating book by Walter White, *A Man Called White* (New York: Viking Press, Inc., 1948).

cepts nationality, cultural group, race, and ethnic minority is important each will be explained according to the way it will be used in this work.

Nationality Group

A *nation* is described usually as a number of people, living in a definite geographic area, under a common government. A national is considered as a person who is a citizen of, a subject of, or who is born in a specific nation. Thus it is logical to define a *nationality group as a number of people who maintain citizenship within or were born under the jurisdiction of a specific government.* In other words nationality groups are characterized by *political membership* and not by any other standard. Therefore, within any nationality group there may be many physical types. This observation is illustrated well in the United States where practically all physical types are considered as nationals of the United States. It is equally true that physical types that are similar enough to be classified as a "race" may be found to have membership in many nationality groups, as the Indians of the United States, the Indians of Mexico, and the Indians of Canada.

Cultural Group

Culture has been defined by Tylor as all knowledge, beliefs, art, morals, law, custom, and any capabilities acquired by man as a member of society.[3] Thus, *cultural groups are characterized by similarity in ways of thinking and doing in some one or more of the basic areas of life.* If we use Wissler's universal culture pattern as a guide, the cultural group will possess similarity in any one or more of the following basic areas of life: language, material traits, mythology and scientific knowledge, family life, religion, art, government, property, or war. The extent to which a person is considered as a member of a cultural group is dependent upon the degree to which he has acquired the cultural complexes that are expected of members of that group. Hence, a cultural group may include members of various racial or nationality groups. For instance, in the United States members of various racial and nationality groups have accepted the ways of thinking and doing that are expected in the United States. These ways of thinking and doing are centered around the belief in the democratic system of government, the Christian religion, the free

[3] Edward B. Tylor, *Primitive Culture* (New York: Brentano, 1924), p. 1.

enterprise economic system, and the importance and dignity of the individual.

Race and Ethnic Minority

For the purpose of this text the most important of the concepts under consideration are race and ethnic groups. During the past several years many students of anthropology have presented articles, monographs, and studies in which they have attempted to clarify the meaning of the concept "ethnic group," and to illustrate how race differs from ethnic group. One of the most interesting and illustrative readings on this subject follows:

ON THE PHRASE 'ETHNIC GROUP' IN ANTHROPOLOGY [4]

M. F. ASHLEY MONTAGU

The objections raised by Huxley and Haddon to the term race seem to me unanswerable. In my book on the subject I fully adopted these authors' views and urged that the term *race* be avoided and the phrase *ethnic group* be substituted in its stead. I suggested that the term race be altogether dropped and that the four great divisions or races of mankind—the Negroid, the Mongoloid, the White, and the Australoid—and the ethnic groups comprising them be spoken of.

These suggestions have created considerable interest, and principally as a result of Huxley and Haddon's admirable treatment of the subject there has been a noticeable tendency to avoid the term *race* and to use the phrase *ethnic group* instead. This is a tendency which should, it seems to me, be encouraged. A number of objections have, however, been privately raised by several interested students both to the phrase *ethnic group* and to the suggestion that the term *race* be eliminated or its use narrowly restricted. Since the matter is rather more than of merely terminological importance, it deserves to be further discussed.

There are two distinct classes of opposition, one is opposed to the suspension of the term *race* on the ground that races do exist within the human species, and that it would therefore be unjustifiable to drop the term. The other agrees that it might be better to drop the term altogether, but is opposed to the use of the phrase *ethnic group*

[4] M. F. Ashley Montagu, "On the Phrase 'Ethnic Group' in Anthropology," *Psychiatry: Journal for the Study of Interpersonal Processes*, Vol. 8 (Feb., 1945), No. 1, pp. 27-33. Used by permission of the author and the William Alanson White Psychiatric Foundation.

because the term "ethnic" in its modern usage has come to possess cultural implications. A more satisfactory term, they suggest, should be found.

In what follows I shall attempt to meet these objections, and show why the term *race* should be dropped when used with reference to man and the phrase *ethnic group* adopted.

"The true meaning of a term is to be found by observing what a man does with it, not what he says about it." By the same token "the proper definition of a concept is not in terms of its properties but in terms of actual operation." Experience defined in terms of experience, in terms of the procedures and instruments used to measure it. By adopting such principles, the concepts used will always be based on experience and will more or less correspond to it. All that is then needed in order to test the validity of the concepts is to reduce them to the terms of experience, and examine them in the light of the range of actual observations and the operations used in arriving at them; for it must be remembered that every observation partakes of the nature of an experiment—a good or a bad experiment in which all experience is subject to error.

Since the concepts are determined by the operations used in making observations, and the concepts are synonymous with those operations, as the operations are so will the concepts be. In examining the meaning of such terms as *race* and *ethnic group* the task then must be to reduce them to the operations which have been performed in arriving at them.

In the case of the term *race* the analysis of the operations by which its meaning has been determined presents no great difficulty. The historical background of these operations constitutes another matter.

Racism and the popular conception of race may, in this paper, be defined as the belief that "heredity" is the prime determiner of all the important traits of body and soul, of character and personality, of human beings and nations. This is "race," a fixed and unchangeable part of the germ plasm which, transmitted from generation to generation, unfolds in each people in a typical expression of personality and culture.

That there is nothing in reality relating to man which corresponds to such a conception has been proven to the satisfaction of all who are prepared to accept the facts of science. Upon this all scientific students of the subject are agreed. Why not say this, then, it is argued, state the facts, and retain the term *race* in its scientific sense? Why throw the baby out with the bath water? There are races, aren't there, so why deny their existence? What is this "racephobia"?

To this, reply may be made that it is not sufficient to state facts, for when facts are confronted by prejudices, the facts are subordinated. A thing may be utterly ridiculous scientifically, and yet have a tremendous force socially, as for example, "race" prejudice. But what is a *race* in the scientific sense? Are scientists agreed and clear upon that point? It is all very well to assert that because there are races of plants and other animals there must be races among mankind. There may be, indeed, but these are words; the operational proof is lacking, and the whole subject, as everyone knows, is in a state of chaos. Where a subject is as confused as is that which deals with the classification and relationships of man it is the better part of wisdom to set no limits to it, but to leave the whole question open until such time as some acceptable conclusion concerning it may be reached. The term *race* as it is customarily used in anthropology begs the whole question from the outset, asserting what in fact requires to be proved.

Professor C. S. Coon, for example, after spending eight pages discussing the term *race,* arrives at the following definition: "A race is ... a group of people who possess the majority of their physical characteristics in common. A pure race, if the term must be used, is one in which the several contributing elements have become so completely blended that correlations fail to reveal their original combinations. At the same time the processes of selection and of response to environmental influences have given the resultant blend a distinctive character."

This is the type of definition of *race* accepted by most physical anthropologists. On the other hand, the conception of a *pure race* as defined by Coon is somewhat original. A pure race, according to this definition, is such a perfect "omelette" that the ingredients entering into it can no longer be distinguished. The reference to the "original combinations" entering into the formation of the *pure race* suggests a mystical belief in pure races in that other sense in which the phrase is customarily used, namely, as groups of human beings that are unmixed or relatively unmixed. All this adds to the confusion.

If the definition of *race* is reduced to the operations which have been utilized in arriving at it, it is found to be based on comparisons of extreme types with one another. This procedure began very early, and proof of it is to be found in the writings of the founder of physical anthropology, Friedrich Blumenbach, and in those of other early writers on anthropology. Blumenbach, for example, in the third edition of his famous work (*De Generis Varietate Humani*), classified mankind into five principle varieties, the Caucasian, Mongolian, Ethiopian, American, and Malay. Later writers took over Blumenbach's classification, and substituting the term *race* for his *variety,* proceeded to elaborate upon his classification by creating more and more *races*. This fractionating method eventually terminated in such extremes as the classification of peoples by the shapes of their heads, as longheaded or broadheaded *races!* The problem appeared much simpler to the early students of the subject than it actually is, and as Linton has remarked, "Unfortunately, the early guesses on these points became dogmas which still have a strong influence on the thought of many workers in this field."

Such a definition of *race* as that quoted from Coon can strictly be applied only to the larger divisions of mankind, the Negroid, the Caucasoid, the Mongoloid, and the Australoid, the latter being a subdivision of the Caucasoid, for it is these groups alone whose members "possess the majority of their physical characters in common." But, it may be asked, are there no distinguishable subgroups within these larger divisions or stocks? Most certainly there are. Let me illustrate the nature of these subgroups by an example. The Australoid or Archaic White division is made up of four distinguishable subgroups, the Australian aborigines, the Pre-Dravidian peoples of India, the Veddas of Ceylon, and the Ainu of Japan and neighboring islands. These four subgroups have been placed in the Australoid division because they share a majority of their physical characters in common. But the Ainu has a white skin, in fact, were he to be seen on any American street no one would turn round to look at him twice, he would pass as a white American. The Ainu could be classed with the Caucasoid division of mankind without doing the slightest violence to the reality or to the logic of systematics. Had he been discovered in Jerusalem instead of Japan the Ainu would most certainly have been so classified. This introduces an important consideration, namely, the factor of geographic distribution in determining racial classifications. The Australian aborigines are restricted to the continent of Australia, no other types of aborigines are there found. The same is true of the Vedda of Ceylon, they being the only surviving aborigines in that island. Similarly, the Pre-Dravidian peoples are for the most part isolated in the jungles of Southern India. The interesting thing about these four groups is that each of them is restricted to a particular circumscribed geographic range or locality, and each of them as a whole is physically distinguishable from the others as a whole, *but only on the basis of a very small number of traits determined by statistical analysis.*

In short, were it not for the fact of their geographic delimitation it would with the exception of the Ainu—and he is a special case, be very difficult, and in a large proportion of cases impossible, to distinguish a Vedda of Ceylon, from an Australian aboriginal, or from a Pre-Dravidian Indian. Furthermore, it would be very difficult to distinguish between a Papuan and an Australian aboriginal, and excessively difficult to distinguish between Veddas, Pre-Dravidians, and innumerable Dravidian peoples in India; finally, it would be equally difficult to distinguish an Ainu from innumerable swarthy whites.

What makes the small number of physical traits by which these groups differ from one another striking is the fact that they are found in these markedly delimited geographic groups. Were any of the members of these groups found freely distributed among, for example, the peoples of India, they could not have been arbitrarily recognized as constituting members of a unique group.

The anthropologist makes a brave attempt to separate out of mixed populations groups of persons who together possess the majority of their physical characters in common, and then refer each such group to some particular *race*. But the fact is that however like the superficial appearance of persons or of groups, their genetic character—genotype—may be very different. As East and Jones put it many years ago, "... one must be very cautious about drawing genetic conclusions in the human race based upon the possession of particular traits, in the absence of proof of a long-continued isolation. Long isolation, it must be assumed, aided in segregating some well-marked human subspecies. It may serve a purpose to continue to accept certain of these types as implied in the terms, white, yellow and black races. Yet one must not forget that real isolation belongs to past epochs. There has been no small amount of interbreeding between even these main types, and the magnitude of the interbreeding between subraces is largely a matter of historical record. Traits originally characteristic of certain peoples because of isolation and the consequent inbreeding have been shifted back and forth, combined and recombined. It is positively misleading, therefore, to classify Englishmen as resembling, Danish, Norman, Pictic, or Bronze Age types, as is done in more than one work of authority. Even if it were known what the average values of the various characters of these early strains were, there is little reason for believing that a present-day individual bearing one or two particularly striking traits should be felt to hold any closer relationship to the strain in which these traits are supposed to have arisen than his neighbors who are without them. He may have outstanding characters which were once peculiar to a comparative pure race; but he probably carries these characters as a mere matter of Mendelian recombination. It is wholly possible, for example, that a tall, blue-eyed, dolichocephalic Frenchman really possesses less of the so-called Nordic factors than a short, dark-eyed round-head."

Where the anthropologist deals with a fairly homogeneous isolated group he is on reasonably safe ground in assuming that regardless of the original elements entering into its formation he is now dealing with a statistically more or less genetic unity. It would be perfectly permissible to call such groups *races*. This cannot, however, be said for groups which have been created by separation out of mixed populations. Anthropologists have attempted to extract Nordic, Alpine, Dinaric, and many other *races* out of such mixed populations. The attempt was certainly worth making, but it has always remained something less than certain that the resulting extracts represented what they were believed to be.

There are, then, three different senses in which scientists have used the term *race*. The first refers to the larger divisions of mankind, the Negroid, Caucasoid, Mongoloid, and Australoid, as races; the second refers to geographically isolated groups exhibiting a similarity of physical characters as races; and the third refers to groups arbitrarily created by selection of persons conforming to the selector's view of what *race* they belong or should belong to.

Customarily used by physical anthropologists these three concepts of *race* are incompatible with one another, and have been responsible for a considerable amount of the existing confusion relating to the classification of mankind. This in itself would not, however, constitute a sufficient reason for rejecting the term *race,* but it would constitute a good reason for demanding a clarification of the whole subject and a more clear-cut definition and restricted use of the term. Were there any promise of success in urging such a view, I should be the first to do so. But in view of the fact that the whole subject has become so fogged and beclouded in the course of the years, it seems to me that the only real clarification which will ever be achieved on this matter will come by way of starting anew, from the very beginning, with a fresh and unbiassed eye, in short, by leaving the whole question of *race* in mankind open until such time as all the relevant facts have been brought to bear upon it. As a first step towards arriving at such a clarification it is highly desirable to banish all question-begging terms from our vocabulary. Because the term *race* is such a question-begging one I, at least, am in complete agreement with Huxley and Haddon that it should be dropped, and the non-committal term *ethnic group* and all that it implies be adopted in its stead.

Another reason for dropping the use of this term is that the scientific, the racist, and the popular senses in which it is used have all become inextricably mixed and confused. It must be the task of the anthropologist to create order and clarity where so much disorder and misunderstanding exists. As Francis Bacon remarked, "Truth comes more easily out of error than out of confusion." The time will come when it will be possible to use the term *race* in a legitimate scientific sense, with clarity and with reason. That time is not now.

It must be realized that in its confused sense the term "race" has become a public possession. The public must be re-educated to look upon the subject in a sensible manner. In its present public sense the term is a meaningless congeries of errors resulting in endless confusion and wrong action. It was Voltaire who said that "As long as people believe in absurdities they will continue to commit atrocities." In discussing the suggestion that the term *race* be dropped in favor of the concept of an *ethnic group* my respected friend Professor Conklin has demurred to the suggestion and asks, "What's in a name?"

I answer with the bare facts that the death of millions of Jews, Poles, Russians, Germans, and millions of others is in the name "race," for it is in the name of "race" that the Nazis have brought death to these millions. In the name of "race" millions of our Negro fellow-citizens are oppressed and deprived of their just liberties, in the name of "race" native peoples all over the world have been, and continue to be, forced to live the life of inferior beings in a world where "white supremacy" is the rule. In the name of "race" lies death and lifelong misery for the greater part of mankind. That, it seems to me, is enough of an indictment for one name to bear.

But, it may be replied, what is to prevent people from developing "ethnic group prejudices," and "ethnic group problems"? By changing names conditions are not changed. By changing names problems are not solved.

All these are more than questionable statements and particularly in view of the fact that it has never been suggested that names be changed. The conception of an *ethnic group* is quite different from that which embraces the usual concept of *race*. The phrase *ethnic group* represents a different way of looking at populations, an open non-question-begging way, a tentative, non-committal, experimental way, based on the new understanding which the sciences of genetics and palaeo-anthropology have brought. One term is discontinued, but another is not merely substituted for it, on the other hand a new conception of human populations is introduced replacing the old one, which is now dropped, and a term suitable to this new conception is suggested. The old concept is *not* retained and a new name given it, but a new concept is introduced under its own name. That is a very different thing from a mere change of names. The new conception embraced in the phrase *ethnic group* renders the possibility of the development of "ethnic group prejudice" quite impossible, for as soon as the nature of this conception is understood it cancels the possibility of any such development. It is a non-contaminating, neutral concept.

What, then, is the concept embraced in the phrase *ethnic group?* Unlike the term *race* the phrase *ethnic group* leaves all question of definition open, it is concerned only with populations said to exhibit a certain undefined amount of physical homogeneity. An ethnic group may be described as one of a number of populations, which populations together comprise the species *Homo sapiens,* and which individually maintain their differences, physical and cultural, by means of isolating mechanisms such as geographic and social barriers. These differences will vary as the power of the geographic and social—ecologic—barriers vary. Where these barriers are of low power, neighboring ethnic groups will intergrade, or hybridize, with one another. Where these barriers are of high power, such ethnic groups will tend to remain distinct from each other or replace each other geographically or ecologically.

One of the important advantages of the term *ethnic group* is that it eliminates all the question-begging emphases on physical factors and differences, and leaves the question completely open, with the emphasis now shifted to the fact—though it is not restricted to it— that man is predominantly a cultural creature. The change in emphasis seems to me a highly desirable one. It does not exclude any possible physical factors, but it leaves the question of the latter open for further dispassionate analysis, omitting any suggestion that the physical factors are determinate, fixed, or definable or that they are in any way connected with mental or cultural factors. This is not simply to replace one term by another, but represents a definite shift in emphasis based upon a fundamental difference in view. It is the view of the person who is anxious to avoid the consequences of thinking in "fuzzy" terms.

The second group of objectors while accepting the description of the kind of human population covered by the phrase *ethnic group* objects to the term "ethnic" on the ground that it "smacks" of the cultural, while that with which the anthropologist is actually concerned represent physical groups which he attempts to delimit on the basis of their physical differences, and not on the basis of their cultural ones.

This is what one might call the perfect objection, for by its very means it is possible to prove the supreme desirability of the phrase *ethnic group.*

In the first place the objection that the term ethnic is too evocative of cultural associations is no objection at all; for while the term "ethnic" is by no means exclusively cultural in its connotation, for the very reason that it retains some cultural associations it is desirable to use it in connexion with man. For what is man if he is not and has not always been a creature of culture? Those who begin their tomes with the declaration "Let us now study man as a physical organism" scarcely ever pause to consider that that is impossible without doing violence to the facts. Man is not a physical organism. He is what he is as a result of the operation of physical *and* cultural factors, and so it has always been. It is necessary continually to emphasize this fact for it is continually being forgotten.

There can be little doubt that man's evolution in his manifold variety has been influenced to an appreciable extent by processes which were primarily cultural in nature, and that the majority, if not all, of the groups of mankind owe something of their present physical character to processes initiated by cultural factors. Furthermore, it is clear that human groups are more or less always in process of change as the result of the operation of such factors. It is desirable to have a term which incorporates within it a recognition of these facts. "Ethnic" is such a term.

SUMMARY

The advantages of the phrase ethnic group are: first, while emphasizing the fact that one is dealing with a distinguishable group, this non-committal phrase leaves the whole question of the precise status of the group on physical or other grounds open for further discussion and research; second, it recognizes the fact that it is a group which has been subject to the action of cultural influences; and third, it eliminates all obfuscating emotional implications.

As for the suggested dropping, restricted, or suspended use of the term "race," there are many parallels for this in science. Possibly the most striking one within recent years is the dropping of the term "instinct" by psychologists for reasons very similar to those which make the term "race" undesirable. Similarly in anthropology the term "savage" has been completely dropped as corresponding to a concept which has no counterpart in reality. Retardative concepts like "phlogiston," of eighteenth century chemistry, have been dropped never to be re-adopted. It may be that the terms "instinct" and "race" may some day be shown to have more than a merely verbal validity, but until that time it would, in my opinion, be more in accordance with the scientific spirit to suspend altogether the use of these terms not alone in psychology and in anthropology, but also in common parlance.

Thus, the most comprehensive and meaningful of the four terms discussed is that of ethnic minority. This group, the ethnic minority, includes characteristics of both the racial and cultural groups. An ethnic group usually possesses some continuity through biological descent, and its members share a distinctive social and cultural tradition.[5] Ethnic groups tend to have cultural attributes in common to a greater degree than biological characteristics. As a result, there are many ethnic groups, but few races. *To qualify as a member of a particular ethnic group, the physical characteristics are kept in the background and the knowledge and values of a particular culture in the foreground.*

Thus, the trend among social scientists is to use the word "ethnic" rather than "race," because race refers to physical characteristics while ethnic implies a combination of physical and cultural uniquenesses. After giving attention to this problem for many years, Reuter concluded more than twenty-five years ago that the term race had changed from a concept involving physical traits to a sociological concept.[6] In emphasizing the use of race as a sociological concept Reuter points out that the term is used largely to determine the status of the individual, and to provide a basis for differential treatment. Regardless of how invalid the concept of race may be from a scientific standpoint, it has come to have a significant meaning as a symbol around which feelings, attitudes, and preferences are clustered. Scientists have discarded the concept of a pure race and prefer to think of the various ethnic groups as important building blocks in the structure known as the *race* of mankind. To preserve the scientific meaning of the concept race, there is no question in the minds of the writers that some word should be adopted that will include the social and cultural implications usually associated with the term race. Because of the broader connotations of the concept ethnic, the writers are using ethnic instead of race wherever possible throughout this work.

Ethnic Minorities Considered

The ethnic minorities discussed in this book are derived from two sources: (1) groups included in the race classification by the Bureau of the Census of the federal government of the United States, and (2) groups that are often referred to as belonging to a distinct ethnic minority in the United States, and are thus considered as "different" from the so-called "typical Americans."

The population of the United States is composed of representatives of each of the major racial, nationality, and cultural groups of the

[5] For an interesting discussion of this point see the work by Robin M. Williams, Jr., *The Reduction of Intergroup Tensions* (New York: Social Science Research Council, 1947), p. 42.

[6] Edward B. Reuter, *The American Race Problem* (New York: Thomas Y. Crowell Company, 1927), pp. 23-25.

world. However, the Bureau of the Census in its population reports included six ethnic groups in 1950, as is indicated in Table I. Thus, the following groups are selected from the classification of the United States Bureau of the Census as ethnic groups for study in this book: native-born whites, foreign-born whites, Negro, Indian, Japanese, and Chinese.

Two other groups are considered by many persons in the United States as being different enough from the "typical Americans" to be socially classified as distinct ethnic groups: Mexicans and Jews. All persons who were born in Mexico, or are descendants of persons who were born under the flag of Mexico, are usually classified as Mexicans by lay persons. The differences accredited to Mexicans are many; including differences in physical appearance, cultural standards, family life, standards of living, religious life, and occupational outlook.

Jews will also be considered as an ethnic minority because they are described operationally as such in the content of the stereotypes of the average layman. Jews are often thought to be different from

Table I: DISTRIBUTION OF THE POPULATION OF THE UNITED STATES BY ETHNIC GROUPS *

Ethnic Group	Number
Total Population	150,697,361
Native-born Whites	124,780,454
Negro	15,042,692
Foreign-born Whites	10,161,168
Indian	343,410
Japanese	141,768
Chinese	117,629
Other races	110,240

* Seventeenth Census of the United States, *Population* (1950). Advance tabulation prepared by Bureau of the Census for this work, Oct. 10, 1952.

"typical Americans." These differences have been ascribed as physical, national, and cultural.[7] Cultural differences, largely religious, seem to be the basic differences between Jews and the "typical Americans." These religious differences have probably, through endoga-

[7] See the chapter "The Jewish Type" in the work by Louis Wirth, *The Ghetto* (Chicago: University of Chicago Press, 1928), pp. 63-74. Note also the statement by the Premier and Defense Minister of the new state of Israel, David Ben-Gurion, which gives some of the differentiations of the Jew from other people: "There have been only two great peoples: the Greeks and the Jews. Perhaps the Greeks were even greater than the Jews, but I can see no sign of that greatness in the modern Greeks." *Time* (August 16, 1948), p. 25.

mous marriages, contributed to the evolution of certain physical traits that are similar among some Jews.[8]

In the process of selection the following groups have been chosen that are distinct enough from "typical Americans" to be classed as out-groups, and as groups that are socially and culturally defined as ethnic minorities in the United States: Negro, Jew, Indian, Japanese, Chinese, Mexican, and foreign-born white. Although it is recognized that most of these are not racial groups, it is difficult to deny that they are considered as *different* from "typical Americans" by most people in the United States. In other words, these ethnic minorities have certain physical or cultural traits that make for *visibility;* and therefore, recognition that affects interpersonal relations with numbers of the majority group.

ETHNIC CONTACTS IN THE UNITED STATES

Ethnic relations arise from two basic factors: (1) consciousness of differences which are defined as ethnic, and (2) contacts among the groups that are regarded as ethnically different.[9] In areas where all persons are considered as members of the same ethnic group, or as persons possessing similar physical and cultural characteristics, there can be no significant ethnic relations. If there is sufficient geographic isolation, groups with marked ethnic differences may live near one another without developing ethnic relations. Thus, physical and cultural differences that are defined as ethnic, combined with contact, are essential for the foundation of most ethnic relations phenomena.

Ethnic relations evolve out of ethnic contacts, and may be thought of as a special type of social relations. MacIver and Page describe social relations as relations, or ties, that have been established and are determined by mutual awareness.[10] Applying this interpretation to this work it is possible to think of ethnic relations as the associations that have evolved among people who are regarded as physically and culturally different. Hence, ethnic relations in any geographic

[8] See R. A. Schermerhorn, *These Our People: Minorities in American Culture* (Boston: D. C. Heath and Company, 1949), pp. 30-32.

[9] Adapted from a definition by Edgar T. Thompson, *Race Relations and the Race Problem* (Durham, N. C.: Duke University Press, 1939), pp. 3-7.

[10] R. M. MacIver and C. H. Page, *Society: Its Structure and Changes* (New York: Rinehart and Company, Inc., 1947), p. 4.

area are better understood if something is known about the nexuses that have been established among the human groups residing in that area, as well as the social factors that have conditioned the development of the existing associations or ties.

Ethnic group contacts are determined to a considerable extent by the statuses which have been assigned the various ethnic groups by each other and by the larger group of which they are a part.[11] Thus, in many ethnic relations situations persons are judged in terms of the status of the ethnic group to which they are assigned rather than in terms of individual attainment. Perhaps the most useful concept describing these group judgments of persons of diverse ethnic affiliation is the functioning of *stereotypes*. A more thorough discussion of stereotypes is presented later, but it is worth noting at this point that social relations referred to as ethnic relations are often based on group derived statuses. As a consequence, individual ethnic relations tend to hinge upon group defined traits that are often not found in other areas of social relations where judgment is more often based on individual merit than upon a group label.

The controversial nature of ethnic relations has become one of the most challenging problems confronting social scientists and interested lay persons in the United States. The constant conflict resulting from ethnic contacts serves as a perpetual warning to democratic minded persons in the United States that there is a long way to go if Americans are to meet intelligently the charges made against our form of democracy. In many written and verbal statements a splendid showing has been made in the attempt to solve this problem. The Bill of Rights has served as an invitation to many oppressed people throughout the world to enter the United States in search of peace and justice. Many Americans have enjoyed the reference that the United States is the great melting pot of the world, accepting members of all racial, nationality, cultural, and ethnic groups, with a variety of physical, religious, cultural, and ethnic characteristics and molding these many variations into a somewhat uniform type.

However, in some outward reactions Americans overlook, or fail

[11] Note the observation of Hiller that the subject of sociology, in its simplest terms, is that of human relations. These relations are social since they consist of the conduct and inclinations of persons, with particular reference to one another. Hence, social relations are discovered through a study of the rules, standards, and usages prescribing conduct between persons and groups. E. T. Hiller, *Social Relations and Structures* (New York: Harper and Brothers, 1947), p. 2.

to consider, the social organization that exists in the nation as a result of the various racial, nationality, cultural, and ethnic groups which constitute the population of the United States. Little consideration is given to the fact that many ethnic groups are deprived of the right to become a part of the *melting process* although they are politically a part of the United States. In fact, the "melting" accomplished in the United States has been somewhat limited when specific reference is made to the Negro, Mexican, Jew, and Oriental. Perhaps for these groups the melting pot has been too similar to the compartmentalized pressure cooker. Such things as laws, attitudes and opinions, economic restrictions, educational limitations, and residential segregation have been used as social partitions, thus forcing many elements of the population of the United States to melt separately from the major parts of the population.

To understand ethnic contacts in the United States today, we must be familiar with the terms "in-group" and "out-group" relations as described by Sumner.[12] The *in-group* is described as the group toward which the persons composing it have attitudes of loyalty, sacrifice, brotherhood, comradeship, peace, lawfulness, and orderliness. *Out-groups* are composed of those who possess characteristics—social, cultural, or physical—that differ in any marked way from those possessed by members of the in-group. Towards out-groups, attitudes of hatred, contempt, hostility, and suspicion are encouraged. *Ethnocentrism* is developed for the in-group, and all out-groups are looked on with contempt.

In the United States the in-group is composed of what Gregory and Bidgood describe as "typical Americans."[13] These authors describe the typical Americans as those persons who cannot be called by any other particular designation except American. They are the native-born white people of native-born parents, who are followers of the Christian religion. The "typical Americans" have been defined by others as the WAP (White-American-Protestants). They are considered as the typical Americans in the sense that they are the most numerous type, and in the sense that they possess the traits that are termed American. All racial, cultural, nationality, or ethnic groups that possess traits differing in any marked way from those possessed

12 William G. Sumner, *Folkways* (New York: Ginn and Company, 1906), pp. 12-13.
13 Edward W. Gregory and Lee Bidgood, *Introductory Sociology: A Study of American Society* (New York: Prentice-Hall, Inc., 1939), pp. 322-325.

by the typical Americans are considered as members of out-groups, and are assigned a general status which differs from that of other ethnic groups in the United States.

There is a tendency in the United States to refer to ethnic minorities that differ from "typical Americans" as racial groups. Hence, as previously indicated, some Americans refer to the Jews as a race, the Germans as a race, the Greeks as a race as though these groups were as distinct biologically as some Negroes and some Mongolians. Not only are these pseudo-races referred to as distinct races by many Americans, but they are socially assigned a status which is lower than that assigned the "typical American" by the average person in the United States. Thus, in order to understand the ethnic relations pattern in the United States, it is almost as essential to give the same consideration to the groups that are socially and culturally *defined* as racial groups as may be given to the human groups that are physically differentiated by scholars as distinct racial groups. In other words, *from the standpoint of common sense it is as important to know what a majority of Americans believe a race to be as to know how physical anthropologists define a race.*

In summary, the concept "race" has three general definitions in the United States: (1) to the zoölogists race may be a matter of a few genes in the chromosomes, (2) to the anthropologists a matter of inherited characteristics that more or less standardize particular sub-groups of man, and (3) to the authors of this book *"race" may be an ethnic group of persons, which because of a combination of physical and cultural characteristics, is assigned a differential status from the majority group in the United States.* The last of these definitions is thought to be the most important in understanding "race" or ethnic, contacts in the United States. This is true since *the relations that are developed among groups in the social order are determined more by the stereotyped thinking of the average person than by scientific definitions and classifications.* Further, the status of individuals is largely determined by the ethnic membership that is *assigned* by other individuals and groups. In fact, for the average person in this country ethnic identification or visibility is a traffic signal of human interaction. Certain ethnic groups pass swiftly along with the green light, other ethnic groups may pass with caution, and for some ethnic groups there is no entry to the main highway of life, except by cautious detours.

A FRAME OF REFERENCE

Although the process of the assimilation of ethnic groups has been going on in the United States for some time, it is evident that few social scientists, and still fewer laymen, have given careful consideration to it in all of its many aspects. [14] Several social scientists have isolated some specific ethnic minority and have given excellent descriptions of the problems confronted by the selected ethnic group.[15] Treatises have also been published that give descriptions of the problems and limitations facing the various minority racial and nationality groups in the United States.[16] Some writers have elucidated on the contributions of various ethnic groups to the social, economic, educational, and cultural development of the United States.[17] Other writers have analyzed the attitudes and opinions of the majority group toward minority groups.[18] Some authors have

[14] Perhaps the best coverage is found in two recent books: (1) Charles F. Marden, *Minorities in American Society* (New York: American Book Company, 1952); and (2) Paul A. F. Walter, Jr., *Race and Cultural Relations* (New York: McGraw-Hill Book Company, Inc., 1952).

[15] Emory S. Bogardus, *The Mexican in the United States* (Los Angeles: University of Southern California Press, 1934); R. D. Dubois and E. Schweppe, *Jews in American Life* (New York: Thomas Nelson and Sons, 1935); Yamato Ichihashi, *Japanese in the United States* (Palo Alto: Stanford University Press, 1932); O. J. Janowsky, *The American Jew* (New York: Harper and Brothers, 1942); Carey McWilliams, *Prejudice: Japanese-American* (Boston: Little, Brown and Company, 1944); Gunnar Myrdal, *An American Dilemma* (New York: Harper and Brothers, 1944); Edward B. Reuter, *The American Race Problem* (New York: Thomas Y. Crowell Company, 1927); Edgar T. Thompson (Durham, N. C.: Duke University Press, 1939); Willis D. Weatherford and C. S. Johnson, *Race Relations* (Boston: D. C. Heath and Company, 1934); E. Franklin Frazier, *The Negro in the United States* (New York: The Macmillan Company, 1949); Leonard Broom and Ruth Riemer, *Removal and Return: The Socio-Economic Effects of the War on Japanese Americans* (Berkeley: The University of California Press, 1949).

[16] F. J. Brown and J. S. Roucek, *One America* (New York: Prentice-Hall, Inc., 1952); Louis Adamic, *A Nation of Nations* (New York: Harper and Brothers, 1945); Carey McWilliams, *Brothers Under the Skin* (Boston: Little, Brown and Company, 1943); Bertram Schriede, *Alien Americans* (New York: Viking Press, Inc., 1936); Donald Young, *American Minority Peoples* (New York: Harper and Brothers, 1932); H. P. Fairchild, *Race and Nationality* (New York: The Ronald Press, Inc., 1947); Charles F. Marden, *Minorities in American Society* (New York: American Book Company, 1952); Paul A. F. Walter, Jr., *Race and Culture Relations* (New York: McGraw-Hill Book Company, Inc., 1952).

[17] Brown and Roucek, *op. cit.;* Lee M. Friedman, *Jewish Pioneers and Patriots* (New York: The Macmillan Company, 1942); Cecil Roth, *Jewish Contributions to Civilization* (New York: Harper and Brothers, 1940); F. F. Schrader, *Germans in the Making of America* (Boston: The Stratford Company, 1924); Harry Sundley-Hansen, *Norwegian Immigrant Contributions to America* (New York: The International Press, 1921).

[18] Emory S. Bogardus, *Immigration and Race Attitudes* (Boston: D. C. Heath and Company, 1928); H. W. Odum, *Race and Rumors of Race* (Chapel Hill: University of North Carolina, 1943); Bruno Lasker, *Race Attitudes in Children* (New York: Henry

made presentations of the multiplicity of laws that have been passed
in an attempt tō define the legal status of minority groups.[19] These
studies have done a splendid job of probing the departmentalized
aspects of American race and ethnic relations.

To understand ethnic contacts in the United States there is a
definite need to synthesize these separate approaches into a single
study that will reflect the many social and cultural partitions in the
American "melting pot." It is believed that this task can be done
best by the formulation of a frame of reference that can be used to
analyze the contacts which exist among the various ethnic minorities
in our population. This frame of reference must of necessity take
into consideration the areas of our social life that provide the material
out of which the previously discussed partitions are constructed. It
should also indicate something of the comparative nature of ethnic
relations.

In retrospect, there have been societies of *structured* ethnic relations throughout the history of man. These structured ethnic relations
or contacts have served to create positions of submission and subordination on the part of some ethnic groups, and positions of dominance and superordination on the part of other ethnic groups. Prior
to the entry of the British into India the caste system in that country
rigidly assigned status upon hereditary group membership. Professor
Kingsley Davis observes that there are at least six common features
in the Indian caste system: (1) membership is dependent upon hereditary factors and is fixed for life; (2) selection of the marriage partner
is endogamous; (3) in general, contact with other castes is further
limited by restrictions on associating with, touching, dining with, or
eating food cooked by outsiders; (4) consciousness of caste membership is emphasized by the distinctive caste name and by the individual's identification with his caste in the eyes of the community;
(5) the caste usually is united by a common traditional occupation;
and (6) for the most part the relative prestige of the different castes
in any community is well established and jealously guarded.[20] How-

---

Holt and Company, Inc., 1929); Samuel A. Stouffer, *The American Soldier,* see especially
Chapter 10 titled "Negro Soldier" (Princeton: Princeton University Press, 1949); Samuel
Tennebaum, *Why Men Hate* (New York: The Beechhurst Press, 1948).

  19 Charles S. Mangum, *The Legal Status of the Negro* (Chapel Hill: University of
North Carolina Press, 1940); Milton R. Konvitz, *The Alien and the Asiatic in American
Law* (Ithaca: Cornell University Press, 1946).

  20 Kingsley Davis, *The Population of India and Pakistan* (Princeton: Princeton University Press, 1951), p. 162.

ever, the lines of demarcation between the various castes seem to be disappearing in the urban areas of India, and under the great leadership of Indian statesmen. In short, there seems to have been a trend toward *flexible* ethnic relations during the last several hundred years in much of the world. Only simple societies have been able to maintain inflexible ethnic contacts because of ignorance. However, with the coming of knowledge concerning the recognition of individual differences regardless of hereditary group membership, such a system becomes difficult to maintain.

It has been especially difficult to perpetuate a structured ethnic system in the United States because of its open class system and firm belief in mobility. Speakers and writers depict with great pride the change of status of an individual; hence, the often quoted quips "from rags to riches," "from log cabin to White House," "from bank clerk to bank president," and "from private to general." Inasmuch as the free enterprise system is defended largely in terms of individual mobility, ethnic contacts in this country must of necessity take on some of this capillarity.

An intensive survey of the many factors that could be used as a frame of reference in presenting ethnic relations in the United States revealed that the following four aspects of *status* seemed significant: (1) attitudes and opinions in the creation of *social status;* (2) laws and the interpretation of legislation in the formation of *legal status;* (3) rates of literacy and grade completion in the gauging of *educational status;* and finally, (4) per capita earning, property ownership, and types of occupation in the determination of *economic status.*

Status is thought of as a position or rating that an individual or group receives from evaluators. Statuses are often thought of as the building blocks in the social structure.[21] These building blocks have been distinguished into two types by professor Ralph Linton, namely, *ascribed status and achieved status.* Linton observes that *"Ascribed statuses are those which are assigned to individuals without reference to their innate differences or abilities. They can be predicted and trained for from the moment of birth. The achieved statuses are, as a minimum, those requiring special qualities . . ."* [22] In other words the factors of sex, age, and ethnic identifiers are probably best thought

---

[21] For a comprehensive discussion of the nature of status see the book by John Bennett and Melvin M. Tumin, *Social Life* (New York: Alfred A. Knopf, Inc., 1948), chap. 6.

[22] Ralph Linton, *The Study of Man* (New York: Appleton-Century-Crofts, Inc., 1936), p. 115.

of as making for ascribed status. If the individual gains recognition in some area of social life by hard work and creative expression, we usually define such behavior as reflecting a superior achieved status. These two types of status are seen in many ethnic relations. Majority members who place the individual of a minority group in a low status category, solely because of his minority group membership, have ascribed that status to him. If on the other hand, he is appreciated as an individual with special abilities and talents, then his status may be defined as an achieved one. Is it always true that the ascribed status tends to be low for an ethnic minority group and that the achieved status usually reflects a high status for the ethnic minority individual?

It is difficult to evaluate individuals and groups in terms of merely one aspect of status; rather, they are to be appreciated in reference to several aspects or components of status. Hence, the caste-class school of ethnic relations is accepted largely in respect to its class aspects rather than its rigid "caste" dichotomy. It must, however, be pointed out that status is a composite position of worth and that an evaluation in terms of one aspect does not present a fair picture. Again, it must be admitted that there is considerable *change* in the status of individuals and ethnic minorities through the realization of ambitions.

The attitudes and opinions possessed by the members of one ethnic group toward another ethnic group serve to explain the role of *social status* in a dramatic way. Attitudes and opinions point out why there may be ethnic group rejection by the majority group. They serve to indicate why social distance is present within and between groups, and the problems involved in minimizing this social distance. They sometimes reflect how personalities of the various groups will act in social situations in which other groups are involved. It is known that all of these attitudes and opinions toward ethnic groups are learned and not inherited. Most nursery school children are devoid of ethnic consciousness. However, as the child passes through the primary grades, he begins to learn about the predominant stereotypes associated with particular ethnic minorities. The home is likely to be the factory of ethnic preference and prejudice, and the school the testing ground for the child's recently acquired attitudes toward ethnic groups. It may not be amiss to suggest that the intercultural education movement is attempting to challenge these home derived ethnic attitudes before they become accepted as facts. One of the great problems confronting the intercultural educational movement is the degree of acceptance of ethnic prejudices.

Laws and proposed legislation are of value in understanding the *legal status* of an ethnic minority. They represent the formal expression of the majority group toward minority groups. On the one hand, laws are a guide as to what the minority groups can expect in the larger group. On the other hand, they serve to regulate and restrict the behavior of minority groups. Laws can also be interpreted as a standard by which justice of the majority group may be measured. In a representative democracy laws are especially important in setting an ideal for fair play that ethnic contact may approach.

The *educational status* of a group is measured largely by its rate of literacy, its degree of schooling, its intellectual reputation, and the educational facilities available to the group. Degrees of literacy and schooling are responsible, to a large extent, for the intellectual achievement of the members of the ethnic group. Thus, the intellectual achievement attained by an ethnic group will aid in determining its status by indicating the extent to which it is capable of participating in the activities of the larger group. Again, the educational facilities available to a minority group will point up the future possibilities of an ethnic group, especially since vertical or upward social mobility is so dependent upon professional and cultural training. Educational status is related in a very direct way to the other facets of status.

The *economic status* of a minority group is best understood by finding out its occupational characteristics, its per capita earning, and the extent of property ownership. Fundamental to the three factors is occupational status, since the per capita earning is largely determined by occupation. Further, the possibility of extending property ownership depends greatly upon earning capacity. All these economic factors play a definite part in determining the general status of any group even where other restrictions are not present. This observation is especially true under a free enterprise system, where an individual's monetary ability plays an important part in one's social mobility.

SUMMARY

As will be shown throughout this book, the several ethnic groups discussed have attained various statuses as judged by the frame of reference criteria. An ethnic group with a low legal status may possess

a high educational status. Or one with a high social status may possess
a low economic status. A similar pattern may be repeated when attention is given to other criteria. Hence, under educational status an
ethnic group might be evaluated as "low" for degree of schooling
attained, but "high" for availability of educational facilities. Another
ethnic group might rank high for occupational status, but low for
home ownership. If careful consideration is given to the possibility
of individuals and groups attaining various statuses as judged by
the suggested criteria, it is manifest that much of the argument over
the caste-class dichotomy in America is wasteful. In summary, instead
of ethnic groups being classified according to one aspect of status,
they should be evaluated in terms of particular statuses with a special
reference for time and regions. It is hoped that the status approach
utilized in this work will give both the dynamics and structure of the
ethnic relations considered.

PROBLEMS FOR STUDY AND DISCUSSION

1. List several of the human groups of which you are a member. Give
the major criteria that are used in determining membership in each of
the groups listed.

2. Point out how the following human groups differ from each other:
nationality group, cultural group, race, and *ethnic group.*

3. List and explain the major criteria that have been used by authorities in classifying humans according to races. Select a classification of races
by some authority, and show which criteria were used in making the
classification.

4. List and explain the major arguments that have been advanced
against the use of the term "race."

5. Keeping in mind Montagu's interpretation of ethnic group, make
a list of the major ethnic groups that you are familiar with, and point
out how these groups differ from each other.

6. Point out the differences between the phrases "melting pot" and
"compartmentalized pressure cooker" as used in this chapter. Select the
one of these phrases which you think gives the best description of the
ethnic relations pattern in the United States, and give reasons for your
selection.

7. Outline and explain the frame of reference that is to be used as a
guide in explaining ethnic relations in this book.

SELECTED READINGS

ASHLEY MONTAGU, M. F., *Man's Most Dangerous Myth: The Fallacy of Race*
(New York: Columbia University Press, 1945), pp. 1-61.

BROWN, Francis J., and ROUCEK, Joseph S., *One America* (New York: Prentice-Hall, Inc., 1952), pp. 1-14.

GILLIN, John, *The Ways of Men: An Introduction to Anthropology* (New York: Appleton-Century-Crofts, Inc., 1948), pp. 97-145.

GOLDENWEISER, A., *Anthropology* (New York: Appleton-Century-Crofts, Inc., 1937), pp. 13-36.

MACIVER, R. M., and PAGE, C. H., *Society: An Introductory Analysis* (New York: Rinehart and Company, Inc., 1949), pp. 384-407.

MARDEN, Charles F., *Minorities in American Society* (New York: American Book Company, 1952), pp. 1-42.

REUTER, Edward B., *The American Race Problem* (New York: Thomas Y. Crowell Company, 1927), pp. 23-37.

ROSE, Arnold and Caroline, *America Divided* (New York: Alfred A. Knopf, Inc., 1948), pp. 256-276.

SCHERMERHORN, R. A., *These Our People* (Boston: D. C. Heath and Company, 1949), pp. 3-53.

SOPER, Edmund D., *Racism: A World Issue* (New York: Abingdon-Cokesbury Press, 1947), pp. 15-49.

WEATHERFORD, W. D., and JOHNSON, C. S., *Race Relations* (New York: D. C. Heath and Company, 1934), pp. 3-21.

WALTER, Paul A. F., Jr., *Race and Cultural Relations* (New York: McGraw-Hill Book Company, Inc., 1952), pp. 3-24.

II

Ethnic Prejudice

Introduction

BASIC TO AN understanding of ethnic relations in the United States
is an insight into the nature and function of prejudices which may be
defined as preconceived judgments toward persons, beliefs, or objects.
It is imperative to know the content of ethnic prejudices and something of their sources. We must recognize that in discussing ethnic
prejudice there is a tendency to give almost complete attention to its
negative aspects. A danger in over emphasizing the negative aspects
of prejudice is to make all prejudgments appear to be directed *against*
persons or groups. Is not strong in-group feeling actually a form of
positive prejudice?

Ethnic prejudice may take the form of covert attitudes with no
overt manifestation of internal feelings. Hence, a person may have a
prejudice against the Chinese, but nevertheless treat persons in this
ethnic group with fairness. His personal feelings are kept in the background of social action. However, these attitudinal prejudices become serious when the feeling reaction is carried into a social situation and discrimination becomes the end product. It is obvious that
when an ethnic prejudice becomes manifest in social action a social
problem has been created.

Considerable discussion has centered on the problem of what to do
about ethnic prejudice. One school of thought suggests that every
effort be made to reduce prejudice. Thus, it is hoped that by exposing
the nature of prejudice the carriers of prejudice would soon discard
them. However, it may be that certain prejudices are integrated into
the personality in such a way that they become major behavior patterns, then the dislodging of these prejudices borders, at least, on the

field of psychiatry.[1] Thus, for prejudices on the level of personality organization, a clinical approach might be necessary. There seems to be no question that some positive gains can be achieved by refuting ethnic prejudice, but it might be a time consuming enterprise for the amount of change resulting.

On the other hand, a second school of thought believes that personal prejudices are in themselves not too significant. *The goal should be to stop discrimination.* This approach to the problem of ethnic prejudice observes that discrimination is in itself a primary cause of related prejudices. Here is a vicious circle. For example, if a particular ethnic group is denied the opportunity to attend public schools, it may as a consequence appear unintelligent. Thus, prejudices against this ethnic group may be perpetuated by its *apparent* low intelligence. However, when schools are opened equally to all members of society, it is no longer possible to link prejudice to conditions resulting from discrimination. It is clear that if acts of discrimination can be controlled, many of the so-called "reasons" for prejudice may disappear. Organized opposition to discrimination may become a serious program, and at some future date destroy the foundations of ethnic prejudices. Yet, such a program can only move as fast as the general public will accept social democracy in the area of ethnic relations. It must not attempt to move so fast that the opposition will become stronger. In many instances the "stop discrimination" school of thought is represented by the fair employment legislation in a number of the states and cities of the nation. Common sense would not suggest initiating such a program in some areas in the deep South, at the present time, but only in such areas as may benefit by the program.

Ethnic *preference* and ethnic *prejudice* are sometimes confused. It is possible to select persons for jobs or as guests without necessarily expressing ethnic prejudice. In some instances persons not selected may jump to the conclusion that there is an ethnic prejudice against them because they were not selected. Upon examination it may be that the *selected* persons are preferred for traits not possessed by the omitted persons. *Preference is usually on an individual basis while prejudice tends to operate in terms of groups of persons.* Actually the omission of a particular ethnic group from some function does not

---

[1] Else Frenkel-Brunswik and N. Nevitt Sanford, "The Anti-Semitic Personality: A Research Report" in Ernst Simmel, ed., *Anti-Semitism, A Social Disease* (New York: International Universities Press, 1946), chap. 6.

in itself prove ethnic discrimination or prejudice. However, if there
are no individuals within a given group who could be invited to the
party, or selected for the occupation, then it may suggest the operation of a group prejudice that discriminates. *When an entire group
has no range of individuals of attraction, the evidence is strong that
the judgment is closed by prejudice.*

Two readings have been selected to illustrate the nature, development, and functioning of prejudice. The first reading, by Joseph B.
Gittler, gives an excellent analysis of the nature and development of
prejudices. The second reading, excerpts from a bulletin distributed
by the Department of the Army, treats some of the practical phases
of the development and functioning of prejudices. These readings
are understandable enough to speak for themselves, therefore the
authors will not attempt any further interpretation of them.

❚ MAN AND HIS PREJUDICES [2]

JOSEPH B. GITTLER

Much has been written about the threat of prejudice in under-
mining our democratic institutions. Specific instances can be cited
in regard to the growth and magnitude of man's antipathy to man.
It seems worth while, therefore, to analyze carefully the fundamental
nature of these antipathies in order more sanely to comprehend
these savage undercurrents in our daily lives and so attack the problem at its most vulnerable point.

The universality of men's aversion for one another is shocking in
its implications. Negativism, once a problem relegated to the confines of early childhood, has become the order of the day among
the adults of every nation. Group is pitted against group: the Protestant attacks the Catholic, the Catholic attacks the Jew, the Jew mis-
trusts the Gentile, the white persecutes the Negro, the Negro turns
on his white enemy. Whatever the manifestations of these antagonisms—whether it be racial, ethnic, religious, or class—a common
thread runs through the entire web of intergroup relations.

There are many general types of prejudices, but two loom largest
on the horizon, dwarfing all others. The first of these is easily recog-
nizable. It is the kind that expresses itself in overt forms of group
opposition. It is the type of prejudice that keeps certain groups from
living in designated areas of a city, bars them from schools, deprives

[2] *The Scientific Monthly,* Vol. 69 (July, 1949), pp. 43-47. Used by permission of the
author and the American Association for the Advancement of Science.

them of voting privileges, and excludes them from hotels, clubs, theater, and so on.

This sort of prejudice is vicious from the standpoint of democratic principles, but it is in a relative sense capable of being handled, since it expresses itself in tangible forms—usually in terms of ordinances and statutes. Given enough people who desire a change, the laws can be repealed. It would appear that there is an ever-growing number of people who are sincerely interested in effecting such a change.

Even if this overt form of prejudice does not express itself in law but in the form of a "gentlemen's agreement" to keep members of various minority groups from obtaining their rights of citizenship—in gaining admittance to hotels, schools, and stores—it is still concrete enough to allow for direct treatment. It involves specific persons who are *principally* responsible for this form of discrimination, and these, skillfully approached through influential community leaders who are truly desirous of mitigating the problem, can be made to modify their rulings.

Thus, by group action to change the law, or through the pressure of public opinion, some of these discriminatory practices may be obviated.

There is another type of prejudice, however, which is more basic and more insidious, difficult to rout from its hidden recesses, and almost impervious to any form of concrete action. It is subtle, covert, and non-institutionalized. An illustration will serve to indicate the nature of this form of prejudice.

I once boarded a city bus and chanced to sit next to two women, residents of a southern city. One lady was telling the other that she had just visited Mrs. R——— at the hospital.

The other lady said, "Oh yes, I know who she is. She is your neighbor, isn't she?" "Yes," was the reply. "And she is a Catholic, isn't she?" "Yes," was the reply again. "And on the other side of you lives Mrs. S———, doesn't she? And I think she is a Catholic too?"

"Yes, she is," the first lady replied. And then, with a sigh of resignation and suffering, she revealed her attitude by adding, "and you know what it feels like to be hemmed in by two Catholics."

No objective listener could deny that here at least was one prejudiced individual. It is true that this type of prejudice is unlike the first. The "hemmed-in" woman would probably not attempt to have instituted laws, ordinances, or even agreements that would keep her Catholic neighbor from visiting any hospital she might please. Their children probably play with one another; they may attend the same school. And one would not imagine that she would be ready to institute, or formally banish, the Catholic children from the neighborhood or theaters.

The revealed prejudice had not reached the form of outright discrimination, true. But prejudice was there. It was not formalized
but rather it existed as a kind of folkway prejudice, a kind of "general feeling of againstness." It reflects the general folk atmosphere.

Although it is unlike the first type, sometimes, if not quite frequently, it may lead into the first type, given an economic or political crisis, when the general negativism might easily turn to outright
discrimination, scapegoating, or persecution.

Nazi Germany has given us our best case in point. In the days of
the Weimar Republic the Jews enjoyed legal freedom and political
tolerance. Laws forbade educational, economic, and legal discrimination. Legal guarantees, however, were not safeguards against folk
feeling. A preponderance of evidence exists to prove that many
Germans continued to feel differently toward the Jew than they did
toward the non-Jew. When a crisis situation arose and a skillful
demagogue appeared on the scene who played on this submerged
feeling of againstness, organized scapegoating and massacre were
easily achieved. In other words, this type of folkway prejudice,
which ordinarily appears merely silly, rude, unfair, unkind, or anti-
democratic, holds within it a submerged threat for the future as well
as unpleasantness—or worse—for the present.

Interestingly enough, it is the nature of folkway prejudice to be
almost universal. Members of primitive tribes manifest a general
feeling of againstness toward the "outsiders," those who are not
members of their own group. The Caribs believe that they "alone
are people." The Lapps call themselves "human beings," implying
that non-Lapps are not. Literally translated, Kiowa is "real, or
principal, people." The Greenland Eskimo believes that Europeans
have been sent to Greenland to learn virtue and good manners from
him. The highest form of praise that the Eskimo can extend to a
European is that he is, or soon will be, as good as a Greenlander.

This feeling of superiority that people feel toward their own way
of life and their own group is not limited to the primitives. The
ancient Greeks referred to the non-Greeks as barbarians. It is of
course true that the Greek word *barbaros* did not have the identical
meaning that our own word "barbarian" has, but it definitely attributed strangeness, rudeness, and inferiority to the non-Greeks.

Nor is this feeling of superiority, or "ethnocentrism," the term
coined by Graham Sumner, limited to ancient peoples. To the query
"Who was the first man?" a youthful patriot answered "Washington." "No," said the teacher, "the first man was Adam." "Oh, I suppose he was," conceded this small isolationist, "if you are going to
include foreigners." Among Western "civilized" peoples we hear
the constant use of such terms as "chocolate drop," "du-donk,"

"nigger," "Dutchy," "flip," "greaser," "dogs," "wop," "kike," "coon," "chee-chee," and others too distasteful to record.

Commenting on the story of Jesus, the Jew, told to a Sunday-school class of ten-year-olds, a pupil declared that she had never known that Jesus was a Jew. After further elucidation by the teacher, this youngster declared that she had always known "that God was a Presbyterian, but not that Jesus was a Jew."

Thus it goes, from one end of the world to the other, even filtering down to the jingles of children at play. A Dutch nursery rhyme tells us that:

> The children in Holland take pleasure in making
> What the children in England take pleasure in breaking.

This strongly rooted attachment to one's own way of life and one's own people has been observed through the ages by poet and scientist, the widely traveled diplomat and the secluded scholar. As Oliver Wendell Holmes so aptly remarked, "The people in every town feel that the axis of the earth passes through its Main Street."

I

It is this very group consciousness, or ethnocentrism, which lays the foundation of group prejudice. If there were no strong feeling for one's own group, there would not be strong consciousness of other groups. An awareness of one's own group as an in-group and of the others as out-groups is fundamental in group relationships. Group tensions are manifested by a sense of distrust or dislike, not to an individual as such, but to an individual as a symbol of an out-group. It does not always follow that a consciousness of one's own group leads to distrust and disharmony with all other groups. The friendly rivalry that exists between athletic teams, or the competition between rival garden clubs, for instance, points to the fact that not all group relations give rise to group tensions.

There appears to be present in all types of group prejudice some degree, whether real or imagined, of struggle or threat. So much of group prejudice, however, is linked up with imagined threat rather than real that a challenge is offered in attempting to understand it. The very universality of group antagonism has led many laymen to accept the inherent, innate, organic nature of these prejudices. So strong was this belief that up to thirty-five years ago it was a valid fact to the psychologists. Psychologically speaking, it was regarded as but one more instinct, along with mother love, pugnacity, curiosity, gregariousness, self-preservation, and fear, to name but a few.

The doctrine of the instinctivists has been pretty well discarded in the light of further and keener psychological research. No longer can the student of human nature accept the thesis that any human attitudes are inborn. No aspect of man's human social nature is inborn. His wishes, his beliefs, his knowledge, and his values all come as a result of his association with other men. They are developmental, not congenital. Attitudes are nurtured, not natured. Prejudice is fostered, not fathered.

We inherit biological traits such as the shape of the skull, the color of eyes and hair, the potentialities of tallness, all of which are carried through the germ plasm. Prejudices—indeed all our attitudes, habits, and emotions—are not carried in the germ plasm. They are developed by the culture that surrounds us: in early years, chiefly through the family groups; in later years, through other institutions —the church, the school, business.

The first few years are the most impressionable ones of our lives. The young child learns primarily from his parents. Children repeat what they find about them rather than invent their own forms of behavior. Thus the child acquires early in life those collective, specific attitudes of prejudice that exist in the family. These tend to remain with him and are often deep-rooted and unconscious.

When these prejudices in the family become further re-enforced by the community, society in general, and later associates, it is easy to see how ingrained and well established one's prejudices can become. And the tendency for prejudices to persist thus becomes comprehensible. For those with prejudices give them to these without them and, once acquired, they become further indelibly stamped. It becomes apparent, too, why it is that for generation after generation prejudices toward certain groups and persons are perpetuated.

This tendency toward perpetuation of group prejudices becomes understandable if we are aware that it is the nature of these prejudices, as well as of most attitudes, to be emotionally loaded. Prejudice consists of a pre-existing emotional tendency to act negatively toward a particular group, idea, or value. The very nature of prejudice presupposes feelings about things. Usually this emotional core is primary in these prejudice tendencies. Often reason supplies the rationalizations for existing prejudices. Emotions lead; reason apologizes and defends the prejudice.

Because attitudes of prejudice are full of emotion, it becomes clear not only why they persist, but also why it is difficult to be emancipated from them. Many instances exist that show how difficult it is to overcome prejudices, even though one is aware of the lack of basis in fact for his prejudice. For example, an intelligent and educated woman in the late fifties, who was born in the South, told the writer that although she was aware that the antiquated

notions about the innate inferiority of the Negro are false rationalizations—that shape of nose, texture of hair, and pigmentation of the
skin have nothing to do with mental ability, human morals, and
interpersonal etiquette—she just could not help herself. By this she
meant that given the stimulus, "Negro," she gets an emotional
negative reaction, which is not reasonable or planned but nevertheless manifested and real. Her prejudice toward the Negro is an
emotionalized phenomenon which appears automatically as a
result of the previously established attitude toward the Negro.
Usually the attitude is developed quite early in life. It often persists
in spite of enlightenment and knowledge. People may "know better"
but still are prejudiced.

Before we suggest what can be done about these emotionalized
prejudices toward specific groups, a further word must be said about
another type of attitude that man is capable of developing. We have
spoken about specific prejudices, specific attitudes—attitudes toward
Negroes, the next-door neighbor, the child on the other side of the
tracks. These are specific attitudes directed toward specific objects.
But there is another set of attitudes that tends to govern man's
behavior and often determines the type of specific attitudes he will
develop. A person has an attitude toward a particular individual,
and he also has an attitude toward people in general. Besides having
an attitude toward a particular member of the opposite sex, one
has an attitude toward members of the opposite sex as a group, or
toward sex in general.

Sometimes one's attitude toward a particular individual may be
the same as the more generalized one. Very often it is not. One may
be sincerely fond of, and favorably disposed toward, a particular
Negro and still possess race prejudice and be anti-Negro. A person
may be in love with a particular member of the opposite sex, but
may have prejudicial attitudes toward members of the opposite sex
as a group. He may elevate the particular member on a pedestal
of social superiority, act obsequiously to her, sincerely feel inferior.
Still, if he be an employer, he may be prone not to hire women. He
could think and believe that a woman's place is in the home, that
this is, and should be, "a man's world."

We can generalize these attitudes even further. Besides having a
certain attitude toward a particular individual or a group, one
also develops attitudes toward people in general; or even toward
life in general. What do we mean when we say a person is not
sociable? Or that he is an introvert? Or a cynic? We do not mean
that he portrays an attitude toward a particular individual or group,
but that he has a *general* tendency to act in a particular way toward
all people and all groups. A cynic is not one who distrusts an

individual as much as one who distrusts all people. The same holds true for an introvert. He is not so much one who "turns inwardly" in particular situations as he is one who practices introversion in most of life's situations. A "prejudiced individual" is one who is generally prejudiced. He may manifest his prejudices toward particulars only; on the other hand, one who is generally prejudiced will act in a prejudiced manner in many of, if not in all, life's social situations.

General attitudes therefore exist and are real, too. How else are we to understand the frequency with which prejudices often come in clusters? An individual who is *anti* a particular group is also anti-group B, C, D, and so on. We find that a tolerant person is not one who limits his tolerance to particulars. Rather, his tolerance usually pervades most of his relationships and experiences. General attitudes are chronic attitudes. The more numerous the situations that arouse a particular mode of behavior, the more general and basic the attitude behind the behavior. One who dislikes Negroes, Jews, Catholics, and children has a tendency to dislike people in general. One who dislikes people is a hostile being. And a hostile person possesses a basic general predisposition of prejudice. How his hostility will express itself depends on the definitions of his society and group. If a community is anti-Catholic, this hostile person will be prejudiced (overtly) toward the Catholic. If the community is anti-Negro, a basic attitude of hostility will arraign him against the Negro. People are what their dominant basic general attitudes are, and people do what the community dictates.

II

Specific attitudes are formed all through life, but basic general attitudes develop quite early in life and are mainly motivated by the family and other primary intimate face-to-face groups, such as the child's play group and the neighborhood. Unlike the specific attitudes, they are less capable of change and alteration, once formed. As long as an attitude is localized, it is capable of change, given a new experience. A person may change his attitude toward a particular individual when he "finds out more about him." A hostile person is not hostile because of a particular experience, but rather because of the fusion of many experiences in early life, until his tendency toward hostility becomes dominant. He has a general tendency to interpret all situations in a hostile manner, and his basic general attitude is not limited to particular objects.

Here again we are faced with an extremely difficult problem if we desire to effect a change, primarily because these attitudes are quite fully developed during the first years of life and, second, because they, too, are emotionally charged. In what other wise can we understand the high incidence of recidivism among criminals and juvenile delinquents? Although antisocial criminal behavior is not inborn, unless powerful reformistic programs are undertaken in our corrective institutions—and even then—one with a criminal bent tends to remains that way. It has often been shown that juvenile experts have ceased trying to alter the basic general attitudes of the bully. Once this aggression-domination tendency develops in an individual, it appears exceedingly difficult to reduce its degree. Without question, it appears even more dubious that a dominating, aggressive individual can ever change fundamentally into a non-aggressive, submissive type. In fact, juvenile experts do not seek basic attitudinal changes. Rather, they seek to constitutionalize the bully. Instead of allowing his bullying to express itself in the un-supervised street-corner gangs, the juvenile gang leader is made president of a club, or the captain of a baseball team. His aggressive tendencies still prevail, but now they are channelized into more acceptable social behavior.

If society could find a way of channelizing the hostile prejudicial tendencies of some people by furnishing outlets for their basic attitudinal drives, we might avoid the group tensions and group antagonisms that have not, of course, a place in democratic societies. If the bigot could be given the opportunity to fulminate his hatred against war, poverty, and disease—against objects of societal dis-approval—the villain might even become a hero in the eyes of society. This is a task for education. Education of construction, that is— not education to reform the basic personality, but to open areas and outlets of satisfaction for already developed basic attitudes.

A more important task for education, of course—and specifically for the family as an educational unit—consists in integrating and normalizing the personality while it is being formed, in supplying the child with primary attitudes of tolerance rather than prejudice, with security, sympathy, and the other human virtues of love, pity, concern, and sociability. This task for the family is the greatest challenge. It is easier to form attitudes *ab origine* than to change them *post maturus*. Baldur von Schirach, the leader of the Hitler youth movement, made an interesting and significant comment when he told an Army psychiatrist at the Nuremberg prison that he believed German children under ten could be directed toward democracy as they were toward Nazism, but that those older than twelve could be considered absolutely lost to democracy. He believed that just as Hitler "pulled young people away from their non-Nazi parents, so American authorities must remove today's children from their Nazi poisoned parents."

Nazism was a general way of life in addition to the specific modes of reaction to particular objects. Nazis possessed basic general traits of social hostility to the outside world, group conceit (extreme ethnocentrism), personal and group aggressiveness, personal and group paranoia, group militance, and a tendency to blame others for their own and the world's ills.

Where do these general tendencies arise so early in life if not in the family? Studies of the development of basic general attitudes suggest that they are not a consequence of immanent mental development, but have their origin in the parents. Toward adolescence, children lose awareness of these origins and often devise rationalizations to support them. A young child, finding that his mother is not on speaking terms with her neighbor, refrains from associating with the neighbor's children. He will often accuse them with words repetitive of his mother's condemnatory remarks. And so he will take over his mother's attitudes toward other people and objects. If the mother portrays a general hostile attitude toward the outside world, her overt acts and expressions gradually fuse in the mind of the child until the imitation of his mother's specific negative habits of behavior becomes a general tendency to behave in a hostile manner. The many acts have become a basic predisposition which is fundamentally the same as the mother's predisposition. As the child matures, this basic dominant trait will force and compel specific behavior in specific situations. In extreme cases he will even offend those particular individuals he sincerely loves. A general tendency to behave colors the specific act itself. Man does not evaluate every stimulus that confronts him; rather, the stimulus becomes for him what he makes of it. And he makes of it what his dominant basic attitudes are. "Children," says George Brock Chisholm, Director General of the World Health Organization, "must be taught to live harmoniously together or mankind will follow the dinosaur into oblivion."

In order for children to develop the "correct" attitudes parents must be made aware of their inherent prejudices. How can this be done? Some self-analysis becomes necessary. It should be pointed out to adults—and here the task for adult education becomes most significant—that persons coming from particular strata and segments in society tend to possess the interests and biases characteristic of that segment. Only the few are the exceptions. A white, urban, Protestant, wealthy, middle-aged, Northern male will not possess the same tendencies to act toward given values, groups, individuals— will not have the same interests, attitudes, and predispositions—as a colored, rural, Catholic, young, poor Southern tenant farmer. Can these two possibly feel the same toward the question of social security, toward equal educational opportunity for all groups, toward taxation, and an endless variety of other social issues? Residence in particular segments of society bring pre-existent reaction patterns.

White persons must be on their guard to avoid slips of the tongue about Negroes—especially in front of children. Protestants can exert special effort in not expressing or showing through divers manners their dislikes of Catholics or Jews—again, especially in the presence of their children. On the other hand, the adults comprising minority groups can minimize their feelings and attitudes of insecurity, withdrawal, resignation, and unnatural aggression by becoming aware of these tendencies.

Only in this way can we break into the perpetual cycle of those who have prejudices passing them on to those who have not, thus making an endless chain of hatred and antagonism among men. Adults can and should be made conscious of their predispositions so that their children need not duplicate their parents in this regard. If the adult avoids specific acts and expressions of prejudice, no groups will consequently become defined in the mind of the child as objects of antagonism. If no groups are thus ill-defined, the child will obtain nothing to integrate into a *general* attitude of prejudice.

People often ask whether there are not any good prejudices, such as prejudices against war, crime, and poverty. Prejudice means prejudgment. If one's beliefs and ideas result from prejudgments it is difficult to see that an attitude for or against any object, group, or value can be condoned. Absence of reason is a poor excuse for any judgment, even if it happens to further the good society. The good society can be and should be reasonable. It surely cannot succeed through capriciousness.

In the preceding reading Professor Gittler outlines, from a theoretical standpoint some of the many aspects of prejudice. The major conclusion that one can deduct from this reading is that prejudices are rarely more than prejudgments that are acquired, many at an early age, from contacts with other persons. Further, he points out that as prejudices are acquired prejudgments they can be prevented, or at least alleviated, if parents and other adults in the community will consciously attempt to avoid the transmission of prejudices from their generation to the next generation.

The reading to follow carries further some of the points introduced by Gittler, and introduces other points that contribute to an understanding of ethnic prejudices. The most important addition is the discussion on the ways by which prejudices might threaten the general welfare of individuals and groups in our social order. Further, this reading was published by the Department of the Army which indicates that the Army recognizes the need for the elimination, or alleviation, of prejudices in military services. The fact that the army has undertaken a frank discussion of ethnic prejudices attests to the assigned importance of this problem.

PREJUDICE [3]

Introduction. Practically every one of us has prejudices. Some of us may shudder at the idea of eating frogs and other foods we've never tasted but which other people enjoy. Or we may be prejudiced against bow ties or purple shirts. But these are meaningless prejudices which are harmless. There are other prejudices, however, which affect our lives very much. A prejudice against a necktie because of its color is harmless—but a prejudice against a person because of his color, race, nationality, or religion can do plenty of damage.

A prejudice is an opinion or emotional feeling which isn't based upon fact or on reason. It is an attitude in a closed mind. Prejudice was used by the Germans to split nations wide open with hate and confusion.

The magic of race prejudice, the Japanese discovered, had performed miracles in Europe. If Hitler could seize Germany and disrupt Europe with the help of race hate, the Japanese saw no reason why they couldn't do the same thing to Asia. About a week after Pearl Harbor, the Japanese were broadcasting: "How can America be fighting for racial equality when it does not exist in America?" During the 1943 race riots in Detroit, the Japanese propagandists had a field day broadcasting the news to hundreds of millions of nonwhites in Asia and throughout the world.

Germany and Japan's "championing" of the Negroes in the United States had only one purpose—to divide us. Negroes form about one-tenth of the American population and are an important minority. Hitler had shown how minority problems could be exploited.

The Nazis assumed that in this country they would find antagonistic groups who would spend their time fighting each other instead of the German armies. Goebbels said to one of his confidants: "Nothing will be easier than to produce a bloody revolution in America. No other country has so many social and racial tensions. We shall be able to play on many strings there."

[3] Slightly edited for reprint purposes from "Armed Forces Talk 210" (Washington, D.C.: Department of the Army).

Any American who "plays on these strings" by spreading prejudices against minorities—Catholics, Jews, Negroes, foreign-born, and others—is, whether he knows it or not, weakening our Nation.

How do prejudices develop? All of us inherit certain characteristics such as the color of our skin and the shape of our head. But we do not inherit our prejudices. When we are born we have only the capacity to develop love and hate and the other human emotions.

Whom we learn to like or dislike, love or hate, depends on our experiences—in our home, in our school, in our neighborhood—and the effect these experiences have upon us. The language we learn, our religion, ideas, feelings, and attitudes, our manners and prejudices—all these come from our environment.

By the time we have grown up we already have "pictures in our mind" of many people with whom we've had little or no contact. Many people have a stereotyped picture of Negroes as lazy, stupid, happy-go-lucky; of Jews or Scots as stingy and money-mad; of Irishmen as hot-tempered, brawling, whiskey-loving. These stereotypes are being constantly reinforced through newspapers, movies, conversations and jokes, books and radio. A single story, comic strip, or movie may not make too deep an impression. However, when time after time the Negro is presented as a crap-shooting, shiftless character; the Latin as a gangster or racketeer; the Oriental as a slinking, mysterious, and crafty person—then deep and lasting impressions are made which go to form attitudes and prejudices.

Are all members of a minority group the same? There is another way that we get false ideas about whole groups of people. As youngsters we may have played games with boys in the neighborhood, and one of them, perhaps a Pole or an Italian, may have cheated. We then conclude that all Poles or all Italians cheat, and we carry this idea with us all through life. We conclude that because one member of a group acted in a certain way, all members of that racial, religious, or national group will act the same way. We usually make these false generalizations about any group but our own. It we're Protestant and a member of our group lies, we don't condemn all Protestants. If we're Catholic and one of our members steals, we don't say all Catholics are thieves. If we're Jewish and one of our group commits a crime, we don't say all Jews are criminals.

How are prejudices developed? It is only natural and human to be curious about things or people about whom we know very little. Curiosity is wholesome. When it leads a man to investigate honestly the thing that arouses his curiosity, he often finds something new and interesting. When he does not make the effort to look honestly into the thing that first called forth curiosity, however—when, instead, he lets the matter dwell and go unanswered—he closes his mind to healthy thinking, and trouble begins. Curiosity gives way to suspicion—suspicion quickly converts itself to fear—and fear grows into hate! One fears the things he suspects, and hates that which makes him afraid. This fear of the strange and unfamiliar is called by a high-sounding name—xenophobia. Primitive tribes usually feared and therefore hated a neighboring tribe because they didn't know them. Unenlightened people today have that same fear and suspicion of the unknown. Only when we've lived and worked with people of different races, cultures, and backgrounds, and learned to know them, can we really overcome these primitive fears.

Prejudices develop, too, from a feeling of insecurity or frustration. We may feel uncertain about our ability or prestige. We may feel insecure in our job or our social position. To strengthen our own confidence and feeling of self-importance, we often search for someone to look down upon as "inferior" or some group to blame for our failure and misfortune. That is why there is more prejudice in times of social stress and economic depression. Depression brings insecurity —and insecure people begin looking around for someone or some group on which they can pin the blame.

Rumors foster prejudice. The man who spreads rumors about any racial, religious, or national group is doing a harm to his community and to the Nation. He may not realize the danger but he is weakening the United States and our way of life, nevertheless.

Why Is Religious and Racial Prejudice a Threat to All of Us?

1. *Prejudice is contagious.* History has taught us that when we discriminate against one segment of the people, we set a pattern that may be used against other groups. Hitler's persecution of the Jews, trade unionists, communists, and socialists was later directed against Catholics, Protestants, liberals, and eventually the people of the world.

In 1855 Abraham Lincoln understood this when he said: "As a Nation we began by declaring all men are created equal. We now read it 'All men are created equal except Negroes.' When the Know Nothings get control it will read 'All men are created equal except Negroes, and foreigners, and Catholics'."

Consideration for the Negro, the Jew, the Catholic, the foreignborn or for any other minority group rests not merely on the grounds of humanity and justice; it rests on the solid base of self-interest.

2. *Prejudice makes all of us poorer.* We can't have an enlightened democracy with minority groups living in ignorance. We can't have a prosperous democracy with minority groups so poor that they can't afford to buy the goods America produces.

If a minority is kept at a low-wage scale in the same field or area in which the majority works, eventually the majority's wages will be reduced because of a smaller demand for consumer goods and the competition of cheap labor. Conversely, a higher standard of living for any group increases the demand for consumer goods and makes for a more prosperous country. Aside from the fact that it is Christian and democratic, it is also to our own selfish interest to help secure better housing, clothing, and nutrition for *ALL* our people.

As Eric A. Johnston, ex-president of the United States Chamber of Commerce, recently declared, "Whenever we erect barriers on the ground of race or religion, or of occupational or professional status, we hamper the fullest expansion of our economic security. Prejudice doesn't pay. Discrimination is destructive."

3. *Prejudice robs us of minority talents.* Prejudice often prevents minority groups from developing their abilities and skills. It limits their achievements and deprives the Nation of their genius. We are all poorer in America today because discrimination prevents members of some minorities from rising to their greatest possible achievements, thus lessening their potential contributions to the general wealth and welfare of America.

4. *Prejudice blinds us to real situations.* Prejudice makes impossible any real solution of economic, social, or personal difficulties. When we blame war or social and economic troubles on some innocent minority group, we are diverting our attention from the real causes. By blaming and hating some scapegoat for our misfortunes, we intensify rather than remove the difficulties. Social ills can be remedied only through acceptance of responsibility and co-operation through democratic means to solve common problems.

5. *Prejudice endangers democracy.* Prejudice means disunity, and disunity plays into the hands of the enemies of democracy. National unity is essential if we are to preserve our way of life. Prejudice is the most formidable weapon of groups that seek to destroy democracy. Hitler used the "hate" technique to divide opposition, to confuse the real issues, to blame national or international ills on innocent scapegoats, and to gain a following by a common hate. "Hate the Jews!" he yelled. "Hate the Negroes!" "Hate the Catholics!" Hate them for their color—their religion—their politics—their nationality. Hate them for any reason—or for no reason—but hate them. For hate meant power—to the Nazis!

6. *Prejudice endangers world peace.* The success of the United Nations and its aim of world peace and security depends a great deal upon how the United States solves its internal problems.

The smaller nations of the world look to the United States for leadership. We cannot afford to lose their confidence.

Three-fourths of the people of the world are what we call "colored." These people naturally look to the treatment of our colored citizens to see what we really mean when we speak of democracy. Racial and religious prejudice alienates the confidence of the vast nonwhite population as well as other peoples, thwarts their hopes and our hopes of peace and freedom, and ultimately creates the conditions from which future global wars can develop.

How we treat minorities is, therefore, more than a matter of mere domestic concern. Almost 13 million people in the United States were born in Europe. The mistreatment of some Mexicans in the United States echoes throughout North and South America; a race riot provokes discussion and resentments in Africa, the Philippines, and among the 800 million nonwhite people in China and India.

Throughout the world there are millions of people who believe that World Was II was a total war against fascism and Fascist ideas. Their concept of peace includes the hope—even the determination—that there will be no such thing as "superior" and "inferior" peoples anywhere in the world.

Conclusion. The story of America is proof that there are no "superior" or "inferior" people. Our country has been made great by people who came from every land under the sun—people with names like Carnegie, Sikorsky, Toscanini, Einstein, Osler—and thousands more. But it isn't only the big names, the Hall of Fame names, that have made America—any more than it is only big names that won the War. We know that the War was fought and won by the little names, by the millions of Joe Doakes who never made the headlines.

The men who built and are building America—who clear her forests, span her rivers, dig her coal, plow her fields, work her machines—the men who made America strong and free are men of every race, color, religion, and nationality. Listen to the names at roll call, or read these names from a casualty list in the *New York Times* of 29 March 1945: Agostinello . . . Cohen . . . Curran . . . Grunwald . . . Hrubec . . . Ivanoski . . . Kuzian . . . Marshall . . . Thomas . . . Warblanski. Were any of these "inferior"?

PROBLEMS FOR STUDY AND DISCUSSION

1. Explain why it is of value to understand the nature of and the functioning of prejudices if one is to understand the ethnic relations pattern in the United States.

2. Point out the differences between *overt* and *covert* prejudices, showing which of these types is most damaging to minority ethnic groups.

3. Explain the meaning of the concept "ethnocentrism" and show how this trait might aid in preventing understanding among the various ethnic groups in the United States.

4. Point out the differences between specific and general prejudices, and show which of these might be more harmful to the personality development of individuals.

5. Explain why the following statement might be considered as true: "There is no such thing as good prejudices."

6. Explain the meaning of the concept *stereotype*. Select one ethnic group that you have acquired a stereotyped picture of and analyze each stereotype that you have of this group from a rational standpoint.

7. List and explain some of the reasons why prejudices develop among people.

8. List and explain some of the ways by which prejudices might be harmful to individuals as well as to the groups that might be involved.

9. Explain why it is difficult for people to eliminate any of the prejudices that they have acquired.

10. Explain what is meant by the word *scapegoat*.

SELECTED READINGS

BROWN, Francis J., and ROUCEK, Joseph S., *One America* (New York: Prentice-Hall, Inc., 1952), pp. 470-481.

FRAZIER, E. Franklin, *The Negro in the United States* (New York: The Macmillan Company, 1949), pp. 665-684.

LIPPITT, Ronald, and RADKE, M., "New Trends in the Investigation of Prejudice," *Annals of the American Academy of Political and Social Science*, 244 (March, 1946), pp. 167-176.

MACIVER, R. M., and PAGE, C. H., *Society: An Introductory Analysis* (New York: Rinehart and Company, Inc., 1949), pp. 407-416.

MARDEN, Charles F., *Minorities in American Society* (New York: American Book Company, 1952), pp. 45-66.

NEWCOMB, T. M., and HARTLEY, E. L., et al., *Readings in Social Psychology* (New York: Henry Holt and Company, Inc., 1947), pp. 503-546.

NORDSKOG, John E., McDONAGH, Edward C., and VINCENT, Melvin J., *Analyzing Social Problems* (New York: The Dryden Press, 1950), chap. 3.

ROSE, Arnold M., Editor, *Race Prejudice and Discrimination* (New York: Alfred A. Knopf, Inc., 1951), pp. 3-85.

SCHERMERHORN, R. A., *These Our People* (Boston: D. C. Heath and Company, 1949), pp. 479-509.

WALTER, Paul A. F., Jr., *Race and Culture Relations* (New York: McGraw-Hill Book Company, Inc., 1952), pp. 25-42.

WEATHERFORD, W. D., and JOHNSON, C. S., *Race Relations* (Boston: D. C. Heath and Company, 1934), pp. 50-64.

III

Sources of Ethnic Attitudes

Introduction

IF ATTENTION is directed to the origin or sources of ethnic attitudes, can a better understanding of ethnic attitudes result? Frankly, a study of the sources of ethnic attitudes should aid in determining the foundation upon which such attitudes are based, and establish whether they are facts or prejudices. If, for instance, it is found that the reactions of persons to ethnic groups are based on objective reason, then they are exemplifying rational behavior. On the other hand, if it is discovered that reactions to ethnic groups are based on feelings, insufficient evidence, atypical experiences, then these reactions can be classed as prejudiced behavior.

In an attempt to trace the origin of ethnic attitudes, a number of personal documents were collected from university students. Hence, the personal documents quoted in this chapter are the verbalizations of students concerning their first awareness of ethnic attitudes. In general, there is a relationship between origin of ethnic awareness and the formation of ethnic prejudice and preference.[1] The acceptance of this view prompted the authors to use this technique in an attempt to determine the origin or sources of ethnic attitudes. However, in the presentation of the data to follow, an effort has been made to select examples that would illustrate the processes and mechanisms involved in the evolution of early reactions to persons who are considered as ethnically different from the respondents. At this point it is necessary to reiterate that there is nothing "innate" about ethnic

[1] These personal documents are episodic and topical rather than complete life histories. Some are almost contemporaneous in time. Professor Clyde Kluckhohn has argued convincingly in behalf of the short statements. See his "Needed Refinements in the Biographical Approach," *Culture and Personality* (New York: The Viking Fund, 1949), pp. 75-89.

prejudices. Note two reasons that Dr. John Cuber advances in this connection:

1. Children—especially very young children—do not show race prejudice. Their likes and dislikes for other children are based upon criteria other than physical appearance. As children get older, of course, and learn more of the adult evalua-tions they take on the characteristic race prejudices of their group.

2. Different cultures have radically different patterns of race attitudes. Many American servicemen, for example, who were recently stationed in England and France, expressed great surprise that Negro men were accepted socially by the "respectable" white women of these societies. Such behavior would be rare indeed in the United States. Apparently in those cultures persons had learned radically different patterns for evaluating Negroes. Even within the United States, of course, there are considerable regional differences in the nature and extent of race prejudice. In the South where race prejudice is regarded as most categorical, it has always been a sign of distinction and high status for white families to employ Negro house servants, even trusting to them such intimate matters as the preparation of food and care of babies. Surely, if there were an innate basis for race prejudice such intimate physical contact would hardly be tolerated by these genteel people.[2]

SOURCES OF ETHNIC ATTITUDES AMONG "TYPICAL AMERICANS"

In this division of the chapter special attention is devoted to a review of the conditions surrounding the origin of ethnic conscious-ness and awareness by members of the "typical American" or the majority group. The majority group often defines itself as "White American Protestants" or, in a slightly different definition, as "the Anglo-Saxons." Some of the minority groups have coined the word WAPS to identify the majority group. It is doubtful if there is an ethnic group without its critical nickname, and the majority group is no exception.

Awareness at the Childhood Level

Ethnic consciousness and awareness tend to have their origins in the experiences of children in a culture that reflects differences. As the child learns the language, he becomes exposed to ethnic preju-dices, if such exist in his group of associates. Excerpts from a number of documents have been selected to depict the recalled reactions of adults toward the initial awareness that in our society there are "differences" in certain groups of the human race. These "differ-

2 John Cuber, *Sociology: A Synopsis of Principles,* 2nd. ed. (New York: Appleton-Century-Crofts, Inc., 1951), pp. 324-325.

ences" take on a social meaning far beyond the child's comprehension and, unfortunately, tend to linger in the mind of the mature adult also.

In the following case the "difference" between white and colored persons is not observed by the child, but is a matter of learning that there *is* a "difference." The child does not detect any difference, but is made to feel that some difference exists:

I was three or four at the time and the street we were living on was in the process of repair. A rather large group of workmen were on the job, a number of whom were Negroes. One day a small group of the colored workers were eating their lunch on the curb in front of our house. I probably was also hungry and asked my mother to fix me a sandwich in a bag. She, without knowing my motive put a sandwich in a sack and I ran out.

As I remember I had been impressed with the workers and wanted to share lunch with them. When my mother saw me out on the curb with the Negro workers eating my sandwich, she called me to come in at once. As I ran to my mother the workers all laughed.

I had no realization that anything was peculiar in my action. I don't believe I even realized that there was a difference in color until my mother mentioned it in her discussion with the neighbor that evening. This was the beginning of a childish prejudice toward a part of the human race.[3]

While the home is one of the chief centers in the diffusion of ethnic attitudes, the school often becomes a testing ground for the integration of ethnic prejudices. Sometimes the home is free from prejudice, but school situations may become a form of compulsory exposure to ethnic attitudes. In the following case, the school setting becomes the field of focus for ethnic consciousness:

The first definite instance I can remember of becoming aware of an ethnic group occurred when I was in about the fourth or fifth grade. At that time a Negro boy of about my age was enrolled in my elementary school. I had been conscious that Negroes existed, but this was the first time an ethnic group was associated in my mind in any way with prejudice or racial tension.

On the day before his first appearance at school, all the classes in the school, especially those of the same grade, were told that the boy was coming. The teachers seemed very sympathetic when they told us that he had attended another school, but had been made so miserable by the jibes of the other pupils his mother had decided to transfer him. We were urged to try to make him as happy as possible so he would not be forced to move again. We were particularly warned not to call names or tease him in any way.

As far as I can remember the majority of the children accepted him quite readily. However, there were a few who were openly hostile. An incident occurred shortly after his entrance which made a deep impression on my mind. One of the boys was caught tormenting the Negro boy, and was forced to apologize not only to the boy himself, but publicly to all the classrooms. Many of the students felt

3 Personal Document of K.S.D.

that the punishment had been unnecessarily harsh and expressed openly their disapproval. The boy soon terminated attendance at this school, but I was the victim of ethnic recognition.[4]

To judge an entire group of persons from one's own experience is considered to be nonlogical, and usually turns out to be inaccurate. However, an interesting aspect of ethnic prejudice and friendliness is the shifting emphasis of attitudes in response to specific experiences. In the case cited below, attention is directed to the early conditioning of attitudes and the formation of new attitudes as the result of one experience:

From the age of three I grew up in a locality in Southern California heavily populated by Jews. So far as I can recall I went through early childhood and elementary school in constant contact with Jewish children, but with no personal conflicts or prejudices. One of my constant companions was, I am sure, Jewish but his family professed to be German.

When about eleven years old, however, my family moved to Indiana where my father had opened a dry-goods store. Prior to this time the only large dry-goods store in town was owned by a Jewish proprietor. On the way home from my first day in the new school, a trying day at best, I found myself waylaid by a gang of very belligerent characters and their leader, a veritable giant, proceeded to beat me to a pulp.

On the second day I managed, by adroit and careful questioning, to determine who my attacker had been and discovered that he was the son of my father's competitor. The fights, or I should say beatings, continued nightly for weeks except on those nights when I managed to elude the gang. It would be impossible to describe the hatred I felt for this Jewish fighter for by this time I had realized that he was Jewish. I honestly believe this to be my first known race hatred because I thoroughly hated anything remotely connected with him. This prejudice existed with me for many years and I automatically connected Jews with this hated Jewish boy.[5]

In the life of children there may develop a conflict between school activities and play activities outside the school situation. The regulatory nature of the school situation tends to minimize ethnic antagonism, while the play situation in the street or park may offer a free area for the *expression* of prejudice. The case cited below is fairly representative of this dualism:

Prior to the second grade I was not conscious of the existence of any differences between the other ethnic groups of my community. As I think back to my early years in elementary school I can remember the various minorities represented in my school. There were Negroes, Japanese, Chinese, Gypsies, Jews, "Anglo-Americans," and Mexicans. We all played and worked together with no animosity displayed because of different backgrounds. However, when school was over, and

4 Personal Document of L.N.
5 Personal Document of J.V.

we were on our way home, the different groups would form cliques, and upon the insistence of older children all in one group would heckle the youngsters of some other group. As the younger children heard name calling on the part of both sides, we slowly became conscious of the existence of differences.

Often hostility was shown toward those minorities who were better off financially, for instance, the Chinese, Japanese, and Jews. But there was no set rule. Sometimes the Gypsies would be made fun of because of their gaily colored dress; the Chinese and Japanese were told that they did not open their eyes until fifteen days after they were born; the Negroes would be called "Little Black Sambos"; the Mexicans were "Pancho Villas"; the Jews supposedly had all the money, and one boy even said: "Yeah, they killed Jesus. I learned that in catechism."

The next day in school, however, every controversy had been forgotten. We would play ball, and we were all playmates again. Slowly we formulated ideas of differences among the various ethnic groups and learned to stick to our own for security and status. It often was a toss up as to what ideas would prevail toward the ethnic groups—those in the school situation or those in our respective ethnic groups.[6]

In the early life of children the role of motion pictures cannot be overlooked as a conveyor of ethnic stereotypes. The movies tend to depict the Negro as amiable and as a person in a servant category, the Jew is the businessman, the Chinese in the mystery play is a deceitful person, the Mexican may run the gamut from the lazy dweller to the owner of a rancho, and so on. The radio and television have been continuing the same process. In fact, the "top" ethnic entertainers are often the persons who can give "realism" to the stereotypes of the designated ethnic groups. At the present time we may note the role of Rochester, Pasquale, Cisco Kid, Pancho, Luigi, Millie, and many others. In some incidents, as in the following case, stereotypes are learned from the various means of communication:

As a youngster the only pictures that I recall were serials which involved a great deal of suspense. Among these was one that I associate with Charlie Chan, but of this I'm not completely sure. However, the central theme involved white girls being abducted by Chinese, induced to smoke opium and being lost forever to white society. Craftiness and underhandedness were characteristic and I soon associated these with the Chinese. They were always shown as quick with the knife, which was well concealed on their person.

When I was about nine or ten years of age a Chinese laundryman came to our town. His establishment was in an inferior building on a side street. Since we walked past his shop on our way home from town we always peeked through his window to try to find out more about him. We had accepted our movie idea of the Chinese villain as characteristic of all Chinese, so as we peeked we were pretty well on our mark ready to run. One day as we peeked into his window he came out and chased us. His queue seemed to trail him and his expletives I'm sure were cursing us. He frightened us sufficiently, so we never bothered him again.

Today I enjoy Chinese food and art objects, but I still have not completely

6 Personal Document of C.U.

overcome the feeling that there is something sinister about the exchange of glances and quiet movements that I notice in those who serve me.[7]

The cases cited are sufficient to suggest that, in many instances, ethnic attitudes are acquired during childhood. These attitudes are acquired from both direct and indirect experiences in the home, the school, the street, the playground, and through the various media of communication. However, it appears that the first four areas of experience are more important as sources of ethnic attitudes, during childhood, than are the various media of communication. Further, the cases cited also suggest that ethnic prejudices may evolve, among children, out of the following conditions or personal reactions: adverse experiences, differences in physical appearance or cultural background, name-calling, superior economic status of members of a minority ethnic group, shame, anger, fear, and envy.

Awareness at the Adolescent-Adult Level

Since the elementary school is usually a neighborhood institution, it usually recruits its school population from a limited range of ethnic groups. In some elementary school districts the population is composed of only one ethnic group, hence, the school population will be obviously from this group. This tends to restrict the ethnic contacts of many children during childhood. Thus, some persons reach the adolescent period acquiring relatively few ethnic attitudes. Also, in some areas, where the population is ethnically homogenous, persons may arrive at the adult period before acquiring definite ethnic attitudes. Some of the sources of ethnic attitudes, among "typical Americans," during the adolescent and adult periods will be presented in the following passages.[8]

As people advance from childhood to adolescence they tend to broaden their areas of interpersonal contact. This is true from an educational, physical, economic, and social standpoint. As the area of contact broadens, the number of contacts with other ethnic groups will increase, and ethnic contacts usually bring with them ethnic attitudes. Therefore, persons who do not acquire ethnic attitudes during childhood usually acquire such "tendencies to act" during the adolescent or adult periods.

It has been pointed out that the school is one of the major sources

[7] Personal Document of D.M.
[8] See S. Andhil Fineberg, *Punishment Without Crime* (New York: Doubleday and Company, Inc., 1949), chap. 1.

of ethnic attitudes. While elementary schools are usually neighbor-hood schools, the secondary school population is drawn from several neighborhoods, and sometimes from several elementary school districts. Thus, in the secondary school situation there is a greater possibility of contacts with various ethnic groups as the following case illustrates:

The elementary schools, of my home community, being rather small and absorbing only the children living within a radius of a very few blocks, naturally, did not make for "ethnic consciousness." Within these elementary schools the composition was of the dominant element living in the surrounding section of the community. This same pattern holds true in relation to shopping districts, amusements, etc.

Not until the age of twelve was it possible for me to become truly ethnic conscious, for at the age of twelve all students would transfer to one of the two junior high schools in the community. Because of the small number of junior high schools in the area, it was necessary for the schools to absorb within their confines pupils from a farther distance than was true in the case of the elementary schools. This produced a co-mingling of the ethnic groups, and in this respect the junior high became the testing ground for better race relations.

The junior high situation placed me in an environment of ethnic differences. These races and groups suddenly emerged to the forefront. I looked at these specimens of humanity that were slightly different than I as if they were "animals in a circus." It was a new phenomenon to me. It was as if I were returning from years of darkness, and in a sense I was. In this school it was not possible to be ethnic conscious of one race or group at a time, but rather of all groups at one specific time. This experience was not disagreeable, but rather agreeable. In retrospection it was much like a movie unfolding—there were actors (the individuals being perceived for the first time), there was a plot (intercultural education), there was a producer (the school system), and the audience (the perceiving students, of which I was one). It seemed difficult to dislike one ethnic group when there were so many differences to be observed.[9]

Some persons may reach the adolescent period without becoming aware of ethnic differences. When this occurs the problem is often complicated by the combination of ethnic contact with adolescent instability, as the following statement shows:

As far back as I can remember, we have always had a colored cook in our home, and this contact was my first with the Negro group. At three years of age (my mother reminds me), I would sit on the stool in the kitchen and watch enthusiastically while Mary prepared the best meals, they were fabulous. I need no reminding of the fact that I was convinced that no one could cook like Mary and on her days off I continually grumbled that mother rated a poor second in the kitchen.

Mary was with us twelve years, covering the complete period of my childhood. Through the twelve years the cook was with us I was aware of no difference between Mary and myself or my parents, except for the fact that Mary's culinary talent far exceeded that of my parents. The idea that Mary was on a lower plane

9 Personal Document of N.M.A.

never entered my mind. She was a dear friend, a confidante and trips to the movies with her were always highly anticipated by me. My mother always encouraged our friendship, and upon Mary's death we all attended the funeral with equally as heavy hearts as those of her immediate family.

At fifteen I entered a large high school where there were four Negro girls enrolled. The attitude of my friends toward these four girls was my first actual introduction to prejudice against colored people. At first, as I recall, I was confused as to why these girls should be treated so unfairly. On one occasion, a close friend of mine pushed one of the Negro girls off the bench at lunch time when the girl attempted to sit beside her. My friend called the Negro a "dirty ——." It made me begin to think and finally I reached the conclusion that my confusion was due to my ignorance of the situation. Having never experienced any discriminatory incidents before, I took it for granted that my friends did know, and gradually I began to adopt their beliefs. So, for the first time, I began distinguishing a dark skin from a white as bad from good. What I failed to realize was the fact that my parents had no prejudices of the negative type, and that my class friends were victims of prejudice in their attempts to dominate on such a weak premise as skin color.[10]

The above case points out a problem that is often overlooked in discussions on ethnic relations. There is a definite need to provide early training that will develop constructive ethnic attitudes, rather than leaving to chance the development of such attitudes.

In a few cases an actual experience with an atypical member of an ethnic group may seem to *confirm* the prejudice learned in the home or on the playground. There are members of every ethnic group who live up (or down) to the worst stereotypes the mind can visualize. It often takes rigorous reflection to disassociate the atypical member of an ethnic group and his misbehavior from the representative members of the designated ethnic group and their good behavior. Some of this difficulty is revealed in the following case:

It was during my first year in junior high school that I first came to realize that there were ethnic differences between myself and our Mexican-Americans. My first contact was not a friendly one, I am sorry to relate.

By way of preface, I might begin by saying that I had heard about the Mexicans and so-called "greasers" from my father who I now know has a very strong prejudice toward this ethnic minority. My father, being a milkman at the time, related stories of his experiences with Mexicans to the family at meal time, and colored these stories stressing unpleasant details. He definitely stereotyped the Mexican as one who couldn't talk "good American," who was dirty, and who always carried a knife. The latter detail I came to have confirmed in my first contact with Mexican-Americans.

Returning to my first contact with Mexican-Americans. I met Joe, a boy of "lanky build" and somewhat taller than I, on the whole friendly, I recall; but he had a fiery temper. He tried to dominate the play activities. It was over this dominating behavior that he and I "got into it." A fist-fight broke out and I knocked

10 Personal Document of R.I.

him down. Then Frank came at me with a very small penknife. We struggled and I finally got him down with my legs pinning his arms to the ground and began "punching his face in." By this time the teacher had noticed the fight and intervened. Frank and I were taken inside the school. I was permitted to go to class and Frank was taken to the office.

However, my senior year in high school and courses in sociology have changed my point of view. I have had to fight against my father's conception of the Mexican. I try to see each person regardless of his ethnic group in terms of himself, and only in terms of his race as merely interesting background information.[11]

In some homes there is a strong doubt thrown on the worthiness of all "foreign groups." Inasmuch as they are "different," it is accepted that they are inferior to the majority group. In the statement below a rather wide ramification of this feeling is dispersed to a number of "foreign or colored groups":

When I first became conscious of the fact that there were different types of ethnic groups, I did not know them by their correct names. I only knew them by the reference to "color." I was told that the "red" people of the Indian race had certain characteristics, the brown Mexicans were different, the yellow folk of the Far East acted differently, and the black Negro race was a race I ought to fear. I was never actually *taught* to treat a person of "another color" in a different manner, but the family put the so-called foreign groups into a certain category, so of course, I did also.

When I lived on an orange ranch during my early high-school days I enjoyed riding horseback through the groves and watching the Mexican pickers at work. My parents saw this and said I was never to go near a Mexican worker. Even at that age, I took that as a view-point on all Mexicans and had a fear of them as a race. It was not a definite fear, but a consciousness of them as a separate group. I considered them as I considered the Japanese during the war time, a completely different people who lived differently and were not to be treated as equals.[12]

During World War II soldiers were sent to various sections of the United States for training. Because of the climate and terrain, the South had many of the larger Army Ground Forces training units. Many soldiers from the North saw, for the first time, the *social distance* practiced in the South. Many of the aspects of the social etiquette seemed absurd to them, especially since the war was being fought partially on the basis of a democracy versus an enemy who proclaimed racial superiority. Likewise, southern soldiers sent to the North were probably surprised at the ethnic patterns found in New York, Chicago, and Detroit. This shift about of soldiers served to broaden the ethnic outlook of many. The surprise at the differential treatment of the Negro in the South is clearly presented in the following statement:

11 Personal Document of V.J.K.
12 Personal Document of G.H.

Nearly all of my life I have lived among diversified ethnic groups. It is possible that at one time I may have become conscious of one or more of these groups, but this is beyond my memory. I have, however, been very conscious of the conditions under which some of these groups live such as housing, employment benefits, and sundry other social conditions.

There was one experience that I had during the war that made it very clear in my mind what the Negro is up against in the South (although this may not be wholly typical). I had the fortune (or misfortune) to be stationed in Jacksonville, Florida for four months in 1943 while I was attending a service school there. I had previously been told of and read about "Jim Crowism" that the Negro contends with in the South, but I had had no concrete idea of just how far this practice was carried.

Separate drinking fountains I had expected, and segregation on busses did not take me by surprise but I was actually thrown off balance when I discovered that there were two separate ticket windows at the railroad station. Possibly such a minor thing, among a large number of situations, should not have impressed me in quite such a way, but it was this point, I think, that really put the lid on a ludicrous though pathetic situation. And all this was happening during the height of the war for "One World."

There were other reactions too—hostile stares I received when I treated a Negro as an equal; and the way in which Negroes were spoken to, as if they were little children, naughty ones at that.[13]

In many instances, soldiers who were sent overseas had their first opportunity to come in contact with members of some of the nationality groups that reside in the United States. Some of these soldiers brought back to the United States *negative* attitudes toward these nationality groups. In some cases these negative attitudes were developed as a result of strained conditions existing. The following case is cited to illustrate how ethnic attitudes may vary when established under favorable and unfavorable conditions:

While living in the United States I had never been in a position to know or to be in contact with any French persons or even second generation French individuals. Perhaps the remoteness of this particular group to my everyday life caused me to be a target for the countless fallacies related to me concerning this group.

The chief source of my indoctrination in regard to the French character and way of life was by way of the soldiers who had been in France for some time at the time of my arrival overseas. I was in my early twenties upon arrival in Europe, and spent only a brief period crossing Northern France, staying in one place and another for but a few days. During this short period the relation of American soldiers to the French population was a most cordial one. For the most part, American soldiers approved of the country and its people.

I shared the view of the majority of the men in my organization during the period described above. However, a new aspect of French-American relations arose as soon as the military personnel became stationary. There was an outbreak of considerable hostility between American and French, and it set in shortly after V-E Day. At this time I was quite resentful, along with others, that the French

[13] Personal Document of J.J.

people should be so unappreciative of the liberation given them by Americans who risked their lives daily. This attitude I held quite strongly when I received an assignment to go to Luxembourg. During a period of a few months in this area my prejudice grew stronger. Comparisons were constantly made to prove how much better people were outside of France. In Luxembourg material things were quite abundant and the country was not very severely touched by war with the exception of the northern areas. We all heartily approved of the country and its people.

In mid-November of 1945 a number of us received an assignment to the Alpine area of France. It was one of these dream assignments that everyone in the Army hopes for. We drove south to Lyon and then into the Alps to a tiny mountain community of two or three hundred persons. The purpose of this assignment was to open a Ski-leave Center. I was back in France again along with my preconceived ideas about French people.

This was the beginning of my education about the people of France. My contact with these people was constant, and not on the formerly superficial basis. By living with a small group of French people over a period of a few months, I saw very soon all that they had to offer in friendship, sincerity, and good will as opposed to my previous concept of the Frenchman as a deceitful, niggardly, and untrustworthy person. Perhaps this transformation would not have as much validity if the population of this mountain community had been strictly rural people. The fact was that large numbers of them were urban dwellers from Paris who either managed hotels and businesses, or were on the staffs of these establishments.

With my old prejudice smashed I made, from time to time, trips to Paris and other cities and found that with my new understanding of the French people I was able to have a most friendly and genuine series of relationships. I became the permanent friend of one family in particular, and several other individuals as well. War conditions are not ideal for understanding anything, peace and leisure afford the best opportunity for friendship around the world.[14]

The concluding personal document, illustrating a source of ethnic attitudes among "typical Americans," is concerned with semantic connotations. This citation is very important since it illustrates how ethnic attitudes may evolve out of unconscious statements that imply metaphorical connotations. It also shows how so-called "friends" of minority ethnic groups might force neutral persons to imply that certain ethnic groups are inferior:

I became suddenly conscious of ethnic groups while participating on a student-faculty panel discussion at one of the large universities in the nation. We were discussing "white Chauvinism," which was defined as a feeling of superiority manifested in ideas and actions by white people toward Negroes generally. Very often people who believe in Negro and white equality are unconsciously guilty of "white Chauvinism."

An interesting example came to light in the discussion. One of the professors who had a long history of struggle for Negro rights made a report on conditions in the South. He unconsciously made this statement: "The picture in Georgia is certainly black."

14 Personal Document of B.K.E.

It was pointed out by one of the student leaders that using the term black in that context was a "white Chauvinist" remark which the professor was perhaps unconscious of. He used the term black as synonymous with bad. This is a hold-over of the feeling that a white person and things that are white are good, and that a black person and things that are black are bad.

It may perhaps be seen better in these two statements: We often say, "I'm free, white and twenty-one," and "It's only a white lie." In stating "I'm free, white and twenty-one," the fact that a person emphasizes that he is white implies that to be black would be a sign of inferiority. Also when a person states, "It's a white lie," he implies that a "white" lie is permissible and superior to a "black" lie as white in his mind perhaps carries the stigma of better to anything that is black. During the war we had the "black" market, and it will be remembered that the "gray" market was not quite so bad.

These and many other words and statements are subtle remains of discriminatory ideas that people in the past knew were derogatory to Negroes. Now, they have remained as clichés and are unconsciously used by people who do not usually intend to imply the inferiority of Negroes to whites.[15]

Thus, those persons who escape the acquisition of adverse ethnic attitudes during the period of childhood may acquire such attitudes during adolescence or the early adult period. To a great extent the sources of ethnic attitudes are similar in all periods of life. The major difference appears to be in a shifting of *emphasis* concerning the importance of particular sources of ethnic attitudes. During the adolescent-adult period, the following sources appear to contribute most to the development of adverse attitudes toward ethnic groups: contacts with a larger number of ethnic groups, varied occupational experiences with other ethnic groups, the acceptance and verbalization of ethnic metaphors and similes, and to a limited extent some of the attitudes may have their origin in the attempt to resolve personal failures by projecting or imagining adverse personality traits in ethnic minorities.

Concluding Statement

It seems clear that persons of the "typical American" group acquire most of their ethnic attitudes through the comments or actions of their parents, playmates, or other associates. *It does not appear that children have any initial aversions to any ethnic group because they recognize physical or cultural differences.* The differences that are recognized are taught through association. This means that, at the present time, persons must depend on their associations with laymen for the development of ethnic attitudes. In other words, ethnic atti-

15 Personal Document of L.R.

tudes among "typical Americans," in most instances, are derived more from unscientific sources that are traditional and emotional in nature than they are from sources that are rational in nature. This poses a problem that will be discussed later.

SOURCES OF ETHNIC ATTITUDES AMONG "MINORITY AMERICANS"

Introduction

In the preceding division attention was directed to the development of ethnic attitudes among persons classified as "typical Americans." To understand fully ethnic relations in the United States, it is also necessary to become cognizant of the reactions of minorities to the multi-ethnic situation, namely, awareness of themselves as "different" from the majority group, as well as from each other. As a result of being defined as "different" from the dominant group, minority groups develop characteristic reactions toward the majority group. *Inasmuch as minority groups have had many more contacts with the majority group than vice versa, the attitudes of minority groups are the result of repetitious contacts with exposed prejudice.*[16] While there are some members of the majority group who may not have the usual prejudices, the members of minority groups have no immediate way of determining this condition. Therefore, the attitudes acquired by minority ethnic groups toward the majority ethnic group are usually colored by those members of the majority group who show some degree of prejudice. Further, *minority ethnic groups acquire attitudes toward each other.* The similarity of the attitudes developed by some minority group members and the majority group toward minority groups should be noted in the documents to be cited. The personal documents cited in this division are illustrative

---

16 In the work by Bruno Lasker, *Race Attitudes in Children* (New York: Henry Holt and Company, Inc., 1929), p. 394 ff., is cited the following forms of expression as typical in early childhood: *fear, cruelty, combativeness, and ridicule.* Typical expressions during adolescence are: *condescension, rivalry, class consciousness, and returning fear.* A recent work by Maurice R. Davie, *Negroes in American Society* (New York: McGraw-Hill Book Company, Inc., 1949), chap. 20, indicates the following reaction patterns of Negroes to their status in the United States that are reflective of adult levels: (1) *acceptance* or the Uncle Tom type of Negro, (2) *resentment* as manifested by the upper-class Negro professional person, (3) *avoidance* or the refusal to be placed in a situation of subordination, (4) *overcompensation* or ego enhancement as indicated in a flashy automobile, (5) *race pride* as observed in constant references to race heroes, and (6) *hostility and aggression,* which take the form of violent displeasure with the selected social relationships between ethnic groups.

of the situations where minority members become ethnically conscious and their reactions to this consciousness.

Awareness at the Childhood Level

Sociologists, and other students of ethnic relations, are certain that prejudice is a learned reaction. In the minority group the learning of an adverse prejudice may take the form of a *traumatic* experience. Naturally, a child is shocked by being made aware that he is a victim of prejudice. As a child he has also been learning some of the essentials of nationalism and the American Creed; hence, the shock of ethnic consciousness may come as an additional personality problem for the growing child.

The personal documents used in this division state with vividness what it means to become aware of being considered "different." In some instances the minority member may have been accepted as "one of the gang" only to be shocked to learn that he must drop his membership in the gang because some parents of "typical American" children protested. In the following case, the emotional blows of segregation and ethnic consciousness are depicted with unusual insight by a young Negro university graduate:

If you are a member of the darker race in the South, as I happen to be, your earliest memories will be full of incidents which define the color line for you. As a child of five you may be thirsty and start to drink from a fountain, but your mother will stop you and warn you not to try that again because a sign on the fountain reads "for whites only." When you reach the "gang age" and want to drop into a drug store with your gang for a soda, you will be stopped, because the tables and fountain are for "white only." If you go to a theater and the balcony is crowded, you have to stand up, even though there are seats on the main floor, because the main floor is reserved for "white only." Having incidents such as these happening constantly, it is hard for you to remember the first time you became ethnic conscious. Yet, there is one incident that is more vivid in my memory than any other.

My parents and I had motored to a small town that is not located on a railroad. After visiting for a week-end my father had to return home. My mother wanted to spend a week in this small town, so my father left us there. When the time came for us to go home we had to ride the bus. When we boarded the bus, all of the seats marked colored, except one, had occupants. However, there were several *vacant* seats in the front of the bus. So my mother had to sit in the one vacant seat in colored section of the bus and hold me, a boy of seven, in her lap for a distance of about ninety-three miles. I asked her if I could sit in one of the vacant seats in the front of the bus. Naturally, she had to say *no*. Then I asked why. She told me that the front seats of the bus were reserved for whites only.

When we arrived home she told my father about the incident. Then they decided that it was time for me to learn *my place* according to the race etiquette of the South. After our conversation that night, I began to develop an inferiority complex toward the white race. I began to envy them for all of the things that they could do and I could not do. I became afraid of them and was not able to conceal my nervousness while in their presence.[17]

Jews who have been reared in Poland and in other European countries where prejudice may take the form of violence also become aware of themselves with fear. Many of our refugee families now residing in America have felt the full impact of ethnic prejudice, especially is this true of the children.[18] One of the encouraging reflections indicated in many personal documents is a sense of understanding and tolerance which minority group members express regardless of their personal status. While the personal document cited below describes a condition preceding the time of Hitler in Germany, many of the same problems are being raised with the migration of displaced persons to the United States, especially, the displaced Jew:

For those who are born to the ghetto as some are "born to the purple" consciousness regarding the existence of a given ethnic group is almost simultaneous with the development of consciousness in its psychological sense. They are like two parallel lines of mental development so that with the growth of one there is an extension of awareness of the other. I was born in Poland during the period of preparation for World War I, and by the time the war had come and gone I had been involved in the life struggle peculiar to the Jewish people in a hostile anti-Semitic environment. I saw the first attacks that I can remember of the Jewish people by Poles who mitigated their military defeats by their victorious onslaught on the ghetto population. I still remember the robberies of the Jewish petty-tradesmen, the burning of our house and the homes of other co-religionists, as well as the beatings and the murderings that went on apace till order was restored in the form of Pilsudski's anti-Semitic nationalism. Hence, my awareness took a bloody form early in life and my consciousness of being a member of a group (which I now have learned to call ethnic) is not foreign to my childhood years.

Perhaps what is more important than my consciousness of my "Jewish belongingness" is my early consciousness that not all members of the Polish people were the same. I never had, thanks to some Poles who befriended us and literally saved our lives while endangering theirs, a stereotype concept of the oppressing group and this lesson I carried with me to the United States where I arrived at the age of ten.[19]

One way children may react to prejudice focused on a given minority is to find a *scapegoat* among another minority group. By transferring the group prejudice to another ethnic group by the scapegoat

[17] Personal Document of H.I.

[18] In this connection see the study by M. R. Davie, *Refugees in America* (New York: Harper and Brothers, 1947), chap. 2.

[19] Personal Document of B.M.

method, a false sense of superordination may result. *We are rarely so low in status that we cannot find a scapegoat to transfer our reactions to, and thus compensate in part for our status.* This process can be seen in the following personal document, in which a young Japanese girl found the Mexican as the scapegoat for her reactions:

It is difficult to establish the exact time of incidence or experience which resulted in the forming of my prejudice against the Mexican, but I must have been five or six years old when I became aware of this group of people as different from my own. During my early childhood I lived on a farm in Fresno County where many Mexican laborers were used. I believe the first thought that entered my head whenever Mexicans were mentioned was the "fact" that they were lazy, dirty, and given to stealing. These ideas were probably gradually absorbed from hearing adults discussing them in my presence. Whenever articles were missing around the farm, whenever the work did not progress according to plans, the Mexicans were blamed. I recall the tales about the daughter of the farmer next door, a Caucasian girl, who used to ride horse back and oversee the Mexican workers. It was said that she was a hard driver, that she would sneak up on the workers with a whip in hand and curse them when she came upon them resting in the orchards. The implications were that she was not to be blamed, but that since Mexicans were lazy one had to keep a close watch in order to get any work done.

In the summertime, during grape and peach-harvesting season, a large group of Mexican workers were hired on the farm. I remember whole families of men, women, and children camped around the edge of the orchards or near the river. Once my mother warned me not to go near the camp as I might be contaminated with lice.

As I became older and began to think for myself a little more, I may have been able to blur the limited and unchanging image of the Mexican which I carried in my head, but nevertheless, there remained a hard core of thinking which always associated the word Mexican with laziness, dishonesty, and uncleanliness. All this was without having any firsthand experience with members of the group. It is ironic, but I held fast to my prejudice without in the least being aware of the fact that I belonged to a minority which was also a victim of similar prejudices. It did not occur to me that my attitudes toward the Mexicans were without basis in fact, and if someone were to challenge my prejudices I could not offer a single concrete evidence to support them. Most of my prejudices were formed through hearsay and were bolstered by seeing and remembering only those features of Mexicans which fitted my stereotypes.[20]

The immediate targets of prejudice may not sense the situation. Thus children may see some incidental item in the situation of planned segregation as an advantage, while the parents are concerned with status and rights. Therefore, a better social situation with an implied lower status is usually not accepted by the parents of minority children. In the following personal document some of this pattern is disclosed:

[20] Personal Document of S.J.K.

It was the first day of school and we had a new school principal. When I arrived home for lunch, I noticed mother was furious. My sister was crying and mother was getting ready to go to school with her. The school principal had sent her home. He had transferred her to the *escuela de bajo* or the "lower school" which was two miles away in the southern part of town. The principal insisted that the class room was overcrowded and he had to transfer some of the students to the other school. He explained that because she was of Mexican extraction and the other school was predominantly attended by Mexican children, it would be more appropriate for her to go there. Mother disagreed. She contacted the school board officials and explained the circumstances. Meanwhile, my sister was absent from school for a month before she was reinstated.

Several years later another sister and myself were confronted with a similar problem. In order to avoid any more unpleasantness and because we wanted to go to this other school, mother finally consented. We were thrilled to think that we could have a picnic lunch everyday.[21]

When a member of a minority group selects friends from the majority group, he is almost certain to gain censure from his minority group. Any person who would rather have friends in the majority ethnic group is not going to be accepted fully in the minority group. For instance, the Mexican may use the term "Gringado" to designate a Mexican who may appear to differentiate himself from his minority group. Minority members are expected to stick together for group survival. In the case cited below this feeling reaction is clearly manifested:

In our neighborhood was an American family who owned the only grocery store. Their small son, Jonny, was the only non-Mexican playmate we had. From the older boys I often used to hear the word "Gringo" which was used to identify this American family. Then, I didn't know what it meant for I was only five years old. Jonny and I grew very fond of each other and the older Mexican boys didn't approve because I was associating with a "Gringo." Many times I was given verbal and physical beatings by the older boys and denounced as an unworthy Mexican.

On our sixth birthday, Jonny and I were to be sent to school but I was told by my mother that Jonny and I were to go to different schools. My mother tried to make me understand that Mexican and American school children could not study together. This only confused me and made me feel bitter toward school.[22]

At times, ethnic attitudes have a slow evolvement during childhood. That is, attitudes are not brought to the surface at once, since a series of events may occur before members of a minority group are made aware of ethnic "differences." The following personal document, although somewhat on the dramatic side, sets forth the possible step-by-step progression of ethnic attitudes among members of minority ethnic groups:

21 Personal Document of H.D.
22 Personal Document of R.M.

You're Jewish. You've been aware of that ever since you can remember. But as a small boy in the pre-school years you aren't particularly conscious of the fact because you're too busy discovering and disciplining the world about you and you have neither the time nor insight to probe the significance of being Jewish.

When you're enrolled in kindergarten you enter another phase of exploration. In the beginning you're both frightened and intrigued. And all the while you take in what you see like a blotter absorbs ink. You play games and make friends in kindergarten. Among your new pals are Billy and Hideo. Billy is Negro and Hideo is Japanese. You're aware that they are different in appearance, but you're indifferent to the differences. Billy and Hideo are swell guys and that's all that counts with you.

Of course, as you grow many days and very few years older you hear the usual remarks about Negroes and Japanese—almost all from adults. You hear a man say that "Japs are smart and they ought to be watched because the yellow slant eyes are too darned smart." Once your father tells a neighbor about a lynching of a Negro that he witnessed. By the time you're eight years old you have been told of past persecutions of Jews and the ever-growing awareness of being Jewish develops, but has not yet formed into a picture.

One day when you are eight you're in the playground after school hours. You and some other boys you know are talking and the conversation shifts to "What are you?" You tell them you are Jewish and one of the toughs spits out he hates Jews. A few remarks pertaining to the reason for the hatred are tossed about and you're in a fist fight. The fight was short. However, you're bruised and shaken, but not from the physical blows you have taken.

Throughout the years you have felt a strong bond with the ethnic under-dog. And you now know the reason. You understand quite early in life that Billy was different because he was dark; Hideo was different because of his features; and at the age of eight you become fully conscious that you are different too.[23]

It is not always necessary to call ethnic groups "nicknames" to make known to all that considerable social distance is intended by the speaker or writer. At times the slur might start out with a phrase that is intended to convey a negative view, but it is later modified. However, the original meaning is implied in the modified statement, and its meaning is understood. The following case is presented to cite how minority groups use "name-calling" in developing ethnic attitudes toward each other:

I was about twelve years old when I became ethnic conscious and had just started to the Junior high school. The school was located in one of the "melting pot" areas of the city and under the circumstances I suppose some friction between the groups might be expected. The Mexican and Jewish groups seemed to have been natural antagonists.

Quarrels during and after school hours were the rule. Although these incidents did not always develop into full-fledged fist fights there were constant slurring remarks made by the participants. At first the remarks: "You dirty Mexicans," or 'You greedy Jews," which later changed to "You Mexican," or "You Jew," with a certain amount of intense feeling; words that in themselves mean nothing, but which under those circumstances were meant to represent insults. It was the

23 Personal Document of S.M.

accepted connotation of the words Mexican and Jew in these cases for each group that there was nothing worse than belonging to that particular ethnic group cited.[24]

Thus, with two exceptions, ethnic attitudes are acquired among children of minority ethnic groups from practically the same sources that they are acquired among children of the majority group. These two exceptions are segregation laws and discriminatory practices. However, children of minority ethnic groups often become conscious of their "differences" in social situations that are extremely emotional and explosive in nature. Social situations of this nature develop reactions of fear, hatred, and inferiority. They also serve to add to the burden involved in the early personality development of children of minority ethnic groups.

Awareness at the Adolescent-Adult Level

The control of economic, social, and political organization in the United States by "typical Americans" makes it difficult, if not impossible, for members of minority ethnic groups to reach the adolescent period without having contacts that stimulate the development of ethnic attitudes toward the majority group. After questioning several hundred Negro college students on this question, over a period of twenty years, it is concluded that most Negro children develop ethnic attitudes between six and ten years of age. Taking into consideration the fact that children of all other minority ethnic groups are forced into contact with the majority group, it is logical to assume that the same is true for these minority groups. *In other words, members of minority ethnic groups are usually forced to acquire ethnic attitudes at an earlier age than members of the majority group.*

The fact that these attitudes are acquired at this early age should provide some understanding concerning the nature of such attitudes. Children are not capable of a rational acceptance of ideas. They are not usually, at this early age, in the hands of capable instructors in human relations and the ethnic attitudes that they acquire are not based on scientific interpretation and analysis. Although the previous statement is made in reference to minority groups, the same is largely true for the majority group. Thus, to understand ethnic relations, we must understand that ethnic attitudes are usually acquired without reference to objective facts or scientific guidance.

Some members of minority ethnic groups reach the adolescent

24 Personal Document of R.W.

period without acquiring definite attitudes toward *other* minority ethnic groups. In fact, it is easy for members of minority ethnic groups to do this, since they may have very little contact with each other. The cases cited will be concerned with the acquisition of ethnic attitudes by minority groups toward each other.

The behavior of members of ethnic groups, in different social situations, serve to establish or modify the ethnic attitudes that might be developed toward that group. An interesting case, showing how ethnic attitudes might change in keeping with varied experiences, is illustrated in the following statement that was made by a Jewish young man:

My earliest recollections of the Negro are ephemeral, intellectual scraps and bits without any basis on actual contact. Family traditions were liberal in the extreme, so that I was not conscious of a Negro race, or people as such. Rather, when I came to recognize a color distinction in the two or more Negro families living just outside my neighborhood, I did not have any discernible or tangible reactions to them.

When I came to work on American ships, I carried a crusading vigor with me. The idealism was beginning to wear off at the ancient age of eighteen, but it was compensated for by a new practicality—working within the National Maritime Union for the extension of the "checkerboard" system of multi-racial manning of union ships, and for principles of racial equality within the Union. I preached tolerance, and personally adopted an attitude rather like bending over backwards in social striving for friendly association with the Negroes aboard ship. Then, all at once, I was put sharply to the test at one shipboard union meeting: without previous warning, one of my Negro friends arose and brought charges (union parlance) against a Scottish friend of mine, claiming that he called him "A lousy N———" or some such thing as that, when he (the Scotchman) was somewhat drunk. The Union, by this time, had some very definite views on name-calling, and in this case it would mean expulsion from the Union and consequent inability to ship out, and eventual withdrawal of the Scotchman's American visa. Seamen being what they are, participation in shipboard union affairs was nominal, and·the men at the meeting were entirely passive: they seemed inwardly to agree with the Scotchman, yet would not contest the Negro on this important Union question. With due modesty, I can say that I almost dominated in this shipboard NMU affair, and I felt that it was incumbent upon me to say something, quite *ad libitum,* when the dead silence fell after the Negro had finished speaking his piece. I first established myself as a friend of both principals— a generally accepted fact—and then went on to excuse (but not condone) the action of the Scotchman, because of the principle that we cannot control men's hearts, however we should like to. Therefore, I suggested, the defendant at this trial should agree to "voluntarily" contribute $25 to the Union welfare fund, in lieu of penalty. He agreed, the meeting adjourned with a sigh of relief, and all was well—except that I did not quite feel sure of my own position on the racial question after that.

Years later, I happened to be on ship which put into a South Carolina port by accident. We took on a crew there, composed of a majority of Negroes: some of them from Harlem (militant NMU men who "knew their rights"), and most of them Guichees (a half-civilized group recently emerged from the isolation of the South Carolina and Georgia Sea Islands). Before the trip was out, there had been a near-mutiny, abundant stabbings both inter and intra-racial, a temporary reversal of the usual racial persecution pattern of America, and eventual rule at gun-point by the ship's officers, of whom I was one. It was an unforgettable experience, and radically altered my views—my prototype—of the Negro people.[25]

In a somewhat similar manner, a young Japanese describes how varied experiences caused him to modify his attitudes toward Jews in the following citation:

When I got to high school, I made friends with a fellow named Cohen. When my parents found this out they said that I must stop associating with him. I could not see any harm so I asked why? They gave me a not too pleasant picture of what they considered a typical "Jew." My oldest brother told me of a recent swindle he had had, so he made the same generalizations that my father had made. When I brought up the Golden Rule "Love thy neighbor," he hemmed and hawed and avoided an answer. I more or less accepted what they said, but I was still not convinced of the attitude which my family tried to instill in me.

When I moved to Chicago, everyone I knew seemed to make a big fuss over whether or not a person was a Jew. I suppose I sort of took up that attitude myself. Later I worked for a family who had Jewish neighbors, and since these people were friendly and did not fit the stereotype which I was developing, I realized that I would have to find out for myself whether or not the so-called "Jews" were as they were supposed to be. I worked for a family in which the husband was Swedish and the wife Jewish. These people were all that my parents had said they were not.

One of my very close friends today is a Jewish fellow whom I met in the Army. I suppose I still have a certain amount of prejudice towards the Hebrew people, and I doubt that I will ever completely get rid of it, but because of several individuals who are my close friends, I doubt that I will ever make the generalities that my parents made. Even the prejudice that I have is not necessarily bad because sometimes it works in a positive direction.[26]

Inasmuch as the Territory of Hawaii has been considered for statehood and presumably will be admitted in the near future, it may be to our advantage to consider briefly the matrix of ethnic groups that live in reasonable harmony on these beautiful islands. The harmony existing in Hawaii has been the subject of many scholarly projects by the late Dr. Romanzo Adams of the University of Hawaii. American sociologists have visited the island to study the social structure that permits so many persons of diverse ethnic backgrounds to be friends and neighbors without the obvious defenses and compensations found among similar peoples on the mainland. The personal document quoted below was written by a university student attend-

[25] Personal Document of R.V.D.
[26] Personal Document of J.M.

ing a mainland institution, and sets forth how ethnic attitudes are often transplanted from one area to another:

I was brought up in a neighborhood of every conceivable ethnic group. There were Hawaiians, Portuguese, Chinese, Japanese, Koreans, Filipinos, Caucasians, and the intermixtures of the various combinations. The groups were composed of so many mixtures that no dominant group stood above any other in my neighborhood. Although, in some areas where an outstanding percentage of the people were of the same ethnic group, especially if Caucasians, there were tendencies of segregation by high prices of land and by restrictive covenants.

My first contact with a Negro was during my high school days. This was the first time that I can remember having met a colored person. His name was known to all the boys in the gang as William. He was the only colored boy in this school and his status was very high. He was a terrific athlete and a real good natured fellow. No doubt William was one of the most popular athletes in school. He was never thought of as a Negro but as one of the gang.

When the war broke out and a great number of war workers were shipped to the islands many were Negroes. Often I would notice that William resented their presence. It seemed that this new migration in great numbers jeopardized his high social status with our group. The great influx of war workers, Negroes and whites, presented many problems. They brought their prejudices with them and tried to transplant them into their new environment. On several occasions bus drivers were asked by white elderly ladies, families of the white workers, to move natives to the rear of the bus. Unfortunately, most of the drivers were natives so they ejected them off the bus with more than a few harsh words.[27]

A second personal document is quoted from Hawaii, which sets forth a slightly different point of view and indicates a situation that has been already implied, namely, that the Caucasians are more likely to be prejudiced than is any other ethnic group. However, the traditional harmony in Hawaii is being tested by the migration of mainland ethnic groups. It is feared by the Hawaiian ethnic groups that the pattern of race prejudice may spread throughout their community. Thus far, "the melting pot of the Pacific" has stood the invasion from the mainland with fair success. However, the ethnic peace of the Territory of Hawaii is being tested. A Chinese respondent sets forth his feeling reactions to the origins of the recognition of ethnic "difference" in the following statement:

Perhaps my first experience in actually having strong consciousness to the problem of ethnic group was when the family migrated to Honolulu, on the Island of Oahu. There I was sent to a boarding school where a majority of the students enrolled were of Caucasian origin. In almost all of our school curricula, the Orientals were somewhat separated from the "haoles" (white in Hawaiian). The "haoles" occupied separate rooms and dining tables from all other "races." Social affairs were limited at times to only the privileged whites.

It was then that I realized that I was different from the whites. I felt inferior

27 Personal Document of E.R.O.

to them in many ways—language, social behavior, and outlook in life. In other words, I felt that there were so much more to gain and offer in being white than being yellow. But the climax of my concept shifted when in the midst of a slight argument between a Caucasian classmate and myself, I was called a "Yellow Jack-ass." The hot-headed expression perturbed me to such an extent that I found it good to rationalize and feel proud to be an Oriental.

If it weren't for World War II, it would hardly be likely that I would have become more conscious of ethnic groups. With rumors about the barbarous and primitive behavior of the Japanese people upon the allied nations, I felt that the Japanese people were culturally inferior to other ethnic groups. In other words, it was relieving to think that at least I was not a Japanese—that I've evolved from a better-liked people inasmuch as the Americans were concerned.

Likewise, Negroes, Mexicans, and Jews were brought to my conscious level. In the Army I was told to keep away from Negroes, Mexicans, and Jews because "You can't trust them."

Admittingly, the result of ethnic conscious has influenced me greatly in the attitude toward life. I've taken the rationalistic point of view that I'm glad I'm Chinese, that I'm no better no worse than the rest of the other races who try to imply superiority over the others.[28]

Ethnic attitudes among minority members reflect the same general pattern as that observed among majority members in the preceding division with some slight modifications. Since minority members are the recipients of prejudice, they usually acquire ethnic attitudes in almost *traumatic* situations. Adverse ethnic attitudes are directed against them. Parents of minority children may attempt to prepare their children for these emotional shocks that can be expected on the playground and in the school; however, this unpleasant task is often neglected until the problem has arisen. Because of the nature of the social situations out of which they acquire ethnic attitudes, minority members may become highly sensitive to ethnic attitudes in general. In some instances they may deflect some of the ethnic prejudice that they experience to other minority groups. By scapegoating another minority group they may feel a false sense of status. Another reaction to ethnic awareness is to attempt to become similar to the majority group as in the case of the so-called "Gringado." Unfortunately, this process tends to leave the personality in a marginal condition. They are rarely completely accepted by the majority group, and may feel a sense of dishonor to their primary ethnic affiliation. Still another prominent reaction of minority children is to disagree with the expressed prejudices of their parents toward ethnic groups. In these situations considerable parent-child conflict is generated, as children may not agree with the stereotypes circulated about the majority group, or other minority groups, by members of their minority

28 Personal Document of J.K.L.

group. In these instances, the emancipated child of a minority group represents a distinct form of marginality, because he disagrees with the prejudices of his own minority group, but may not be accepted by the very groups he defends.

SUMMARY

If the personal documents cited in this chapter show anything, they point out the need for a systematized educational program if constructive ethnic attitudes are to be developed. As it is, most ethnic attitudes are transmitted without plan and usually from sources that are unscientific in nature. Not only are these sources unscientific, but they tend to lean toward the opposite extreme and are highly charged with emotional content. One can easily guess the kinds of attitudes that will evolve from such social situations. Imagine, for instance, the confusion that would exist in this country if all human relations were dependent upon attitudes thus derived. As an illustration, suppose that attitudes toward property rights were derived from sources that were highly emotional, based on ethnocentrism, and transmitted by members of the specific group with very few guides or restrictions. Under a situation like this, property rights would be determined more by numbers or by entrenched power than by individual rights or group welfare. The documents cited indicate that ethnic attitudes are determined more by numbers and entrenched power than by individual rights or group welfare. Is such a practice democratic?

PROBLEMS FOR STUDY AND DISCUSSION

1. Make a list of the ethnic groups which you consider as "different" from the ethnic group of which you are a member, and write a short statement reflecting your first feeling reaction to each of these groups.

2. Write a short essay explaining in detail your first feeling reactions toward a selected ethnic group, and describe the social situation surrounding the first time that you were made aware of this group.

3. Make a list of the sources of ethnic attitudes that are presented in the various personal documents cited in this chapter. Classify these sources according to whether they are emotional or rational in nature.

4. Compare the usual social situations out of which the majority and minority ethnic groups acquire ethnic attitudes. Point out which social situations might contribute most to personality disturbances.

5. Point out the weaknesses inherent in the use of personal documents as the sources of attitudes. Suggest what you think would be a better procedure to use.

6. Develop a plan that you believe would aid young people in acquiring constructive ethnic attitudes.

SELECTED READINGS

ADORNO, T. W., FRENKEL-BRUNSWIK, Else, LEVINSON, Daniel J., SANFORD, R. Nevitt, *The Authoritarian Personality* (New York: Harper and Brothers, 1950), pp. 19-27.

BROOKOVER, Wilbur B., and HOLLAND, John B., "An Inquiry Into the Meaning of Minority Group Attitude Expressions," *American Sociological Review,* Vol. 17 (April, 1952), pp. 196-202.

DAVIE, M. R., *Negroes in American Society* (New York: McGraw-Hill Book Company, Inc., 1949), chap. 20.

GOODMAN, Mary Ellen, *Race Awareness in Young Children* (Cambridge: Addison-Wesley Press, Inc., 1952).

LUNDBERG, George A., and DICKSON, Lenore, "Inter-ethnic Relations in a High School Population," *American Journal of Sociology,* Vol. 58 (July, 1952), pp. 1-11.

LAPIERE, R. T., and FARNSWORTH, P. R., *Social Psychology* (New York: McGraw-Hill Book Company, Inc., 1949), pp. 45-56.

LASKER, Bruno, *Race Attitudes in Children* (New York: Henry Holt and Company, Inc., 1929).

LINDESMITH, A. R., and STRAUSS, A. L., *Social Psychology* (New York: The Dryden Press, 1949), pp. 384-415.

MARDEN, Charles F., *Minorities in American Society* (New York: American Book Company, 1952), pp. 433-460.

ROSE, Arnold and Caroline, *America Divided* (New York: Alfred A. Knopf, Inc., 1948), pp. 256-276.

IV
Patterns of Ethnic Adjustment

Introduction

IN THIS CHAPTER the concept *adjustment* is used to refer to any process followed by an ethnic group in its attempt to establish harmonious (i.e., nonconflicting) intergroup relations. In some instances the adjustment process is a conscious one, in others it may go on without the participants being aware of the process. Almost from the earliest history of ethnic contacts in the United States, minority ethnic groups have accepted, or have been compelled to submit to, various patterns of adjustment. Since these patterns of adjustment have played an important part in determining the nature of ethnic relations at any given time, it is impossible to understand ethnic relations without some knowledge of the several patterns of adjustment that have prevailed.

From the many statements that have been written in which adjustments have been described, three were selected for presentation in this chapter. In the selections that follow the writers have presented descriptions that illustrate patterns of adjustment that have occurred in the past, as well as at the present time, and in a number of geographic areas. In the first selection Park presents a schematic description of Negro-White relations. In the next selection Warner outlines the class-caste concept of ethnic adjustment. The final selection, by Bogardus, indicates the process of adjustment he observed in his studies of ethnic relations on the Pacific Coast.

▌ THE BASES OF RACE PREJUDICE [1]

ROBERT E. PARK

Prejudice, even race prejudice, no matter how reprehensible in itself, is a profoundly human phenomenon. As such, it deserves,

[1] *The Annals of The American Academy of Political and Social Sciences*, Vol. 130, No. 229 (Nov., 1928), pp. 11-20. Used by permission of the American Academy of Political and Social Sciences.

perhaps, to be defended against those who inveigh against it, as if it were not a common human weakness in which we all, more or less, share. It is not, however, in precisely this sense that President John Grier Hibben, of Princeton, wrote some years ago his "Defense of Prejudice." He sought to show that prejudice was, as he says, "a natural factor in any thinking, and not to be regarded in any sense as an abnormal and disturbing element."

DEFENSE OF PREJUDICE

When the matter is stated in this fundamental way, it serves merely to call attention to the fact that primarily men are practical creatures; that thought is, after all, merely an incident of action, and that reflection arises, and gets its justification, in our efforts to achieve ends. We are biased by our own purposes, and in the final analysis, knowledge is relative to them. The fact is, we come into the world with certain predispositions, and we acquire others. Tradition into which we are born, and which we imbibe with our mothers' milk, is infused with prejudices. "There is," as President Hibben puts it, "no thought, however original, that does not rest upon a credit basis." A man without prejudice is a man without conviction, and ultimately without character.

Common sense, "that diffuse sagacity which eludes all attempt at definition," is a tissue of hunches and prejudices that have been, in most cases cannot be, justified on general and rational grounds. Our friendships, our hobbies, our amiable but irrational predilections for certain places and certain persons—all are manifestations of what, under certain circumstances, we are likely to condemn as prejudices. It is notorious, for example, that friendships corrupt politics. The situation has been defined in the phrase, "What is the constitution among friends?" What, indeed, is the constitution or any other formal principle of action in the presence of the elementary claims of friendship, and the personal prejudices, which such friendships imply?

As it seems impossible to conceive of a world without friendships, so it seems improbable, in such a world, that life should go on without enmities, for these two things are, in some sense and in some degree, correlative, so that the bias with which we view the qualities of our friends makes it difficult if not impossible to do justice to the virtues of our enemies and theirs. There is always and everywhere the inevitable dichotomy between those who call each other "we" and the outsiders whom one refers to as "they." As William Graham Sumner puts it,

The relation of comradeship and peace in the "we-group" and that of hostility and war toward the "other-groups" are correlative to each other.

... Sentiments are produced to correspond. Loyalty to the group, sacrifice for it, hatred and contempt for outsiders, brotherhood within, warlikeness without—all grow together, common products of the same situation.

All our sentiments, love, loyalty, patriotism, homesickness, contempt, arrogance, hate, are based upon and supported by prejudices. Furthermore, mankind is incurably sentimental, and sentiments and prejudices are part of the stuff from which our human life is made.

The thing reduces itself to this, that prejudice, defined in this broad and inclusive way, has its source and origin in the very nature of men and their relation to one another. It gets itself fixed and sublimated in the habits of individuals, and enters into the very structure of society. In short, prejudice is an attitude, a social attitude.

RACE PREJUDICE

There is no reason to believe that attitudes based upon race are fundamentally different from any other attitudes. Race prejudice is like class and caste prejudices—merely one variety of a species. So far as it can be described in these terms, race prejudice may be regarded as a phenomenon of status. Most of us are familiar with the fact that thought, particularly scientific thought, proceeds by the method of classification. According to the rules of Aristotelian logic—which is the logic of common-sense—we may be said to know a thing when we are able to classify it. We have not always recognized that the thinking of the ordinary man proceeds, if less consciously still substantially, in the same manner.

We are all dependent, to a degree that we do not recognize, upon our categories, and this is true in a very special sense with respect to our knowledge of human beings. Every individual we meet inevitably finds a place in our minds in some category already defined. He is either a friend, a neighbor, a mere acquaintance, or, as we determines, more or less automatically, and with very little conscious often say, a complete stranger. The category into which he falls reflection on our part, the attitude we assume toward each individual figure in the changing scene of our daily experiences. Furthermore, our attitudes, our fundamental attitudes at any rate, are substantially alike. Each of us has, of course, his own preferences and his own opinions, and we are all likely to be a little proud of our independence of thought. On the other hand, any very marked divergence from the generally accepted opinion is invariably shocking, and frequently quite unintelligible. Most of our "opinions" are merely justifications and apologies for what are, after all, rather slight deviations from views that are orthodox in the society in which we happen to live. Opinions are individual, but the attitudes upon which they are based are collective.

On the whole and in the large, in every society, things have very much the same meaning. That is merely to say that every society has its own universe of discourse, and that is what Walter Lippmann means when he says that the public thinks only in stereotypes. There is, in fact, no other way in which the public can think. Where there is substantial agreement as to the categories, as there is bound to be in every stable society, there the status of every individual is defined by the class in which, by tradition or general consensus, he happens to find himself. The individual who is in no class at all is a pariah and an outlaw. The man who seeks to rise, or who rises suddenly, from a lower to a higher class is an upstart and a parvenu. The man who loses his status and sinks to a lower class is what the French describe as *déclassé*.

The point is that every change in status, whether of an individual or of a group, involves a change in social organization. Prejudice— that is caste, class and race prejudice—in its more naive and innocent manifestations, is merely the resistance of the social order to change. Every effort of the Negro—to take the most striking example—to move, to rise and improve his status, rather than his condition, has invariably met with opposition, aroused prejudice and stimulated racial animosities. Race prejudice, so conceived is merely an elementary expression of conservatism.

As a matter of fact, changes in status are constantly taking place in every society. Certain individuals and certain classes rise and invade the higher levels of society. As a consequence the prestige of other individuals and other classes is diminished, with the result that they are forced to decline and to accept a lower position. In America, where changes in underlying conditions proceed more rapidly than they do elsewhere, changes in status are correspondingly rapid. There seems, under ordinary conditions, to be no barrier in America to advancement—except failure to succeed. Lindbergh, a small town boy from the Middle West, flies across the Atlantic and becomes a national hero. Gene Tunney, yesterday a prize fighter, today moves in the most exclusive circles. Prohibition has created a new generation of plutocrats, composed of retired "bootleggers." The spectacle of American life is amazing and inspiring. No man, it seems, is so far down that he cannot hope to rise. Every boy born in America may aspire to be president, even if he be a Catholic.

It may strike the disinterested observer as a little strange that in America, where, humanly speaking, there are no class distinctions, there is still so much race prejudice, particularly when we consider that as far as race relations are concerned, racial minorities are merely social classes. What is the answer?

First of all we ordinarily confuse racial prejudices with racial antagonism. There is probably less racial prejudice in America than elsewhere, but there is more racial conflict and more racial antagonism. There is more conflict because there is more change, more progress. The Negro is rising in America and the measure of the antagonism he encounters is, in some very real sense, the measure of his progress. The fact seems to be that racial prejudices do not always and everywhere express themselves in racial animosities. Animosities arise in conflict, and racial animosities are an incident of the struggles in which racial classes are formed. When, however, conflict ceases; when some sort of accommodation of the contending is achieved, animosities subside. In that case the sentiments change. They are no longer hostile, or are only potentially so. On the other hand, the racial prejudices, which are the basis of this hostility, may and often do persist.

RACE RELATIONS

Where there are social classes there will invariably be corresponding attitudes and sentiments. Racial distinctions, when they exist, will always be supported by racial prejudices. But where distinctions based on class, caste, and race, are part of the established social order, as they invariably are in a static society, each caste and class lives within the limitations of its own world and accepts the definition imposed upon it as if it were a part of the order of nature. Under such circumstances each class and caste, having its own internal organization, maintains its own norms of conduct, and each expects and demands that every individual will live up to the standards of his own class. So far as this normal expectancy is maintained, good-will will exist, and each class will respect the other.

Something approaching this condition existed in the southern states before the Civil War, particularly in the far South, where slavery was firmly established and race relations, especially the relation of master and slave, assumed that fixed and irrevocable character which simulated the permanence of physical nature.

It was, however, during this period, and under the influences of the associations thus established, that those intimate and friendly relations between master and slave were established which are still so unintelligible to those who have looked upon slavery as if it were, always and everywhere, something inhuman and monstrous.

It was, nevertheless, during this same period that there grew up, out of the daily experience of master and slave, that conception of the Negro, according to which he was predestined by God and

Nature, to be forever a hewer of wood and a drawer of water, "a servant of servants unto his brethren."

There is evidence to show that, on the whole, the black man accepted the position which the white man assigned him. Negro servants spoke habitually in a proprietary sense of their masters' families as "our white folks." And, on the other hand, the masters' families thought of the slaves on their plantations as "our Negroes." In short, the plantation population, in spite of differences of race and status, constituted what I have described as a we-group. This was conspicuously the case of the members of the families and the house servants, between whom a lifelong intimacy existed.

Every large plantation in the South tended to assume the character of a little feudal state, each relatively independent of the others. In the intimacy of that isolated life, racial antipathy, such as existed elsewhere, and especially in the North, disappeared. Nathaniel S. Shaler, who knew this life intimately says:

> It is an interesting fact, if my observations on the matter are correct, that the instinctive dislike to the Negro disappears more quickly than prejudices against others less remote in quality of body from ourselves. I have never known an instance in which it persisted, provided contacts were intimate.

On the other hand, race and class distinctions within this feudal society were rigidly enforced. Writing of the plantation overseer, John Spencer Bassett says:

> It was not even his fortune to be esteemed for what he did. He was patronized by the benign planters and condemned by the heedless. He might belong to the same church with the planter, but he usually preferred some plain form of worship, as in the churches of Methodists or Baptists. If the two found themselves worshiping in the same place they sat apart quite distinctly. Their children did not visit one another nor intermarry. Each was a class in society, and between them in social matters was a frozen ocean.
>
> When there was illness in the overseer's family there was much kindness for him in the mansion. The mistress on a Southern plantation knew no caste in time of distress. . . . But she knew, and the overseer knew, that her visits of mercy were not visits of social equality. And he suffered nothing in his mind because of his lower place on the ladder. He was born to it. His wife was born to it. His children would never have aught else so far as the existing environment was concerned. Being a sensible man, he was not discontented. He took the best he could get of what life offered to overseers, finding his wife and marrying off his children in the ranks of such people as himself. If he did not like this prospect, and sometimes he was in revolt against it, he might turn to the frontier, which always had a welcome for a man with courage and industry.

One may suspect that the distances which separated the families of the planter and the overseer, if they were not so great as those between master and slave, were more rigidly maintained. However, the very definiteness with which the position of the overseer was defined within the plantation hierarchy, is an indication of the solid character of the institution. The structure within which master and slave had lived for two hundred and fifty years was not at once dissolved by the publication of the emancipation proclamation. The old order, which was fixed in the habits and customs of both races, persisted long after the institution of slavery had been deprived of its legal sanctions. In many of its characteristic features it exists today; but it is crumbling.

EFFECTS OF SOCIAL DISSOLUTION

The effect of the gradual dissolution of the traditional social order was to release interests and passions which, on the plantation if not in the cities, had achieved something like a stable equilibrium. The resulting struggles and conflicts, with the incidental disorganization, released all the latent animosities in the old social order, and created antipathies and prejudices between the races which previously did not exist.

Prejudices against the Negro in the South were, and are still, prejudices in favor of an order that is changing or no longer exists. "The Negro," Southern people were wont to say, "is all right in his place." On the whole, and so far as one may make any general statement of the matter, race prejudice in the Southern States is caste prejudice. If the Negro were content to remain in a subordinate position to which the white man's prejudices—prejudices which have grown up through long and intimate association—assigned him, racial animosities would probably not exist.

As far as the South is concerned, it is where racial prejudices, and the social order which they perpetuated, are breaking down, that racial animosities are most intense. It is when the Negro invades a new region that race riots occur; it is when he seeks a place in a new occupation or a new profession that he meets the most vigorous opposition; it is when he seeks to assume a new dignity that he ceases to be quaint and becomes ridiculous.

The Negro achieved in slavery a definite position in the social organization and the cultural life of the South. In the South the black man is a native and has his roots in the soil; he has a place in tradition and is a figure in literature. The folk-songs of the South are Negro songs. Tradition assigns him a place in the social order, and race prejudice has made it difficult for him to get out of it.

Not so in the North. There, until very recently, the Negro has been, in the main, a sojourner and a stranger. He has had more freedom, but his status is precarious and undefined. It is true that, in the more liberal atmosphere of the Northern cities, the Negro has contributed something of his tradition to literature and something of his temperament to the stage. On the other hand, as a serious figure either in literature or on the stage, he is still a good deal of a novelty and his contributions to our culture have the interest of something exotic.

Antagonism to the Negro in the North is different from that which he meets in the South. In the North it is less prejudice than antipathy, which is something more elementary and more insidious.

Racial antipathies, in a somewhat more positive sense than is true of racial prejudices, have their sources in fundamental human nature. This does not mean, however, that any particular prejudice nor the antipathies with which it is so often associated are instinctive; that is to say, biologically fixed and inalterable, so that the individual who grows up without the customary and expected race consciousness and the corresponding race prejudice, is to be regarded as in some sense abnormal—an aberrant individual.

Race consciousness, like the racial reserves, antipathies, and tabus in which it finds expression, is invariably, as far as observation goes, an acquired trait, quite as much as the taste for olives or the mania for collecting stamps. Children do not have it. They take the world of human beings in which they find themselves as part of the order of nature and respond to a black or yellow face as readily as they do to a white, depending upon the character and intimacy of the association. In the South it is a mark of distinction to have had a "black mammy," and the lasting affections which have so frequently grown out of that early intimacy are unquestionably the normal and natural consequences of human associations of this description everywhere.

RACE INSTINCTIVENESS

The fact seems to be that what we ordinarily regard as instinctive and biologically determined in our behavior and attitudes toward peoples and races other than our own, is merely, in the first instance at least, the spontaneous response of most sentient creatures—including men and dogs—to what is strange and unfamiliar. We are always keenly conscious of whatever in our experience is novel and undefined, and we are invariably interested in other creatures like ourselves, especially if they are at the same time different. Man is notoriously the most unstable and unpredictable element in the environment. Nature, physical nature, is changing and moody; but behind those brooding human faces that men wear, and particularly behind those faces that we do not know, who can tell what things are going on?

On the whole, we may define the situation in which races meet, as one of vague apprehension tinged with and qualified by curiosity. The first effect is to provoke in us a state of tension—a more vivid awareness and readiness to act—and with that a certain amount of reserve and self-consciousness which is incident to every effort at self-control. In all this there is so far neither prejudice nor antipathy, but merely expectancy. The strange new creature may prove to be attractive, even fascinating. The reports of the first meetings of primitive peoples with Europeans are instructive on this point. The first Europeans to reach Mexico were received ceremonially and regarded as superior beings.

On the other hand, if we seek to get at the very core of this so-called instinctive element in race prejudice, it seems to have its locus just here. If the strange creature approach too suddenly, or if on further acquaintance he seems to behave in outlandish and in-calculable ways, we may retain our interest, but we maintain our distance. In that case, anything approaching intimacy may leave us with a vague sense of insecurity and malaise which effectually limits intercourse and understanding.

It is in such situations, I suspect, that those antipathies arise which seem to constitute the most irrational, and at the same time the most invincible, elements in racial prejudice. The sense of insecurity which the presence of the stranger inspires, when not dispelled by more intimate acquaintance, crystallizes into an atti-tude. Sentiments grow about it which give it substance and support. The racial mark becomes a symbol of these sentiments, the core of which is a sense of insecurity. We do not know what, under certain circumstances, a creature so unlike ourselves will do. Even after a prolonged and rather intimate acquaintance with an individ-ual of another race, there usually remains a residue of uncertainty and vague apprehension, particularly if the stranger maintains a reserve that we cannot fully penetrate. Under such circumstances it is inevitable that rumors and legends will arise and gain general currency which purport to describe and explain racial differences, but in fact serve merely to give support to apprehensions and vague terrors for which there is no real ground in fact. Anything that tends to make a mystery of divergent and alien races, even biological theories which suggest remote and ill-defined dangers of contact and intimacy, tends to intensify antipathies and lend support to racial prejudices. For racial differences in which we are ultimately inter-ested are not the obviously physical and biological marks by which one race is distinguished from another, but the less obvious mental and moral traits of which these physical characters are assumed to be an index and a symbol. The more obvious the differences in physical traits, the greater the presumption of fundamentally divergent moral characteristics.

ANTIPATHIES

Racial antipathies are intensified by anything which arouses disgust. For this reason we tend to contract many of our racial antipathies, so to speak, through the nose. Some writers have gone so far as to suppose that the sense of smell is, in some subtle way, a guide to moral differences in individuals. At any rate, it seems to be a fact that races and individuals have each a distinctive smell, and this odor becomes, in certain cases, the sensuous basis for racial antipathies. The Hindu, for example, who are so meticulous about their contacts with aliens, as well as with members of the different castes of their own people, profess a special abhorrence to the smell of the Anglo-Saxon. A few years ago a Hindu acquaintance of mine, in explaining the opposition of his family to his marriage to an American woman, confessed that his father had written him saying he hoped, if no other considerations were sufficient, that the smell of an Anglo-Saxon would be sufficient to prohibit such a mesalliance. W. H. Hudson, in his volume "A Hind in Richmond Park," discussing the sense of smell in animals, devotes a chapter to the explanation of the fact that those who have a nose for these things are sensitive to the smell of other races, but quite oblivious to the odor of their own. He relates an incident, by way of illustration, which I quote in his own words:

Many and curious are the tricks our olfactories play us ... A young army doctor in India and at Bombay zealously set himself to win a good private practice. He made himself well known in the society of the place, and his servant had strict instructions to come always into the church where he attended Sunday morning services to call him out to a supposed urgent case.

The natives just then were in a state of political excitement, and he was desirous of finding out all he could about their aspirations, intentions, and so on. One day he told his servant that he wished to attend a big meeting about to be held in a quarter of the town he was not well acquainted with, to listen to the speeches of the orators, and he asked his man to take him there and get him admitted. Accordingly, they went on an oppressively hot evening, and he sat in a huge densely packed hall for about half an hour, then came out. After taking a few deep breaths he exclaimed: "What a relief to get out! In another ten minutes I should have collapsed. The smell!"

To which his servant promptly replied: "Ah, Sahib, *now* you will understand what I suffer every Sunday when I have to go right to the middle of the church to call you out! ..."

The extraordinary readiness, the candour, the spontaneity, and even the glee, with which he brought out his words made it impossible for his master to doubt his perfect sincerity. He had taken it for granted that his master *would* understand, and after his own unhappy experience at the native meeting would be ready to sympathize with his servant's sufferings in the performance of that painful Sunday duty. . . . And what did it mean? Why, that we white-skinned Westerners, lords of creation, have our smell just as the blacks and bi-colored races and the lower animals have theirs; that we are unconscious of this fact with regard to ourselves—our own race—but are quite conscious of it with regard to the others.

It is because smell is so definitely associated with the organic reactions that it is the least intellectual of the senses. For the same reason, no doubt, it is so intimately related to the antipathies and the sentiments generally. At any rate, racial antipathies are frequently concerned with touch and smell. If these antipathies have, as many persons contend, a biological significance, it is because they seem to inhibit intimate and ultimately sexual contacts. They are a bar to miscegenation. There seems to be just as good reason for adopting, as some writers do, the opposite view. It is the strange woman who is sexually the more stimulating; and it is the man from abroad to whom the most romantic interest attaches. This is one explanation of exogamy.

The facts seems to indicate that racial antipathies and tabus have a conventional rather than a natural and instinctive origin. The man who arrives with a strange, new, pungent odor may arouse disgust, but he may, under other circumstances, evoke a sentiment of awe and respect. We are most of us familiar with the odor of sanctity that attaches to saints and sacred edifices. It seems, therefore, that antipathy and prestige may, and perhaps often do, rest on the same sensuous basis. To a Hindu, the mere thought of eating meat is disgusting. The Japanese are shocked to see men and women embrace in public. Whether a stranger entering an unfamiliar society will be treated with consideration or contempt, is apparently uncertain, except in so far as the situation is controlled by ceremonial and etiquette. It is notorious that representatives of every race and color have been received at one time and another in the most select and intimate circles. Marco Polo was received with distinction at the court of Kublai Khan, and Booker T. Washington dined with President Roosevelt at the White House. It seems as if there were no instinctive racial antipathies that cannot be overcome by scrupulous adherence to etiquette.

CEREMONIAL AND SOCIAL RITUAL

While etiquette and ceremonial are at once a convenience and a necessity in facilitating human intercourse, they serve even more effectively to maintain social distances and to preserve the rank and order of individuals and classes, which seems to be essential to social organization and effective collective action. This is the significance of the ceremonial and social ritual so rigidly enforced in the South, by which racial distinctions are preserved amid all the inevitable changes and promiscuity of an expanding industrial and democratic society. Thus white folk and colored, in the small town at any rate, eat at the same restaurant, if it is conducted by a Negro, but not at the same tables.

A colored nurse may ride, without objection, in a Pullman coach if she has a white baby in her arms. On the other hand, if a white nurse should appear in the same car with a colored baby, no one knows what would happen. There is no provision in the social ritual for the unprecedented.

Southern people have difficulty in addressing a colored man as "Mr.," even though he may have achieved an eminent position in the world. In that case it is possible to avoid the difficulty, as one man is reported to have done in the case of Booker T. Washington, by calling him "Professor." A distinguished clergyman in the Southern Episcopal Church, after some mental conflict, announced a few years ago that he had resolved that thenceforth when a colored woman was decently married, to address her as "Mrs.," "out of respect," as he explained, "for the holy estate of matrimony."

On the other hand, in a little Negro town in Oklahoma, Boley, where at the time no separate provision was made for white visitors, a traveling salesman appealed to the Negro hotel keeper to give him a table apart, because, as he said, with a certain amount of pathos in his voice, "I am from Mississippi, and I just can't eat with you niggers."

These are illustrations of what Ogburn calls "cultural lag." The situation changes, but the cultural form persists.

There exists in the South, and in the North too, for that matter, a great body of materials which no student of race problems has, so far as I know, seen fit or found time to collect and interpret. These are the legends, anecdotes, and racial myths current in the South in which each race, in perfect good faith, and often with very real insight, has characterized the follies and foibles, and occasionally the more excellent qualities, of the other. These materials, because they do not get into print, are a kind of folklore, a form of verbal literature which passes sometimes for history, and sometimes for scientific fact. In this as in every other form of literature, the wishes—and particularly the conflicting wishes—of the two races are unconsciously reflected. As might be expected, the stories which circulate among white people concerning Negroes tend to support the traditional social order, which assigns every Negro to a position inferior to that of every white man. On the other hand, the stories which circulate among Negroes are those which show that the old order is cracking or exhibit the traditional racial distinctions in some paradoxical or logically untenable and ridiculous form.

For example, a white farmer in Alabama, one of the so-called "poor whites," became greatly interested in the farm demonstration work which a colored agent was carrying on among the Negroes. The white man invited the colored agent to come over and look at his place and advise him about his crops. Eventually he invited him to stay to dinner. He arranged the matter simply. The colored man sat at one table, and the white man at another, close enough to continue their discussions. The white man's wife waited upon them both. This was merely reversing the situation in which a white man visits a Negro planter and perhaps remains all night. In that case, the white man eats in the dining room, and colored more than likely eats in the kitchen. In both cases the social amenities are served, and what amounts, in these cases, to caste distinctions are preserved. They are part of the etiquette which makes intercourse and cooperation among the races in the South possible.

CHANGE IN RACE RELATIONS

Originally race relations in the South could be rather accurately represented by a horizontal line, with all the white folk above, and all the Negro folk below. But at present these relations are assuming new forms, and in consequence changing in character and meaning. With the development of industrial and professional classes within the Negro race, the distinction between the races tends to assume the form of a vertical line. On one side of this line the Negro is represented in most of the occupational and professional classes; on the other side of the line the white man is similarly represented. The situation *was* this:

All white

All colored

It is *now* this:

White	*Colored*
Professional occupation	Professional occupation
Business occupation	Business occupation
Labor	Labor

The result is to develop in every occupational class professional and industrial bi-racial organizations. Bi-racial organizations preserve race distinction, but change their content. The distances which separate the races are maintained, but the attitudes involved are different. The races no longer look up and down: they look across. These bi-racial organizations, so far as I know, are a unique product

of the racial struggle in this country; they do not exist outside the
United States.

The previous reading by Park has shown the mobility of the classes
and implied some equality of status for members of both ethnic
groups based on a common occupation. We now turn to an analysis
of the caste and class statement of white-Negro relations as interpreted
by Professor Warner. A dichotomy of ethnic relations is presented for
analysis. Warner suggests that ethnic relations may reflect a class and
caste status. It is worth realizing that caste is a more permanent status
than class.

▌ AMERICAN CASTE AND CLASS [2]

W. LLOYD WARNER

The social organization of the Deep South consists of two different
kinds of social stratification. There is not only a caste system, but
there is also a class structure. Ordinarily the social scientist thinks
of these two different kinds of vertical structures as antithetical to
each other. It is rare that the comparative sociologist finds a class
structure being maintained together with a caste structure.

Caste as used here describes a theoretical arrangement of the
people of the given group in an order in which the privileges, duties,
obligations, are considered to be higher and lower. There are social
sanctions which tend to maintain this unequal distribution. Such
a definition also describes class. A caste organization, however, can
be further defined as one where marriage between two or more
groups is not sanctioned and where there is no opportunity for
members of the lower groups to rise into the upper groups or of the
members of the upper to fall into the lower ones. In class, on the
other hand, there is a certain proportion of interclass marriage
between lower and higher groups, and there are, in the very nature
of the class organization, mechanisms established by which people
move up and down the vertical extensions of the society. Obviously,
two such structures are antithetical to each other, the one inflexibly
prohibiting movement between the two groups and intergroup marriage, and the other sanctioning intergroup movement and at least
certain kinds of marriage between higher and lower classes. Nevertheless, they have accommodated themselves to each other in the
southern community we examined.

Perhaps the best way to present the configurations of the two kinds

[2] *American Journal of Sociology*, Vol. 42, No. 2 (Sept., 1936), pp. 234-237. Used by
permission of The University of Chicago Press.

of vertical structure is by means of Figure 1. The diagonal lines separate the lower Negro caste (N) from the upper white caste (W), and two broken lines in each segment separate the three general classes (upper, middle, and lower) in each caste from each other. The two double-headed vertical arrows indicate that movement up and down the class ladder in each caste can and does take place and

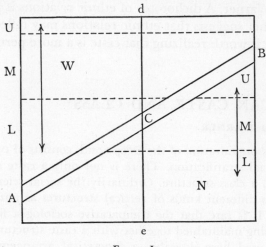

FIGURE I

is socially sanctioned, but that there is no movement of marriage between the two segments. The diagonal arrangement of the parallel lines which separate the two castes expresses the essential skewness created by the conflict of caste and class in the South. The gradual elaboration of the economic, educational, and general social activities of the Negro caste since slavery (and to some extent even before) has created new groups which have been vertically arranged by the society until certain fairly well-marked class groups have developed within the Negro caste. As the vertical distance of the Negro group has been extended during the years, the top Negro layer has been pushed higher and higher. This has swung the caste line on its axis (c), so that the top Negro group is higher in class than the lower white groups and is so recognized. (This recognition is expressed in circumlocutions and by unconscious actions, but is at times also consciously and openly stated by the members of both the white and the Negro groups.) If this process continues, as it seems to be doing at the present time, it is possible, and indeed probable, that the lines AB might move on the axis c until they approximate the hypothetical line de. (Theoretically, of course, this process could go farther, but it seems unlikely.) This tendency to bring the two groups out of vertical opposition and organization into a horizontal arrangement is being reflected at the present time in such movement as "parallelism," as expounded by Dr. DuBois. Such terms as "parallelism" are kinds of collective representations which have come into existence and approximately express the social facts of the changing social structure; at the same time, of course, allowing the sentiments of some of the people who live in the structure also to find expression. Should the line AB reach the position *ed*, the class situation in either group would not be fundamentally disturbed, except that the top Negro group would be equivalent with the top white, while the lower classes in each of the parallel groups would also be equivalent. Even the present approximation of this gives the top Negro group certain advantages over his lower class fellows which he is anxious to maintain.

On the other hand, the social skewness created by the present class-caste conflict which results in the process of changing the social location of the caste line has placed the upper-class Negro in a decidedly difficult situation. The Negro who has moved or been born into the uppermost group (see the chart) of his caste is superior to the lower whites in class, but inferior in caste. In his own personality he feels the conflict of the two opposing structures, and in the thinking and feeling of the members of both groups there is to be found this same conflict about his position. He is known to be superior to the "poor white" (he is a doctor, say), but he is still a "nigger" or "Negro," according to the social context in which the words are used. Metaphorically speaking, although he is at the top of the Negro class hierarchy, he is constantly butting his head against the caste line. He knows himself to be superior to the poor white, yet to the poor white the upper-class Negro is still a "nigger," which is a way of saying the Negro is in a lower caste than himself. Furthermore, if it ever came to an issue, the supraordinate white class would maintain the solidarity of the white group by repudiating any claims by any Negro of superiority to the lower-class whites. This would be true even though the admission might be made privately that the Negro was superior to certain of the lower-class whites.

The present and past political behavior of the South has to be understood, it seems to me, in terms of the maintenance of the caste lines, and as an effort to prevent the continued elaboration and segmentation of the class groups within the lower caste. The unequal distribution of school funds and privileges are an excellent example of how the system tends to maintain itself through the changing generations. The operation of the courts and the activities of the police also reflect the same conscious or unconscious maintenance of control by the supraordinate white caste. For that matter, all

social institutions in the South, including the family, school, association, clique, and church, are formed to fit the dominant caste social
situation of the dominant social caste.

An interesting hypothesis may be built out of the skewed social
position of the upper-class Negro. It seems possible that the instability of many of the individuals in this group (as compared, let us say,
with the Negroes of the lower positions) may be due to the instability
and skewness of the social situation in which they live.

Park and Warner have described ethnic relations in terms of
diagrams indicating the importance of class status. To them many of
the problems in ethnic relations result from attempts to change the
class structure. Professor Bogardus sees ethnic relations in terms of
sequences of reactions, actually an ethnic social process. To him ethnic relations often run a characteristic sequence of typical reactions.

▌ A RACE-RELATIONS CYCLE [3]

EMORY S. BOGARDUS

A cycle as used here is a recurrence of group behavior, and a race-
relations cycle may be conceived as a recurrence in the behavior of
natives toward immigrants. While the history of the behavior of
native Americans toward newcomers would doubtless show many
race-relations cycles, only one will be described in this article.

The history of treatment by Americans of races conspicuously
different from themselves in one or more particulars reveals several
recurring stages. By conspicuously different races is meant those
made distinctive by color, religion, political and economic doctrines,
or by other physical and cultural factors. The conclusions of this
analysis are drawn from first-hand studies of American reactions
toward oriental and Mexican immigrants: first, of reactions toward
Chinese immigrants extending back to about 1868; second, of reactions toward Japanese immigrants beginning in the early nineties;
and, third and fourth, of reactions now taking place with reference
to the Filipinos and Mexicans, but extending back ten or twelve
years. The main cycles of American behavior toward the Chinese
and Japanese appear to be concluded, but the cycles relating to
Filipinos and Mexicans are in actual process at the present moment
and are reaching climaxes. They are, therefore, especially significant
for observation and research. The natural history of American
responses to the Chinese, Japanese, and now to Filipino and Mexi-

[3] *American Journal of Sociology*, Vol. 35 (Jan., 1930), pp. 612-617. Used by permission
of The University of Chicago Press.

can immigrants reveals sufficient recurrences in each case, as well as
similarities in the behavior recurrences, to justify the label of a race-
relations cycle.

1. *Curiosity.*—The first comers of these culturally strange races
have been uniformly viewed with curiosity. Sympathetic responses
have been widely generated by the lone stranger far away from his
home base. His strangeness coupled with his original fewness of
numbers make him appear helpless. Defense mechanisms and mores
were not aroused against him. With a certain supposedly secret air
of superiority, Americans have met and greeted him, curious as to
who and why he is. His strange culture traits have invited passing
comments, while he, seeing the culture traits of Americans, has
responded cautiously at first but with rising hopes.

2. *Economic welcome.*—The strange newcomers have put in an
appearance sometimes because of a spirit of adventure, sometimes
because of a luring halo attached to the United States, but more
often because of high wages. To make "big money," to save as much
as possible, to return wealthy is often the plan which has led on
occasion to long hours of labor in this country and to a willingness
to work for less than American standards permit.

Employers of labor, therefore, have been quick to employ, and
at least indirectly to encourage these immigrants to send for relatives and friends. American wages have seemed unusually high, and
the immigrants have sent the good news home. Relatives and friends
have responded with alacrity. Increasing numbers of kinsfolk have
come. There has been great rejoicing because of the golden opportunities offered by the economic welcome in the United States.

3. *Industrial and social antagonism.*—Suddenly and perplexingly
to these immigrant peoples, reactions have broken out against them.
They have hardly been prepared for the vicious propaganda that
has been spread against them, especially in this land of the free,
where brotherhood of man, a square deal, and a high degree of
enlightenment are boasted. First, sporadic outbursts of prejudice
against them have occurred, and then organized movements have
gained a tremendous momentum, reaching to the farthermost cor-
ners of the nation. At the time these immigrants seemed to be getting
a footing and to be reaching a degree of economic independence for
which Americans are noted, they have heard the roar of an oncoming
storm. Organized labor has usually been the leader in protesting
against the conspicuously different immigrants, on grounds of protecting labor against unfair competition and the pulling down of
standards built up at great sacrifice by American workers. Organized
labor has had the prompt co-operation of patriotic societies of one
kind or another, who usually are the watchdogs of the national

mores. Silver-tongued politicians and crowd-exciting chauvinists have stood forth in this hue-and-cry phase of the race-relations cycle.

The organized opposition to conspicuous immigrants acquires momentum because the immigrants have come in such increasing volume. There has seemed to be uncounted millions on the way. It is easy for the imagination of natives to picture this country being overrun and overwhelmed by literal millions of these foreigners. It is natural for the latter to immigrate faster than they can be assimilated. Because of wide differences in culture traits, assimilation must necessarily take place slowly.

The high birth-rate of both orientals and Mexicans is disturbing to many Americans. All these numerous children, it is asserted, will soon grow up, will be citizens, will outvote the natives, and will take control of political affairs. Seen in a teeming perspective, these strange peoples arouse every conceivable type of defense mechanism of the natives. Their very conspicuousness seems to multiply their numbers manifold. Sheer numbers of immigrants plus high birth-rates constitute a tremendous threat against the established order.

The fact that the assimilation of these immigrants is hindered if not prevented by natives is not considered. The related fact that the acculturation of the children of these immigrants is in the hands of natives is also but vaguely conceived. Natives do not appreciate how they may bring about the assimilation and acculturation of both the first- and second-generation immigrants, and thus avoid foreign usurpation.

A special type of antagonistic expression is found in the reactions of a neighborhood invaded by the conspicuous foreigner. Like other immigrants, the Chinese, Japanese, Filipinos, and Mexicans all tend on arrival to live together in groups or immigrant settlements. After a time, however, some of the more progressive, catching the progressive spirit of natives, seek a higher status for themselves and better homes for their families. They acquire the worthy idea of moving out of the despised (by Americans) foreign quarters, and of moving into a "respectable" American neighborhood. At once adverse opinions are heard. Signs go up: "Japs are not wanted," or "Japs get out." Danger to property values looms up. Realtors who have taken a part in the selling or leasing of property to these conspicuously different people are threatened by the irate neighbors.

The native considers that his status, or the status of his neighborhood, is lowered by "race invasions." His friends raise invidious questions when they visit him. A few strange neighbors may soon lead to an "influx," and an influx may mean ultimately a complete change of population. Old and well-established sentiments are aroused; crowd psychology and even mob psychology may become

rampant. Neighborhood antagonism joins with patriotic or chauvin-
istic antagonism.

4. *Legislative antagonism.*—The next phase of the race-relations
cycle logically follows. Bills are introduced into legislatures and into
Congress. A full-fledged campaign is organized against the "undesirable" immigrants. The latter are openly, publicly, and sometimes
viciously denounced. Only one side of the case is presented to the
general public. Politicians attempt to make their legislative berths
secure by campaigning in behalf of the public, the state, and the
nation—against the invaders. These tirades are inexpensive, for
orientals are ineligible to vote, and Mexicans are unnaturalized to
any extent and hence cannot vote. The legislative phase gains
momentum until its objective is reached or until the threatened
danger is past.

5. *Fair-play tendencies.*—Belatedly but invariably a "fair-play"
movement develops. Broadminded Americans initiate a counter-
movement, not only because of friendship for the immigrants but
because the latter are being attacked unjustly. This counterphase
operates under serious handicaps. It is usually not well organized,
is lacking in financial support, is not steadily aggressive, is hampered
by the zealots and dreamers among its numbers who bring it into
disrepute. It is, however, a source of comfort and understanding to
many of the immigrants in question. It helps them to retain confidence in American life and principles. It holds somewhat in check
the anti-race reactions and prevents the race antagonists from going
to ultimate extremes. It serves as a balance wheel to an otherwise
one-sided mechanism. It maintains the idealistic reputation of the
nation in the eyes of the world.

6. *Quiescence.*—After the sought-for restrictive or prohibitive
legislation was passed, in both the Chinese and Japanese race cycles,
there was a sudden slowing up of the antagonistic activities. Assured
that the impending danger is safely thwarted, the antagonistic organizations modify their attitudes. After the Japanese were excluded in
1924, the anti-Japanese groups announced a friendly but guarded
attitude toward the Japanese in the state and nation.

If the anti-race movement goes to the extreme of complete exclusion, as it did in dealing with both Chinese and Japanese immigration, then the protagonist groups express sympathy for the unjustly
treated immigrants and silently vow to secure justice for the latter
some day. If needed restriction, but not exclusion had been adopted
in both the Chinese and Japanese race-relation cycles, it is probable
that the protagonistic phase would have passed away entirely.

7. *Second-generation difficulties.*—Another important phase develops later if needed restriction, but not exclusion, had been called

the second-generation problem. This has developed serious proportions in the case of the Japanese and the Mexicans, who have come
to the United States with their wives and families. The children of
the Japanese and Mexicans have been undergoing assimilation in
the schools and through many other contacts. They have been losing
contact with the home-country culture, and have been partially
ostracized. But because of their conspicuous nature (color or culture
heritage), they have been only partially accepted in the land of their
birth and citizenship.

This statement of a race-relations cycle has developed naturally
out of the study of Chinese-immigrant and Japanese-immigrant experiences in the United States. It is significant as a measuring stick
for considering the developing Mexican and Filipino situations in
this country. At first (1) Mexican immigrants were viewed with some
curiosity and with pity; (2) they were, and are, being sought as
laborers by large-scale employers; (3) reactions against them have
developed, and are still in process. Bills have been introduced
(4) in Congress against them; (5) and a fair-play movement in their
behalf is in operation. There are strong indications that the sixth
and seventh phases are materializing. The Filipinos likewise have
experienced the first five phases of the race-relations cycle. They will
doubtless experience the sixth, but will escape the seventh, for their
numbers are so largely male.

SUMMARY

One of the chief adjustment problems emerges when there is a
change in the status of an ethnic group. Social organization structures
ethnic groups in certain status categories. As long as each ethnic
group accepts the existing pattern of adjustment, few problems
develop. However, when an individual or a group challenges the
entire pattern of adjustment by demanding a change in the status
quo, then the problem of adjustment becomes acute and borders on
conflict. Sociologists have attempted to describe the patterns of
adjustment in order to throw light on the social organization maintaining ethnic relations.

Both Professors Park and Warner have attempted to indicate the
status areas by diagrams. Professor Park sees the new pattern as one
of biracial adjustment. The whites and Negroes look across at each
other with respect to a class structure. Under slave conditions Park
suggests that all whites looked down on all Negroes, but this pattern
of adjustment has been changed with a different class structure of
the two ethnic groups. A very different point of view is maintained

by Professor Warner who depicts ethnic relations in terms of caste and class. He believes, in summary, that the races look across each other on class lines, but certainly not on caste lines. Caste separates the white medical doctor from the Negro physician no matter how similar the status may be in class or occupational status. *The caste status is an inherited status, whereas the class status implies that there is a certain mobility possible.* Class status fits in with the popular conception of democracy.

It must be recognized that Professor Warner has critics, such as Professor Oliver Cox who does not agree with Warner's analysis of white-Negro relations in the South. Cox definitely challenges Warner's conception of a caste system. He doubts that a caste system prevents *all* intermarriage between selected members of different castes. In addition, there is considerable evidence of ethnic intermixture in the South; hence, the interracial marriage barrier can be circumvented. The Warner thesis may be defended, in part, that ethnic relations in the South *appear* to resemble the antithetical elements of a caste system.

Professor Emory S. Bogardus describes the progression of ethnic relations through a cycle of adjustment starting with curiosity, and including, economic welcome, industrial antagonism, legislative antagonism, fair-play tendencies, quiescence, and finally, second-generation difficulties. Dr. Bogardus' cycle of ethnic relations was designed particularly to indicate the adjustment steps of immigrants to this country.

PROBLEMS FOR STUDY AND DISCUSSION

1. Explain the meaning of the concepts *class* and *caste*. Express whether or not you think that there is a caste system in the United States.

2. List and explain the patterns of ethnic adjustment that you have knowledge of. Evaluate each of these in keeping with the principles of reason.

3. Explain the meaning of "biracial organization" as used by Park. Discuss the extent to which you think this form of organization exists among the various ethnic groups in the United States.

4. Explain the ethnic relations diagram that is presented by Warner. In keeping with your knowledge of ethnic relations in the United States, express your agreement or disagreement with Warner's diagram.

5. List and explain the meaning of each of the stages in the race relations cycle that is presented by Bogardus. Select one minority ethnic group that you are familiar with and apply this cycle to its relations in the United States.

SELECTED READINGS

BERRY, Brewton, *Race Relations* (Boston: Houghton Mifflin Company, 1951), pp. 157-351.

BOGARDUS, Emory S., *Immigration and Race Attitudes* (Boston: D. C. Heath and Company, 1928), chap. 4.

BROWN, Francis J., and ROUCEK, Joseph S. *One America* (New York: Prentice-Hall, Inc., 1952), chap. 23.

COX, Oliver, *Caste, Class and Race* (New York: Doubleday and Company, Inc., 1948).

GALLAGHER, Buell G., *American Caste and the Negro College* (New York: Columbia University Press, 1938).

HALSEY, Margaret, *Color Blind* (New York: Simon and Schuster, Inc., 1946).

WARNER, W. L., and SROLE, Leo, *The Social Systems of American Ethnic Groups* (New Haven: Yale University Press, 1945).

II

ANALYZING ETHNIC RELATIONS

V

The Negro in the South

Introduction

FOR MANY REASONS it is impossible to understand the status struggle of ethnic groups in the United States without giving considerable attention to the position of the Negro in the social scheme of ethnic groups. From a numerical standpoint, the Negro is the *largest minority* ethnic group in this country. Chronologically, the Negro is the *second oldest* group that has challenged the ability of leaders in the United States to deal "justly" with minority ethnic groups. In color, the Negro represents the *greatest variation* from what is considered to be the "typical American" in the United States.

Throughout most of our history, and at the present time, the Negro has been the largest specific minority ethnic group residing in the United States. In making this statement it is recognized that Caucasians have always predominated in the total population, but this group has included representatives from many cultural and nationality groups. Although the proportion of the Negro population in the total population has decreased since 1790 (the first census report), the number of Negroes in the United States has increased from 757,208 in 1790 to approximately 15,042,692 in 1950. In 1930 the total number of foreign-born whites in the United States was greater than that of Negroes, but the number included representatives from more than fifty nationality groups. In 1950 the total number for the Negro was definitely higher than that for any other minority ethnic group, including other racial, cultural, or nationality groups.

Chronologically, the Negro is third in importance among the ethnic groups in the United States which are discussed in this book. The Indians were occupying the area when foreign-born whites arrived, and Negroes came in with foreign-born whites or were brought in a few years later. Historical data point out that Negroes entered what is now the United States from two directions. During the first half of the sixteenth century, Negroes accompanied Spanish explorers on expeditions into the southwestern part of the country.[1] However, the first Negroes to enter the area as permanent residents were the twenty Negroes left at Jamestown, Virginia in 1619.[2] Thus, considered from the standpoint of temporary or permanent entrance, the Negro was the third ethnic group to come into the area now included in the United States.

In color the Negroes represented the greatest possible variation from the population residing in the area when they arrived. The first Negroes brought into the United States are described as black. Since this beginning the color of the Negro population has been modified through a process of miscegenation. Nevertheless, today the Negro is distinguished from other ethnic groups by color more than by any other factor.

Present Negro Population

The present Negro population in the United States is a mixture of the many racial, cultural, and nationality groups that constitute the total population. Because of the inadequacies of scientific measurements it is difficult, if not impossible, to determine the exact extent to which the various ethnic groups in the total population have contributed to the composition of the present Negro population. However, observation of any large group of Negroes will disclose the presence of some physical characteristics that are ascribed to each of the major racial, nationality, or ethnic groups.

The degree to which the Negro is mixed with other ethnic groups varies in different areas of the United States. In most rural sections of the South, Negroid characteristics appear to predominate. In southern Louisiana, and other areas that were settled by the French, there is an abundance of the physical and cultural characteristics usually ascribed to the French. In the Southwest one can easily recognize characteristics that are considered as Indian or Mexican. As this color mixture of black with red and white will usually result in some shade of brown, it is easy to agree with Embree in classifying Negroes in the United States as brown Americans. Embree describes brown Americans as a hybrid racial group that is indigenous to the United

[1] John Hope Franklin, *From Slavery to Freedom: A History of American Negroes* (New York: Alfred A. Knopf, Inc., 1947), p. 46.
[2] *Ibid.*, p. 70.

States and that has developed as a result of mixtures of the many racial, nationality, and ethnic groups which have made up the total population of the United States from its origin to the present time.[3]

Location of the Negro Population

The greatest concentration of the Negro population is in the region designated as the South by the Census Bureau of the United States. Table II shows 68.5 per cent of the total Negro population in the United States resided in the sixteen southern states and in the District of Columbia in 1950. This leaves a scattering of 31.5 per cent in the other thirty-two states. Although it is recognized that some shifting of the population distribution in the United States will occur, it is believed that this shifting will not be sufficient to disturb, to any extensive degree, the concentration of the Negro population in the South.

This concentration of the Negro population is more impressive if consideration is given to the proportion of the Negro population to the total population in several of the southern states. According to Table III, the percentages of the Negro population to the total population in the southern states ranged from 5.7 per cent in West Virginia to 45.2 per cent in Mississippi. The percentages for states outside the South range downward from around 5 per cent to less than 0.1 per cent. In nine of the southern states the percentage for the Negro is approximately 22 per cent or more: Mississippi, South Carolina, Louisiana, Alabama, Georgia, North Carolina, Arkansas, Virginia, and Florida in the order listed. Further, from the standpoint of numbers four of these states have a Negro population of approximately one million or more: North Carolina, Georgia, Alabama, and Mississippi in the order listed. Thus, from the standpoint of proportions or numbers the Negro population in the United States is concentrated in the South, with the most intense concentration in the states that are usually referred to as the "deep south."

This concentration of the Negro population is one of the factors that has contributed to the differentiated statuses of the Negro in the United States. At the present time it is impossible to refer to the status of *"the Negro"* in the United States. The fact is he has many statuses. These statuses vary in keeping with the different regions, the many states, and even within any one state in the United States.

[3] Edwin R. Embree, *Brown America: The Story of a New Race* (New York: Viking Press, Inc., 1931), pp. 3-10.

Table II: PERCENTAGE DISTRIBUTION OF THE NEGRO POPULATION OF THE UNITED STATES BY REGIONS *

Region	Per Cent of Negro Population
South	68.5
North Central	14.3
Northeast	13.3
West	3.9
United States	100.0

* Seventeenth Census of the United States, *Population* (1950), Preliminary Report.

Table III: PERCENTAGE OF THE NEGRO POPULATION TO THE TOTAL POPULATION IN SIXTEEN SOUTHERN STATES AND THE DISTRICT OF COLUMBIA *

State	Per Cent Negro
Mississippi	45.2
South Carolina	38.8
District of Columbia	35.0
Louisiana	32.9
Alabama	31.9
Georgia	30.8
North Carolina	25.7
Arkansas	22.3
Virginia	22.1
Florida	21.7
Maryland	16.4
Tennessee	16.1
Delaware	13.7
Texas	12.6
Kentucky	6.8
Oklahoma	6.5
West Virginia	5.7

* Seventeenth Census of the United States, *Population* (1950). Percentages computed from an advance Report prepared by the Bureau of the Census for this work, Oct. 10, 1952.

However, it seems as if there is a high correlation between points of concentration and low status. Where the concentration is most intense the status of the Negro is lowest. On the other hand, in the areas where they are few in number Negroes appear to be accorded a higher status. In a text of this nature, however, it is impossible to give attention to the many status aspects of the Negro. Still, to illustrate the point it is necessary to make some division of the United States. The most convenient division that the writers could find is that provided by the Census Bureau, in which the United States is divided into four regions: the South, the North Central, the Northeast, and the West. As the concentration of the Negro population is in the South, this region will be separated from the other three regions in presenting data on the Negro. In doing this it is recognized that the status of the Negro is not the same throughout any region or state, but it is essential to make some division to gain a comparative picture of the varied statuses of the Negro in the United States. In this chapter the Negro in the South will be considered. In the chapter to follow the Negro in the North Central, the Northeast, and the West will be discussed.

Early Negro-White Relations in the South

The first Negroes to be brought into the United States as permanent residents landed in a southern colony, Jamestown, Virginia in 1619.[4] It is consensus among historians that these first Negroes were accepted as indentured servants, a system of securing workers that was in existence at that time in Virginia. In keeping with this system Negro servants were placed in a temporary status of servitude from which they were removed after serving for some definite period. Through a gradual process the status of the Negro in Virginia was changed during the latter part of the seventeenth century from that of indentured servant to that of slave. Since this degrading process was going on in all of the southern colonies, Negro slavery was well established as an economic system by means of which the labor needs of the South could be alleviated by the end of the seventeenth century.

With the development of slavery in the South, there was established a vertical stratification of whites and Negroes according to which all whites were considered superior to all Negroes. In keeping with this stratification Negroes were forced to accept always an inferior status in all contacts between whites and Negroes. The extent to which the inferior status of the Negro was recognized is illustrated by the majority opinion of the United States Supreme Court in the Dred Scott Case, when it was declared that the Negro had no rights which the white man was bound to respect.[5] Since slavery continued in the South for about two hundred years, this superior-inferior pattern of race contacts became so deeply entrenched that more than eighty years of Negro freedom have not been able to remove it, and in some areas have not modified it to any considerable extent.

4 For an excellent analysis of the early status of the Negro in Southern Colonies, see Franklin, *op. cit.,* pp. 70-87.
5 *Dred Scott v. Sanford,* United States 506 (1859).

Contacts based on master-slave relations between whites and Negroes were the accepted pattern until after the Emancipation Proclamation was issued by President Lincoln in 1862. According to this proclamation "all persons held as slaves within any State, or designated part of the State, the people whereof shall be in rebellion against the United States, shall be then, thenceforward, and forever free" on January 1, 1863. As most of the southern states were in rebellion against the United States on January 1, 1863, this proclamation decreed a sudden and abrupt change in the status of the Negro in the South—a change from an extremely inferior status to a status of potential equality. Within eight years after the Emancipation Proclamation was issued the Thirteenth, Fourteenth, and Fifteenth amendments had become a part of the Constitution of the United States. In these amendments the equal status for the Negro that was decreed by the Emancipation Proclamation was given the sanction of the federal government. The extent to which the Negro has been able to gain an equal status in the South will be analyzed in the following pages.

SOCIAL STATUS

The social status of the Negro in the South will be determined by the nature of the attitudes and opinions of whites in the South toward Negroes. In an attempt to point out the attitudes and opinions of whites in the South toward Negroes, many studies have been made by students of ethnic relations in the United States. Five of these studies have been reviewed for the purpose of determining the predominant attitudes of whites in the South toward Negroes; and the attitudes reported most frequently have been tabulated in Table IV. The studies selected are representative and authoritative enough to indicate some of the general attitudes of whites toward Negroes. The studies by Myrdal and Johnson included the whole of the United States, but the attitudes accredited to whites in the South were selected for this study. The study by Odum centered on the South. The study by Davis and Dollard was made in one urban community in Louisiana and one in Mississippi. The study by Powdermaker was made in a small urban community in Mississippi. As these studies include data that were collected throughout the South, they should be sufficient to describe the attitudes and opinions of whites in the South toward Negroes.

Table IV shows the predominant attitudes that were reported in at least four of the five studies. The following six attitudes were reported in all five of the studies reviewed as attitudes of whites toward Negroes: (1) are mentally inferior, (2) social equality is impractical if not impossible, (3) are lazy and shiftless, (4) are incapable of self-discipline, (5) segregation is necessary, and (6) are criminally

Table IV: ATTITUDES OF WHITES IN THE SOUTH TOWARD NEGROES AS REPORTED IN FIVE STUDIES OF RACE RELATIONS IN THE UNITED STATES

Attitude	Myrdal[6]	Odum[7]	Johnson[8]	Davis & Dollard[9]	Powder-maker[10]
Are mentally inferior	X	X	X	X	X
Social equality is impractical if not impossible	X	X	X	X	X
Are lazy and shiftless	X	X	X	X	X
Are incapable of self-discipline	X	X	X	X	X
Segregation is necessary	X	X	X	X	X
Are criminally inclined	X	X	X	X	X
Are all right in their place	X		X	X	X
Intermarriage should be prohibited	X	X	X		X
Possess a low moral standard	X	X	X		X
Are happy-go-lucky and carefree	X	X	X		X
Are not capable of assuming responsibility and leadership	X	X	X		X
Are highly sexual	X		X	X	X
Will lie	X	X		X	X
Are satisfied with their present status		X	X	X	X

[6] Gunnar Myrdal, *An American Dilemma: The Negro Problem and Modern Democracy* (New York: Harper and Brothers, 1944), pp. 50-112.
[7] Howard W. Odum, *Race and Rumors of Race: Challenge to American Crisis* (Chapel Hill: University of North Carolina Press, 1943), pp. 3-31.
[8] Charles S. Johnson, *Patterns of Negro Segregation* (New York: Harper and Brothers, 1943), pp. 194-227.
[9] Allison Davis and John Dollard, *Children of Bondage: The Personality Development of Negro Youth in the Urban South* (Washington, D. C.: American Council on Education, 1940), pp. 17-20, 237-255.
[10] Hortense Powdermaker, *After Freedom: A Cultural Study in the Deep South* (New York: Viking Press, Inc., 1939), pp. 23-42.

inclined. The following eight attitudes were reported in four of the five studies reviewed: (1) are all right in their place, (2) intermarriage should be prohibited, (3) possess a low moral standard, (4) are happy-go-lucky and carefree, (5) are not capable of assuming responsibility and leadership, (6) are highly sexual, (7) will lie, and (8) are satisfied with their present status.

A study of the attitudes included in Table IV reveals that whites in the South assign the Negro to a very low social status for at least four reasons. In the first place, the Negro is considered as inferior from a mental and moral standpoint. In the second place, the Negro is believed to possess several traits that denote a low social status in the American social order, such as being lazy and shiftless, criminally inclined, happy-go-lucky and carefree, highly sexual, and very un-truthful. In the third place, since he is not capable of assuming responsibility and leadership and is incapable of self-discipline, social equality is impractical if not impossible. Therefore, segregation is necessary, and intermarriage should be prohibited. In the fourth place, the Negro is all right in his place, which the preceding atti-tudes indicate is a very low place, and is satisfied with his present status. In summary, whites in the South assign Negroes to a very low social status because they believe that they have certain inferior characteristics, possess several traits that denote a low social status, are not capable of full participation in the American social order, and are satisfied with their present low social status.

The attitudes and opinions of the majority group in the South toward the Negro are best expressed in the various forms of discrim-ination that exist in this area. These forms of discrimination reflect in a vivid way the social status assigned to Negroes by whites. This is true in most instances since these forms of discrimination, although without a legal foundation, serve to restrict the extent to which the Negro can advance his social status in the South. Not only do these forms of discrimination restrict the social advancement of Negroes, but they also serve as barriers to their mobility along educational, economic, political, and all other essential areas of life. In fact, it is difficult, if not impossible, to understand the general status of the Negro in the South without an insight into the various forms of discrimination. It is for this reason that the following reading, by Professor Gunnar Myrdal, is presented. In this reading Myrdal presents the views of both Negroes and whites to the various forms of discrimination that exist in the South at the present time.

▌ THE "RANK ORDER OF DISCRIMINATION" [11]

GUNNAR MYRDAL

The anti-amalgamation doctrine represents a strategic constella-tion of forces in race relations. Their charting will allow us a first general overview of the discrimination patterns and will have the advantage that white Americans themselves will recognize their own paths on the map we draw. When white Southerners are asked to rank, in order of importance, various types of discrimination, they

[11] From *An American Dilemma* (New York: Harper and Brothers, 1944), pp. 60-67. Used by permission of the publisher.

consistently present a list in which these types of discrimination are ranked according to the degree of closeness of their relation to the anti-amalgamation doctrine. This rank order—which will be referred to as *"the white man's rank order of discriminations"*—will serve as an organizing principle in this book. It appears, actually, only as an elaboration of the popular theory of color caste sketched above. Like that theory, it is most clearly and distinctly perceived in the South; in the North ideas are more vague, but, on the whole, not greatly divergent. Neither the popular theory of caste nor the rank order of discriminations has been noted much in scientific literature on the Negro problem.

The rank order held nearly unanimously is the following:

Rank 1. Highest in this order stands the bar against intermarriage and sexual intercourse involving white women.

Rank 2. Next come the several etiquettes and discriminations, which specifically concern behavior in personal relations. (These are the barriers against dancing, bathing, eating, drinking together, and social intercourse generally; peculiar rules as to hand-shaking, hat lifting, use of titles, house entrance to be used, social forms when meeting on streets and in work, and so forth. These patterns are sometimes referred to as the denial of "social equality" in the narrow meaning of the term.)

Rank 3. Thereafter follow the segregations and discriminations in use of public facilities such as schools, churches and means of conveyance.

Rank 4. Next comes political disfranchisement.

Rank 5. Thereafter come discrimination in law courts, by the police, and by other public servants.

Rank 6. Finally come the discriminations in securing land, credit, jobs, or other means of earning a living, and discriminations in public relief and other social welfare activities.

It is unfortunate that this cornerstone in our edifice of basic hypotheses, like many of our other generalizations, has to be constructed upon the author's observations. It is desirable that scientifically controlled quantitative knowledge be substituted for impressionistic judgments as soon as possible. It should be noted that the rank order is very apparently determined by the factors of sex and social status, so that the closer the association of a type of interracial behavior is to sexual and social intercourse on an equalitarian basis, the higher it ranks among the forbidden things.

Next in importance to the fact of the white man's rank order of discriminations is the fact that *the Negro's own rank order is just about parallel, but inverse, to that of the white man.* The Negro resists least the discrimination on the ranks placed highest in the white man's evaluation and resents most any discrimination on the lowest level. This is in accord with the Negro's immediate interests.

Negroes are in desperate need of jobs and bread, even more so than of justice in the courts, and of the vote. These latter needs are, in their turn, more urgent even than better schools and playgrounds, or, rather, they are primary means of reaching equality in the use of community facilities. Such facilities are, in turn, more important than civil courtesies. The marriage matter, finally, is of rather distant and doubtful interest.

Such reflections are obvious; and most Negroes have them in their minds. It is another matter, however, whether the white man is prepared to stick honestly to the rank order which he is so explicit and emphatic in announcing. The question is whether he is really prepared to give the Negro a good job, or even the vote, rather than to allow him entrance to his front door or to ride beside him in the street car.

Upon the assumption that this question is given an affirmative answer, that the white man is actually prepared to carry out in practice the implications of his theories, this inverse relationship between the Negro's and the white man's rank orders becomes of strategical importance in the practical and political sphere of the Negro problem. Although not formulated in this way, such a relationship, or such a minimum moral demand on the ordinary white man, has always been the basis of all attempts to compromise and come to a better understanding between leaders of the two groups. It has been the basis for all interracial policy and also for most of the practical work actually carried out by Negro betterment organizations. Following to its logical end, it should fundamentally change the race situation in America.

It has thus always been a primary requirement upon every Negro leader—who aspires to get any hearing at all from the white majority group, and who does not want to appear dangerously radical to the Negro group and at the same time hurt the "race pride" it has built up as a defense—that he shall explicitly condone the anti-amalgamation maxim, which is the keystone in the white man's structure of race prejudice, and forbear to express any desire on the part of the Negro people to aspire to intermarriage with the whites. The request for intermarriage is easy for the Negro leader to give up. Intermarriage cannot possibly be a practical object of Negro public policy. Independent of the Negroes' wishes, the opportunity for intermarriage is not favorable as long as the great majority of the white population dislikes the very idea. As a defense reaction a strong attitude against intermarriage has developed in the Negro people itself. And the Negro people have no interest in defending the exploitative illicit relations between white men and Negro women. This race mingling is, on the contrary, commonly felt among

Negroes to be disgraceful, and it often arouses the jealousy of
Negro men.

The required soothing gesture toward the anti-amalgamation
doctrine is, therefore, readily delivered. It is iterated at every convenient opportunity and belongs to the established routine of Negro
leadership. For example, Robert R. Moton writes:

> As for amalgamation, very few expect it; still fewer want it; no one advo-
> cates it; and only a constantly diminishing minority practise it, and that
> surreptitiously. It is generally accepted on both sides of the color line that
> it is best for the two races to remain ethnologically distinct.[12]

There seems thus to be unanimity among Negro leaders on the point
deemed crucial by white Americans. If we attend carefully, we shall,
however, detect some important differences in formulation. The
Negro spokesman will never, to begin with, accept the common
white premise of racial inferiority of the Negro stock. To quote
Moton again:

> ... even in the matter of the mingling of racial strains, however, undesir-
> able it might seem to be from a social point of view, he (the Negro) would
> never admit that his blood carries any taint of physiological, mental, or
> spiritual inferiority.[13]

A doctrine of equal natural endowments—a doctrine contrary to the
white man's assumption of Negro inferiority, which is at the basis
of the anti-amalgamation theory—has been consistently upheld. If a
Negro leader publicly even hinted at the possibility of inherent
racial inferiority, he would immediately lose his following. The
entire Negro press watches the Negro leaders on this point.

Even Booker T. Washington, the supreme diplomat of the Negro
people through a generation filled with severe trials, who was able
by studied unobtrusiveness to wring so many favors from the white
majority, never dared to allude to such a possibility, though he
sometimes criticized most severely his own people for lack of thrift,
skill, perseverance and general culture. In fact, there is no reason
to think that he did not firmly believe in the fundamental equality
of inherent capacities. Privately, local Negro leaders might find it
advisable to admit Negro inferiority and, particularly earlier, many
individual Negroes might have shared the white man's view. But it
will not be expressed by national leaders and, in fact, never when
they are under public scrutiny. An emphatic assertion of equal
endowments is article number one in the growing Negro "race
pride."

12 *What the Negro Thinks* (New York: Doubleday and Company, Inc., 1929), p. 241.
Used by permission of the publisher.
13 *Ibid.*, p. 239.

Another deviation of the Negro faith in the anti-amalgamation doctrine is the stress that they, for natural reasons, lay on condemn-ing exploitative illicit amalgamation. They turn the tables and accuse white men of debasing Negro womanhood, and the entire white culture for not rising up against this practice as their expressed antagonism against miscegenation should demand. Here they have a strong point, and they know how to press it.

A third qualification in the Negro's acceptance of the anti-amalga-mation doctrine, expressed not only by the more "radical" and out-spoken Negro leaders, is the assertion that intermarriage should not be barred by law. The respect for individual liberty is invoked as an argument. But, in addition, it is pointed out that this barrier, by releasing the white man from the consequences of intimacy with a Negro woman, actually has the effect of inducing such intimacy and thus tends to increase miscegenation. Moton makes this point: [14]

The Negro woman suffers not only from the handicap of economic and social discriminations imposed upon the race as a whole, but is in addition the victim of unfavourable legislation incorporated in the marriage laws of twenty-nine states, which forbid the intermarriage of black and white. The disadvantage of these statutes lies, not as is generally represented, in the legal obstacle they present to social equality, but rather in the fact that such laws specifically deny to the Negro woman and her offspring that safeguard from abuse and exploitation with which the women of the white race are abundantly surrounded. On the other side, the effect of such legislation leaves the white man, who is so inclined, free of any responsibility attend-ing his amatory excursions across the colour line and leaves the coloured woman without redress for any of the consequences of her defencelessness; whereas white women have every protection, from fine and imprisonment under the law to enforced marriage and lynching outside the law.

But even with all these qualifications, the anti-amalgamation doc-trine, the necessity of assenting to which is understood by nearly everybody, obviously encounters some difficulties in the minds of intellectual Negroes. They can hardly be expected to accept it as a just rule of conduct. They tend to accept it merely as a temporary expedient necessitated by human weakness.

.   .   .   .   .   .

Negroes have always pointed out that the white man must not be so certain of his woman's lack of interest when he rises to such frenzy on behalf of the danger to her and feels compelled to build up such formidable fences to prevent her from marrying a Negro.

With these reservations both Negro leadership and the Negro masses acquiesce in the white anti-amalgamation doctrine. This

[14] *Ibid.*, pp. 208-209.

attitude is noted with satisfaction in the white camp. The writer has observed, however, that the average white man, particularly in the South, does not feel quite convinced of the Negro's acquiescence. In several conversations, the same white person, in the same breath, has assured me, on the one hand, that the Negroes are perfectly satisfied in their position and would not like to be treated as equals, and on the other hand, that the only thing these Negroes long for is to be like white people and to marry their daughters.

Whereas the Negro spokesman finds it possible to assent to the first rank of discrimination, namely, that involving miscegnation, it is more difficult for him to give his approval to the second rank of discrimination, namely, that involving "etiquette" and consisting in the white man's refusal to extend the ordinary courtesies to Negroes in daily life and his expectation of receiving certain symbolic signs of submissiveness from the Negro. The Negro leader could not do so without serious risk of censorship by his own people and rebuke by the Negro press. In all articulate groups of Negroes there is a demand to have white men call them by their titles of Mr., Mrs., and Miss; to have white men take off their hats on entering a Negro's house; to be able to enter a white man's house through the front door rather than the back door, and so on. But on the whole, and in spite of the rule that they stand up for "social equality" in this sense, most Negroes in the South obey the white man's rules.

Booker T. Washington went a long way, it is true, in his Atlanta speech in 1895 where he explained that: "In all things that are purely social we (the two races) can be as separate as the fingers, yet one as the hand in all things essential to mutual progress." He there seemed to condone not only these rules of "etiquette" but also the denial of "social equality" in a broader sense, including some of the further categories in the white man's rank order of discrimination. He himself was always most eager to observe the rules. But Washington was bitterly rebuked for this capitulation, particularly by Negroes in the North. And a long time has passed since then; the whole spirit in the Negro world has changed considerably in three decades.

The modern Negro leader will try to solve this dilemma by iterating that no Negroes want to intrude upon white people's private lives. But this is not what Southern white opinion asks for. It is not satisfied with the natural rules of polite conduct that no individual, of whatever race, shall push his presence on a society where he is not wanted. It asks for a general order according to which *all* Negroes are placed under *all* white people and excluded from not only the white man's society but also from the ordinary symbols of respect. No Negro shall ever aspire to them, and no white shall be allowed to offer them.

Thus, on this second rank of discrimination there is a wide gap between the ideologies of the two groups. As we then continue downward in our rank order and arrive at the ordinary Jim Crow practices, the segregation in schools, the disfranchisement, and the discrimination in employment, we find, on the one hand, that increasingly larger groups of white people are prepared to take a stand against these discriminations. Many a liberal white professor in the South who, for his own welfare, would not dare to entertain a Negro in his home and perhaps not even speak to him in a friendly manner on the street, will be found prepared publicly to condemn disfranchisement, lynching, and the forcing of the Negro out of employment. Also, on the other hand, Negro spokesmen are becoming increasingly firm in their opposition to discrimination on these lower levels. It is principally on these lower levels of the white man's rank order of discrimination that the race struggle goes on. The struggle will widen to embrace all the thousand problems of education, politics, economic standards, and so forth, and the frontier will shift from day to day according to varying events.

Even a superficial view of discrimination in America will reveal to the observer: first, that there are great differences, not only between larger regions, but between neighboring communities; and second, that even in the same community, changes occur from one time to another. There is also, contrary to the rule that all Negroes are to be treated alike, a certain amount of discretion depending upon the class and social status of the Negro in question. A white person, especially if he has high status in the community, is, furthermore, supposed to be free, within limits, to overstep the rules. The rules are primarily to govern the Negro's behavior.

Some of these differences and changes can be explained. But the need for their interpretation is perhaps less than has sometimes been assumed. The variations in discrimination between local communities or from one time to another are often not of primary consequence. All of these thousand and one precepts, etiquettes, taboos, and disabilities inflicted upon the Negro have a common purpose: to express the subordinate status of the Negro people and the exalted position of the whites. They have their meaning and chief function as symbols. As symbols, they are, however, interchangeable to an extent: one can serve in place of another without causing material difference in the essential social relations in the community.

The differences in patterns of discrimination between the larger regions of the country and the temporal changes of patterns within one region, which reveal a definite trend, have, on the contrary, more material import. These differences and changes imply, in fact, a considerable margin of variation within the very notion of American caste, which is not true of all the other minor differences between the changes in localities within a single region—hence the reason for a clear distinction. For exemplification it may suffice here to refer only to the differentials in space. As one moves from the Deep South through the Upper South and the Border states to the North, the manifestations of discrimination decrease in extent and intensity; at the same time the rules become more uncertain and capricious. The "color line" becomes a broad ribbon of arbitrariness. The old New England states stand, on the whole, as the antipode to the Deep South. This generalization requires important qualifications, and the relations are in process of change.

The decreasing discrimination as we go from South to North in the United States is apparently related to a weaker basic prejudice. In the North the Negroes have fair justice and are not disfranchised; they are not Jim-Crowed in public means of conveyance; educational institutions are less segregated. The interesting thing is that the decrease of discrimination does *not* regularly follow the white man's rank order. Thus intermarriage, placed on the top of the rank order, is legally permitted in all but one of the Northern states east of the Mississippi. The racial etiquette, being the most conspicuous element in the second rank, is, practically speaking, absent from the North. On the other hand, employment discriminations, placed at the bottom of the rank order, at times are equally severe, or more so, in some Northern communities than in the South, even if it is true that Negroes have been able to press themselves into many more new avenues of employment during the last generation in the North than in the South.

There is plenty of discrimination in the North. But it is—or rather its rationalization is—kept hidden. We can, in the North, witness the legislators' obedience to the American Creed when they solemnly pass laws and regulations to condemn and punish such acts of discrimination which, as a matter of routine, are committed daily by the great majority of the white citizens and by the legislators themselves. In the North, as indeed often in the South, public speakers frequently pronounce principles of human and civic equality. We see here revealed in relief the Negro problem as an American Dilemma.

An evaluation of the attitudes of whites in the South toward Negroes will show that these attitudes include some of the stereotypes that are commonly held concerning Negroes. Many of these stereotypes are traditional in nature, and represent a carryover from the period of slavery in the United States. As stereotypes these attitudes have been handed down from generation to generation without much reflection or evaluation. It is therefore valid to assume that many of these attitudes are fallacious concerning Negroes at the present time. *Whether these attitudes are fallacious or valid, the social status of the Negro will be determined by these attitudes as long as they are held by whites in the South.* Thus, until efforts are exercised in an attempt to change the present attitudes of whites in the South toward Negroes, the Negro will continue to be assigned a low social status in the South. A program for changing attitudes will be discussed in a later section in this book.

LEGAL STATUS

The legal status of the Negro in the United States is and has been very elastic and flexible. During the colonial period this status of the Negro differed among the several colonies, and changed much from the time of his entrance into the area now known as the United States to the time that the federal government was established. Since the establishment of the federal government, the best legal minds in the United States have not been able to agree in their interpretations of the legal status of the Negro in keeping with federal laws. Also, there is much variation in the legal status of the Negro, if federal laws are compared with state laws, and even more variation if the laws of the forty-eight states are contrasted. These many variations must be kept in mind, if one is to understand the present legal status of the Negro in the South or in the United States.

Since the ratification of the Thirteenth Amendment, which abolished slavery; the Fourteenth Amendment, which guaranteed to the Negro citizenship and certain other personal rights; and the Fifteenth Amendment, which protects the Negro in his right to vote, the Negro has had the same legal status as other citizens according to the Constitution of the United States. An intensive study of federal statutes will show that these statutes are in harmony with the principles of the Federal Constitution in so far as the Negro is concerned. Although some racial and nationality groups are legislated against by federal statutes, Negroes born in the United States are accorded by federal laws [15] the same legal status as whites born in the United States.

[15] See Milton R. Konvitz, *The Alien and the Asiatic in American Law* (Ithaca, N. Y.: Cornell University Press, 1946).

In other words, if the legal status as stated or implied by federal laws were recognized, there would be very little, if any, difference between the legal status of Negroes and that of whites in the South. However, the principles included in some federal laws are written in such general terms that it is possible for many interpretations to be given to them. Even the United States Supreme Court at different times

Table V: MAJOR LEGAL PROVISIONS REQUIRING THE SEPARATION OF NEGROES FROM WHITES IN THE SOUTH *

States	Prohibit inter-marriage of races	In public schools	In colleges	In institutions for juvenile delinquents	In penal institutions	In mental institutions	On railways	On busses	On streetcars	In places of amusement	In institutions for physical defectives	Miscellaneous	Waitingrooms
Alabama	X	X	X	X	X	X	X	X				12	X
Arkansas	X	X	X	X	X		X	X	X	4		12	X
Delaware	X	X	X	X	X							12, 13	
Florida	X	X	X	X	X		X	X	X			10	X
Georgia	X	X	X	X	X	X	X	X		5		11	
Kentucky	X	X	X	X			X	X			6	13	
Louisiana	X	X	X	X	X	X	X	X	X	1	6		X
Maryland	X	X	X	X			X	X				12	
Mississippi	X	X	X	X	X	X	X	X	X			11	X
North Carolina	X	X	X	X	X	X	X	X	X		6	9, 10, 13	X
Oklahoma	X	X	X	X			X	X	X	3	6	12, 13, 14	X
South Carolina	X	X	X	X	X		X	X	X	3, 5, 1		11	X
Tennessee	X	X	X	X	X	X	X	X	X	2	7, 8		
Texas	X	X	X	X			X	X	X		6	9, 12, 13	
Virginia	X	X	X	X	X	X	X	X	X	2	6		
West Virginia	X	X	X	X	X	X				5	7, 8	12, 13	

* The data in this table were compiled from Charles S. Mangum, Jr., *The Legal Status of the Negro* (Chapel Hill: The University of North Carolina Press, 1940), 436 + viii pp.; and Milton R. Konvitz, *The Constitution and Civil Rights* (New York: Columbia University Press, 1947), pp. 133-141 and 230-241.

1 Circuses	2 Theaters	3 Parks, playgrounds, beaches	4 Racetracks
5 Billiard parlors and poolrooms	6 Deaf, dumb, and blind	7 Blind	
8 Deaf	9 Libraries	10 Separate textbooks	11 In hospitals
12 Tubercular patients	13 In homes for orphans and aged		
14 Separate telephone booths			

has given varied interpretations to the principles of the Federal Constitution. The many interpretations of federal laws have provided states with opportunities to enact state laws that are in keeping with these interpretations, but contrary to what many authorities consider the fundamental principles of federal laws.

The extent to which the legal status of the Negro in the South varies from that prescribed by federal law is illustrated in Table V. *Although the Negro is accorded by federal laws the same legal status as other citizens, this sameness fades when attention is directed to the laws of the states in the South.* Many laws exist that provide for the separation of Negroes and whites. These laws range from the possible separation of the races in telephone booths in Oklahoma, to laws prescribing separation in the most intimate of all social relations —that of marriage—in all of the states of the South. As with marriage, all of the states of the South have required separation of the races in public schools, in colleges, and in institutions for juvenile delinquents. The following are areas where separation is required by law in most of the states in the South: on railways, in penal institutions, in mental institutions, on busses, on streetcars, in waiting-rooms, and in institutions for physical defectives. Some of the other areas of activity in which separation is required in the South are: in places of amusement, in institutions for tubercular patients, in homes for orphans and the aged, in hospitals, in libraries, and in the use of textbooks.

To remain within the framework of the principles of the Federal Constitution, state laws that require the separation of Negroes and whites usually indicate that the separate facilities shall be equal. The principle of "separate but equal" facilities has been brought before the Supreme Court of the United States many times, and this body, to the present time, has decreed in favor of the principle.[16] *These decisions imply that separation is legal and in keeping with the police power of the states as long as this separation is on the basis of equality.* In these decisions, however, the Supreme Court of the United States has not attempted to define or give a description to the concept equality. As a result, legal separation is a well-established policy in the South; but very little, if any consideration has been given to interpreting the principle of equality. Thus, the concept of "equality" has received many interpretations in the South, and these interpretations have varied from state to state and among the various areas within the states in the South.

It is the consensus among students of ethnic relations in the South that separation has led to "separate but not equal" facilities,[17] instead of separate but equal facilities. Separate but not equal prevails in practically all localities and for most activities where separate facilities are required. In schools and colleges the facilities are so far from

16 See the decisions of the Federal Supreme Court rendered in the following cases: McLaurin v. Oklahoma State Regents for Higher Education; and Sweatt v. Painter, *The United States Law Week,* Vol. 18 (June 13, 1950), pp. 4405, 4407.

17 For a discussion on this point, see Charles H. Thompson, "Separate But Not Equal: The Sweatt Case," *The Southwest Review,* Vol. 33 (Spring, 1948), pp. 105-112.

equal that comparisons are almost impossible (this problem will be discussed later). Other institutions where separation is required are equally as inferior, or are not provided for Negroes. On transportation facilities Negroes are generally assigned the least desirable sections. Where separate waitingrooms are required, the upkeep of the Negro waitingroom is usually inferior to that of the white waitingroom. Almost without exception studies of facilities where separation is legal have shown that facilities for Negroes are absent or inferior to those provided for whites. Thus, separation is practiced where it is legally required in the South, but equality is neglected to the extent that facilities are inferior or are not provided for Negroes.

In the South the separation of Negroes and whites is required in the use of many facilities that are not included in the laws as compiled in Table V. Areas where separation is practiced but not required legally, in many instances, include employment, hotels, tourist camps, cafes and restaurants, churches, Christian Associations, boys' and girls' clubs, residences, social clubs, professional and occupational organizations, and many other activities where social contacts are involved. On the other hand, most economic enterprises in the South, in which profit is the major motive, will deal with the Negro on a basis of equality. A Negro can go into most stores and other economic enterprises with the expectation of receiving equal attention, and in most instances he will not be disappointed. *In other words, functional democracy is frequently practiced more in private economic enterprises than in social, religious, or governmental agencies.*

A great difference exists between the legal status of the Negro as defined by federal laws and that as defined by state laws in the South. Federal laws guarantee an equal legal status to Negroes and whites in the United States. State laws in the South modify this equal legal status by requiring a *separate* but equal legal status. Social and political practices in the South have further modified this legal status by assigning the Negro to an inferior status. State courts, in their decisions favoring the status assigned to the Negro by social and political practices, have added legal sanctions to this low legal status for Negroes. As a result, the legal status of the Negro in the South is much lower than that of the majority population group in the South —the native whites. However, it should be remembered that the actual legal status of the Negro in the South is contrary to both state and federal laws, but in keeping with the attitudes and opinions of whites in the South toward Negroes. This fact is sufficient to support the contention that the actual status of the Negro in the South can be improved more rapidly by changing attitudes and opinions than by changing the present laws. In other words, if the present laws were enforced, there would be little, if any, significant difference between the legal status of Negroes and whites in the South.

EDUCATIONAL STATUS

The educational status of the Negro in the South will be evaluated by three criteria: (1) the availability of educational facilities, (2) the number of years of school completed, and (3) the professional training of the population. However, the first fact that should be recalled is that separate schools for whites and Negroes are required by law in all of the states in the South. This separation makes it easy to compare the available facilities for the two ethnic groups in keeping with the criteria used.

Educational Facilities

Although the public school facilities available for Negroes in the South have increased at a rapid rate since 1930, they were still inferior to those for whites in all of the states in the South in 1945.[18] In the study cited the public school facilities available for whites and Negroes in the South are compared. Among the conditions compared are accreditation by regional agencies, value of school property, teaching load, size of schools, transportation of pupils, expenditure per pupil, and many others. Several illustrations selected at random will be presented to show the extent to which differences exist between white and Negro schools in the South.

In Arkansas only two Negro schools were accredited by the regional accrediting agency, while seventy white schools were accredited by this agency.[19] In Georgia the value of school property per pupil enrolled was $35.00 for Negro schools and $160.00 for white schools.[20] In Louisiana there was one white teacher to every thirty pupils registered and only one Negro teacher to every fifty-one pupils.[21] In Mississippi 2,015 (61.2 per cent) of the Negro schools were one-

---

[18] See "The Availability of Education in the Negro Separate School," *Journal of Negro Education*, Vol. 16, No. 3 (Summer, 1947), pp. 263-479, for an intensive presentation of this problem in each of the states in the South.

[19] *Ibid.*, p. 323.

[20] *Ibid.*, p. 349.

[21] *Ibid.*, p. 361.

teacher schools, while only 105 (less than 5 per cent) of the white
schools were one-teacher schools.[22] In North Carolina 45.58 per cent
of the white pupils were transported to and from school, while 17.76
per cent of the Negro pupils were transported.[23] In South Carolina
the expenditure per pupil enrolled was $37.00 for Negro pupils, but
$113.00 for white pupils.[24] Although the Negro school population
in Texas was 15.3 per cent of the total school population, Negro
schools received only 5.7 per cent of the appropriations for facilities
and special instructional programs in 1945.[25] These illustrations
should be sufficient to warrant the conclusion that, from the standpoint of facilities, the status of Negro education in public schools
is on a very low level, even much lower than the level for white
education in the South.

If attention is directed to facilities for higher and professional education for Negroes in the South, the situation is much worse than it
is in public schools.[26] In the sixteen states included in the South in
this study there was not a Negro institution that was qualified to offer
work for the Doctor of Philosophy degree in 1948, and only two of
the Negro universities that offered work leading to the Master's
degree were on the approved list of the Association of American Universities. One medical school was recognized by the American Medical Association in the sixteen states in 1948, and one school of social
work was recognized by the American Association of Schools of Social
Work. On the other hand, not a single recognized school for Negroes
existed in the professional areas of engineering and architecture.
Although several universities in a few southern states have admitted
Negroes to graduate and professional schools during the past few
years, Negroes with the desire and ability to pursue professional
training are still very restricted in their choice. In most instances,
they have to seek entrance into the few professional schools that
exist for Negroes, or into professional schools in states outside the
South. In either case, they find it very discouraging. Usually, the few
professional schools that exist for Negroes are overcrowded, and
Negro students find it very difficult to gain admission to professional
schools outside the South.

22 *Ibid.*, p. 375.
23 *Ibid.*, p. 391.
24 *Ibid.*, p. 407.
25 *Ibid.*, p. 430.
26 "Negro Higher and Professional Education in the United States," *Journal of Negro
Education,* Vol. 17, No. 3, pp. 221-436.

In so far as college education is concerned, Negroes in the South are hampered by the lack of available facilities. Junior colleges are almost nonexistent, colleges are poorly located, most of the colleges are small private colleges, most Negro colleges are poorly financed, and the colleges that exist do not have a broad curriculum or the staff to offer a broad curriculum.[27] In 1946 Oklahoma had twenty-six white junior colleges, of which twenty-two were supported by municipal or state governments; but this state did not have even one junior college for Negroes.[28] In 1945 whites were offered college training in forty-three fields of study that were not available to Negroes in Arkansas.[29] In Florida white students were offered work in eighteen divisions, while Negro students were offered work in seven divisions.[30] In Georgia there were twenty professional schools in which white students could study, but only four available for Negroes.[31] In Oklahoma white students could receive degrees in one hundred and eighty-nine different fields of study, while only twenty-four fields of study were available for Negro students.[32]

Since the publication of the study cited several state universities, that were formerly all-white, have admitted Negroes to enroll for graduate and professional training. Also, a number of colleges and junior colleges in the South have agreed to admit Negroes. During the school year 1951-52 about 1,000 Negroes were enrolled in colleges and universities in the following states in the South: Arkansas, Delaware, Kentucky, Louisiana, Maryland, North Carolina, Oklahoma, Tennessee, Texas, Virginia, and West Virginia. However, these admissions have been at the top of the educational ladder, and are of little value in equalizing the inequalities in the educational facilities that exist in the public schools and in many undergraduate colleges. Further, the inferior educational facilities that are available for Negroes on the lower levels make it difficult, if not impossible, for many of them to qualify for admission to the graduate and professional universities to which they are now eligible for admission.

The preceding facts should be sufficient to indicate a low educational status for Negroes in the South in so far as facilities are con-

27 *Ibid.*, pp. 221-430.
28 *Ibid.*, p. 344.
29 *Ibid.*, p. 259.
30 *Ibid.*, p. 274.
31 *Ibid.*, p. 286.
32 *Ibid.*, p. 345. See also Maurice R. Davie, *Negroes in American Society* (New York: McGraw-Hill Book Company, Inc., 1949), chap. 6.

cerned. They show that the status of Negro education is far below that for whites in the South. When this fact is combined with the observation that educational facilities in the South are on a much lower level than those in any other region of the United States, it is logical to conclude that the educational status of the Negro in the South, in so far as facilities are concerned, is on the lowest level in the United States. This is true if the status is judged from any standard for facilities, or on any level from kindergarten through professional schools.

Years of School Completed

The educational status of the Negro, as reflected by the number of school years completed by persons 25 years old and over, is very low for the Negro in the South. The percentages for no school years completed ranged around 11 per cent for Negroes and 3 per cent for whites in 1940. Percentages for both groups decreased by 1950, but the percentages for Negroes were still much larger than those for whites. As examples, the rates in South Carolina for 1950 were 10.5 per cent for nonwhites and 2.6 per cent for whites. In Arkansas the rates were 7.8 per cent for nonwhites and 1.7 per cent for whites. The average for all states in the South was around 9 per cent for nonwhites and 2 per cent for whites.

On the higher levels the educational status of the Negro is much lower than that for whites in the South. In 1940 the rates for four years of high school were approximately 13 per cent for whites and 3.0 per cent for nonwhites. In 1950 the rates in Arkansas were 15.5 per cent for whites and 3.2 per cent for nonwhites, and in South Carolina they were 10.9 per cent for whites and 1.7 per cent for non-whites. A similar picture was evident in 1950 for four years or more of college completed. In Arkansas the rates were 3.6 per cent for whites and 1.2 per cent for nonwhites, and in South Carolina they were 7.2 per cent for whites and 1.7 per cent for nonwhites. These figures indicate that the educational status of the Negro in the South is much lower than that for whites as far as years of school completed are concerned.

The median number of school years completed is also much lower for Negroes than for whites in the South. In 1940 the range for Negroes was from 2.8 years in Louisiana to 6 years in Oklahoma, while it ranged from 6.3 years in Louisiana to 8.1 years in Mississippi for whites. In 1950 the median number of school years completed in

Arkansas was 8.7 years for whites and 5.6 years for nonwhites, and in South Carolina it was 9.0 years for whites and 4.8 years for non-whites. On the average, whites in the South have completed between three and four more years of formal schooling than Negroes.

Professional Training

The educational status of the Negro in the South is also low if judged by the proportion of the trained professional personnel to the total Negro population. As illustrations, there is one Negro physician and surgeon to about every 5,000 Negroes, but one white physician and surgeon to about every 800 whites. There is one Negro dentist for about every 12,000 Negroes, but one white dentist for about every 2,500 whites. There is one Negro lawyer for about every 25,000 Negroes, but one white lawyer for about every 700 whites. The number of lay persons for Negro professionals is five times or more the number for white professionals. There are more Negroes trained as physicians, dentists, and social workers, these being three of the professions in which training has been available to Negroes in the South. On the other hand, there is a very poor representation in the professions of lawyers, architects, and engineers, professions in which training has not been provided for Negroes in the South.

According to the criteria used, it is evident that the educational status of the Negro in the South is on a very low level when compared with that of whites in the South. This is true if the status of education is examined by the availability of educational facilities, the number of years of school completed, or the extent of professional training. When consideration is given to the fact that the status of education for whites in the South is much lower than that for other regions of the United States, it is valid to conclude that the educational status of the Negro in the South is on the lowest possible level when compared with that of whites in the South, and with that of other ethnic groups in other regions of the United States.

ECONOMIC STATUS

The economic past of the Negro in the South presents a very dismal picture. During the period of slavery the economic status of the Negro was defined as that of economic property, which was handled and controlled as any other economic property. With the emancipation of slaves there was a change from controlled economic activity to a certain degree of economic freedom. However, when the Negro in the South was granted economic freedom he was without the

Table VI: PERCENTAGE DISTRIBUTION OF MALE EMPLOYED WORKERS BY MAJOR OCCUPATIONS *

Occupation	Nonwhite in South	Total for South	Total for U.S.
Laborers, except farm and mine	23.4	8.8	8.0
Farmers and farm managers	19.1	16.6	10.7
Operatives and kindred workers	19.1	18.3	20.0
Farm laborers (wage workers)	10.3	5.0	3.5
Service workers, except private household	9.0	4.6	5.6
Craftsmen, foremen, and kindred workers	6.4	15.5	18.3
Farm laborers, unpaid workers	5.1	3.2	1.5
Professional, technical, and kindred workers	1.8	5.8	7.4
Managers, officials, and proprietors, except farm	1.5	9.9	10.8
Clerical and kindred workers	1.5	5.3	6.5
Sales workers	1.2	5.6	6.2
Private household workers	0.5	0.1	0.2
Occupation not reported	1.2	1.2	1.2

* Seventeenth Census of the United States, *Employment and Income, By Regions* (1950). Preliminary Report, Series PC-7, No. 2, April 11, 1951.

necessary educational background to make the most profitable use of this freedom. The Negro was without land or capital, he lacked economic training and experience, and he found himself in an area where the thinking of the majority group was antagonistic to his economic advancement. With these, and many other economic obstacles, the Negro in the South made his start toward acquiring the economic freedom that had been made possible from a legal standpoint. The following criteria will be used to evaluate the extent to which the Negro in the South has made use of his economic freedom up to the present time: (1) occupational distribution, (2) income, and (3) home ownership.

Occupational Distribution

Table VI shows the occupational distribution for Negro males as compared with the distribution for males in the South, and in the United States. A review of this table will show that most of the non-white male workers in the South are engaged in occupations that require little formal training and grant small economic returns. More than 38 per cent of the nonwhite male workers are engaged as laborers, while for the South only 17.0 per cent are engaged as laborers and in the United States only 13 per cent are so engaged. From the standpoint of income, laborers are among those on the lowest level. In 1949 the average yearly income for male civilian workers was $2,634, while the average yearly income for laborers was $2,025 and that for farm laborers $781.

The next leading occupation for Negro male workers in the South was farmers and farm managers. The average income for this group of workers was $1,027 in 1949, which was less than one-half of the average income for all workers. Considering the fact that about two-thirds of the Negro farmers in the South are tenant farmers, and in a lower economic class than laborers, it is reasonable to conclude that more than 57 per cent of the Negroes in the South are in or below the laboring class. For the whites in the South about 33 per cent of the male employed population was classified in the laboring and tenant farming classes. In other words, white male workers in the South are engaged in a much greater number of occupations that pay higher wages than those in which Negro male workers are engaged. Also the occupations in which white male workers are engaged are accorded a higher occupational status than is accorded to those in which Negro male workers are engaged.

Private household and service occupations account for 59.9 per cent of all Negro female workers in the South, and farm or other labor for 17 per cent according to Table VII. These percentages denote a concentration of Negro female workers in a few occupations. Only 33.8 per cent of the white female workers in the South are engaged in the occupations in which 77.5 per cent of the Negro female workers are engaged. Again, there is a much wider distribution among white workers than among Negro workers. Also, a low economic status for Negro female workers is indicated by the fact that the occupations in which Negro female workers are concentrated are the occupations that pay the lowest wages, and are accorded the lowest social status. In 1949 the average yearly income for female civilian workers in the United States was $1,522, but the average yearly income for the occupations engaging the majority of the Negro female workers was far below this average: $458 for private household workers, and $997 for other service workers.

As far as occupational distribution is concerned, the Negro in the South is on a low economic level since he is engaged in the occupations that return the lowest economic income, and that carry with them a low occupational status. At the present time two factors are serving to continue this low occupational status. On the one hand, facilities for training and experience are not available for Negroes in the occupations that make possible a high economic status. On the

Table VII: PERCENTAGE DISTRIBUTION OF FEMALE EMPLOYED WORKERS BY MAJOR OCCUPATIONS *

Occupation	Nonwhite in South	Total for South	Total for U.S.
Private household workers	43.7	13.6	8.9
Service workers, except private household	16.2	12.1	12.2
Operatives and kindred workers	10.1	17.1	19.2
Farm laborers, unpaid workers	7.5	3.8	2.1
Professional, technical, and kindred workers	7.1	11.9	12.6
Farm laborers, wage workers	6.3	2.2	0.9
Farmers and farm managers	3.2	1.6	0.8
Clerical and kindred workers	1.8	21.7	26.7
Sales workers	1.3	7.7	8.0
Craftsmen, foremen, and kindred workers	0.6	1.0	1.6
Managers, officials, and proprietors, except farm	0.7	4.6	4.3
Laborers, except farm and mine	0.6	0.5	0.7
Occupation not reported	0.9	2.3	2.0

* Seventeenth Census of the United States, *Employment and Income, By Regions* (1950). Preliminary Report, Series PC-7, No. 2, April 11, 1951.

other hand, Negro youth is often discouraged from training for higher occupations. He is told that there is no place for him in higher occupational activities and, therefore, he resigns himself to occupations that are on a low economic level.

Income

The reported family incomes of workers in 1949 are shown in Table VIII. It is recognized that present incomes might be a little higher than these, but the very low incomes for 1949 are amazing. For nonwhites in the South 43.9 per cent of the family incomes were below $1,000, while for the South 24.2 per cent were below this sum. In all of the income brackets under $2,500 the percentages for non-whites are larger than those for workers in the South, while in all income brackets over $2,500 the percentages are larger for the total population. The incomes for 86.5 per cent of the nonwhites in the South were below $2,500, while the income of 55.1 per cent of all southern families and 39.5 per cent of all families in the United States were below this sum. The median income for nonwhite families in the South was $1,168, for the South it was $2,248, and for the United States it was $3,068. These figures support the statement made previously, that the low status occupations in which Negro workers are engaged in the South carry with them low wages or salaries. It is impossible for persons on the low income levels reported for Negroes in 1949 to acquire anything other than a low economic status.

Table VIII: REPORTED INCOME BY FAMILIES, 1949 *

| | Per Cent Distribution | | |
Income	Nonwhite in South	Total for South	Total for U.S.
Under $500	20.8	12.4	8.6
$500 to $999	23.1	12.0	6.8
$1,000 to $1,499	18.3	10.8	7.3
$1,500 to $1,999	14.1	10.0	7.5
$2,000 to $2,499	10.2	9.9	9.3
$2,500 to $2,999	4.8	8.0	9.0
$3,000 to $3,499	3.4	8.6	10.9
$3,500 to $3,999	1.3	6.1	8.7
$4,000 to $4,499	1.1	4.9	7.2
$4,500 to $4,999	0.5	3.7	4.9
$5,000 to $5,999	1.1	5.3	7.9
$6,000 to $6,999	0.6	3.0	4.3
$7,000 to $9,999	0.7	3.3	4.7
$10,000 and over	—	2.0	2.9
Median income	$1,168	$2,248	$3,068

* Seventeenth Census of the United States, *Employment and Income, By Regions* (1950). Preliminary Report, Series PC-7, No. 2, April 11, 1951.
— Less than 0.1.

Property Ownership

The extent to which Negroes in the South are home owners is illustrated in Table IX. In the metropolitan areas presented in this table the percentages for home ownership for nonwhites ranged from 25.9 per cent to 40.1 per cent in 1950. A liberal estimate would be that about one-third of the Negroes in the South are owners of the houses in which they reside. For whites the percentages ranged from 43.5 per cent to 61.8 per cent for home ownership. A conservative estimate would be that at least one-half of the whites own the houses in which they reside. In 1940, 73.6 per cent of the houses owned by Negroes in the South were valued at below $1,000, while 39 per cent of those owned by whites were valued below this figure. The value of houses has increased at a rapid rate since 1940, but this increase has been for both white and nonwhite houses. Thus, it is reasonable to conclude that the percentage for home ownership in the South is much higher for whites than for Negroes, and that the houses owned by whites are of greater value than those owned by Negroes.

At the present time most of the Negro farmers in the South are tenant farmers. As tenant farmers they are subject to the plight of all tenant farmers, a condition which has been described in several studies.[33] These studies show that the income of all tenant farmers

Table IX: OWNER-RENTER DISTRIBUTION OF DWELLINGS IN SEVEN METROPOLITAN AREAS IN THE SOUTH *

Metropolitan Area	Per Cent for Owners		Per Cent for Renters	
	Nonwhite	White	Nonwhite	White
Atlanta, Ga.	29.1	56.8	70.9	43.2
Birmingham, Ala.	31.2	59.5	68.8	40.5
Memphis, Tenn.	34.8	49.3	65.2	50.7
Nashville, Tenn.	34.0	61.8	66.0	38.2
New Orleans, La.	25.9	43.5	74.1	56.5
Norfolk, Va.	32.1	48.5	67.9	51.5
Richmond, Va.	40.1	57.9	59.9	42.1

* Seventeenth Census of the United States, *Housing* (1950), Preliminary Report, Series HC-5, No. 5, November 30, 1951.

in the South is on a very low level, and that the income of Negro farmers is the lowest among tenant farmers. When consideration is given to the fact that about 20 per cent of the Negro male workers were farmers in 1950, and that about two-thirds of these were tenant farmers, it is evident that Negroes in the South are owners of very little farm property.

In most localities in the South there are a few Negroes who have attained a certain degree of economic success and who are recognized by whites as being moderately wealthy. These few are accorded a fair degree of economic equality by whites in their business dealings, a degree of economic equality superior to that of whites on a low economic level. It is true that the few Negroes who have attained economic success are accorded more equality in reference to economic relations than Negroes are accorded in connection with social, educational, religious, or legal contacts. At least they are accorded equality in the spending of money in most white business places.

As with the other aspects of status examined in this chapter, the Negro is on a low economic level in the South. He is engaged in occupations that require little formal training and pay low wages or salaries. His median income is about one-half that of whites in the South. He owns very little property, and that which he owns is valued

33 Among these studies are Charles S. Johnson, *Shadow of the Plantation* (Chicago: University of Chicago Press, 1934); Arthur F. Raper, *Preface to Peasantry* (Chapel Hill: University of North Carolina Press, 1936); and T. J. Woofter, Jr., *Landlord and Tenants on the Cotton Plantation* (Washington: Works Progress Administration, Research Monograph V, 1936).

much lower than that of whites. However, it is true that the Negro's economic status has advanced and is advancing. Some few Negroes have been able to attain a degree of economic security that places them on a higher economic level than many whites. If this trend continues, the Negro in the South will probably be accorded a fair degree of economic equality long before he attains equality in other areas of group life.

SUMMARY

The Negro's social status is low because whites have accepted many attitudes and opinions that are degrading to the Negro, and that tend to make him socially unacceptable to whites. There are many laws that serve to restrict the advancement of the Negro in the South, and to relegate him to a position much lower than that of whites. Educationally, he is segregated in schools, and the schools and facilities provided for him are far inferior to those provided for whites. Also, he has acquired a much lower educational status than whites, as measured by the years of school completed. Economically, he is on the lowest level in the South, but the trend is in the direction of upward mobility.

PROBLEMS FOR STUDY AND DISCUSSION

1. Explain how the status of the Negro has changed since he was first brought into the South, and list some of the factors that have contributed to this change.
2. List and discuss the possible influences of the concentration of Negroes in southern rural communities on the attitudes of whites toward Negroes in the South.
3. Evaluate the common attitudes of whites in the South toward the Negro (see Table IV), showing which of these attitudes are supported and which are refuted by scientific data and logical thought.
4. Study the "rank order of discrimination" that is presented in the reading by Myrdal, and point out any changes that you would make in these ranks.
5. Evaluate the "separate but equal" principle that is included in the legislation of most southern states, showing the extent to which this principle is actually put into practice.
6. Study the major legal provisions requiring the separation of Negroes and whites in the South (see Table V). Make a list of the facilities not included in this table but where separation is practiced, and try to find the laws supporting this separation in one southern state.
7. Point out the ways by which the educational status of the Negro

differs from that of the whites in the South. Suggest a program that might aid in modifying these differences.

8. Explain how the occupational distribution of Negro workers in the South might be used to support the contention that the Negro occupies a low economic status in the South.

SELECTED READINGS

DAVIS, A., and DOLLARD, J., *Children of Bondage* (Washington, D. C.: American Council on Education, 1940).

DONALD, Henderson H., *The Negro Freedman* (New York: Henry Schuman, 1952).

FRAZIER, E. Franklin, *The Negro in the United States* (New York: The Macmillan Company, 1949).

GILMORE, H., and WILSON, L., "Negro Socioeconomic Status in a Southern City," *Sociology and Social Research,* Vol. 26 (May 1, 1945), pp. 361-373.

MARDEN, Charles F., *Minorities in American Society* (New York: American Book Company, 1952), pp. 225-256.

MYRDAL, Gunnar, *An American Dilemma* (New York: Harper and Brothers, 1944).

SOPER, Edmond D., *Racism: A World Issue* (New York: Abingdon-Cokesbury Press, 1947), pp. 220-246.

STERNER, Richard, et al., *The Negro's Share* (New York: Harper and Brothers, 1943), pp. 10-46, 59-88.

WALKER, Harry J., "Changes in the Structure of Race Relations in the South," *American Sociological Review,* Vol. 14 (June, 1949), pp. 377-383.

WALTER, Paul, Jr., *Race and Cultural Relations* (New York: McGraw-Hill Book Company, Inc., 1952), chap. 15.

VI

The Negro in the North and West

Introduction

FOR SEVERAL centuries Negro-white relations in the North and West have differed from those in the South. During the colonial period there was considerable change in Negro-white relations in the North, and the trend of this change was almost the reverse of the change in the South.[1] While slavery was becoming entrenched as an economic system in many of the southern colonies, it was becoming less economical in northern colonies and was being slowly eliminated in some. In fact, in some of the northern colonies slavery was never entrenched as an economic system, and in many of these colonies it was a constant cause of conflict between economic and religious groups. At the time the present federal government was established in the United States several organizations had been initiated, largely in the North, to fight for the elimination of slavery. On the other hand, much capital had been invested in slavery in the South, which caused many of the southern states to develop a movement to resist the elimination of slavery. Thus, at the beginning of the federal government the North and the South were not in agreement concerning the status of the Negro in the United States.

The interval between the beginning of the federal government and the emancipation of slaves was a period of great change in so far as the status of the Negro in the United States was concerned.[2] In the North and West slavery was being eliminated state by state, and many leaders in these regions had organized to fight for the elimination of

[1] See John H. Franklin, *From Slavery to Freedom* (New York: Alfred A. Knopf, Inc., 1947), pp. 88-110, for a discussion of the Negro in northern colonies during the colonial period.

[2] *Ibid.*, pp. 239-266; and see E. Franklin Frazier, *The Negro in the United States* (New York: The Macmillan Company, 1949), pp. 59-81, for interesting discussions on this point.

slavery throughout the United States. On the other hand, the cotton gin, and other inventions, served to increase the profitableness of slavery in the South. In other words, the North and West were losing interest in slavery, while slavery was becoming an important economic asset in the South. *Thus, at the beginning of the Civil War the Negro had acquired a very different status in the North and West from what he had acquired in the South.* The extent to which this difference in status exists at the present time will be analyzed in this chapter.

Negro Population in the North and West

In 1950, 31.5 per cent of the Negro population of the United States resided in the thirty-two states classified as North and West by the United States Census Bureau. Of the number residing in these states more than 90 per cent are inhabitants of the eight states listed in Table X. A further concentration of the Negro population in the North is illustrated in Table XI. This table indicates that 76 per cent of the nonwhites in this region are concentrated in cities with a population of over 100,000, and that 68.4 per cent are concentrated in fifteen of these cities.

Table X: STATES IN THE NORTH IN WHICH MORE THAN 170,000 NEGROES RESIDED *

State	Number
New York	918,191
Pennsylvania	638,485
Illinois	645,980
Ohio	513,072
Michigan	442,296
Missouri	297,088
New Jersey	318,565
Indiana	174,168
Thirteen other states	298,599
Total in North	4,246,444

* Seventeenth Census of the United States. Advance Report prepared for this work by the Bureau of the Census, October 10, 1952.

From the standpoint of population distribution, there are several conditions that vary the position of the Negro in the North and West from that of the Negro in the South. The first condition is that a smaller number are scattered over a larger geographic area, which means that Negroes do not reside in many localities and the number residing in many other localities is negligible. *Thus, Negro-white contacts do not exist or are very few in numbers in many localities in the North and West.* With few or no contacts, the pattern of relations that exists is not so fixed as it is in the South. Further, where contacts are few the pattern of relations that develops is based largely on individual relations instead of group relations; or the ability of the individual usually replaces relations based on group membership.

Table XI: DISTRIBUTION OF NEGROES IN CITIES WITH A POPULATION OVER 100,000 IN THE NORTH *

City	Number
New York City	775,529
Chicago, Ill.	509,437
Philadelphia, Pa.	378,968
Detroit, Mich.	303,721
St. Louis, Mo.	154,448
Cleveland, Ohio	149,547
Pittsburgh, Pa.	82,983
Cincinnati	78,685
Newark, N. J.	75,626
Indianapolis, Ind.	64,091
Kansas City, Mo.	56,023
Columbus, Ohio	47,131
Boston, Mass.	42,744
Gary, Ind.	39,326
Buffalo, N. Y.	37,700
Forty-four other cities	420,765
Total for cities over 100,000	3,216,724

* Seventeenth Census of the United States, *Population* (1950), Preliminary Report, Series PC-14, No. 1, December 16, 1951.

A second condition that tends to make Negro-white relations differ is the urban concentration of Negroes in the North and West. In the North 92.5 per cent and in the West 92 per cent of the Negro population reside in urban areas, whereas 46.9 per cent of the Negro population in the South is urban. Then, too, this urban Negro population in the North and West resides in the larger urban centers. In other words, Negroes in the North and West reside largely in urban centers where secondary group relations predominate, while in the South they reside in areas where primary group relations are important.

Also, in the North and West the Negro is only one of several minority ethnic groups, while in the South he is *the* minority ethnic group. In the North and West one or several foreign nationality groups outnumber the Negro in many localities. In the West, Mexicans, Japanese, Indians, Chinese, or Filipinos, or a combination of two or more of these ethnic groups outnumber the Negro in many areas. Thus, instead of being *the* minority ethnic group as he is in the South, the Negro is *one among several minority ethnic groups in the North and West*.

SOCIAL STATUS

In the North and the West attitudes and opinions toward the Negro differ in several ways from those in the South.[3] It is recognized that basically there is much similarity in the attitudes and opinions toward the Negro in all sections of the United States. Yet, as discussed previously, three conditions serve to modify these attitudes and opinions to an important degree in the North and West: (1) limited contacts of whites and Negroes resulting from a scattered Negro population, (2) the urban concentration of the Negro population, and (3) the presence of other minority ethnic groups in these regions. These conditions make for somewhat superficial Negro-white relations, since in many instances these relations are based on vicarious experience instead of actual contacts.

Nevertheless, it has been pointed out that several attitudes and opinions are well fixed in the North and West.[4] Among these attitudes and opinions accepted by whites are: (1) residential segregation is necessary and should be continued, (2) social equality is impractical if not impossible, (3) Negroes should be segregated in close social relations, (4) Negroes are best fitted for unskilled labor and domestic work and should be denied white-collar jobs, (5) close personal contacts with Negroes should be avoided, and (6) interracial marriages are taboo and should be avoided.

It should be noted that most of these attitudes imply the use of what Johnson describes as the *avoidance technique* in race relations.[5] This technique is used by both whites and Negroes in the North and the West. In using this technique, the attitude of whites seems to be centered around avoiding situations that might necessitate close personal contacts or close social relations. Whites seek to avoid these contacts or relations in an attempt to maintain status, or to keep from offending other whites who might consider close relations with Negroes as degrading. Negroes use the technique of avoidance in

---

[3] See Otto Klineberg, Editor, *Characteristics of the American Negro* (New York: Harper and Brothers, 1944), pp. 185-208, for a discussion on "Attitudes and Sectional Differences in the United States."

[4] See St. Clair Drake and Horace R. Cayton, *Black Metropolis: A Study of Negro Life in a Northern City* (New York: Harcourt Brace and Company, Inc., 1945), pp. 266-270; and Charles S. Johnson, *Patterns of Negro Segregation* (New York: Harper and Brothers, 1943), pp. 194-227.

[5] *Ibid.*, pp. 267-293.

order to spare themselves possible embarrassment by whites who strive to avoid contacts with Negroes.

The extent to which avoidance is practiced by whites in the North and West can be illustrated in many ways. Although segregation is illegal in most of the states in these regions, voluntary segregation is practiced in all; and whites who transcend this voluntary segregation must pay the price in some way. According to the principles of voluntary segregation, Negroes are not supposed to reside in the same hotels as whites. They are not supposed to eat in the same cafes, unless in a secluded portion of the building. They are not to act on familiar terms with whites unless in privacy. They are not to intermarry as this will lower the status of offspring of the union. They are not to be employed in positions of respectability, or positions that will make them superior to whites. They are not to live in residential areas occupied by whites as this will lower the value of property. They are to be restricted to certain schools, or in specific classrooms, as contact in school might lead to closer social contacts in other areas of social life. Surely, there is an etiquette of race relations in the North and West that is almost as fixed as that described by Doyle as existing in the South.[6] This etiquette is followed by both whites and Negroes—whites to maintain status and Negroes to avoid embarrassment. Above all, the etiquette that exists denotes a low social status for the Negro in the North and West when compared with the social status of native whites in these regions.

Yet, it should be kept in mind that the Negro is not the only large minority ethnic group in the North and West as he is in the South. Although the social status of Negroes is lower than that of native whites, it is as high if not higher than that of other minority ethnic groups in some areas. In a few localities in the North the Negro may be accorded a social status equal to or higher than that of some white nationality or cultural groups. In many localities in the West the social status of the Negro is equal to or higher than that of Mexicans, Indians, Japanese, Chinese, or Filipinos. Thus, in the North and West the Negro is not always on the lowest social level as he is in the South. In many instances he has a social status equal to that of other ethnic groups, and in some instances he is accorded a higher social status than other minority ethnic groups.

As in the South, the social status of the Negro in the North and

6 Bertram W. Doyle, *The Etiquette of Race Relations in the South* (Chicago: The University of Chicago Press, 1937).

the West is reflected, to a large extent, by the many forms of social segregation and discrimination that exist in these areas. Although these forms of social segregation and discrimination are carried on in subtle ways, most Negroes are made aware that they exist. It might be that they will attempt to purchase property, but find that a property agreement prevents this. They might desire membership in some organization, but are informed that the organization has a "white membership" clause in its constitution. They might attempt to secure a hotel room, and are told that all rooms are occupied, while a white person arriving later will be assigned a room without question. They might desire a meal, but must be careful and select a cafe or restaurant where they know they will be served without being slighted. They might enter a theater and, when the lights are turned on, find that the ushers have seated all Negroes in the same area. These, and many other forms of social segregation and discrimination confront Negroes daily in most northern cities. Although the forms of social segregation and discrimination are not as structured in the North as they are in the South, they are practiced enough for anyone to recognize that Negroes are accorded a low social status by "typical Americans" in the North. In the following reading, Professor Myrdal gives an interpretation of some of the forms of social segregation and discrimination as they exist in the North.

▌ SOCIAL SEGREGATION AND DISCRIMINATION IN THE NORTH [7]

GUNNAR MYRDAL

At the outbreak of the Civil War, most Northern states were nearly as far removed in time from actual slavery in their own realms as the Southern states are now. Their Negro populations were comparatively small in numbers. But slavery was a living institution within the nation. Though conditions were rather different in different Northern states, the general statement can be made that wherever Negroes lived in significant numbers they met considerable social segregation and discrimination. The Abolitionist propaganda and the gradual definition of emancipation as one of the main goals of the War undoubtedly tended to raise the status of Negroes somewhat. Still, one of the difficulties congressional leaders had in passing the Reconstruction legislation was the resistance in some Northern

[7] From *An American Dilemma* (New York: Harper and Brothers, 1944), pp. 599-604. Used by permission of the publisher.

states where people found that they would have to change not only their behavior but also their laws in order to comply with the new statutes.

In the social field—as in breadwinning, but not as in politics and justice—the North has kept much segregation and discrimination. In some respects, the social bars were raised considerably on account of the mass immigration of poor and ignorant Negroes during and immediately after the First World War. In the latter part of the 'twenties this movement was perhaps turned into a slight tendency in the opposite direction, namely, an appreciation of "The New Negro." After a new wave of unpopularity during the first years of the depression, there seems again to have been a slow but steady development toward less social discrimination during the era of the New Deal. But quite apart from these uncertain fluctuations during the last couple of decades, it is obviously a gross exaggeration when it is asserted that the North is getting to be "like the South."

Even in the realm of social relations it is of importance that the average Northerner does not think of the Negroes as former slaves. He has not the possessive feeling for them and he does not regard their subservience as a mark of his own social status. He is, there- fore, likely to let the Negroes alone unless in his opinion they get to be a nuisance. Upon the ideological plane the ordinary North- erner is, further, apparently conscious that social discrimination is wrong and against the American Creed, while the average South- erner tries to convince himself and the nation that it is right or, in any case, that it is necessary. The white newspapers in the North ordinarily ignore the Negroes and their problems entirely—most of the time more completely than the liberal Southern press. But when they have to come out in the open on the Negro problem, they usually stand for equality. Back of this official attitude, of course, is the fact that most Northerners are not in direct contact with Negroes. The patterns of social discrimination in the South have originally formed themselves as rural ways of life. In the North the rural sections are, and have always been, practically free of Negroes. Even in the big cities in the North, where there are substantial Negro populations, only a small part of the white population has many contacts with Negroes.

Lacking ideological sanction and developing directly contrary to the openly accepted equalitarian Creed, social segregation and dis- crimination in the North have to keep *sub rosa*. The observer finds that *in the North there is actually much unawareness on the part of white people of the extent of social discrimination against Negroes.* It has been a common experience of this writer to witness how white Northerners are surprised and shocked when they hear about such things, and how they are moved to feel that something ought to be done to stop it. They often do not understand correctly even the implications of their own behavior and often tell the interviewer that they "have never thought of it in that light." This innocence is, of course, opportunistic to a degree, but it is, nevertheless, real and honest too. In this situation *one of the main difficulties for Negroes in the North is simply lack of publicity*. It is convenient for the Northerners' good conscience to forget about the Negro.

In so far as the Negroes can get their claims voiced in the press and in legislatures, and are able to put political strength behind them, they are free to press for state action against social discrimination. The chances are that they will meet no *open* opposition. The legislatures will practically never go the other way and attempt to Jim Crow the Negroes by statutes. The federal Reconstruction legislation has taken better root in the North. When the Supreme Court in 1883 declared the Civil Rights Bill of 1875 unconstitutional, most states in the Northeast and Middle West, and some in the Far West, started to make similar laws of their own, while the Southern states, instead, began to build up the structure of Jim Crow legislation.

With the ideological and legal sanctions directed *against* them, social segregation and discrimination have not acquired the *strength, persuasiveness or institutional fixity* found in the South. Actual discrimination varies a good deal in the North: it seems to be mainly a function of the relative number of Negroes in a community and its distance from the South. In several minor cities in New England with a small, stable Negro population, for instance, social discrimination is hardly noticeable. The Negroes there usually belong to the working class, but often they enter the trades, serve in shops, and even carry on independent businesses catering to whites as well as to Negroes. They belong to the ordinary churches of the community, and the children attend the public schools. Occasional intermarriages do not create great excitement. They fit into the community and usually form a little clique for themselves beside other cliques, but nobody seems to think much about their color. The interracial situation in such a city may remain even today very similar to that of Great Barrington, Massachusetts, some sixty years ago, which W. E. B. DuBois portrays in his recent autobiography, *Dusk of Dawn*.

In the bigger cities, even in New England, the conditions of life for the Negroes have probably never been so idyllic. Since the migration beginning in 1915, the status of Northern Negroes has fallen perceptibly. In the Northern cities nearer the Mason-Dixon line there has always been, and is even today, more social segregation and discrimination than farther North.

One factor which in every Northern city of any size has contributed to form patterns of segregation and discrimination against
Negroes has been residential segregation, which acts as a cause as
well as an effect of social distance. This fundamental segregation
was caused by the general pattern for ethnic groups to live together
in Northern cities. But while Swedes, Italians, and Jews could become Americanized in a generation or two, and disperse themselves
in the more anonymous parts of the city, Negroes were caught in
their "quarters" because of their inescapable social visibility; and
the real estate interest kept watch to enforce residential segregation.
With residential segregation naturally comes a certain amount of
segregation in schools, in hospitals, and in other public places even
when it is not intended as part of policy. Personal contacts become,
as a matter of course, more or less restricted to Negro neighborhoods.
As the Negro sections grew during the northward migration, it
became more and more possible for Negroes to have their entire
social life in Negro neighborhoods, and white people became conditioned to look upon this as a natural and desirable situation.

In this process white Southerners who also moved northward have
played a crucial role. To make a manager of a hotel, a restaurant, or
a theater interested in trying to keep Negroes out of his establishment, it is not necessary that more than a tiny minority of customers
object, particularly if they make a scene. Time and again, I have,
in my interviews with managers of various public places in the
North, been told this same story: that they, themselves, had no
prejudices but that some of their customers would resent seeing
Negroes around. The fact that most Negroes are poor and residen-
tially isolated and, hence, do not patronize white places often, and
the further fact that upper class Negroes, who could afford to,
abstain voluntarily from visiting places where they are afraid of
being embarrassed, solidifies the situation. I have also noticed that
Negroes often have an entirely exaggerated notion of the difficulties
they would meet. They are conditioned to suspect discrimination
even when there is no danger of it. So they abstain from going to
places where they actually could go without any trouble. When once
this pattern is set by themselves the result might later be discrimination when some Negro tries to break it.

The migrating Negroes have been probably even more influential
in spreading Southern patterns in the North than the Southern
whites. The low cultural level and poverty of the average Southern
Negro stand out even more when he comes North where general
standards are higher. If he comes without any other education, he is
at least thoroughly trained in the entire ceremonial system of scrap-
ing his foot, tipping his hat, and using self-abasing vocabulary and

dialect, and generally being subservient and unobtrusive in the company of whites. A Negro recently from the South is characterized as much by his manners and bearing as by his racial traits. He might get some ideas of a new freedom of behavior in the North and actually try his best to behave as a full man; and he might, indeed, easily succeed in becoming aggressive and offensive. But fundamentally it takes a radical reeducation to get him out of his Southern demeanor or the reaction to it. For a long time after migrating he will invoke discrimination by his own behavior. The submissive behavior of lower class Southern Negroes is usually not appealing at all to the white Northerner, who has not been brought up to have a patronizing attitude and who does not need it for his own self-elevation. The white Northerner also dislikes the slovenliness and ignorance of the Southern Negro. Thus the Negro often seems only strange, funny or repulsive to the white Northerner.

Even the poor classes of whites in the North come to mistrust and despise the Negroes. The European immigrant groups are the ones thrown into most direct contact and competition with Negroes: they live near each other, often send their children to the same schools, and have to struggle for the same jobs. Obviously attitudes among immigrants vary a good deal. Recent immigrants apparently sometimes feel an interest solidarity with Negroes or, at any rate, lack the intense superiority feeling of the native Americans educated in race prejudice. But the development of prejudice against Negroes is usually one of their first lessons in Americanization. Because they are of low status, they like to have a group like the Negroes to which they can be superior. For these reasons, it should not be surprising if now, since new immigration has been restricted for a considerable time, a study of racial attitudes should show that the immigrant groups are on the average even more prejudiced than native Americans in the same community.

I have an impression that the resentment against Negroes in the North is different from that in the South, not only in intensity, but also in its class direction. It does not seem to be directed particularly against the rising Negroes. In the more anonymous Northern cities, the Negro middle and upper classes do not get into the focus of public resentment as in the South. More important is the Yankee outlook on life in which climbing and social success are generally given a higher value than in the more static Southern society, and the ambitious Negro will more often be rewarded by approval and even by admiration, while in the South he is likely to be considered "smart," "uppity" or "out of his place."

Otherwise, the North is not original in its racial ideology. When there is segregation and discrimination to be justified, the rationalization is sometimes a vague and simplified version of the "no social equality" theory of the South which we have already discussed. It is continuously spread by Southerners moving North and Northerners who have been South, by fiction and by hearsay. But more often the rationalizations run in terms of the alleged racial inferiority of the Negro, his animal-like nature, his unreliability, his low morals, dirtiness and unpleasant manners. The references and associations to amalgamation and intermarriage are much less frequent and direct. This does not mean that the Northerner approves of intermarriage. But he is less emotional in his disapproval. What Paul Lewinson calls "the post-prandial non-sequitur"—if a Negro eats with a white man he is assumed to have the right to marry his daughter—practically does not exist in the North.

In this situation, however, not only is intermarriage frowned upon, but in high schools and colleges there will often be attempts to exclude Negroes from dances and social affairs. Social segregation is, in fact, likely to appear in all sorts of social relations. But there is much less social segregation and discrimination than in the South: there is no segregation on streetcars, trains, and so on, and above all, there is no rigid ceremonial governing the Negro-white relations and no laws holding the Negro down. The fact that there are no laws or defined rules of etiquette is sometimes said to cause friction and bitterness because some whites in the North will want Negroes to keep away from them, and Negroes cannot tell which whites these are. But the absence of segregating laws also keeps the system from being so relatively locked as in the South. It allows Negroes to be ambitious. And since Negroes in the North have the vote and a reasonable amount of justice in court, and since they can go to good schools and are, in fact, forced to get at least an elementary education, they can struggle for fuller social equality with some hope.

LEGAL STATUS

The legal status of the Negro in the North and West is much higher than the legal status of the Negro in the South. As was presented in the preceding chapter, there are many laws that serve to restrict the Negro to a low legal status in the South. On the other hand, in the North and the West there are laws in many states that are intended to remove all legal or social differences which might exist among the many ethnic groups in these regions. These laws make many types of segregation and discrimination illegal and provide criminal and, or, civil punishments for those in violation of these laws.

Table XII reveals the major areas in which segregation and discrimination are prohibited in eighteen of the thirty-two states in the North and West. While the Negro is legally denied the use of many of the same facilities as whites in the South, in these eighteen states segregation is legally prohibited. In most of the fourteen states in the North and West without civil rights provisions the Negro is granted the legal rights provided for in the Federal Constitution. Thus, the

Table XII: MAJOR CIVIL RIGHTS PROVISIONS IN STATES IN THE NORTH AND WEST *

States	Inns	Restaurants and eating houses	Hotels	Barbershops	Bathhouses	Theaters	Public conveyances	All other places of public accommodation or amusement
California	X	X	X	X	X	X	X	X
Colorado	X	X		X		X	X	X
Connecticut		X	X			X	X	X
Illinois	X	X	X	X	X	X	X	X
Indiana	X	X		X				X
Iowa	X	X		X	X	X	X	X
Kansas	X		X				X	X
Massachusetts	X	X	X	X	X	X	X	X
Michigan	X	X	X	X	X	X	X	X
Minnesota		X	X	X	X	X	X	X
Nebraska	X	X		X		X	X	X
New Jersey		X	X			X	X	X
New York		X	X	X		X	X	X
Ohio	X	X		X		X	X	X
Pennsylvania							X	X
Rhode Island	X	X			X	X	X	X
Washington								X
Wisconsin	X	X		X			X	X

* The data in this table were compiled from a bulletin entitled *Defending Your Civil Rights* (1950), that was prepared by the Legal Department of the National Association for the Advancement of Colored People. Segregation is prohibited in the use of facilities in states where "X" appears.

right of political participation, which is guaranteed by the Federal Constitution, is granted to Negroes in all of the states in the North and the West, while many legal restrictions of this right are found in some of the states in the South. In addition, the states with civil rights provisions have made it illegal to deny many other rights to Negroes.

In some states the areas in which segregation is prohibited are very specific, while in others they are general in nature. For instance, in Illinois the law specifies thirty-two areas in which segregation is illegal, while according to the Washington law segregation is illegal in "any place of public resort, accommodation, assemblage or amusement." The most common provision included in these laws is "all places of public accommodation or amusement." Other places mentioned in these laws are: public conveyances, restaurants and eating houses, theaters, inns, barbershops, hotels, and bathhouses. The extent to which voluntary segregation is accepted among Negroes in the North and West is illustrated by the fact that Negro businesses in the states in these regions have developed most in five of the areas in which segregation is legally prohibited: inns, eating places, hotels, barbershops, and theaters.

It is evident that the legal status of the Negro is the same as that of other ethnic groups in the North and the West. Not only is the Negro accorded the legal status granted by the Federal Constitution, but in many states special laws have been enacted to guarantee these rights to all ethnic groups. In other words, the differences that exist between the status of the Negro and other ethnic groups in the North and the West are not legal differences, but differences based on the attitudes and opinions that have developed, or are accepted, among members of the majority ethnic group in these regions.

EDUCATIONAL STATUS

There is a wide range in the laws and practices governing the educational status of the Negro in the thirty-two states included in the North and the West by the Federal Census Bureau.[8] In 1945 the school laws of one of these states required separate schools (Missouri);[9] five states had laws that made it possible for separation to be practiced on some level, or under certain conditions; twelve states by law prohibited the segregation of ethnic groups; and fourteen states did not mention separation in public schools in their constitutions or statutes.[10] In other words, there are twenty-six states in the North and West in which separate schools for minority ethnic groups are not legal or are actually illegal.

Although separate public schools do not have a legal foundation in

[8] For a discussion on this point see L. D. Reddick, "The Education of Negroes in States Where Separate Schools Are Not Legal," *Journal of Negro Education*, Vol. 16 (Summer, 1947), pp. 290-300; and Reid E. Jackson, "The Development and Character of Permissive and Partly Segregated Schools," *Ibid.*, pp. 301-310.

[9] Since Missouri requires separate public schools for Negroes, it will not be included in the discussion of the educational status of the Negro in the North and West.

[10] Jackson, *op. cit.*, p. 301.

most of the states in the North and West, it is a recognized observation that they do exist in these regions; and some of these separate schools are in states that legally prohibit separate public schools.[11] It is estimated by Reddick that the distribution of Negro pupils in these regions is as follows: "One-fourth of them in schools that are thoroughly mixed, another two-fourths (or one-half) attend schools partially mixed, and a final one-fourth attend schools as distinctly separate as in the South."[12] Or, according to this estimate, three-fourths of the Negro pupils are in schools that are separate or in which "the ideal of complete integration is departed from in one or more particular."

Two conditions have served to continue separate public schools for Negroes in the North and West. The first condition is ecological, in that a number of factors have restricted Negroes to certain residential areas. Among these factors are: restrictive property covenants, the Negroes' economic position, and the greater freedom found in Negro communities. The second condition is a problem of educational administration and guidance. Some educational leaders still emphasize the need for a different kind of education for Negroes, and strive to provide an educational program that will satisfy the special needs of Negroes. Both of these conditions contribute to the number of separate schools that exist in the North and West. The first condition is responsible for Negroes residing in geographic areas that are served by specific schools. The second condition, though of doubtful validity, is used as an excuse for assigning Negro pupils to separate classrooms, or encouraging them to attend schools that will contribute to what is thought to be their special needs. Since Negroes are compelled to live in crowded slum areas in many cities in the North because of social and economic conditions, they are required to attend schools that reflect the areas in which they live. These schools are often overcrowded, and more often the buildings are in a somewhat dilapidated condition, making it difficult for Negroes to obtain an education that is equal to that in other areas of the city.

In theory the facilities available to whites for higher and professional education are also available to Negroes in all of the states in the North and West with the exception of Missouri. However, if the study conducted in the state of New York is representative, Negroes

---

[11] *Ibid.*, pp. 302-304 and 307-309. Jackson cites specific separate schools in Illinois and New Jersey, two of the states with laws prohibiting separate public schools.
[12] Reddick, *op. cit.*, p. 296.

are discriminated against for many reasons when they apply for admission to colleges and universities.[13] In this study, 16 of the 39 high schools (41 per cent) having some Negroes in their student bodies, reported that Negro graduates had encountered some form of discrimination in seeking admission to the colleges and universities in the state of New York. Although they were not denied admission, many excuses were offered in discouraging Negro high school graduates from entering many colleges and universities in New York. Among the most common excuses were: (1) social life for Negro students is negligible, (2) parents object to Negro students, (3) the institution is not interested in Negro students, (4) the situation might not be happy for Negro students, and (5) scholarship or work aids are not available. To these reasons might be added the following: (6) most Negroes lack the economic resources necessary to attend many of these schools, (7) Negro youth receives little encouragement from their elders, and (8) many schools are not ready to admit Negroes into their dormitories. Thus, although Negroes are not denied admission to many of the colleges and universities in the North and West, they are confronted with many discouragements when they seek it. This means that only the courageous will follow through and many capable students who can be misled or discouraged will drop by the wayside. As a result, Negroes in the North and West are not able to make the best use of the facilities for higher and professional education that are available to them.

The educational status of the Negro in the North and West, as measured by the number of school years completed, is indicated for selected states in Table XIII. This table shows that the Negro in these regions has, on the average, completed many more years of schooling than the Negro in the South and, in most instances, more than whites in the South. For median years of school completed there is some difference in most of these states between the schooling of native whites and Negroes, the greatest difference (2.5 years) being in California in which the median school years completed is much higher for whites than in any of the other states. As in the South, however, the proportions for high school graduation and for four years or more of college are much higher for whites than for Negroes. Also, the proportions for high school and college graduation are much

<hr />

13 David S. Berkowitz, *Inequality of Opportunity in Higher Education* (Albany: Williams Press, Inc., 1948), pp. 159-174, 191-195.

higher for whites in the South than for Negroes in the North and West.

The logical conclusions that can be drawn from these facts are:

Table XIII: YEARS OF SCHOOL COMPLETED BY PERSONS 25 YEARS OLD AND OVER IN THE NORTH AND WEST BY RACE AND STATE *

State and Race	Percentage of population 25 years old and over				Median school years completed
	No school years completed	1-4 school years	4 years high school	4 years college or more	
California:					
Native white	0.6	3.0	24.3	7.6	10.8
Negro	3.9	12.2	14.4	2.5	8.3
Illinois:					
Native white	0.6	3.9	16.8	5.3	8.8
Negro	4.3	16.0	8.4	2.0	7.7
Indiana:					
Native white	0.7	5.3	16.4	4.0	8.6
Negro	5.2	17.3	7.1	1.8	7.6
Michigan:					
Native white	0.6	4.1	17.3	4.8	9.0
Negro	3.9	17.4	8.0	1.5	7.6
New Jersey:					
Native white	0.7	3.4	16.8	6.5	8.8
Negro	5.6	19.7	5.4	1.4	7.2
New York:					
Native white	0.8	2.4	16.9	7.1	9.0
Negro	3.7	13.6	9.0	1.9	7.8
Ohio:					
Native white	0.6	3.8	18.0	5.0	8.8
Negro	5.3	19.1	7.2	1.6	7.4
Pennsylvania:					
Native white	0.8	4.8	15.0	4.9	8.6
Negro	5.6	20.0	5.7	1.2	7.1

* Sixteenth Census of the United States, *Population* (1940), Vol. 2, Parts 1-7.

The educational status of the Negro in the North and West is far above that of the Negro in the South; it approaches that of whites in the South; but it is far below that of whites in the North and West. The general conclusions that these facts will support are that the educational status of the Negro in the North is above that of foreign-born whites, but below that of native whites; in the West the educational status of the Negro is above that of several minority ethnic groups, but, again, below that of native whites.

ECONOMIC STATUS

Occupational Distribution

The economic status of the Negro in the North and West will be analyzed in keeping with the following standards: (1) occupational distribution, (2) home ownership, and (3) retail businesses. The occupational distribution of Negro workers in the North and West, as compared with that for white workers, is illustrated in Tables XIV and XV. In these tables the occupational distribution in the North Central division is presented. One-half of the Negroes living in the North and West reside in the North Central division. Also, a comparison of the occupational distribution in this division with that in other divisions indicated that its occupational distribution is representative of that in the other divisions in the North and West.

The outstanding fact illustrated for Negro male workers in Table XIV is what Sterner calls "The Negro's Flight from Agriculture." [14] In the South 49.6 per cent of the Negro male workers were engaged as farmers or farm laborers in 1940, while in the North and West the proportion ranged from 2.6 per cent in the Northeast to 5.7 per cent in the West. [15] The occupation group that supplants farming among Negro males in the North and West is service workers, except domestic and protective, as the proportion engaged as laborers is approximately the same in all divisions in the United States. In 1940 almost two-thirds of all Negro male workers in the North and West were engaged in the following specific occupations: laborers, janitors and porters, servants, and chauffeurs and truck drivers, in the order listed. [16] There is a much better distribution of white male workers among the major occupational groups; and there is a larger concentration of white workers in occupations that require special training, pay higher wages and salaries, and carry with them a higher social status. On the other hand, *the occupations in which Negro male workers are concentrated are those that require very little training, pay low wages and salaries, and generally carry some social stigma.*

Occupational concentration is much more evident among Negro female workers in the North and West. As illustrated in Table XV,

[14] A detailed description of this flight is presented in Richard Sterner, *The Negro's Share* (New York: Harper and Brothers, 1943), pp. 10-28.
[15] Sixteenth Census of the United States, *The Labor Force* (1940), Vol. 3, Part 1, p. 97.
[16] *Ibid.*, pp. 91-92.

Negro female workers are concentrated in service occupations. More than one-half (56.7 per cent) are engaged as domestic service workers, and 21.5 per cent as service workers, other than domestic and protective. Thus, 78.2 per cent are engaged in service occupations. The specific occupations in which approximately two-thirds of the Negro female workers are engaged are: domestic workers, servants other than in private families, and laundry operatives and laundresses, in the order listed. White female workers are distributed in larger proportions among several occupational groups, with the greatest concentration being for clerical, sales, and kindred workers (33.8 per cent). The real difference in the existing status of the occupation in which Negro female workers are concentrated (domestic workers) and that in which white female workers are concentrated (clerical and sales) is well known. The economic difference is equally as great, for in 1939 more than three-fifths of the domestic workers in the North Central states earned less than $400 for twelve months' work, while one-half or more of the clerical and sales workers earned $1,000 or more for the year's work.[17]

Table XIV: PER CENT DISTRIBUTION BY MAJOR OCCUPATION GROUPS FOR EMPLOYED MALES BY RACE FOR THE NORTH CENTRAL DIVISION *

Major Occupation Group	Negro	White
Service workers, except domestic and protective	26.3	3.5
Laborers, except farm	25.8	7.2
Operatives and kindred workers	19.4	18.1
Craftsmen, foremen, and kindred workers	8.1	15.5
Clerical, sales, and kindred workers	4.9	13.1
Farm laborers (wage workers)	2.9	4.7
Domestic service workers	2.8	0.1
Professional workers	2.6	4.4
Proprietors, managers, officials, except farm	2.4	10.0
Farmers and farm managers	2.1	17.3
Protective service workers	1.2	1.5
Semiprofessional workers	0.5	1.1
Farm laborers (unpaid family workers)	0.3	2.9
Occupation not reported	0.7	0.7

* Sixteenth Census of the United States, The Labor Force (1940), Vol. 3, Part 1, p. 97.

In the North and West, as in the South, Negro workers are engaged in occupations that require the least training, pay the lowest income, are the least desirable, and are accorded the lowest social status.[18]

17 Ibid., p. 167.
18 An intense analysis of Negro jobs is given in Gunnar Myrdal, An American Dilemma, Vol. 2 (New York: Harper and Brothers, 1944), pp. 1079-1124.

Because the wage level is higher for most occupations in the North and West than it is in the South, the money income of Negro workers in these regions is larger than it is in the South. In other words, Negroes in the North and West may be better off than Negroes in the South from the standpoint of income, but in all regions of the United States they are engaged in occupations that denote a lower economic

Table XV: PER CENT DISTRIBUTION BY MAJOR OCCUPATION GROUPS FOR EM-PLOYED FEMALES BY RACE FOR THE NORTH CENTRAL DIVISION *

Major Occupation Group	Negro	White
Domestic service workers	56.7	12.9
Service workers, except domestic and protective	21.5	12.7
Operatives and kindred workers	9.0	16.1
Professional workers	4.3	13.8
Clerical, sales, and kindred workers	3.9	33.8
Proprietors, managers, officials, except farm	1.4	4.1
Laborers, except farm	1.2	1.1
Semiprofessional workers	0.5	0.9
Craftsmen, foremen, and kindred workers	0.3	1.1
Farm laborers (wage workers)	0.2	0.1
Farm laborers (unpaid family workers)	0.1	0.7
Farmers and farm managers	0.1	1.1
Protective service workers	—	—
Occupation not reported	0.8	1.3

* Sixteenth Census of the United States, *The Labor Force* (1940), Vol. 3, Part 1, p. 97.

status than those engaged in by whites. Occupations engaged in by Negro workers pay an income much smaller than that required to maintain a minimum standard of living, they provide little economic security, and they offer few chances for occupational advancement.

Home Ownership

As judged by home ownership, the economic status is much lower for Negroes than for whites in both the North and the West. This is true if the economic status is measured by the proportion of owner occupied homes or by the value of the homes owned. In the North 45 per cent of the whites and 17.6 per cent of the Negroes owned the homes that they occupied, while the proportions for the West were 48.8 per cent for whites, and 33.4 per cent for Negroes.[19] These figures indicate that the economic status of the Negro, as measured by home ownership, is lower than that for whites in the West, and much lower in the North. When consideration is given to the fact that 94.2 per cent of the Negroes in the North and West reside in the North, it is

[19] Sixteenth Census of the United States, *Housing* (1940), Vol. 2, Part 1, p. 7.

evident that the Negroes' economic status is much lower than that of whites, the proportion for home ownership for whites being 2.5 times that for Negroes.

If attention is directed to the value of the homes owned prior to the inflation of World War II, the economic differential is about the same. The average value of homes owned in the North was $3,528 for whites and $2,084 for nonwhites.[20] Further, only 14.6 per cent of the homes owned by whites in the North were valued at less than $1,000, while 32.9 per cent of those owned by nonwhites were valued at less than this figure. On the other hand, 22.6 per cent of the white homes were valued at $5,000 or more, and only 8 per cent of the non-white homes were valued at this figure or more.[21] Thus, if measured by home ownership or the value of homes, the economic status of the Negro in the North and West is far below that for whites.

Business Enterprises

Business enterprises among Negroes in the North and West are practically of the same kind as those among Negroes in the South. The businesses operated are restricted largely to barbershops, beauty parlors, retail food businesses, cleaning and pressing shops, and eating and drinking places.[22] That these businesses are small is attested by the fact that the average sales for these businesses was $3,566 in 1939, and the average stock on hand at the end of the year was valued at $167.[23] As in the South, the Negro has developed a few large or middle-size businesses in the North and West, such as insurance companies, newspapers, funeral homes, manufacturing of toilet goods and cosmetics, real-estate establishments, and banks; but these businesses depend largely on Negro patronage and influence the larger business system very little, if any.

The fact is, Negro business enterprises have not been able to influence Negro purchasing power to any great extent. An excellent illustration of this is presented by Drake and Cayton, and could be duplicated in almost any city in the North or West.[24] The most desirable business sites in Negro communities are usually owned by whites, and Negroes have a difficult time renting any of these for

---

20 *Ibid.,* p. 45.

21 *Ibid.,* p. 48.

22 See Drake and Cayton, *op. cit.,* pp. 430-494; and Frazier, *op. cit.,* pp. 387-413, for discussions on Negro business.

23 Sixteenth Census of the United States, *Retail Trade* (1940), Part 1, p. 142.

24 Drake and Cayton, *op. cit.,* pp. 437-439 and 448-453.

business purposes. As whites own the buildings, they usually operate the businesses, or employ Negroes to operate them. As an example, it has been estimated that white business enterprises receive more than nine-tenths of the money spent in Negro neighborhoods in one northern city.[25] The businesses in which Negroes are most successful are usually those enterprises whites have not entered to any large extent in Negro communities, such as barbershops, beauty parlors, cleaning and pressing shops, taverns, and cafes, or businesses in which whites have refused or discouraged Negro clientele such as funeral homes, insurance companies, newspapers, real-estate offices, and the manufacturing of toilet goods and cosmetics to be used especially by Negroes.

Hence, if the economic status of the Negro is measured by his business enterprises, he is on a very low economic level. His businesses are usually very small and unstable from an economic standpoint. His enterprises have very little, if any, influence on the larger economic system. He has been able to acquire only a small part of the purchasing power of the Negro, and this is, in most instances, in businesses that whites have not entered in Negro communities.

Thus, the economic status of the Negro in the North and West is lower than that of native whites when measured by the standards used in this chapter, and it is believed that the same would be true if any other set of economic standards were used. *The Negro is engaged in the occupations that pay the smallest wages and salaries, and are accorded the lowest social status.* The Negro owns a much smaller proportion of the houses that he occupies, and the houses that he owns are of a much lower value. The Negro has not been able to gain much ground in competition with whites in business. However, the economic status of the Negro in the North and West differs much from that of the Negro in the South. In the South the Negro, as the only large minority ethnic group, is on a low economic level by himself. In the North he finds many foreign-born whites who are on as low, or a lower, economic level than he is. In the West the Negro has attained a higher economic level than other minority ethnic groups, as will be pointed out later.

25 *Ibid.*, p. 438.

SUMMARY

Three demographic conditions serve to differentiate the Negro population in the North and West from the Negro population in the South. In the North and West the Negro population is smaller in proportion to the total population, it is more urban, and other minority ethnic groups reside in these regions. Nevertheless, the Negro is accorded a social status much lower than that of "typical Americans," but equal to, if not superior to, that of some of the other minority ethnic groups in these regions. Legally, the status of the Negro is the same as that of members of all other ethnic groups that are citizens of the United States. Although the educational status of the Negro is equal to that of whites if judged by laws, it is lower if measured by educational attainment. From an economic standpoint, the status of the Negro is lower than that of native whites, but approaches that of several other minority ethnic groups.

In general, the status of the Negro is low in the North and West when compared with that of native whites. Although the laws in many of these states prohibit differential treatment between ethnic groups, the fact remains that differences are made. The source of these differences seems to be the attitudes and opinions that are common among members of the majority ethnic group. These attitudes and opinions relegate the Negro to a low social status, and this low social status predominates in all other areas of group life. *This fact strongly suggests the conclusion that attitudes and opinions are more important than laws in determining the general status of an ethnic group.* Therefore, if ethnic relations, in the United States, are to be improved, it is essential that constructive programs and procedures be established that will modify attitudes and opinions. These programs and procedures should be so planned that they will serve to modify the many fallacious attitudes and opinions that are accepted, and to reinforce the democratic attitudes and opinions that science and logic have been able to prove valid.

The data presented in Chapters V and VI should be sufficient to show that it is impossible to refer to *the* status of the Negro in the United States. Rather, existing laws and conditions indicate *many* statuses for Negroes in the United States. He has one status in areas where segregation is legal, and another in areas where segregation is prohibited or not mentioned. He has one status in areas where he is the only minority ethnic group, and another in areas where several minority ethnic groups reside. He has one status in areas where Negroes reside in large numbers, and another in areas where only a few reside. He has one status in southern rural communities, and another in northern urban communities. However, as it is impossible to consider all of these variations, data have been presented to point out the differences in the status of the Negro in the larger regions in the United States—the North and West as compared with the South.

The factual material in Chapters V and VI indicate that there is much difference between the status of the Negro in the North and West as compared with the Negro in the South. The Negro in the North has a higher social status, as attitudes and opinions toward the Negro are not so degrading, fixed, or embedded in the thought and action of the people as they are in the South. The Negro's legal status is higher in the North and West as many laws in these regions prohibit separation and discrimination, while in the South many laws exist that require separation and make possible discrimination. The Negro's educational status is higher in the North and West as, theoretically, all educational facilities are available to Negroes, while in the South they are legally denied access to or are not provided with many of the educational facilities that are available for whites. The Negro's economic status is higher in the North and West because he has more educational and occupational opportunities, the income level is higher, he has been able to acquire more valuable homes, and the yearly sales of the average Negro business enterprise are larger.

PROBLEMS FOR STUDY AND DISCUSSION

1. Compare the early Negro-white relations in the North with those in the South showing how these differences have contributed to the development of different patterns of ethnic relations.

2. Point out some of the ways by which the urban concentration of the Negro population in the North has served to accord the Negro a higher status in the North than he is accorded in the South.

3. List and explain the ways by which social discrimination, against the Negro, differs in the North and the South.

4. List some of the principles of the "etiquette" of race relations in the North that are implied in this chapter.

5. Discuss the legal status of the Negro in the North, showing how this differs from his social status.

6. Explain how it is possible for discrimination to continue in many states in the North and West although laws exist in these regions that intend to prohibit discrimination.

7. Compare the occupational distribution of Negroes and whites in the North, showing which occupational distribution indicates the lowest economic status.

8. Evaluate the status of the Negro in the North under the following points, and outline a program by which his status might be improved: (1) social, (2) economic, and (3) educational.

SELECTED READINGS

DRAKE, St. Clair, and CAYTON, H. R., *Black Metropolis* (New York: Harcourt, Brace and Company, Inc., 1945).

KARDINER, Abraham, and OVESEY, Lionel, *The Mark of Oppression* (New York: W. W. Norton and Company, Inc., 1951).

KLINEBERG, Otto, *Characteristics of the American Negro* (New York: Harper and Brothers, 1944), pp. 185-208.

LEE, Alfred M., and HUMPHREY, Norman, *Race Riot* (New York: The Dryden Press, 1943).

MARDEN, Charles F., *Minorities in American Society* (New York: American Book Company, 1952), pp. 256-285.

RATONA, A., et al., "A Survey of Race Relations in a Northern Town," *Journal of Educational Sociology*, Vol. 20 (Nov., 1946), pp. 129-151.

SCHERMERHORN, R. A., *These Our People* (Boston: D. C. Heath and Company, 1949), pp. 131-151.

WALTER, Paul A. F., Jr., *Race and Cultural Relations* (New York: McGraw-Hill Book Company, Inc., 1952), pp. 3-24.

WARNER, W. L., JUNKER, B. H., and DAVIS, W. A., *Color and Human Nature: Negro Personality Development in a Northern City* (Washington, D. C.: American Council on Education, 1941).

WEAVER, R. C., *The Negro Ghetto* (New York: Harcourt, Brace and Company, Inc., 1948).

VII
Jews

To THE sociologist, the attitudes of preference for and prejudice against the Jews as an ethnic group are very real, although many of these attitudes may be fallacious in terms of their scientific bases. Few social scientists would define the Jews as a distinct race, especially if the term is to have any biological significance. Yet, despite the facts, the Jews, in the minds of the prejudiced, constitute a different race from "typical Americans."

Some scholars have vigorously refuted the assumption that the Jews constitute a race.[1] It is assumed that much of the "race" prejudice against the Jews may be challenged and restricted with the proof that the Jews should be defined as a cultural group generally united by a common religion and welded together through the centuries by the combined forces of out-group persecution and in-group preference. Hence, the Jews are, in terms of sociological analysis, an ethnic group, but often defined by lay persons as a race. If the Jews are considered to be a religious unit, then many persons have reactions, not against the Jews as an ethnic group, but against the Jews as a people with a distinct religion. In the United States, as well as in most other countries, the prevailing method for estimating the number of Jews is through a census of religious bodies. At the present time there are slightly over 5,000,000 persons in the United States designated as Jews, or approximately 4 per cent of the nation's population.

Some of the Jews in the United States manifest the operation of at least five major definitions, including religious, racial, linguistic, ideological, and economic identifiers. For instance, comments may be

---

[1] Note the following statement: "In actual fact there is a Jewish question not because of Jewish blood, but because of Jewish history." James Parkes, *The Jewish Problem in the Modern World* (New York: Oxford University Press, 1946), p. 5.

overheard concerning the importance of religious tolerance and understanding between Christians and Jews. Almost any discussion of minority groups will evoke a reference to Negroes and Jews. The Jews are sometimes thought of as a distinct linguistic group.[2] In an ideological setting the impression may be reflected that the Jews are communists, and, finally, they may be regarded as capitalists in an economic sense. *No doubt these contradictory facets and definitions are vital to an understanding of the several statuses of these people.*

The Jews are a race only in the sense that they may be defined so by their critics. Professor Frank H. Hankins[3] observed some years ago that Jews seem to have a certain biological specialization, but that a person is struck by the fact that even a moderate-sized gathering of these people will indicate Teutonic, Mediterranean, Mongoloid, and Negroid traits. It may be of interest to note what Dr. C. S. Coon of Harvard University has to say on this point:

> The Jews, therefore, are not a race, in that one could place them in a list like the following: Nordic, Alpine, Dinaric, Jewish, or Mediterranean. To do so would be comparable to listing English or French in the same way. They are a group of people as united biologically as is the average intermarrying social or geographical unit found among the white peoples; they have racial peculiarities which serve to differentiate the majority of them anthropometrically from their non-Jewish compatriots and neighbors.[4]

While the Jews have a culture of Judaism in common, they can be thought of as a people, some of whom aspire to be a nation. No doubt the question may be now raised as to whether the Jews represent a distinct nationality with the formation of the Government of Israel and its recognition by the United States. A survey of several statuses of the Jews may throw some light on these contradictory facets.

SOCIAL STATUS

Social status is a composite rating that designates the relative standing a person or group receives when compared with others. Each status, according to Hiller, is a place or position in the scheme

2 For a scholarly analysis of the role of language and religion as cultural identifiers, see A. H. Hourani, *Minorities and the Arab World* (New York: Oxford University Press, 1947), p. 140.

3 Frank H. Hankins, *The Racial Basis of Civilization* (New York: Alfred A. Knopf, Inc., 1926), p. 84. Also see *The Hebrew Impact on Western Civilization* by Dagobert D. Runes (New York: Philosophical Library, 1951), p. 784.

4 From *Jews in a Gentile World*, Isacque Graeber and Steuart Henderson Britt (New York: The Macmillan Company, 1942), p. 35. Used by permission of the publisher.

of social relations.[5] One of the most objective measures of social status has been developed by Professor Bogardus in his study of social distance.[6] *It is our contention that slight distance is actually commensurate with high social status, and, conversely, marked distance in most instances, refers to low social status.* Hence, the ethnic groups that rank at the top of an array of such groups tend to occupy the highest social status or standing. Thus, evaluators accord status to the groups toward whom they have little "farness."

In 1926 Dr. Bogardus asked 1,725 Americans in the United States on a roughly stratified basis to participate in a survey of attitudes toward forty ethnic groups. He found that the German Jews ranked twenty-sixth from the top and that Russian Jews ranked twenty-eighth from the top. Less than 8 per cent of the persons indicated that they would marry into a Jewish family. American Jews placed German Jews first, Russian Jews second, and English Jews third.[7] In 1946 Dr. Bogardus gave his social distance scale to 1,950 persons in six regions of the United States and found that the Jews ranked in twenty-third place in a list of thirty-six ethnic groups.[8] In both social distance surveys by Bogardus, the Jews ranked in the lowest third of the ethnic groups evaluated by this means.

In the Richards' study involving approximately 1,672 white university students,[9] the Jews were accorded fifth place in the nine ethnic groups evaluated. The Jews received 64.3 per cent positive items checked by the evaluators. Perhaps some insight into the significance of the social status of the Jew may be attained by observing the following five traits checked most frequently as characterizing Jews: (1) "will cheat you out of money," (2) "are industrious," (3) "are interested in educational advancement," (4) "are thrifty," and (5) "are clean and neat."

In May of 1947, an exploratory study was made by the writers to determine the relative social status of sixteen ethnic groups. The sub-

---

[5] E. T. Hiller, *Social Relations and Structures* (New York: Harper and Brothers, 1947), p. 330.

[6] Dr. Bogardus defines "social distance" as the amount of sympathetic understanding existing between persons or groups, or between persons and groups.

[7] Emory S. Bogardus, *Immigration and Race Attitudes* (Boston: D. C. Heath and Company, 1928), p. 25.

[8] Emory S. Bogardus, "Changes in Racial Distances," *International Journal of Opinion and Attitude Research*, 1:58, December, 1947.

[9] Eugene S. Richards, "Attitudes of College Students in the Southwest Toward Ethnic Groups in the United States," *Sociology and Social Research*, Vol. 35, No. 1 (Sept.-Oct., 1950), pp. 22-30.

jects in this study were two samples of university students, one white group and the other Negro.[10] The subjects were asked to react to a modified social distance scale as developed by Bogardus. The results were surprisingly similar to established ratings and suggest that white and Negro students accord the American Jew somewhat comparable status. White students from the University of Oklahoma ranked the Jewish group eighth from the top, and Negro students from Langston University ranked the Jews thirteenth. White students accorded more status to the Jews than to the Chinese, Mexicans, Mulattoes, Filipinos, and Negroes. On the other hand, Negro students gave the Jewish group higher status than Japanese, Scotch, and German.

A second test of social distance was then administered to the two Oklahoma groups. The subjects were asked to react to each of the sixteen ethnic groups, not in terms of the average representatives, but in terms of the outstanding representatives of each group. With this modification, the white and Negro samples accorded the American Jew comparable status, namely, rank eleven.[11] The similar status assigned to the Jews by white and Negro evaluators may suggest a biracial pattern of limited social status for the Amercian Jew. A low social status to the Jews is perhaps objective evidence of the role of particularistic experience, hearsay, and the diffusion of anti-Semitism.

Anti-Semitism is one of the outstanding problems confronting the Jews in the United States. Recognition of this belief has initiated many interesting studies in an attempt to determine the extent to which anti-Semitism is actually present in the United States. These studies have reflected that there is a core of anti-Semitism, and that this core might be used to mobilize a more intense program of anti-Semitism. One of the most objective studies on this problem was conducted in New York City. As New York City contains one of the largest Jewish population concentrations in the world, this study is presented to illustrate the nature and extent of anti-Semitism in the United States.

10 Sample of students was approximately 100 from each of the two institutions. Ethnic groups considered were American Indian, Chinese, English, Filipino, French, German, Irish, Italian, Japanese, Jewish, Mexican, Mulatto, Negro, Russian, Scotch, and Spanish.

11 White students ranked outstanding Jews ahead of Mexicans, Filipinos, Japanese, Negroes, and Mulattoes. Negro students rated outstanding Jews ahead of Chinese, Japanese, and Scotch. Several ethnic groups tied for the same rank; hence, the apparent discrepancy in rank orders.

▌ ANTI-SEMITISM IN NEW YORK CITY [12]

DUANE ROBINSON AND SYLVIA ROHDE

Anti-semitism expresses itself in several forms of overt action. These include discrimination in industry, quotas in professional schools, acts of gangsterism and hoodlumism such as the defacing of synagogues and the beating up of Jewish youngsters, to mention a few. A considerable body of public opinion tacitly approves of these activities and accepts the prejudices which are characteristic of anti-semitism. This study of anti-semitic opinions in New York City examined some of these attitudes, with special attention being paid to apparently contradictory differences found between some of the economic and educational groups within the major religious groups.

To study the anti-semitic feelings of the population several questions were chosen which were considered suitable as reflectors of these feelings. The questions sought for expressions of disapproval of the number of Jews holding government jobs, judgments on the relative honesty of Jewish business men, criticism of the patriotism of Jews, and fear of the power of Jews in the United States. A schedule was constructed containing direct questions on these subjects, along with a number of background items.

The sample selected to be analyzed was stratified on five characteristics, random samples being drawn from three rental groups, two education groups, two nativity groups (native and foreign born), and Negro and white groups, proportional in the relative size of these groups in the New York City population, as found in the Sixteenth Census of the United States. Samples were drawn from four religious groups, based upon the estimated proportions from each group listed in the religious census of the state of New York.

It has been demonstrated that in interviewing on anti-semitism the appearance of the interviewer might influence the respondent's answers. Therefore two equal groups of interviewers were selected, one group in which each interviewer's appearance was supposed to correspond to the common stereotype of Jewish appearance, and the other in which the appearance did not correspond to the stereotype.

Findings: The number of Jewish respondents was large and their opinions differed markedly from those of the non-Jewish respondents, so the over-all findings for 1165 cases were examined with this fact in mind. Whole percentages were considered as adequate for the analysis made here, and unnecessary refinements were eliminated.

[12] Duane Robinson and Sylvia Rohde, "A Public Opinion Study of Anti-Semitism in New York City." *American Sociological Review,* Vol. 10, No. 4 (Aug., 1945). Used by permission of the American Sociological Society.

In answer to the question, *Do you think Jewish business men are as honest as other business men?* 24 per cent of the respondents answered "No," while 65 per cent answered "Yes," and 11 per cent gave qualified or non-committal answers. The "No" answers were more numerous on this question than on the others analyzed below, and reflect the centuries-old stereotype of the dishonesty of Jewish business men.

The next question was, *Do you think there are too many Jews holding government offices and jobs?* 17 per cent answered "Yes," with corresponding percentages of "No" and other answers. Then the question was asked, *Do you think that the Jews have too much power in the United States?* 18 per cent of the answers were "Yes." This question was intended to determine the extent of anti-semitism as it applies to a subject with fascist overtones, the implications being the same "threat of power" which the Nazis used in their onslaught against the Jews.

The last question to be analyzed asked, *Do you think that Jews are as patriotic, more patriotic, or less patriotic than other citizens?* 11 per cent of the total answered "Less." Of the four questions this stimulated the smallest proportion of anti-semitic answers. A favorite rumor during the war has been that the Jews are draft-dodgers and profiteers, but this view has not been accepted as readily, apparently, as the older, more traditional forms of anti-semitism. Another factor making for the relatively small number of anti-semitic responses may be that this is an immediate and practical war issue, and people in the city have more information and are less confused.

These preliminary findings indicate that in the city anti-semitic opinions were expressed by a minority of the citizens, and that the anti-semitic group varied with the subject, with relatively few taking the view that the Jews are not patriotic, but with a large number believing in Jewish business dishonesty.

Religious and Economic Differences. The next step was to investigate the relation between economic and religious factors and anti-semitism. The 1165 cases were divided into religious groups, then subdivided into economic groups, and answers within each of these categories were studied.

On the question of Jewish honesty in business the per cent of "No" or anti-semitic answers are shown in Table I.

Table I shows that:

1. The non-Jewish respondents answer "No" much more than the Jewish respondents, although a number of Jewish respondents answered in like fashion.
2. The differences between economic groups among Protestants and "Others" are statistically significant.

3. The differences between Catholics and Protestants in the lower economic group is significant, and the middle economic group is worth noting as the two differences are not consistent:
   a. The lower economic Protestants are relatively more anti-semitic than the other major groups.
   b. The middle economic Catholics conversely tend to be more anti-semitic than middle economic Protestants and lower economic Catholics.

Table I

	Jewish	Catholic	Protestant	Other *
Upper economic				
per cent	8%	33% †	41% †	48% †
total sample	50	18	17	7
Middle economic				
per cent	7	40	29	29 †
total sample	250	131	91	28
Lower economic				
per cent	11	28	50	53
total sample	200	236	97	40

* "Other" group consists largely of non-religious persons, that is, persons unable to be classified in a religious group.
† These samples are under 30 respondents, too small for reliability, except, perhaps, in the one sample of 28 cases.

The interesting fact here is the emergence of the lower economic Protestants, and the middle economic Catholics as relatively more anti-semitic than the middle Protestants and lower Catholics.

Table 2, showing the per cent of "Yes" answers to the question of "too many government jobs," presents somewhat the same picture: Table 2 shows that:

1. The Jewish respondents give practically no anti-semitic responses.
2. The differences between economic groups are significant among the Protestants.
3. The differences between Catholics and Protestants are significant in the lower groups and again are not consistent between lower and middle groups:

Table 2

	Jewish	Catholic	Protestant	Other *
Upper economic				
per cent	2%	33% †	52% †	57% †
total sample	50	18	17	7
Middle economic				
per cent	2	31	22	14 †
total sample	250	131	91	28
Lower economic				
per cent	3	27	39	30
total sample	200	236	97	40

* See footnote, Table 1.
† See footnote, Table 1.

a. The lower Protestants indicate more anti-semitism than any of the other groups.
b. The middle Catholics again tend to be more anti-semitic than middle Protestants and lower Catholics, although not at the level of statistical significance in either case. The same pattern of relations emerged here as in the previous question.

The "No" answers to the question "Do Jews have too much power," provides a further corroboration of some of these findings (Table 3):

In this question the lower Protestant group is even more anti-Jewish, almost half claiming that the Jews have "too much power." The two Catholic groups agreed in this case, the anti-semitism of the middle-Catholic group thus not appearing as consistently as those of the lower Protestants.

Why do the lower economic Protestants and, conversely, the middle economic Catholics (with the exception of the "power question), seem to be most affected by anti-semitic feeling? It seems likely that these lower economic Protestants compose a group of relatively insecure and frustrated members of America's native-born Protestant majority whose advantaged position is part of this country's tradition. Under such economic and cultural pressures they might readily accept propaganda antagonistic toward traditionally discriminated-against groups, against whom they vent their unrecognized anger at their own situation. The lower Catholics represent, conversely, immigrant groups who are similarly discriminated against, and they might be more tolerant of other groups and more inclined to respect the American democratic traditions.

Table 3

	Jewish	Catholic	Protestant	Other *
Upper economic				
per cent	0%	33%	18% †	43% †
total sample	50	18	17	7
Middle economic				
per cent	0	27	20	18 †
total sample	250	131	91	28
Lower economic				
per cent	2	29	49	40
total sample	200	236	97	40

* See footnote, Table 1.
† See footnote, Table 1.

The anti-semitism of the middle economic Catholics in this city of immigrants may indicate that some of them are reacting to Jewish competition in business. It was in regard to the question on Jewish business men that they reacted most sharply. It may be that the propaganda of clerical fascism also has had some influence among them. Possibly also a *nouveaubourgeois* status among such a group in a community with such heterogeneous groups, many striving for such status, might have stimulated some of the narrowness of which these attitudes are an index. These guesses do not substitute for more thorough analysis. The findings, however, suggest such conclusions and provide a basis for further thought.

Religious and Educational Differences. An analysis was made next of the answers by religious and educational groups. The question on honesty of Jewish business men produced the following "No" responses:

Table 4

	Jewish	Catholic	Protestant	Other *
Upper education				
per cent	10%	35%	37%	38%
total sample	305	162	121	46
Lower education				
per cent	7	30	43	48
total sample	195	223	84	29

* See footnote, Table 1.

From Table 4, one can observe that:

1. The differences in anti-semitism between the upper educated and lower educated were small and not statistically significant, but again were reversed in the two religious groups as in the economic analysis. However, both Protestant groups tended to be more anti-semitic than the Catholics. The reason for this probably is that upper economic status and educational status are rather highly correlated, and a number of upper economic persons, who in the economic analysis earlier were shown to give relatively anti-semitic responses, were in this case probably included in the upper-education group, thus enlarging the anti-semitic group.
2. A statistically significant difference appeared between Protestant and Catholic lower educated groups, the Protestants being more anti-semitic than the Catholics.

On the question of Jews having too many government jobs no significant difference appeared between the groups except for the Jewish and non-Jewish differences. On the question "do the Jews have too much power," significant differences appeared in the "Yes" answers (Table 5).

Table 5, like Table 4, points out that the poorly educated Protestants were the most anti-semitic of the four main non-Jewish groups. It would seem to corroborate the analysis given earlier regarding economic and cultural pressures, and stands out as the most significant fact in the study, one which it would be well to study further.

Table 5

	Jewish	Catholic	Protestant	Other *
Upper education				
per cent	0%	29%	28%	26%
total sample	305	162	121	46
Lower education				
per cent	2	29	42	41
total sample	195	223	84	29

* See footnote, Table 1.

Conclusions. In drawing conclusions from these findings it is correct to recall that the study was limited to New York City, which is
atypical of communities in the United States. It is possible also that
because of the reluctance of respondents to give their opinions on a
subject such as this, the findings indicate too little anti-semitism.
It is our opinion that this would be a small error.

Within such limitations the following conclusions are suggested
by the data:

1. While a majority of the non-Jewish persons in the sample expressed non-anti-semitic answers, a minority seemed ready to agree
to the anti-semitic suggestions in the questions. This indicates that
in the community as a whole there is at least a considerable minority
who boldly and possibly quite naively accept the anti-semitic opinions as their own.

2. The lower economic and educated Protestants expressed more
anti-semitism than the other groups studied. It was suggested that in
this group there are many persons whose positions in the dominant
religious group, and perhaps as native-born "Americans," contrast
painfully with the economic disadvantage and insecurity which they
experience. Such a position might lead to feelings of frustration and
antagonism which could be channelized readily into anti-semitic
views.

3. The somewhat less extensive anti-semitic views expressed by
middle economic Catholics probably arise from other causes, among
which might be a certain amount of anti-Jewish propaganda available to them, and their position in business competition with Jews.

4. New York City, with its large minority of Jews, may indicate
certain unique characteristics of anti-semitism, but it is likely that
several of these are common to other communities. One might ask
whether, if a fascist movement were to develop further in America
it would find its bases in some of these poorly educated and economically disadvantaged Protestant groups who as the "American"
majority are apparently somewhat willing to violate both Protestant
and American principles and accept such an excrescence of fascism
as anti-semitism.

LEGAL STATUS

The legal status of the Jews is somewhat difficult to comprehend with any degree of clarity. There is a long history of low legal status for Jews, which is perpetuated through "private action" by non-Jews in this nation.

James Parkes has observed that from the tenth century to the nineteenth the Jews had no share in the gradual evolution of political institutions, no rights of citizenship, no security of tenure; they were forced to reside in segregated neighborhoods, and were compelled to serve as royal usurers as the price for residence.[13] *It was not until the middle of the nineteenth century that the Jews in western Europe secured equal legal status with other citizens.* In fact, the American Revolution offered the Jews in this country complete legal equality before European nations were willing to do so.

The European example of differential legal status for Jews was revived with horrible exactitude by the Nazis. Jews were removed from civil service positions, their attendance in public schools was limited, all identification papers were stamped with a conspicuous "J." The lowered legal status of the Jew was symptomatic of coming pogroms and the systematic massacre of millions of these people in Germany and Poland.

Although there is little evidence in this country of differential legal status between Jews and non-Jews, yet there is a differentiation expressed informally through the mores. Without legal prohibitions the Jew may yet find it difficult to purchase certain residential property, to gain access to specific recreational areas and clubs, and to enter certain professions and businesses. A sign posted over the entrance to a recreational area reading "Gentiles Only" tests the significance of American freedom. When "private actions" are sanctioned by the courts, they have the power of legal expressions. Racial restrictive convenants have been written to exclude Jews as well as Negroes, Orientals, and American Indians.[14] However, on May 3, 1948, the United States Supreme Court handed down the decision

---

13 James Parkes, *op. cit.,* pp. 8-23.

14 Special analysis of the Nature of restrictive covenants may be found in the following sources: Tom C. Clark and Philip B. Perlman, *Prejudice and Property: An Historic Brief Against Racial Covenants,* (Washington, D.C.: Public Affairs Press, 1948), 103 pp.; Herman H. Long and Charles S. Johnson, *People Versus Property* (Nashville: Fisk University Press, 1947), pp. 10-57; James S. Roberts, "Racial Restrictive Covenants," *Sociology and Social Research,* Vol. 32 (Nov.-Dec., 1947), pp. 616-624.

that restrictive real-estate covenants are lawful, as private agreements; but under the terms of the Fourteenth Amendment and the Civil Rights Act of 1866 they *cannot be enforced* by either state or federal courts.[15] This important decision may stimulate the discrimination of Jews and other minority groups on a purely quasi-legal basis.

Lemert and Rosberg have analyzed the administration of justice to ethnic groups in Los Angeles County for the year 1938.[16] Their study tends to suggest that minority groups are arrested for particular types of crimes. Perhaps the following table will disclose the legal status of the Jew compared with seven other ethnic groups in the percentage distribution of felonies. It appears from this table that the Jews are arrested for crimes bordering on economic matters, and such felonies as "not sufficient funds," "grand theft," "bookmaking," and "receiving stolen property," seem to be conspicuous. If the student will compare the rates of Jews and whites in the foregoing table, other differences in crime rates will become manifest. In a few metropolitan areas gang wars have received wide publicity in which the participants were persons with surnames thought to be Jewish. No doubt some writers would designate the type of crime Jewish persons are arrested for as an indication of their business pursuits and proximity to white-collar crime activities. However, such explanations have little support in verified evidence at this time.

A hopeful and promising improvement of the legal status of American Jews has been made in New York, Massachusetts, and New Jersey.[17] These states have legislation which help assure equal rights to all Americans. In many respects it is a significant trend that legislation is being enacted to invalidate some of the narrow and biased aspects of "race conscious" mores. *America is attempting to guarantee to the Jews and other minority groups the human rights that the Germans under Hitler legally abolished.* It may not be amiss, however, at this point to observe that Jewish refugees are often shocked by the degree of ethnic consciousness existing in the United States. In fact, some

[15] A popular statement of the United States Supreme Court's decision may be found in *Time*, Vol. 51 (May 17, 1948), pp. 25-26.

[16] Edwin M. Lemert and Judy Rosberg, *The Administration of Justice to Minority Groups in Los Angeles County* (Berkeley: University of California Press, 1948), p. 27.

[17] Robert E. Cushman, "The Laws of the Land," *Survey Graphic*, Vol. 34 (Jan., 1947), p. 18. The question is asked whether or not these "fair practices acts" achieve their purpose without creating additional resentment in the minds of the prejudiced. This problem deserves study. Perhaps the best statement on the effectiveness of fair employment practices is the work of Malcolm Ross, *All Manner of Men* (New York: Reynal & Hitchcock, 1948), 413 pp.

Table XVI: PERCENTAGE DISTRIBUTION OF FELONIES BY POPULATION GROUPS, LOS ANGELES COUNTY, 1938 *

Felony	Negro	Mex-ican	Jewish	Japa-nese	Chinese	Fili-pino	Indian	White
Burglary 1st degree	2.4	2.8	—	—	—	12	—	3.5
Burglary 2nd degree	19.6	15.8	6.8	4.7	11.1	12	35.2	14.0
Robbery 1st degree	2.4	2.5	2.3	4.7	—	8	—	4.9
Robbery 2nd degree	5.9	2.8	—	—	—	4	—	1.7
Narcotics Act Violation	8.3	5.3	6.0	—	44.4	—	—	1.7
Grand theft plus 503	10.0	26.0	3.4	—	—	—	11.7	12.6
Receiving stolen property	3.8	2.5	4.3	—	—	—	5.9	1.7
Forgery	5.9	4.0	12.8	19.0	—	12	—	14.9
Not sufficient funds	0.3	—	6.0	—	—	—	5.9	7.5
Petty theft plus prior	9.3	4.3	1.7	—	—	8	—	1.7
Grand theft	3.8	2.3	6.0	4.7	—	8	—	4.2
Rape, Incest, 288a	7.2	12.6	1.7	—	—	4	17.2	7.0
337a (bookmaking)	0.03	0.8	43.6	28.5	11.1	—	—	10.0
Assault with deadly weapon	8.0	7.0	1.7	9.5	11.1	20	5.9	3.4
Deadly Weapon Act violation	2.8	1.8	—	—	11.1	8	—	1.8
Assault	1.3	2.8	—	—	—	—	—	1.8
Bigamy	0.7	—	—	—	—	—	—	—
Vehicle Code violation	1.7	5.5	—	19.0	—	4	17.6	3.9
Murder	0.3	0.5	—	4.7	—	—	—	1.0
Manslaughter	3.1	—	—	—	—	—	—	—
Perjury	1.7	0.3	0.8	—	—	—	—	—
Alcoholic Beverages Act violation	—	0.8	—	4.7	11.1	—	—	0.2
False claims	—	0.3	—	—	—	—	—	—
Bribery	—	—	1.7	—	—	—	—	—
375	—	—	1.7	—	—	—	—	—

* Edwin M. Lemert and Judy Rosberg, *op. cit.*, p. 7. Used by permission of the University of California Press.

of the refugees report about the same amount of ethnic prejudice against the Jews in this country now as was prevalent in Germany before the advent of Hitler.[18] If this estimate is correct, it is all the more clear that legal action may have to come to terms with the mores which collectively deny human rights to Jews and others, not as individuals, but as groups of persons.

EDUCATIONAL STATUS

The academic success of the Jews reflects their high status as scholars and the prejudice against them as competitors. *In the United States the Jews are predominantly an urban people with a strong*

[18] Maurice R. Davie, *Refugees in America* (New York: Harper and Brothers, 1947), p. 64. There is some evidence that in countries controlled by the Soviet Union there has been a revival of anti-Semitism. *Time* (Jan. 26, 1953), pp. 28-30.

tradition of scholarship. There are some bases for believing that they are the most academic-minded ethnic group in the United States. For instance, Terman found twice as many very bright boys and girls who were Jewish as the percentage of Jews in the general population of California at the time of the study.[19] Historically, some of the great men of the arts and sciences have been Jews; and such names as Spinoza (philosophy), Mendelssohn (music), Freud (psychiatry), and Einstein (physics) immediately come to mind. The desire among the Jews for academic achievement has its historic roots in their great men, and is currently manifest in the disproportionate demand for professional training among Jewish students.

One of the fascinating sociological characteristics of the American Jew, which has a distinct relationship to his interest in academic status, is his proclivity to live in urban areas. In the following five cities with over 1,000,000 population 75 per cent of the Jews in the United States reside—New York, Chicago, Philadelphia, Los Angeles, and Detroit. These five cities account for only one-eighth of the general population, as contrasted with three-fourths of the Jewish population.[20] Table XVII indicates the relative Jewish population in selected American cities. While New York City has the highest per cent of Jews in its population, St. Louis has the lowest.

The strong desire of Jewish students to enter medical schools has met with antagonism by the majority group. Inasmuch as the Jews have not developed their own professional schools in the United States, they find themselves at a marked disadvantage in securing admission to medical schools under the auspices of Christian denominations. Private and state universities in varying degrees have adopted the "quota system" as an arbitrary method of excluding a very large percentage of the applications by Jewish candidates. Of particular interest is the fact that the percentage *of Jewish candidates admitted each year has been declining.*

According to the study by Frank Kingdon, the percentage of Jewish graduates of City College of New York, where almost 80 per cent of the student body is Jewish, admitted to a medical school dropped from 58.4 per cent in 1925 to 15.0 per cent in 1943. The College of Physicians and Surgeons of Columbia University admitted 46.92 per cent of the class of 1920 as Jewish, but in the class of 1940 only

19 L. M. Terman, *Genetic Studies of Genius* (Palo Alto: Stanford University Press, 1925), p. 648.

20 Sophia M. Robison, "How Many Jews in America," *Commentary,* Vol. 8 (Aug., 1949), p. 189.

6.40 per cent of the class was Jewish.[21] Walter R. Hart writing in 1947 purported that, in six of the past ten years, not a single Jewish graduate of the College of City of New York was accepted in the Cornell University School of Medicine and, in the remaining four years, a

Table XVII: CITIES WITH ESTIMATED JEWISH POPULATION OF 40,000 AND OVER RANKED BY SIZE OF JEWISH POPULATION *

City	Estimated Jewish Population 1948	Total Population 1940 (Rounded)	Percentage of Jews
New York	2,000,000	7,500,000	28
Chicago	300,000	3,396,000	8.8
Philadelphia	245,000	1,931,000	12.7
Los Angeles	225,000	1,504,000	15
Boston	137,000	771,000	17
Detroit	90,000	1,623,000	5.5
Cleveland	80,000	878,000	9.1
Baltimore	75,000	859,000	8
Newark	56,000	430,000	13
Pittsburgh	54,000	671,600	8
San Francisco	50,000	634,000	8
St. Louis	44,000	816,000	5.4
Miami	40,000	172,000	24

* *Ibid.*, p. 189. Used by permission of the Magazine.

total of nine were admitted. In fact, from 1942 to 1946 inclusive, 218 graduates of City College applied for admission to Cornell Medical School and only five were admitted. Forty-eight of these applicants had an average of A-minus or better.[22] About the same story prevails for other municipal colleges in the City of New York. On September 11, 1946, the Council of the City of New York voted to authorize the organization of a committee to determine the underlying difficulty of city college graduates in securing admission to nonsectarian professional schools in the City of New York. In many instances the deans of the medical schools attempted to defend the quota system on the bases of secondary factors of selection, such as, geographical selection and personality characteristics. One of the basic questions in the quota system that demands an answer: Is it designed to keep Jews out of the practice of medicine because it is a profession of high social

[21] Frank Kingdon, "Discrimination in Medical Colleges," *The American Mercury*, Vol. 61 (Oct., 1945), pp. 4-5. Related articles to this subject in *The American Mercury* are: Philip Wylie "Memorandum on Anti-Semitism," Vol. 60 (Jan., 1945), pp. 66-73, and Dan W. Dodson, "Religious Prejudice in Colleges," Vol. 63 (July, 1946), pp. 5-13.
[22] Walter R. Hart, "Anti-Semitism in New York Medical Schools," *The American Mercury*, Vol. 65 (July, 1947), p. 56.

and economic status or because Gentile patients would protest a larger proportion of Jewish physicians? It is usually understood that, if administrators of medical schools are asked whether or not they have a quota system of admission, almost all of them deny the charge. *It may seem ironic in this scientific age that ethnic attitudes determine the selection of prospective physicians rather than objective measures of abilities.*

Table XVIII: PERCENTAGE DISTRIBUTION OF JEWS IN SELECTED COLLEGES *

College	Total Students	Jews	Per Cent Jews
Allegheny	442	4	1
Bennington	224	9	4
Bowdoin	580	37	6
Bryn Mawr	486	30	6
Bucknell	1,231	34	3
Colgate	971	10	1
Dartmouth	2,422	140	5
Hamilton	483	7	2
Hobart	293	4	2
Kenyon	242	0	0
Knox	543	5	1
Lehigh	1,541	85	5
Midland	667	0	0
Mt. Holyoke	928	15	2
Oberlin	1,696	50	3
Ohio Wesleyan	1,350	3	.002
Princeton	2,295	51	2
Purdue	4,534	88	2
Skidmore	635	42	6
Syracuse	6,726	527	8
Vassar	1,216	66	5
Washington and Jefferson	622	15	3
Washington and Lee	874	47	5
Yale	5,362	525	9

* Adapted and abbreviated from the study by Dan W. Dodson, "Religious Prejudice in Colleges," *The American Mercury*, Vol. 63 (July, 1946), p. 8.

The restriction of Jewish students in selected colleges is indicated in Table XVIII. One important caution must be kept in mind in interpreting these figures for 1936: colleges located in rural communities probably had very few Jewish applicants. In Table XIX are shown figures for predominantly urban universities where less prejudice is manifest.

An examination of the 1946 application blanks from thirty-nine "grade A medical schools" disclosed that *all* wanted to know the applicant's religion, church preference, or church membership. In addition to church affiliation, ten applications asked for the religion of the mother and father. Fifteen of the schools asked the race of the applicant, and twenty-eight asked the race of the applicant's mother or father. Eleven applications called for information concerning change of name. Of course, such application questions in themselves may prove nothing, but they suggest much.[23]

Table XIX: PERCENTAGE DISTRIBUTION OF JEWS IN SELECTED URBAN COLLEGES *

College	Total Students	Jews	Per Cent Jews
Boston	10,031	1,258	12
Brooklyn	9,162	6,856	75
Brown	2,016	286	14
Chicago	6,158	1,087	17
City College of New York	22,175	17,752	80
Cooper Union	1,417	534	37
Hunter	11,892	7,920	66
Illinois	10,523	1,325	12
New York	28,291	12,709	44
New School for Social Research	5,000	3,000	60
Pennsylvania	9,126	1,825	20

* *Ibid.*, p. 8. The base year is again 1936. A few colleges were omitted in this table.

The demand for high educational status by Jewish persons has developed into a sharp issue. In fact, in a recent survey B'nai B'rith disclosed that the percentage of Jewish students in graduate and professional schools dropped from 14.2 in 1935 to 10.6 in 1946, and in dental colleges from 28.2 to 18.9.[24] Both the demand and the percentage attending professional schools attest to the very high status Jews accord formal education. Discrimination against Jews by the establishment of quotas may be an attempt to limit their status by this means. Would anti-Semites admit that the limiting of the educational opportunities of the Jews is one way of limiting the economic status of these people?

There has been considerable argument as to the reported advantages and disadvantages of enacting a state law that attempts to com-

[23] In one of the states with a fair employment practice law, the candidate to a medical school must present a character reference from his minister with his application papers. Jews are thus easily discerned. This practice is as effective as the fraternity that invites a group of rushees to a pork dinner served Friday. Catholics and Jews thus are tested by indirection.

[24] *The Key Reporter of Phi Beta Kappa*, Vol. 13 (Winter, 1947-48), p. 3. This source also reported that the "Combined totals for the five medical colleges in New York revealed that of 2,439 students admitted from 1921 to 1925, 1,094 or 44.9 per cent were Jewish. By the period 1941-44, when 2,809 students were admitted, the figures had dropped steadily to 24.2 per cent Jewish." About 15 per cent of the population of the state of New York is reported to be Jewish.

pel fair treatment of all ethnic groups in matters of employment and educational opportunities. However, the effectiveness of the New York State law raises some doubt as to the efficiency of this approach. The American Jewish Congress Commission on Law and Social Action, after a survey of the admission rates of Jewish students into medical schools in New York, concluded that there is considerable discrimination against Jewish students, even those who had won in 1951 full-tuition state medical scholarships. It was found that the 41 Jewish students, who had won state scholarships, had to file a total of 214 applications with the nine state medical schools in order to gain admittance, or twice as many per capita as the 16 non-Jewish winners who filed 39 applications, or a ratio of 5.4 to 2.4. One medical school rejected the application of every Jewish scholarship winner living in New York City—21 in all.[25]

ECONOMIC STATUS

No doubt one of the chief factors in the development of critical attitudes toward the Jew has been his alleged economic success, not his real economic status. For many Americans, the Jews are stereotyped as great financiers, who control much of the wealth in the United States. Ethnic relations have been limited between Jews and non-Jews because many of the latter have believed that the former decide the great economic issues of the day. Fortune magazine, not long ago, asked the following question: "Do you think any of these groups are getting more economic power anywhere in the United States than is good for the country?" The following results were found: Protestant, 2 per cent; Catholic, 12 per cent; Jews, 36 per cent; Negroes, 8 per cent; none, 39 per cent; blank or confused statement, 11 per cent.[26] This poll disclosed the interesting finding that most of the critical reactions against the Jews came from rural areas and in sections of the country where the Jews are not particularly numerous.

Perhaps the most reliable study of the economic status of the Jews in the United States was made by the editors of *Fortune* and published in 1936. *This study revealed that at that time the Jews played*

25 A complete text of the letter of Herman L. Weisman, chairman of the American Jewish Congress' Commission on Law and Social Action, to John P. Myers, chancellor of the state's Board of Regents may be found in *Valley Jewish News*, Vol. 9, No. 42 (July 9, 1952).

26 *Fortune* (Oct., 1947), p. 6.

little or no part in the great commercial houses of this nation. Of the 420 listed directors of the nineteen members of the New York Clearing House in 1933, only 30 were Jews, and interestingly, about half of these were in the commercial National Bank and Trust Company and the Public National Bank and Trust Company. No Jewish directors were found in the Bank of New York and Trust Company, National City, Guaranty Trust, Central Hanover, First National, Chase, Bankers Trust, or New York Trust.[27] The percentage of Jewish employees of any kind in the largest commercial banks is very low in spite of the large number of Jewish customers and the high percentage of Jews in the population of New York.

Among the large Jewish houses in the investment field, those of Kuhn, Loeb & Company, Speyer & Company, J. & W. Seligman & Company, Landenburg, Thalman & Company, and Lehman Brothers are the best known; they do not compare in power with the great houses owned by non-Jews. A ranking of these houses on March 1, 1935, in terms of the amounts of foreign loans outstanding indicated the following: J. P. Morgan with 19.87 per cent, National City Company with 11.71, Dillon, Read with 11.44, Chase, Harris, Forbes with 8.45, Guaranty with 6.68 per cent, Bancamerica-Blair with 6.18 per cent, and Lee, Higginson with 4.23 per cent; all rank above the highest Jewish house, which was Kuhn, Loeb with 2.88 per cent.[28]

In heavy industries Jews do not occupy a prominent place; in the light industries, particularly in the sale of merchandise, they are more numerous. However, almost the whole wearing-apparel business is in Jewish hands. About 85 per cent of men's clothing, about 95 per cent of women's dresses, and about 95 per cent of the fur merchants are said to be Jews. Some of the large retail department stores in New York are under Jewish control; yet, a national comparison of this control indicates its diffusion rather than centralization. In the grocery field, where the greatest number of chains operate, 95 to 99 per cent including A and P are non-Jewish.

The interest of Jews in American newspapers remain small. The four newspaper chains in which Jews have a considerable economic influence do not compare in daily circulation with the chains of Hearst, Patterson-McCormick, and Scripps-Howard. In the periodical field *Esquire* may be the only major publication with prominent

27 *Jews in America,* by the editors of *Fortune* (New York: Random House, Inc., 1936), pp. 130-133.
28 *Ibid.,* p. 130.

Jewish support; however, such a magazine featuring men's clothing fits logically into the pattern of Jewish interest of the wearing apparel industry. A few of the large publication houses are owned and operated by Jews, but again the part played by Jews is not conspicuous.

In the radio broadcasting field, a stronger statement can be made for Jewish managers than in the publication world. The Columbia Broadcasting Company is not owned by Jews but has been managed by a Jew. The theater is centralized in New York, and it is not surprising that Jews should play a prominent part in this occupation. In the realm of motion picture, the part played by Jews as pioneers must not be forgotten in evaluating their present status. Some of the best known pioneers in the production of motion pictures are: Marcus, Lowe, Adolph Zukor, Sam Goldwyn, Carl Laemmle, Louis Selznick, Louis B. Mayer, Jesse Lasky, and William Fox. The control of motion pictures is clearly indicated in the following observation:

Three of the eight principal companies are owned and controlled by Jews, two are probably owned and controlled by non-Jews, and in three management and ownership are divided. But though Jews do not monopolize the industry moneywise they do nevertheless exert pretty complete control over the production of pictures.[29]

It seems reasonable to conclude that the Jews do not dominate the American economic scene, although in some particulars they exercise considerable control over some industries.

An interesting study is quoted by Karpf on the occupation status of Jewish and non-Jewish persons in New York City. It was found that about 17 per cent of the Jewish persons were engaged in retail and wholesale occupations, while for Gentiles the percentage was only 6; in broker and sales work Jews accounted for 16.2 per cent and non-Jews 8.3 per cent; in skilled and unskilled jobs the Jews were 13.8 per cent and the non-Jews 22.4 per cent. In clerical, sales, and professional positions the percentages were about the same for both groups. In domestic occupations the percentages were 3.7 per cent Jewish and 13.5 per cent non-Jewish.[30] An exploratory study under the senior author's direction by Dorothy Coleman and Toby Wolchin, students at the University of Southern California, attempted to determine whether a relationship existed between ethnic surnames and occupational status. The *1942 Los Angeles City Directory* was the

29 *Ibid.,* p. 133. Used by permission of *Fortune* magazine.
30 M. J. Karpf, *Jewish Community Organization in the United States* (New York: Bloch Publishing Company, 1938), p. 12.

source for typical surnames. The names chosen were Gonzales and Hernandez for the Mexican group, Goldberg and Friedman for the Jewish group, and Jones and Wilson for the "American group." A hundred persons of each surname selected in alphabetical order were listed, with their designated occupations. Thus, altogether 600 names were used. Table XX presents a breakdown of the ethnic names and

Table XX: ETHNIC AFFILIATION AND OCCUPATION *

	Mexicans			American non-Jewish			Jewish		
Occupations	Hernandez No.	Gonzales No.	Total Per Cent	Jones No.	Wilson No.	Total Per Cent	Friedman No.	Goldberg No.	Total Per Cent
Unskilled	57	53	55.0	23	19	21.0	5	5	5.0
Semiskilled	9	12	10.5	7	15	11.0	10	4	7.0
Skilled	16	16	16.0	26	17	21.5	16	21	18.5
Clerical	11	10	10.5	25	28	26.5	37	34	35.5
Managerial	5	2	3.5	7	6	6.5	18	18	18.0
Professional	1	2	1.5	10	10	10.0	13	16	14.5
Entertainment	1	4	2.5	1	5	3.0	0	2	1.0
Military Service	0	1	.5	1	0	.5	1	0	.5
Total	100	100	100.0	100	100	100.0	100	100	100.0

* Unpublished data collected by Dorothy Coleman and Toby Wolchin, students at the University of Southern California. Under the direction of Edward C. McDonogh.

their occupational classifications. These data must be accepted with great *caution*, inasmuch as the surname does not always indicate the correct ethnic ancestry of affiliation. It must also be noted that the Directory does not indicate the racial background of those listed. However, a cursory study of the table will indicate that the Jewish names tend to be associated rather definitely with clerical and managerial callings and are not represented in the unskilled and semi-skilled jobs. There also seems to be a slight clustering of Jewish surnames and the professions. This table suggests that there may be some occupational differences between Jew and Gentile, but also that the differences are by no means so great as quoted from some sources.[31]

In the United States the occupational distribution of Jews and non-Jews seems to have been more comparable than it was in Germany

[31] Jacob Lestchinsky says that "the economic structure of the American Jews appears to resemble that of the Americans of old stock and those deriving from western and northern Europe, rather than that of the Slavic and a few other groups among whom trade and the professions are still at a very low stage of development. As a whole, however, the position of the Jews in the business world and even in the professions, as intimated above, does not measure up to that held by British-Americans and groups of old immigrant stocks. Jewish businessmen include many more petty shopkeepers and struggling professionals than do those groups." Quoted in Graeber and Britt, *op. cit.*, p. 415.

preceding World War II. In 1933 a German census indicated that
61.3 per cent of all gainfully occupied Jews were engaged in trade
and commerce in contrast to 18.4 per cent among the total population; but altogether they constituted only 2.5 per cent of all engaged
in these fields in Germany. In law and medicine Jews made up comparatively large proportions, 16.3 per cent and 10.9 per cent, respectively.[32]

Nathan Reich sums up the economic status of American Jews in
an interesting manner:

> The Jewish contribution to the imposing American economic edifice has been
> very substantial. The Jews brought into America at the "right" time a reservoir
> of manpower and entrepreneurial skill which the economy urgently needed.
> The economic structure of Jews is normal in the sense that it is the "natural"
> product of economic tendencies. It may sound paradoxical but it is nevertheless
> correct to say that the occupational structure of the whole modern world is
> moving in the direction of the Jewish occupational structure, i.e., in the direction
> of urbanization and professionalization and not in the opposite direction of
> agrarianization and industrial proletarianization.[33]

Liston Pope concludes that the *class* composition of the Jewish
congregations approaches that of Presbyterian, Episcopalian, and
Congregational churches, so-called upper class Protestant denominations.[34]

Finally, in a study made of the occupational distribution of Jews
in Los Angeles for the year 1951 the following classifications were
found: 15 per cent professionals and semi-professionals, 36 per cent
proprietors, managers, and officials, 28 per cent clerical and sales
people, and 21 per cent craftsmen, operatives, and laborers. These
previous figures may be compared with the *general* population in
Los Angeles County by utilizing the same categories and data from
the 1950 census preliminary report: 12 per cent professionals and
semi-professionals, 12 per cent proprietors, managers, and officials,
26 per cent clerical and sales people, and 49 per cent craftsmen, operatives, and laborers.[35] This study confirms the judgment that Jews

[32] Davie, *op. cit.*, p. 6.

[33] From Nathan Reich, "The Role of the Jews in the American Economy," *YIVO
Annual of Jewish Social Science*, Vol. V (1950), pp. 197-205. Used by permission of the
Yiddish Scientific Institute.

[34] Liston Pope, "Religion and the Class Structure," *The Annals of the American
Academy of Political and Social Science*, Vol. 256 (March, 1948), pp. 84-91.

[35] *A Preview of the Greater Los Angeles Jewish Community, 1951* under the technical
direction of Fred Massarik, research associate, for the Los Angeles Jewish Community
Council. This study indicates that the Jewish population in Los Angeles almost doubled
since 1941 making Los Angeles perhaps the largest Jewish community in the nation
outside of New York.

tend to be represented more heavily than the general population in the professional and business callings.

SUMMARY

The social status of the American Jews appears to be within the range of other white nationality groups, but on one of the lowest levels within this principal category. His educational status seems to be high, but not so high as perhaps his ability and desire might suggest, inasmuch as prejudice against the Jew precludes his entrance into some colleges and restricts his progress in some professions. Legally, the Jews who are citizens of the United States are accorded the same legal status of other citizens, with minor variations occurring in the interpretation of the laws by some officials and private agreements. In economic status he tends to be found in the business and merchandising fields which reflects a status similar to the middle class in the United States.

PROBLEMS FOR STUDY AND DISCUSSION

1. List and explain the different ways by which the Jews have been classified as different from "typical Americans."

2. List some of the reasons why you think the Jews are accorded a somewhat low social status in the studies cited, and discuss why you include each of the reasons listed.

3. In the reading on anti-Semitism in New York City it is shown that anti-Semitism varies among religious and economic groups. Explain these differences and give reasons why you think each exists.

4. List the different ways by which Jews are discriminated against in the United States, and show how this discrimination differs from that against the Negro.

5. Explain why there is a tendency for Jews to have a high educational status in the United States.

6. It is the belief among most people that the Jews are largely in control of the economic system of the United States. Evaluate this belief in keeping with the information that is available at the present time.

SELECTED READINGS

BERNSTEIN, Peretz, *Jew-Hate As a Sociological Problem* (New York: Philosophical Library, 1951), especially chap. 6.

BETTELHEIM, Bruno, "The Dynamism of Anti-Semitism in Gentile and Jew," *Journal of Abnormal Social Psychology*, Vol. 42 (1947), pp. 153-168.

FINEBERG, S. Andhil, *Punishment Without Crime*, (New York: Doubleday and Company, Inc., 1949).

DUKER, Abraham G., "Emerging Culture Patterns in American Jewish Life," *American Jewish Historical Society,* Vol. 39 (June, 1950), pp. 351-388.

FORSTER, Arnold, *A Measure of Freedom* (New York: Doubleday and Company, Inc., 1950).

FORSTER, Arnold, and EPSTEIN, Benjamin, *The Troublemakers* (New York: Doubleday and Company, Inc., 1952).

GAER, J., "Jewish Problem Myth," *North American Review,* Vol. 234 (Nov., 1932), pp. 457-462.

KAPLAN, M. M., *The Future of the American Jew* (New York: The Macmillan Company, 1948).

ROSE, Arnold M., *Race Prejudice and Discrimination* (New York: Alfred A. Knopf, Inc., 1951), chap. 43.

SCHERMERHORN, R. A., *These Our People* (Boston: D. C. Heath and Company, 1949), pp. 377-445.

WALTER, Paul A. F., Jr., *Race and Cultural Relations* (New York: McGraw-Hill Book Company, Inc., 1952), pp. 342-359.

VIII

Mexicans

AMERICANS OF MEXICAN ancestry constitute about 3,500,000 persons in the United States, nearly ninety per cent of whom reside in the western states. Recent data of a comparative nature are difficult to obtain inasmuch as the Mexican was omitted from Census Reports after 1930. As indicated in Chapter I, Mexicans were classified in the 1940 census as either Indian or white; hence, some interpolation of fragmentary sources is imperative when considering this ethnic group.

The Mexicans are found chiefly in the following five states: Texas, California, Arizona, New Mexico, and Colorado. These states probably account for at least two-thirds of the Mexican population in the United States. There are, at least, four types of Mexicans: (1) the old native group, (2) the new native group, (3) the "wetbacks," and (4) the Mexican Nationals. Briefly, the old native group consists of those Mexicans who lived in the Southwest territory before this region became a part of the United States. This group is, in most instances, the result of miscegenation of Indian and Spanish parentage. These persons are often thought of as the pioneers of the Southwest. The new native group is composed of those persons born in the United States of parents who migrated from Mexico. This group of Mexicans reflects many of the assimilation problems of the second generation. The "wetbacks" are Mexicans who have crossed the Rio Grande or the United States border illegally. Some estimates have placed the number of "wetbacks" coming to the United States as high as 50,000 per month. Mexican Nationals are the contract laborers who enter the United States legally from Mexico for a stipulated wage and time period. While there are these four types of Mexicans in the United States, most people fail to make the distinctions that are necessary for a clear understanding and appreciation of these ethnic groups.

SOCIAL STATUS

The social status of the Mexican may be approximated by reference to the findings of several studies, especially a study by Dr. E. S. Bogardus. In 1926 Bogardus found that the Mexican was ranked in twenty-seventh place, and in 1946 he found that the Mexican had been assigned to the twenty-sixth rank in a list of some thirty-six ethnic groups.[1] It is of special importance to observe that the Spanish were rated in twelfth place in 1926 and sixteenth place in 1946. On the other hand, the Indian occupied twenty-first place in 1926 and twenty-fourth place in 1946. Of sociological interest is the finding that the hybrid group resulting from miscegenation (Spanish-Indian) occupies a lower status than either of its parent ethnic groups. In some particulars this lower social status of the Mexican is similar to that assigned other hybrid ethnic groups.

A recent study of the social status of nine ethnic groups disclosed that the Mexican was ranked lowest.[2] Approximately 1,800 white university students from the states of Texas, Oklahoma, Arkansas, and Louisiana were asked to check statements that were either positive or negative, and might be used to describe the ethnic groups under consideration. Of the statements checked for the Mexican, 61.5 per cent were negative and 38.5 per cent were positive. It may be of special interest to note the statements checked most frequently for the Mexican. Of the forty statements considered, the following five were those most often marked as depicting the Mexican: (1) "possess a low moral standard," (2) "will steal," (3) "are dirty and filthy," (4) "help to keep wages low," and (5) "are spreaders of disease."

The low social status of the Mexican may be appreciated by observing the reticence of many to refer to these people as Americans. In a number of social situations these people are designated as Mexican or Spanish Americans, but rarely as Americans. It appears that "typical Americans" assume that Americans are Anglo-Americans. Another sidelight on the social standing of the Mexicans may be appreciated by observing the tendency to refer to the favorable aspects of Mexican culture as *Spanish,* and thus to relegate to the background many of

[1] Emory S. Bogardus, "Changes in Racial Distances," *International Journal of Opinion and Attitude Research*, Vol. 1, No. 4 (Dec., 1947), p. 58.

[2] E. S. Richards, "Attitudes of White College Students in the Southwest Toward Ethnic Groups in the United States," *Sociology and Social Research*, Vol. 35 (Sept.-Oct., 1950), pp. 22-30.

the Indian patterns as primitive and unimportant. One rarely sees an advertisement for Mexican food, but "Spanish dishes" are a commonplace on the menus of restaurants in the Southwest. Since corn is the matrix of most so-called "Spanish foods," it is rather obvious to whom the credit ought to go. A Mexican university student states: "I am ashamed of my own group. So many of my Mexican friends in the university claim to be Spanish. We are Americans in the sense of ancestry and pioneer background." [3] As Mexican students are graduated from the high schools, it is usually expected that they should assume the role of an American of Spanish ancestry. This role-playing has a tendency to make it appear that intellectual superiority and Spanish ancestry are definitely related. It becomes easy for the majority group to observe that "Mexicans never finish high school." *Hence, the Mexicans become stereotyped in the minds of the Anglo-Americans as persons of low abilities and cultural attainments.*

Another item reflecting the social status of the Mexican American may be found in the development of the "zoot-suit" cult and the resulting friction in Los Angeles during World War II. This peculiar garb seems to have won wide acceptance because of its attention-getting qualities, as a symbol of emancipation, and for some as a fashion. The zoot-suit was also accepted by some Negroes, Filipinos, and Anglo-Americans of the "jitterbug cult."

The Mexican gangs in Los Angeles involved only a small percentage of the total Mexican population. Bogardus estimates that about one in thirty-six Mexican youths was associated actively with a zoot-suit gang.[4] For the most part, these Mexican gangs fought one another; however, the daily press frequently featured a story depicting conflict between zoot-suit gangs composed of Mexicans and Negroes. Too often the metropolitan newspapers described the ethnic gangs in much the same language as the Normandy landing or the Battle of the Bulge. Reporters failed to state that these gangs of American Mexican youth were the products of low social and economic status. These Americans of Mexican ancestry were logical candidates for zoot-suit associations, especially if they had been denied war jobs, failed to meet the physical standards for military service, or had been rather poor students in school. The zoot-suit gave an immediate status

[3] From the statement of R. L., a senior at the University of Southern California, Aug. 4, 1948.

[4] One of the most penetrating analyses of the zoot-suit problem is to be found in the article by E. S. Bogardus, "Gangs of Mexican-American Youth," *Sociology and Social Research,* Vol. 28, No. 1 (Sept., 1943), pp. 55-66.

to the wearer and a consciousness of kind quickly developed among the Mexican youth. A unique garb gave the wearer an esoteric status.

The conflict between American sailors and Mexican zoot-suit wearers received generous coverage from the Los Angeles metropolitan press. Sailors, and other men in service, represent persons living under restricted conditions and exacting discipline. The Articles of War with their universal coverage for all human deviation certainly serve to repress the normal impulses of the service man. From a sociological point of view, the uniforms of the two groups represent the freedom of the civilian as a zoot-suiter, and, on the other hand, the strict discipline of the sailor in his garb, sometimes referred to by sailors as a "monkey suit." In retrospect, it is certainly true that many of the Mexican boys desired the approved status of the military uniform, and many of the sailors wanted the freedom symbolized by the zoot-suit. Service men, in some instances, did bodily harm to the wearers of zoot-suits on the ground of "protecting American womanhood." Some of the zoot-suiters were doing nothing to bring criticism upon themselves; but, when the sailors moved in on Main Street "on liberty," some "innocent bystanders" were roughed up a bit. A vivid account is to be found in the following statement by a Negro university student of a sailor and zoot-suit fracas:

Late one Saturday afternoon a few months prior to my induction in the Army, I was walking down one of the principal streets of Pasadena with three Mexican friends. A cab drove up to the curb and four Marines hopped out. One of the Marines a PFC, said "let's give these 4-F zoot-suiters some combat training." There was nothing else to do but fight. Since I had been an amateur boxer, I guess I did more than my share. I broke the jaw on one of the USO commandos just as the police arrived. The police took me into custody. My guilt as a zoot-suiter was determined by a careful measurement of my trousers! My trousers proved me innocent. However, one of the officers phoned my mother and warned her that I should not be seen in public with Mexicans who apparently were zoot-suiters. Uncle Sam solved my clothing problem, a complete G.I. outfit in a short time.[5]

No doubt one of the major factors in assigning a low social standing to the Mexican-American is the habit of the majority group to define him as a peon. He is too often depicted as a person sleeping against a shady wall. In a go-getting culture such as ours, this stereotype cannot offer much status. The American-Mexican as an artist, a writer, or a scientist is omitted from this visualization of role. It must not be forgotten that the successful Mexican-American is likely to

[5] From the statement of R.L.B. a senior at the University of Southern California, January 28, 1948.

define himself as Spanish, which adds status to the Spanish and de-
tracts from the natural abilities of the Indian ancestry.

A recent study of status stratification in a Southern California
town of 4,200 persons, about one-third of whom were of Mexican
descent, reported that a number of discriminatory practices against
the Mexican-Americans had been modified or discontinued since
World War II, although the status of the group as a whole remained
quite low. It was the opinion of a number of the non-Mexican residents that the more "progressive" members of this ethnic group had
been able to raise their status *among the Mexicans* by speaking English on the street, moving out of the old "Mexican Town" into an
adjacent new tract with superior housing but also inhabited by
Mexican-Americans, "going on" in school, attending a Protestant
mission for Mexicans rather than the traditional Catholic church,
and seeking other values generally thought to constitute attempts
to emulate the non-Mexicans. However, the evidences of caste feelings were persistent—intermarriage was unthinkable, residents were
contrasted as either "white" or "Mexican," and the expression "a
good Mexican can do a lot for his people," was typical of non-Mexican
thought. Even the most liberal residents were found to think in terms
of "the Mexican community" as a distinct and definitely inferior
subdivision of the total community.[6]

LEGAL STATUS

The legal status of the Mexican-American varies from state to
state. Perhaps one of the interesting aspects of the legal status of the
Mexican is his lack of desire to become a citizen of the United States.
It is well known that most of the Americans of Mexican ancestry were
born in the United States and were *not* naturalized. For instance, in
the community study by Ruth Tuck she found that, out of 277 immigrant Mexicans interviewed, only one had taken out his first papers.[7]
Some of the reasons why Mexicans fail to become naturalized citizens
may be reviewed: (1) cost of securing the necessary documents, (2)
difficulty of speaking in a foreign language, (3) inability to furnish
adequate proof of legal entry into the United States, (4) and deep

6 Thomas E. Lasswell, "A Study of Status Stratification" (Los Angeles: The University
of Southern California, 1952), unpublished Doctor's dissertation.

7 Ruth Tuck, *Not with the Fist* (New York: Harcourt, Brace and Company, Inc.,
1947), p. 207.

loyalty to a land only a few hundred miles away. Perhaps a fifth reason of signal importance might be added, namely, the foreign-born Mexican cannot see how he will benefit from the naturalization status. He has heard Mexicans born in this country remark that Anglo-Americans make no distinctions as to the citizenship of the Mexican-American. He is just a Mexican, whether a citizen of the United States or of Mexico. *In fact, some of the foreign-born Mexicans feel, by way of rationalization or justification, that they have more protection and effective legal status as aliens than as potential citizens of the United States.* The National of Mexico, when in trouble, can seek the aid of his government through official channels of respective state departments.

Prior to the United States Supreme Court decision on restrictive covenants in the spring of 1948, the Mexican had been legally defined as "white," and the usual "Caucasian clauses" thus could not apply to them. Also, it is to be remembered that the 1940 census classified Mexicans as Indians or whites. The American of Mexican ancestry has few legal prohibitions against him. In fact, there is little "Jim Crowism" expressed against the Mexican. True, there may be isolated examples of discriminatory treatment but not as a legal policy of separation, as is found in the case of the Negro in the deep South. *Hence, the Mexican and the Jew find themselves discriminated against largely by persons of prejudice rather than by laws.* Official legal discrimination against the Mexican at the present time is a difficult case to prove.

While official discrimination against the Mexican is not sanctioned by the courts, there are many instances of personal discrimination. Malcolm Ross, formerly director of the Fair Employment Practices Committee, cites an example. In a drugstore in a Texas town a waiter refused to serve a dish of ice cream to a Mexican veteran. This American-Mexican who had been refused service had won the Congressional Medal of Honor at the hand of the President of the United States for extraordinary heroism under enemy fire.[8] The same pattern of discrimination is cited by Pauline R. Kibbe[9] in the case of a young Sergeant from Mission, Texas. The soldier had completed twenty-five missions over enemy territory as an aerial gunner on a B-17 bomber. He was returned to the United States because of an injury.

[8] Malcolm Ross, *All Manner of Men* (New York: Reynal and Hitchcock, 1947), p. 272.
[9] Pauline R. Kibbe, *Latin Americans in Texas* (Albuquerque: University of New Mexico Press, 1946), p. 213.

At an open-air meeting the community of Mission gave him a watch as a token of appreciation for his courage. In a matter of a few months he married one of the local Mexican girls and a small wedding party went to a night club near Mission. The doorman refused to admit the young couples. Later, upon questioning, the doorman said he would have permitted the soldier in but not his Mexican wife. The dramatic point of this story is that not long after this incident the soldier was sent overseas to the Pacific Theater—and was killed in action. This treatment was not typical of the average Mexican in Texas, but is illustrative of the degree to which the prejudice against the Mexican may be expressed.

The Good Neighbor Commission of Texas received from Mexican Consuls, Latin American Organizations, and individuals one hundred seventeen complaints of discrimination during the first four months of its existence.[10] One hundred ten of these complaints involved refusal of admission to or service in public places of business and amusement. Sixty-seven of these complaints occurred in West Texas, four in East Texas, and forty-four in South Texas. Few complaints were to be noted near the border where the heaviest concentration of Mexican population resides. The cotton-growing section of Texas had the most frequent number of complaints. By superimposing the migratory labor routes and the places of incident upon a map, a very close relationship was found between cotton, migratory labor, and refusal of service. Most of the complaints were in small towns and in fourth and fifth rate establishments.

An insight into the differential legal status of the Mexican as compared with other ethnic groups may be observed in a report by E. M. Lemert and Judy Rosberg.[11] They investigated the arrest-felony conviction ratios, the number of arrests on felony charges in Los Angeles County and City being divided by the number of felony convictions. In rank order the ratios were: Negroes, 7.7; Filipinos, 5.7; Mexicans, 5.3; Chinese and Japanese, 3.7; white (including Jewish) 2.7. It is purported by these writers that these high arrest rates of the minorities should not be regarded as objective measures of criminality, but as indicating differences in the amount of putative deviation.

There is a history of differential treatment toward the Mexican

10 *Ibid.*, p. 208.
11 Edwin M. Lemert and Judy Rosberg, "Crime and Punishment Among Minority Groups in Los Angeles," *Proceedings of the Pacific Coast Sociological Society* (June, 1946), p. 133.

in the Southwest and on the Pacific Coast. It was not so long ago that a white man might harm a Mexican and suffer no great penalty, but the reverse was almost never true. A rather long list of examples of differential legal status between "whites and Mexicans" is cited by Paul S. Taylor.[12] These make it clear that the Mexican had little protection under the law. In California some of the automobile insurance companies refuse to accept applications from Mexicans. Two devices are used for the screening of applicants: (1) a statement concerning race and (2) ability to speak English clearly. Upon questioning as to why Mexicans are not insured, one of the underwriters gave the writers the following reasons: (1) Mexicans drive old automobiles, (2) we think they are poorer drivers, (3) we have no chance of defending ourselves in a court case since the Mexican cannot make himself understood, and (4) the jury may be prejudiced against him.[13]

The American-Mexican and Mexican National do not freely utilize the services of the court, inasmuch as they have the feeling that "justice" is for Anglo-Americans. In some instances they fear the threat of deportation as a consequence of any kind of court action. No doubt Americans of Mexican ancestry feel that their services on the battle fields have not been appreciated. Because of their large families, low-skilled jobs not qualifying them for war deferment, and perhaps the tendency of some draftboard officials to send Mexicans ahead of other Americans, there is some reason to believe that the Mexican family contributed more generously to the war effort than "typical American" families. Is a contribution of life on the altar of freedom worth equal treatment for all Americans?[14]

EDUCATIONAL STATUS

The educational status of the American-Mexican is not high. Since American culture places a premium on the amount of formal schooling an individual has, the Mexican finds himself at considerable disadvantage. His culture has been geared to an agricultural tempo, and

12 Paul S. Taylor, *An American-Mexican Frontier* (Chapel Hill: University of North Carolina Press, 1934), pp. 167-173.

13 From a conversation with a representative of a prominent California underwriter. Aug. 20, 1948.

14 It is our opinion that Mexicans served in the combat divisions of the army in greater proportion than any other ethnic group, with the possible exception of the American Japanese. A Mexican name and a military occupational speciality of 745 (riflemen) stand out vividly in retrospection. Some excellent studies could be made on this question if the Adjutant General Department believed it worthwhile.

the conflict between rural and urban values is part of the problem. A number of studies are available that point up the fact that the educational status of the Mexican is low because of poor school attendance, limited average grade completion, and frequent school failures. Some of this low educational status may be explained in terms of high mobility necessitated as transient workers, difficulties centering upon bilingualism, and perhaps a less pressurized culture that does not stress formalized schooling. Table XXI presents a com-

Table XXI: SCHOOL ATTENDANCE FOR THE POPULATION 5 TO 20 YEARS OF AGE IN THE UNITED STATES *

Ethnic Groups	Per Cent in School
All classes	69.9
White	71.5
Native parentage	71.8
Foreign parentage	71.9
Foreign born	55.6
Negroes	60.0
Mexicans	52.1
Indians	60.2
Chinese	75.6
Japanese	84.0

* Fifteenth Census of the United States, *Population* (1930), Vol. II, p. 1094: Filipino, Hindu, and Korean omitted. This is the last Census Report in which the Mexican was given a separate classification.

parative statement of the standing of the Mexican with several other ethnic groups. A glance indicates that the Mexican ranks lowest in the population groups compared. To some students it may seem strange that the Mexican does not attend school with the same frequency as the Negro. The Mexican's need for schooling is appreciated when it is recalled that these people may have a special language problem which has direct bearing on their general acceptance in the American culture. In the United States the foreign-born Mexican ranks high in the population groups unable to speak English. It must be recognized that a superior command of English adds status and a poor command of the chief language of communication results in a lower evaluation. No doubt some of the first- and second-generation problems result from a differential command of English. Mutual suspicion may be encouraged when there is an inability to comprehend the verbalization of either generation.

What factors account for the Mexican's retardation in school and in the use of English? Some of the prominent factors underlying the low educational status of the Mexican alien are: (1) frequent shifts back and forth between this country and Mexico decrease the value of becoming Americanized; (2) the high mobility of Mexican labor interrupts regular school attendance; (3) the low wage scale of the Mexican forces the entire family to participate in the common task of working; and (4) there is a somewhat futile attitude toward formal schooling which may be expressed in the statement: "Why is José going to high school? Isn't he going to pick grapes anyway?"

A few psychologists and educators have hinted that the Mexican does poorly in school due to inferior intelligence. One must remember that the paper and pencil tests of intelligence are measuring insight in terms of American culture, not Mexican. Before we can accept the proposition that the Mexican does not measure up to other ethnic groups in intelligence, we must certainly keep the following qualifications in mind: (1) American tests of intelligence place a premium on speed, (2) the tests are strongly urban biased, (3) command of English is imperative, and (4) the Mexicans who are best educated may be *passing* for "Spanish" or "white." Cultural factors and certain selective factors probably account for the differential scores made on tests on intelligence better than any difference in native ability between ethnic groups.

Another reason for the poor use of English and its related problems is the segregated school for the Mexican. Most of the states have abolished the segregated school by court action; however, the segregated school persists through the operation of certain "natural factors." The Mexican may live in a predominantly Mexican neighborhood; hence, nearly all his contacts will be with other Mexican children. The few non-Mexican children residing in that neighborhood may attend a different school.

Until recently in Texas the segregated school worked to the advantage of the majority groups rather than the Mexican. Texas formerly appropriated a sum of about $30 per capita for children between the ages of six and seventeen who were enumerated in the census. This sum of money was turned over to the individual school districts whether the children attended school or not. If the attendance laws were not enforced in the Mexican districts, there was a greater sum of money to be spent for teachers' salaries, buildings, and other state improvements in the non-Mexican community. Other states paid individual school districts on the basis of average daily attendance and the same problem did not arise. This method of paying the school districts has been changed in Texas. Another variety of this problem in the South has been the counting of Mexicans and Negroes for the purposes of securing representatives in the Congress and then denying the Negro and sometimes the Mexican the right to vote. However, progress is underway to eradicate the poll tax.[15]

One of the famous test cases on the segregation of Mexicans from other Americans concerned the Gonzalo and Others vs. Westminister School District of Organge County on February 18, 1946. In this case United States District Judge Paul J. McCormick, of the Southern District of California, granted an injunction restraining further discriminatory practices against Mexican pupils. It was decided that the paramount requisite under "equal protection of the laws" in California's system of public education was social equality. Segregation implied social inferiority for pupils of Mexican descent.

ECONOMIC STATUS

The low economic status of Mexicans is well known and is perhaps the chief problem confronting this group and all interested persons. The economic status of a group has tremendous value in terms of other statuses. Poverty is a factor in poor housing, inadequate health protection, deferred social acceptance, and inadequate school attendance. The American of Mexican ancestry may receive less money than other ethnic groups because of (1) prejudice, (2) low occupational skills, (3) seasonal working conditions, and (4) perhaps a lack of aggressive enterprise.

It is not easy to secure reliable data on the economic status of the Mexican that has a comparative reference. However, a number of studies will be reviewed to afford some insight into this phase of human relations. The Los Angeles Coördinating Council reported before the advent of war work that the median Mexican family income did not exceed $800, or about $500 less than the minimum required for decent living.[16]

Reference may be made to Table XX published in Chapter VII on American Jews. It will be recalled that the persons with predominantly Spanish or Mexican names were to be found in the low-skilled jobs. Poor wages and low occupational skill are likely to be correlated with each other to a great degree. Persons with typically

15 See the explicit statement in the special issue of *Survey Graphic* with the theme "Segregation," Vol. XXXVI, No. 1 (Jan., 1947).

16 Quoted by R. D. Tuck, *Not with the Fist* (New York: Harcourt, Brace and Company, Inc., 1947), p. 174.

Mexican names were represented in the unskilled occupations by the large proportion of 55 per cent; persons of typically "American" names were modestly represented by 21 per cent in unskilled jobs; and the Jewish ethnic names were infrequently represented by 5 per cent in such callings. By way of comparison, it is well to realize that perhaps no other ethnic group is more urban centered than the Jews, while to a large extent, Mexicans are newcomers to the city.

In a study of Mexicans in San Diego during the depression it was found that about 80 per cent of the family income was derived from the husband's earnings. The Mexican worker earned a little more than $1,000 annually. This annual income was about $300 less than the average of workers in manufacturing industries in that community. Close to half the wives worked for wages and they augmented the family income by about $300 per year. Most of the women were employed in the canneries. About half of the families "broke even" at the end of the year, and the rest went behind financially.[17]

Another statement of the economic status of the Mexican may be found in a report of the U. S. Department of Labor concerning agricultural laborers of Hidalgo County, Texas, during the first three months of 1941. The report states:

> In most households the father and mother and also several children were wage earners. Employment was, however, so irregular and rates of pay were so low that the combined earnings of all the workers from agricultural labor, supplemented to some extent by earnings from non-farm work, were too small to provide adequate food, clothing, and shelter for the family group. During the year preceding the date of interview, the families had a median cash income from all sources of only $350 to provide for their large households, averaging 6.6 persons. This is considerably less than the minimum annual income of $480 estimated by the Texas Social Welfare Association to be necessary to maintain relief families, averaging only 4.2 members, at a level of health and decency. Yet very few of the families had received any assistance from public or private agencies during the year.[18]

Pauline Kibbe cites a study made by the University of Texas that throws additional light on the comparison of family income of Latin-Americans and Anglo-Americans. About 1,600 questionnaires were analyzed from parents of children in six Texas communities that have

17 Constantine Panunzio, *How the Mexicans Earn and Live* (Berkeley: University of California Publications in Economics, 1933), p. 68.

18 Amber A. Warburton, Helen Wood, and Marian M. Crane, M.D., *The Work and Welfare of Children of Agricultural Laborers in Hidalgo County, Texas* (Washington, D. C.: U. S. Department of Labor, Children's Bureau, 1943), pp. 4-5. (It is an open question that $500 per year could maintain a family of four on a decent standard of living.)

a majority of Latin-Americans as residents. In no case did a Mexican-American family report an annual income of more than $2,249. The average size of Mexican families was 6.2 individuals, whereas Anglo-American families averaged only 4.6 persons, and reported incomes ranging as high as $5,000 per year.[19]

Carey McWilliams, a very critical and partisan student of minority problems, says the extensive use of Mexican labor in California began during the First World War. Newspapers and farm journals were replete with references to the great need for additional workers. Mexican Nationals were considered to be ideal. Large groups of Mexicans were brought in units of 1,500 from San Felipe to the Imperial Valley. Another impetus to Mexican labor was the closing of immigration from most of the world in 1924. While health authorities and organized labor protested the importation of Mexican labor, farm operators were persistent in their urgent demands for a cheap source of labor. One of the newspapers observed that a Californian was sent to Congress "to get us Mexicans and keep them out of our schools, and out of our social problems." [20]

It was generally believed that the Mexican was not property minded to the same degree that the Japanese was and, therefore, was easier to handle. The Mexicans with their Indian communal conception of property appeared almost docile to the land-hungry ranch owners and fruit growers. Perhaps the "docility" of the Mexican was due to a different set of culture patterns and definitions of the goals of living. Mexicans were not eager for unionization, because a show of organized strength might bring the threat of deportation. The Mexican defined his role in the United States as superior to his homeland; hence, an appearance of docility was insurance against trouble and actual deportation. Almost as high as 70 per cent of the Mexican field hands might be deported on technical grounds.

The most recent statement concerning the economic status of this ethnic group may be found by a review of the contracts which were in effect during World War II. These contracts indicate the prevailing conditions of Mexican labor in the fields and on the railroads.

In the first quarter of 1942 the California fruit growers urged the United States Employment Service that Mexican Nationals be

19 *Comparison of Family Income and Expenditures for Five Principal Budget Items in Twenty Texas Cities.* (Austin: The University of Texas, Bureau of Business Research, 1943).

20 Carey McWilliams, *Factories in the Field* (Boston: Little, Brown and Company, 1939), p. 123.

brought to California to aid in the harvesting and processing of fruit.[21] The scarcity of labor for the fields resulted from the drafting of Mexican Americans and the migration of other Mexican-Americans to defense industries where more money might be earned. No doubt the mass evacuation of 110,000 Japanese from the coastal states also contributed to the need for agricultural workers. It was assumed that the introduction of Mexican Nationals would not upset the existing ethnic accommodation in the fields. Few growers and railroad managers would admit the fact that the Mexican National during a war period was ideal inasmuch as he was draft free, an asset of great value for labor continuity.

On September 29, 1942, the first group of Mexican Nationals arrived in California for the sugarbeet harvest. These Nationals of Mexico were selected on the basis of good health, good character, and some knowledge and skill in agriculture. It is Dr. Jones' opinion that most of these Nationals were motivated by the following factors in coming to this country: (1) a desire to contribute to the war effort, (2) an opportunity to increase their earnings, (3) the possibility of learning English, and (4) in some Nationals by a spirit of adventure.[22]

An underlying principle of the labor contract was that no National worker was to displace an American worker or was to lower the wage rates currently being paid. The Mexican National was assured 75 per cent employment during the contract period of six months at a rate of pay of not less than thirty cents per hour. However, an estimate placed the amount actually paid to Mexican Nationals at 61 cents per hour.[23]

Some of the problems experienced by these Mexican Nationals centered upon homesickness, diet changes, isolation from other Americans, thus making it impossible to assimilate the language or other parts of the culture, barracks-living, and inadequately organized recreation. Some of the growers developed special classes in English and extension classes in agricultural subjects. Others attempted to give the National a clean place to sleep and some organized recreation. Too often recreation as a sustainer of morale was lost in the rush of war production.

From official records it is disclosed that 4,203 agricultural workers

[21] The best statement on the Mexican labor contracts may be found in the work by Robert C. Jones, *Mexican War Workers in the United States* (Washington, D. C.: Pan American Union, 1945), p. 1.

[22] *Ibid.*, p. 6.

[23] *Ibid.*, p. 9.

were brought to this country in 1942, 52,098 in 1943, and 62,170 in 1944. These workers were distributed over twenty-one states. The summer of 1944 found 32,280 agricultural workers in California; the remainder were distributed in the following states: Montana, 4,434; Washington, 4,332; Oregon, 3,670; Colorado, 3,335; Idaho, 2,410; Michigan, 2,006; Arizona, 1,850; Nebraska, 1,495; Minnesota, 1,299; Wyoming, 961; Nevada, 691; Utah, 689; North Dakota, 432; South Dakota, 300; Kansas, 298; and Wisconsin, 191. A little over half of the 118,471 workers who were brought to the United States to help meet the shortage of agricultural workers during the first two years that the program was in operation were to be found in California.[24]

A second war program where Mexican Nationals were used was in the maintenance of the railroads. This program was initiated by the Southern Pacific Railroad Company of San Francisco when, in the late months of 1941, it requested permission from the Immigration and Naturalization Service to bring Mexican Nationals for a temporary maintenance program. Immediate opposition to this suggested program was voiced by organized labor in California. But in May, 1942, this railroad again filed an application for foreign workers inasmuch as there were 949 unfilled positions on its lines. While railroads were losing men to the armed forces, the ton-mile freight traffic had almost doubled in 1943 over 1939.[25]

About the same requirements as to health and character were in operation for the recruitment of railroad workers as had been the case with agricultural workers. The workers were guaranteed a minimum of 75 per cent full-time employment in each pay period. They were assured of at least 46 cents per hour, and later this base pay was raised to 57 cents. The average hourly earnings for Nationals on the railroads were probably higher than either of these figures reported.

Principal problems that confronted the Mexican National encountered as a railroad worker were: (1) they were disappointed as to the real wages in terms of the cost of living, (2) some of the workers had misconceptions as to the actual base pay to be paid and had naively accepted rumors of pay as high as $25 per day, (3) housing accommodations in bunkhouses were modest at best, (4) and some of the Mexican Nationals found the climate in the northern parts of the United States a terrific problem of adjustment.

Up to December 31, 1944, 80,137 Mexican Nationals had been

24 *Ibid.,* pp. 24-25.
25 *Ibid.,* pp. 26-27.

delivered to employers for railroad work. Over half of the Nationals were employed by the Southern Pacific and the Atchison, Topeka, and Santa Fe Railroads. One estimate placed the percentage of Mexican Nationals as track workers at 72 per cent on the Southern Pacific Railroad.[26]

During the first three years of the war about 120,000 Mexican Nationals came to the United States to work in the fields and about 80,000 augmented the labor supply on the railroads. The latest figures obtainable place the number of Mexican Nationals as agricultural workers in the United States at 26,577.[27] Of course, this number of Mexican Nationals varies greatly with the seasons of the year.

Pauline R. Kibbe, a well known student of the Mexican-American in the United States, presents an excellent description of the economic status of Mexicans and the general reaction of Texans to these people in the following reading. Kibbe was the first executive secretary of the Good Neighbor Commission of Texas, which was established in 1943 by former Governor Coke R. Stevenson. About one-half of all Mexicans in the United States reside in Texas, and this reading reflects the conditions under which a considerable proportion of the Mexicans in the United States live and work.

▌ THE ECONOMIC PLIGHT OF MEXICANS[28]

PAULINE R. KIBBE

The scope and seriousness of the problems of Mexican Americans in Texas is not generally understood. They have always had a national as well as an international significance. But developments during the past two or three years have set out, in bold relief, the absolute necessity for a concerted attack on the problems from two directions: regulations by the federal government, and energetic activity on the part of organized labor.

A great many Texans are not going to like either approach. Nevertheless, the government of the state has proved its impotence and actual disinclination to remedy the situation. The time has come for action of a different kind.

Let's see what this is all about.

It is the wetback who has brought matters to a focal point. "Wet-

---

26 See the article in *Business Week*, October 1944.

27 *Immigration and Naturalization Service Monthly Review*, Oct., 1947.

28 Pauline R. Kibbe, "The American Standard—For All Americans," *Common Ground,* Vol. X, No. 1 (Autumn, 1949), pp. 19-27. Used by permission of the Common Council for American Unity.

back" is the term used to describe a Mexican citizen who effects an illegal entry into this country by wading, swimming, or rowing across the Rio Grande. His name is legion. He is disrupting thousands of American citizens of Mexican descent, forcing their migration to slum areas of towns and cities in and out Texas where they, in turn, glut the skilled and unskilled labor market, depressing wages for all workers.

There have always been wetbacks in Texas and throughout the border area, but the real invasion began during the war years when many of the seasonal agricultural laborers who had perennially harvested the fruit and vegetable and cotton crops of the state were serving in the armed forces. Workers from Mexico came in illegally, rather than under contract, for a very good reason. In June, 1943, the Mexican government flatly refused to contract labor to Texas farmers and growers because of the many forms of discrimination practiced against Mexicans and persons of Mexican descent within the state.

The fact that the wetbacks came in, by the hundreds and by the thousands, despite the widely publicized discrimination, was due to a number of pressures on both sides of the Rio Grande.

The cost of living in Mexico was going up even more rapidly than in this country, and in May 1948 stood at 314.2, with a norm for 1939 of 100 as a basis. The agrarian program in Mexico had not developed to the point where it could provide a living wage for more than a fraction of the rural population. People on the verge of starvation are not likely to consider discrimination too seriously when rosy promises of food are held out to them from the other side of a river that is dry, or nearly so, much of the year.

Adamant though it was in its determination that agricultural workers should not come into Texas, the Mexican government was powerless to effectively patrol the river, and petty officials both along the border and in the interior were easily induced for a price, to assist the agents of Texas farmers and growers in rounding up and herding to the border droves of peons and peasants.

Enforcement of Mexico's ban from this side of the river was the responsibility of the U. S. Immigration and Naturalization Service. While it can be conceded that the Service was undermanned during the war, it must also be admitted that the pleas of citrus, vegetable and cotton growers, individually and through their respective associations, fell upon receptive ears. The Immigration Service accepted the assertions of the growers that the shortage of labor on the farms and in the fields was so acute that the decree of the Mexican government must be ignored if the crops were to be harvested.

It was an easy matter for the Immigration Service to comply with the wishes of the growers. Wetbacks were unmolested except when they appeared openly in the towns or on the highways. In that event, they were rounded up, taken to the nearest port of entry, and released on the other side. Sometimes the wetbacks would beat the Immigration officer back across the river. There are instances on record where one wetback was deported as many as four times in a twenty-four hour period.

But the real villains of this international conspiracy were, and are, the growers themselves. Not even during the war years did they ever succeed in proving a real shortage of labor in agriculture. Their concern has always been, and continues to be, cheap labor in abundance.

The citrus groves, the extensive vegetable farms, the vast expanse of cotton acreage—in combination, a very important segment of Texas economy—all have been developed by cheap Mexican labor. Year after year, beginning about 1900, Texas growers recruited labor in Mexico. The wages promised were not always paid, and even when paid proved woefully inadequate for the support of families, many of them, each year, elected to remain in Texas. The following year, it would be necessary for the growers to recruit new workers in Mexico, since those of previous years had learned the value of American money and knew it could be stretched just so far and no farther.

Thus the Mexican American population of Texas increased from approximately 70,000 in the year 1900 to an estimated 1,250,000 in 1948. This figure is exclusive of the wetbacks now in the state. One out of every six Texans is of Mexican descent. At least half of the total is dependent upon agriculture, in one form or another, for its livelihood.

These are the people who not only chop and pick the cotton, harvest and pack the citrus fruits, cultivate and cut the spinach, and pull and bunch the onions, carrots, beets, and radishes of Texas; they are the same people who, in large measure, tend and harvest the sugar beets of many northern and northwestern states, help to pick the cotton in Arkansas, New Mexico, and numerous other states, and assist in many areas outside Texas during the fruit and vegetable season.

Nominally, these migratory Texans are residents of the state—80 per cent are United States citizens by birth or naturalization, and the others are legal residents—but actually they constitute a floating population of the country as a whole.

Many acute problems are inherent in the seasonal and migratory nature of their employment: problems in economic, education, health, sanitation, and civil rights. Because they are of the same national origin, and because there is not and cannot be any clear-cut line of demarcation, the remaining 600,000 or so Mexican Americans in Texas, who through the years have found permanent employment in other fields and have attained a certain educational and economic status, suffer, to a greater or less extent, the same inequalities, the same social ostracism, the same denial of civil rights.

At the root of all other problems of Mexican Americans in Texas is the economic situation. Enforced "cheap labor" in Texas has bred the same evils that cheap labor breeds any place: a tuberculosis death rate among Mexican Americans which is seven times that of Anglos; a third-grade level of education; a fantastically high mortality from diarrhea in Mexican American infants under two years of age; rural and urban slums that are unspeakable; segregation of Mexican American children in the public schools (until the decision of a federal judge abolished it in the summer of 1948), effective in the first three grades in some schools, extending through twelve grades in others; refusal of service in some public places of business and amusement, regardless of social or economic status or the number of generations of U. S. citizenship the victim may be able to claim; denial of the right to vote, or to serve on juries, or to own or rent real estate in certain areas.

These were the conditions which existed even before the real invasion of wetbacks began.

Late in 1946 the Mexican government admitted that at least 119,000 of its citizens were illegally resident in the border area of the United States. Of that number, a minimum of 50,000 were conceded to be in the Lower Rio Grande Valley of Texas.

Lacking the power and the means through which to secure the return of these 119,000 wetbacks to Mexico, and being equally powerless to provide for their upkeep should they all go home, the Mexican government, on January 31, 1947, entered into an agreement with the U. S. Immigration and Naturalization Service by the terms of which the presence of the 119,000 aliens was to be legalized through the signing of contracts with employers. Among other things, such contracts were to provide for the payment of the "prevailing wage" in each area. Three Mexican ports of entry—Reynosa, Ciudad Juarez, and Mexicali—were designated as the points to which employers would take their wetbacks for the legalization process, which began at Reynosa on April 21, 1947. (This was, perhaps, symbolic, for April 21 is the date celebrated in Texas as San Jacinto Day, commemorating the final defeat of the Mexican forces under Santa Ana at San Jacinto, near Houston, on April 21, 1836.)

On that and succeeding days, Texas growers acquitted themselves in a manner typical of their long history of dealing with Mexican

labor. They certified that the prevailing wage rate in the Lower
Rio Grande Valley was 25 cents an hour: this in the face of the fact
that employers in the El Paso-New Mexico area were certifying to
a wage rate of from 37½ to 45 cents an hour, and in California to
as much as 65 cents an hour, for the same labor, to produce the same
crops, to be sent to the same markets, to bring the same prices.

What the Valley employers failed to make clear, of course, was
that 25 cents an hour was the prevailing wage for wetback labor.
Even that admission would not have been accurate, since 25 cents
an hour was the exception rather than the rule. Many employers
confided that they were actually paying 10 cents, or 15 cents, at the
most, for wetback labor.

The war was well over by April of 1947. The thousands of Mexican American boys who had served in the armed forces had long
since returned to their homes; and, for all but a few of them, the
52-20 payments had about run their limit. Their jobs had been
usurped by 50,000 wetbacks, whose status was now being legalized,
and at an accepted wage rate of 25 cents an hour. On the basis of
a ten hour day, six days a week, that would mean a maximum possible income of $15 a week; only one doesn't work a regular ten-hour
day or six-day week in agriculture. The work is seasonal and entirely
dependent upon the weather.

Nevertheless, the situation was made clear to resident agricultural
workers, including veterans and their families: We can get all the
Mexican labor we want for 25 cents an hour. You will accept the
same wage, or else. The majority chose "or else."

The signing of contracts continued until early in September 1947,
when the Mexican government, convinced that the wage rate agreed
upon was too low and that Texas growers were not living up to
other provisions of the contract such as those calling for suitable
housing and sanitary facilities, firmly put an end to the legalization
process so far as Texas was concerned, and cancelled all existing
contracts with Texas growers.

The wetbacks, again illegal, not only stayed put, but their ranks
were swollen daily by new arrivals. Only now there was no minimum
wage, not even on paper. The growers were having—and are still
having—a field day.

A migration of unprecedented proportions and of a new character
began in the Valley and in South Texas generally. Some families of
resident agricultural workers left early for northern and eastern
states, intending to return again to their homes; but many others
embarked upon a quest of another sort. They carried their household goods with them with the intention of founding new homes in
towns and cities. Some stopped in Corpus Christi, San Antonio,

Austin, Dallas, and Fort Worth; some in the smaller towns in between. Some left Texas behind entirely.

In each instance they crowded into the already overcrowded slum areas or threw up new, makeshift dwellings on the fringes of the slums. Being totally inexperienced in any work except agriculture, they began, through force of circumstances, to undercut on unskilled and semi-skilled jobs of many kinds. Employers, broadly speaking, are never slow or reluctant to take advantage of a kind fate which offers an opportunity to reduce operating costs. Furthermore, a surplus of workers is always an effective threat in keeping one's employees in line, and particularly in preventing the organization of a plant. It is, apparently, an exciting game to play off a desperate man against one whose economic security is being threatened so that wages may remain "fair."

The process of displacement, reaching out in ever-widening circles across the nation, is by no means new. It has merely become greatly accelerated in the last two or three years. Mexican colonies have sprung up in states that heretofore had no Mexican population whatever. The long-established colonies in Chicago, Detroit and other large cities have increased in size.

As one concrete example of what is happening, we can look at Arkansas. In the 1930's, the cotton crop of Arkansas was harvested almost entirely by Negroes resident in that state. By 1948, however, according to the U. S. Employment Service, 12,838 Mexican Americans from Texas and contract laborers from Mexico were picking Arkansas' cotton. This meant that the Negroes who formerly did the work had been forced to migrate to the cities, or out of the state altogether, where they, too, aggravated existing slum conditions and undercut on jobs in business and industry.

In Texas, the wetbacks have been used to defeat organizational efforts of labor unions. The National Labor Relations Board confirms the fact that on November 10, 1948, and with the cooperation of the Border Patrol, wetbacks were used to interfere with an NLRB election at the Rio Grande Valley Gas Company, Harlingen, Texas. Almost all of the 140 employees in the plant were Mexicans or of Mexican descent. It was no secret to the employer that many of them were illegally in this country. About ten minutes before the NLRB official was to open the polls on the morning of the election, Border Patrolmen entered the plant, rounded up ten or more of the aliens, and deported them. All were back on the job the day after the election.

This is only one instance. With the assistance of the Immigration Service and the United States Consul in Nuevo Laredo, Mexican Nationals were imported into Laredo in 1947 to break a strike of the employees of four import-export firms. The Amalgamated Clothing Workers had the same experience in El Paso, also in 1947.

The spotlight of national publicity was trained, if but briefly, upon the wetback situation in Texas in October 1948, when the U. S. Immigration Service made an amazing move.

The cotton growers of West Texas had been badgering the Mexican Consuls General in San Antonio and El Paso for months with their demands for contract labor. As usual, they offered no proof of any shortage of domestic labor. Even if they had been able to do so, their demands would still have been denied in view of the Mexican government's steadfast refusal to permit laborers to enter Texas legally. Not only did they demand special dispensation from the Mexican government, but they also wanted a reduction in the contractual wage rate. Cotton pickers under contract to growers in Arkansas, Mississippi, and other cotton-producing states last year were guaranteed a wage rate of $3 per hundred pounds on the first picking, and a rising scale for each additional picking. The West Texas growers insisted upon contract labor from Mexico, but they likewise insisted that the wage be $2 per hundred pounds.

When their demands were unequivocally refused, the cotton growers hatched out a neat scheme. It worked, too.

They poured their troubles into the sympathetic ears of the Chief of the Immigration Service at El Paso and the Director of the U. S. Employment Service and convinced them that without a plentiful supply of labor from across the river West Texas cotton would rot in the fields. These soft-hearted officials of the United States government apparently agreed that in the face of such an imminent catastrophe an international treaty and the goodwill of nations were of no significance whatever. Accordingly, the glad tidings were carried across the river and before dawn one morning in the early part of October a horde of shadowy figures began a wholesale invasion of the El Paso area. No one tried to stop them. Once on this side, they were placed under technical arrest by Immigration officers, immediately paroled to the U. S. Employment Service, and loaded into waiting trucks driven by agents of West Texas cotton growers.

More than 7,000 wetbacks crossed the river before the border was closed again three days later. It took that long before the Chief of the Immigration Service became convinced either that his friends in West Texas had a plentiful supply of labor or that he had exceeded his authority.

Neither the Governor of Texas nor that state's official agency especially charged with protecting and furthering the interests of persons of Mexican descent—the Good Neighbor Commission—

registered any protest with the federal government concerning the break-through at El Paso. The Good Neighbor Commission, as it was originally constituted in 1943 and during the first four years of its life, did much to advance the cause of Mexican Americans in the state and to bring about an intelligent understanding of their problems on the part of Anglo Texans.

But with the advent of a new governor in 1947—a governor elected with the financial support of large interests such as the oil and sulphur industries, the citrus and vegetable growers' associations, and the cotton growers' association—the Commission has, to all intents and purposes, ceased to function. The fact that 7,000 destitute workers had been added within a three-day period to the already clogged labor market in Texas was obviously of no concern whatever to the Governor or the Commission. One might reasonably conclude that the break-through was a matter of prior knowledge to them.

Vigorous protests were registered with President Truman and Attorney General Tom Clark by the Mexican Consular Service, the League of United Latin American Citizens and other Mexican American Organizations, the Texas State Industrial Union Council —CIO, the American Federation of Labor, and a number of individual union heads.

The Mexican invasion continues. The number of wetbacks now in the state of Texas, according to reliable authorities, exceeds 100,000. Great as is the economic need of the Mexican workers in their own country, they are, on the whole, an humble group, and it is not conceivable that they would so openly and consistently violate the laws of two countries without strong encouragement from what cannot be called anything but a fifth column in Texas.

It should be abundantly clear from all the foregoing that the state of Texas cannot, or will not, do anything to stem the tide. The remedy must be administered by the federal government.

There can be no question but that our immigration policy and program on the Mexican border is bankrupt and a shocking disgrace to the entire country. Open connivance with private interests, at extreme variance with the public policies of two governments; overt violation of an international treaty; individual and collective insult to the dignity and sovereignty of a friendly and neighboring republic—these are sins on the part of a federal agency which cannot be overlooked or condoned.

Bear in mind that in this vicious progression—wetbacks displacing domestic agricultural labor and depressing wages; displaced agricultural workers invading towns and cities and, in turn, displacing workers in business and industry, at substandard wages, etc., etc.—

we have the pretty spectacle of the breakdown of our immigration system on the border interfering with the wage scales in both agriculture and industry for Anglos and Negroes as well as for Mexican Americans.

The recommendations which follow may very well revive (if, indeed, it has ever died down) the old battle cry of "states' rights." There is no better smoke screen for bigotry, or avarice, or failure. The state of Texas has had the "right," as well as the obligation, for at least fifty years to rectify the unsavory conditions under which its Mexican American population has always labored. Now the time has come when the implications, not to mention the stench, of those conditions reach far beyond the boundaries of the state.

First, I respectfully recommend that the President of the United States appoint a Presidential Commission, similar in composition to his Committee on Civil Rights, and instruct it to investigate, thoroughly and painstakingly, all aspects of this complex problem, from both the domestic and international standpoints. The conclusions and recomemndations of such a Commission would serve as a blueprint for action by the federal government.

Secondly, I urge the Congress of the United States to make the employment of illegal aliens a federal offense, punishable by a heavy fine and/or imprisonment. No other measure could so effectively and immediately terminate the flow of wetbacks across our borders. The wetback himself cannot be punished, except by informal deportation from which he rebounds like a rubber ball. So long as employers are crying for his services, he is coming across the river. Only the employer can be controlled by legislation, and it must be federal legislation. The powerful lobbies of the citrus, vegetable, and cotton growers' associations would kill such a bill in the embryo stage in the Texas legislature.

Concurrently, or beforehand, the U. S. Immigration and Naturalization Service, and the U. S. Employment Service, should be transferred to the U. S. Department of Labor to which they both, by their very nature belong.

So far as the Mexican American citizens and residents of Texas are concerned, nothing would go farther toward the solution of their economic problems and thereby the eventual solution of all their other problems, than an all-out organizing drive on the part of trade unions. Unity on any front, for any purpose, is something the Mexican Americans have been successfully prevented from achieving up to now. Organization is imperative if economic security is to be attained.

Increasingly, during the past few years, Mexican Americans have been accepted into trade unions all over Texas. But organized labor has been able to make almost no headway in the field where it is most desperately needed: in agriculture. Nor can organization be effected until the wetback—a potent weapon of fear and intimidation in the hands of the employer—is permanently disposed of. Once the wetback has been removed from the scene and the agricultural workers united in a strong trade union, corporate farms and other apparently soulless employers will find themselves forced to the collective bargaining table.

The mere mention of organized labor conjures up nameless terrors for some people. For the citrus and vegetable growers' association in the Valley, where the need for organized labor is perhaps most urgent, it hangs as the Sword of Damocles. This fear is understandable, for organized labor is the natural enemy of any feudal system.

But those who produce the citrus fruits, the vegetables, and the cotton of Texas, as well as the gentleman mentioned in the first paragraphs of this article, might much more profitably concern themselves with the real threat which lurks in the un-American conditions of life they are perpetuating (and ignoring) among the Mexican Americans in Texas. No longer ago than the summer of 1948 I had occasion to attend various meetings of Mexican Americans at widely separated points in Texas. These were workers' meetings. Those in attendance were, for the most part, United States citizens, many of them of the second or third generations. But they were, nevertheless, downtrodden, underprivileged people—people who had never had anything and who saw no prospect of making anything of themselves, the situation being as it is in Texas. Much of the conversation and most of the speeches were in Spanish, and my blood ran cold at the recurrence of such expressions as the "proletariat," the "masses," the "workers of the world," etc. These people were *not* Communists. They did not know it was the Communist line they were parroting. But their neverending frustrations had made them ripe for insidious Communist propaganda.

The simple logic of the thing is that, in a land of plenty, when one is deprived of an education, poverty-stricken, denied civil, social, and economic rights, and subjected to all manner of indignities, one automatically looks for relief from some quarter. To the uninformed and underprivileged, the Communist line sounds good, even when they have never heard of the Communist Party.

I agree that the slave-labor camps in the Soviet Union are a blot upon the face of the earth and should be eliminated. At the same time, I am much more concerned that the conditions in Texas which are rapidly preparing the soil in which communism can easily take root and flourish be corrected once and for all.

The magnitude of the problem of "wetbacks" has probably become more acute. In 1951 it was claimed that more than one million nationals of Mexico illegally entered the United States. Almost half a million of these people were arrested and deported. However, the number of Mexican laborers in the United States on approved contract was perhaps less than 150,000. It has been noted that when these "wetbacks" apply for work they have at least two strikes against them. They are technically fugitives from the law and they are forced to accept the employer's working and living conditions. Some of these workers have been known to accept jobs at from ten to twenty-five cents per hour. If these people are apprehended by American immigration officials, they may be sent back home—sometimes by airlift to a point a thousand miles South of the border.[29]

SUMMARY

At the present time the Mexican's statuses may be indicated as follows: (1) his social status is probably in the lowest quartile of a representative list of ethnic groups, if this is judged by the many negative attitudes expressed toward Mexicans, (2) his official legal status seems to be equal to that of the majority group, inasmuch as the Mexican is defined as "white" in most of these relationships; however, the Mexican finds himself discriminated against in many social situations and by the police, who accord him a low legal status, (3) his educational status is very modest in terms of formal schooling completed and ability to use the English language, and (4) his economic status is probably in the lowest quartile of ethnic groups in terms of pay rates and the low percentage of Mexicans in skilled jobs and the professions. In general, the Mexican is accorded a low status in the United States at the present time. However, the statuses reported in this chapter relate to the present situation. The chances seem very good that in the United States the general status of the Mexican will improve in the future.

PROBLEMS FOR STUDY AND DISCUSSION

1. List and distinguish the different types of Mexicans that reside in the United States at the present time.
2. List at least five of the attitudes that you have acquired concerning

29 From *The Commonweal* (Feb. 22, 1952), p. 485.

Mexicans, and analyze these attitudes showing the source, nature of, and validity of each.

3. Point out how the social status of Mexicans differs from that of the ethnic groups that have been discussed.

4. Explain why Mexicans seem to have a very low educational status when compared with other ethnic groups in the United States.

5. It is said that "Mexican labor is essential in the economic system of the United States." Explain why you think this statement to be true or false.

6. Make a list of the reasons why you think that Mexicans are accorded a low general status in the United States.

7. Outline a program that you think would aid in advancing the general status of Mexicans in the United States.

SELECTED READINGS

BOGARDUS, E. S., "Gangs of Mexican-American Youth," *Sociology and Social Research,* Vol. 28 (Sept., 1943), pp. 55-56.

BROOM, Leonard, and SHEVKY, Eshref, "Mexicans in the United States" *Sociology and Social Research,* Vol. 36 (Jan., 1952), pp. 150-160.

BROWN, Francis J., and ROUCEK, Joseph S., *One America* (New York: Prentice-Hall, Inc., 1952), pp. 350-355.

HANDMAN, M. S., "Economic Reasons for the Coming of the Mexicans," *American Journal of Sociology,* Vol. 35 (Jan., 1930), pp. 601-611.

JONES, R. C., *Mexican War Workers in the United States* (Washington, D. C.: Pan American Union, 1945).

KIBBE, Pauline R., *Latin Americans in Texas* (Albuquerque: University of New Mexico Press, 1946).

McWILLIAMS, Carey, *North from Mexico* (Philadelphia: J. B. Lippincott Company, 1949).

MARDEN, Charles F., *Minorities in American Society* (New York: American Book Company, 1952), pp. 128-154.

Migratory Labor in American Agriculture (Report of the President's Commission on Migratory Labor, 1951), 188 pp.

SANCHEZ, George I., *The Forgotten People: A Study of New Mexicans* (Albuquerque: University of New Mexico, 1940).

SCHERMERHORN, R. A., *These Our People* (Boston: D. C. Heath and Company, 1949), pp. 175-198.

TAYLOR, Paul S., *An American-Mexican Frontier* (Chapel Hill: University of North Carolina Press, 1934).

TUCK, Ruth, *Not With the Fist* (New York: Harcourt, Brace and Company, Inc., 1947).

WALTER, Paul A. F., Jr., *Race and Cultural Relations* (New York: McGraw-Hill Book Company, Inc., 1952), pp. 342-360.

IX

Indians

Introduction

WHEN WHITE Europeans arrived in the territory now known as the United States, they found a strange group of "red men" there to meet them. Without previous knowledge of this ethnic group, and because of its resemblance to known natives of India, they classified these strange people as "Indians." The introduction extended to white Europeans by this strange red group took many forms: in some instances it was hostility, in others it was one of curiosity, and in still others it was one of friendliness. All these forms of welcome were extended to the white Europeans in this land and were responded to in various ways. As McWilliams points out, many of the present reaction patterns toward minority groups can be traced to the early responses of white Europeans to the welcome that they received from this "odd" red group when they arrived in America.[1]

Two factors were important in determining the form of initial ethnic contacts that were established: (1) the nature and purposes of the white Europeans that came to the United States, and (2) the kind of tribe that was located in the area where white Europeans landed. Among the whites who came to America were groups of persons of widely different purposes and ambitions. Some were political and religious outcasts looking for a place where they could settle in a peaceful manner. Others were explorers seeking an area where they could add fame to their nation. And still others were wholly mercenary, and thus seeking a location where they could easily profit. These European groups, with varying purposes, found themselves in contact with several kinds of Indian tribes.

When white Europeans landed a number of Indian tribes inhab-

[1] Carey McWilliams, *Brothers Under the Skin* (Boston: Little, Brown and Company, 1944), p. 50.

ited America. These tribes were scattered throughout the territory destined to become the United States. Some of these Indian tribes were nomadic and roamed from area to area; others attempted to develop a stable home life. The tribes that developed a stable life concentrated in areas where waterways provided means for transportation, fishing, and a bountiful supply of plant and animal life. Thus, the early Europeans, arriving by water routes, had their first contact with Indians who had developed some stability in domicile. An early ambition of many white European settlers, therefore, was to find some means by which they could disturb this stability and acquire land from Indians who were then residing on it.

Several techniques were used by the Europeans in acquiring land from the Indian. In some areas, as in Virginia and Pennsylvania, cooperation and friendliness were used. In other areas, as in New York, land purchase was used. And in still other sections, as in the area surrounding the Great Lakes, intimidation and force were used. Each of these methods and many combinations of all of them were used indiscriminately by white Europeans in acquiring land from the Indian. In deciding on the method to be used in gaining land, little, if any, consideration was given to the welfare of the Indian or to the culture that he had developed. From the beginning it was thought that the Indian way of life was inferior, or that it provided an obstacle which had to be removed if civilization was to advance. Thus, the first basic pattern of ethnic relations in the United States was established in keeping with the will of one group: the early white European settlers. However, the Europeans who were establishing the pattern were ignorant concerning Indian life and culture and did very little, if anything, to become informed about the group with whom they were establishing contacts.[2]

As white Europeans moved westward, they carried with them the techniques previously mentioned, and used these as means by which they acquired more lands from the Indian. Although many techniques were used, most reports show that intimidation and force were employed more liberally than the other techniques. Not only did white Europeans use intimidation and force, but the westward movement served to increase the use of force among Indian tribes toward one another. Collier points out that the westward movement increased strife among Indian tribes as the whites usually pushed one tribe onto the hunting, fishing, and planting grounds of another

[2] *Ibid.,* pp. 51-53.

tribe.[3] The number of Indians in this country was decreased by two means. First, the lives of many thousands of Indians were expended through massacres and wars initiated by white Europeans. Then, too, as one Indian tribe was forced onto the territory of other Indian tribes, many intertribal conflicts served to contribute to the "killing off" process that was directed toward the Indian.

Many Indians who were not "killed off" started disappearing from the area then occupied by whites. Some of these disappeared into mountain and desert areas, where they thought they could avoid contact with whites. As the spearhead movement of European frontiersmen forced Indians to the north or south, many continued the northward movement by entering Canada and others continued to the south by migrating into Mexico. In both Canada and Mexico, Indians fared much better than they did in their former homes. Because of the "killing off" and disappearing processes, it is ironic to speak, as many do, about the "dying Indian." Rather, it would be more logical to refer to the exterminated or disappearing Indian.

The preceding sketch provides a background of the social situation out of which the early pattern of Indian-white relations evolved. Any critical examination of this sketch will show that the evolving pattern was not based on humane principles. Furthermore, it is easy to see that the early pattern was not the kind to initiate, or contribute to, a pattern of ethnic relations that one would expect to find in a democratic social order. *In other words, the early contacts of white Europeans and Indians contributed to the development of a pattern of ethnic relations that was very undemocratic in nature.*

The Indian Population

It is impossible to ascertain the size, distribution, and exact points of concentration of the Indian population at the time that the first white European settlers arrived in the geographic area now designated as the United States. The size of the Indian population, at that time, has been estimated as varying from 500,000 to several millions. As these were only loose estimates they are of little scientific value. However, the first census of Indians, made in 1860, accounted for 44,021 Indians as residents of the United States. To this number one could add the uncounted ones who lived in territories, or who had temporarily disappeared into mountain and desert areas and who

[3] John Collier, "United States Indian Administration as a Laboratory of Ethnic Relations," *Social Research,* Vol. 12 (Sept., 1945), p. 270.

reappeared at a later date when social and economic conditions had improved for Indians.

The Census Bureau and the Bureau of Indian Affairs use different criteria for classifying persons as Indians. For this reason it is difficult to determine the exact number of Indians in the United States at the present time. Recent reports, however, show a decided increase of the Indian population since 1860. In 1945 the Commissioner of Indian Affairs reported that 393,622 Indians resided in the United States. As shown in Table XXII, this population group is concentrated largely in ten states, with 87.1 per cent of the Indian population residing in these states. This concentration of the Indian population is further illustrated by the fact that 53.1 per cent resided in three states: Oklahoma, Arizona, and New Mexico in the order listed. However, the percentage of the Indian population to the total population is highest in Arizona, where Indians constituted 8.8 per cent of the total number in 1950. Thus, if the concentration of population is indicative of ethnic relation problems, emphasis on the Indian problems should be centered in the ten states listed in Table XXII, with special emphasis given to Oklahoma, Arizona, and New Mexico.

Table XXII: TEN STATES IN WHICH THE INDIAN POPULATION WAS CONCENTRATED, 1945 *

State	Number
Oklahoma †	110,864
Arizona	55,194
New Mexico	43,005
South Dakota	30,745
California	24,100
Montana	18,800
Minnesota	18,188
Washington	15,270
Wisconsin	13,780
North Dakota	12,863
Total in ten states	342,809
Per cent of total population	87.1

* United States Department of Interior, "Tables on Hospitals, Population, and School Census," *United States Indian Service*, Pamphlet III (1950), pp. 18-33.
† Includes population for members of the Five Civilized Tribes not residing in Oklahoma.

As with most ethnic groups in the United States, the present Indian population is very heterogeneous. It is a composite of approximately two hundred tribes, each with variations in language, customs, and physical appearance. Then too, as Indians have intermixed with whites and Negroes, the population classified as Indian includes persons with many degrees of mixed blood from these racial groups. Also, many persons from Canada and Mexico, with various mixtures of blood, were classified as Indian in the United States. Thus, the population classified as Indian is composed of persons with many degrees of mixed blood, derived from most of the racial and nationality groups that made up the total population.

For a better understanding of the concentration of the Indian population in the United States, some knowledge of Indian reservations is imperative. Indian reservations are geographic areas that have been set aside for Indians by the federal government and on which they reside under the supervision and partial control of the federal government. *These reservations provide a voluntary form of ethnic segregation sponsored by the federal government.* Indians have the right to select or refuse to live on these reservations, which are financed by the federal government, and supervised by one of its agencies.

In 1945 there were approximately two hundred reservations, located in 26 states in the United States.[4] Some 220,000 of the Indians lived on these reservations. This number represented almost 60 per cent of the Indians living in the United States at that time. Thus, the majority of the Indian population is concentrated on Indian reservations, which are racially segregated geographic areas. Because of this fact, there is very little contact between Indians and the majority of the population that inhabit the United States. This fact also indicates why the Indian is often omitted from discussions of ethnic problems in the United States. In addition, it indicates why most of the inhabitants of the country know very little about and give little consideration to the problems confronted by the Indians.

SOCIAL STATUS

It is difficult to determine accurately the social status of any group, but it is a more difficult task insofar as the Indian in the United States is concerned for at least two reasons: (1) most of the population has had little actual contact with Indians and (2) very few studies have been designed for the purpose of ascertaining the attitudes and opinions of other population groups toward Indians. The first of

[4] United States Department of the Interior, *Statistical Supplement to the Annual Report of the Commissioner of Indian Affairs* (June 30, 1945), pp. 4-13.

these reasons became more vivid to the authors as a result of several years' work in Oklahoma, the state embracing the largest number of Indians. Discussions with numerous residents of this state revealed that many had had no direct contact with Indians. This lack of contact was due to the fact that most Indians resided on reservations far removed from the more populous parts of the state, or resided in communities that were largely Indian in their make-up.

Without direct contact with Indians, the majority of the population of the United States must depend on literature and hearsay as their major source of information concerning the "red" man. Much of the literature that has been published on the Indian has been written by apologists for the Indian. As Strong points out, these apologists have glorified and glamorized the Indian to such an extent that the attitudes and opinions which one might develop from reading literature are more mythical than real.[5] In such literature it is probable that the opinion about the Indian has changed more during the past fifty years than it has changed toward any other minority group. A review of the literature published, concerning the Indian, during this period will show the following major changes: (1) instead of being regarded as sneaking savages, they are now often considered very brave; (2) instead of being a group to be exterminated, they are portrayed with forms of life and culture to be preserved and appreciated; and (3) instead of being a group incapable of becoming civilized, they are now recognized for having developed a civilization many centuries ago.

Specific attitudes and opinions of the majority group toward Indians have been expressed by several writers. These attitudes and opinions differ very much from those expressed in the previous paragraph. La Farge, a student of Indian life and former president of the American Association on Indian Affairs, states that the Indian is usually thought of as "a befeathered, half-human creature of unnatural dignity with a habit of saying 'ugh.' "[6] Locke and Stern point out that Indians are usually considered as inferior to whites, and in the same class with Negroes.[7] In our study of the attitudes of college students in the Southwest toward ethnic groups in the United States,

---

[5] Ester B. Strong, "The White Man and the Indian in the United States," *International Review of Missions,* Vol. 32 (April, 1943), pp. 141-155.

[6] O. La Farge, "Plea for a Square Deal for the Indian," *New York Times Magazine* (June 27, 1948), pp. 14-15.

[7] Alain Locke and B. J. Stern, *When People Meet: A Study in Race and Culture Contacts* (New York: Hinds, Hayden and Eldredge, Inc., 1946), p. 576.

we found the following attitudes to predominate in the order listed:[8] (1) are very brave, (2) are artistic, (3) are peaceful and friendly, (4) are loyal and trustworthy, and (5) are ignorant people. These five statements were selected from forty statements as the expressions most descriptive of Indians by more than 50 per cent of 1,672 white college students.

Table XXIII: RANK OF THE INDIAN AS REFLECTED BY STUDIES OF ETHNIC GROUPS IN THE UNITED STATES *

Conductor of Study	Year of Study	No. of Respondents	Classification of Respondents	No. of Population Groups Included	Rank of the Indian
Bogardus	1926	1,725	Stratified sampling of the U. S.	36	21
Bogardus	1946	1,950	As above	36	24
McDonagh & Richards	1947	100	White college students in Oklahoma	16	7
McDonagh & Richards	1947	100	Negro college students in Oklahoma	16	4
Richards	1946-47	1,672	White college students in Okla., Ark., La. and Tex.	9	5
Richards	1946-47	337	Negro college students in Ark., Okla., and Texas	9	8

* Bogardus, *op. cit.*, p. 58.
McDonagh and Richards. An unpublished study conducted among 200 college students in Oklahoma.
Richards, *op. cit.*, p. 26.

Table XXIII reports the rankings for the Indian as compared with other ethnic groups, and as reported in a number of studies. The study by Bogardus was based on his social distance scale, which was planned to measure the amount of sympathetic understanding the evaluators would accord the average members of a number of ethnic, religious, and occupational groups.[9] In the part of his study that was

8 Eugene S. Richards, "Attitudes of College Students in the Southwest toward Ethnic Groups in the United States," *Sociology and Social Research*, Vol. 35 (Sept.-Oct., 1950), p. 25.
9 Emory S. Bogardus, "A Social Distance Scale," *Sociology and Social Research*, Vol. 17 (Jan.-Feb., 1933), pp. 265-271.

concerned with ethnic groups, thirty-six groups were used.[10] In this study, rank 1 denotes the highest degree of social nearness and the highest social status, rank 36 the greatest degree of social farness and the lowest social status. In the 1926 report Indians ranked twenty-first from the top, and in the 1946 report they ranked twenty-fourth from the top. *These rankings denote a high degree of social farness, thus a low social status for Indians in the United States.*

The unpublished study by McDonagh and Richards was exploratory in nature and was conducted to gain insight concerning the reaction of college students in Oklahoma toward sixteen racial and nationality groups.[11] This was a social distance study, and the scale used was a modified form of the scale that Bogardus had developed. The scores accorded the Indian by both groups were practically the same (1.87 for white students and 1.83 for Negro students), but indicated definite social distance between the Indian and both groups. White students ranked six groups above the Indian: Irish, Scotch, French, Russian, German, and English. Negro students ranked three groups above the Indian: Negro, Mulatto, and Filipino. In other words, white students ranked members of white ethnic groups above the Indian, while Negro students ranked members of other colored ethnic groups above them. Thus, according to this sample, the Indian has a moderate social status among both groups. It is below that of several racial and ethnic groups, but above that of many other groups.

The findings in Richards' study were based on the extent to which college students evaluated twenty statements that had been rated as negative, and twenty statements that had been rated as positive by a number of sociologists and psychologists. The rankings in this study were based on the predominance of the positive or negative statements that were checked by the students. Among the nine groups used, Indians were ranked in fifth place by white students, and in eighth place by Negro students.[12] The findings of this study also indicate a low social status for the Indian.

The studies cited point out that the Indian is accorded a somewhat low social status by population groups in the United States. The Indian is not placed in the lowest social status by any of the

[10] E. S. Bogardus, "Changes in Racial Distance," *International Journal of Opinion and Attitude Research,* Vol. 1, pp. 55-62 (Dec., 1947), p. 58.

[11] Approximately 100 students from each of two institutions were used in the sample: the University of Oklahoma for whites, and Langston University for Negroes.

[12] Richards, *op. cit.,* p. 26.

groups responding; however, in most of the studies cited the Indian is placed in the lower half of the racial and ethnic groups included.

LEGAL STATUS

The legal status of the Indian has been and is different from that of any other ethnic group residing within the boundaries of the United States. The first difference is determined by the place of birth of Indians. If they were born in Mexico, they are usually granted the legal status of Mexicans; if they were born in India, they acquire the legal status of Asiatics; and, if they were born in the United States, they have a legal status that is different from that of any other group residing in the United States. In our discussion, foreign-born Indians will be eliminated, and attention will be centered on those Indians who were born in and now live in the United States.

Throughout the history of the United States, Indians born in the nation, or territory now included in the United States, have remained largely outside the bounds of state and local laws. The original Federal Constitution granted Congress the right to regulate all relations with Indian tribes. According to this provision, the tribes were placed in a position similar to that of foreign nations. At first this was advantageous to the Indian, since it removed him from the orbit of the many illogical and discriminatory laws that had been passed by state and local governments. Because of this advantage, most Indians found it best to maintain tribal membership, but in accepting this tribal membership they were denied citizenship and naturalization rights in the United States. The legal status that they did possess was within the tribe, or depended on treaties made between the tribes and the federal government. It is difficult to determine the legal status of Indians within the tribe since this varied much among tribes. However, it is possible to imagine to some extent the nature of the early treaties made with Indian tribes by the federal government by recalling that the Indian Bureau, the agency that was responsible for treaties with Indian tribes, was under the War Department from 1824 to 1849.

The policy of making treaties with Indian tribes continued to 1871, when Congress prohibited further treaty-making with tribes. Thereafter, many judicial opinions were rendered that involved the legal staus of the Indian.[13] The prevailing idea of these opinions

13 See Milton R. Konvitz, *The Alien and the Asiatic in American Law* (Ithaca: Cornell University Press, 1946), pp. 110-114, for a discussion on this point.

placed the Indian in a very peculiar legal status. Although born in the United States, he was declared ineligible for citizenship or naturalization rights—the Fourteenth Amendment did not apply to Indians born in the United States. In keeping with the treaty-making power of Congress with Indians, citizenship or naturalization rights could be granted only if Congress enacted legislation granting them these rights. In 1924 Congress passed an act granting citizenship rights to all Indians born in the United States before or after the passage of the act.[14] This act was augmented by a judicial decision of the Arizona Supreme Court in 1928, when it decreed that citizenship was compatible with the wardship that the federal government exercises over Indians [15] and by the Nationality Code of 1940. Hence, according to law and judicial decision, all Indians born in and now living in the United States are legal citizens of the United States. *However, the citizenship of the Indian is different from that of any other group born in the United States in that it is based on an act of Congress, while the citizenship status of other groups born in this country is based on the Federal Constitution.*

With the establishment of the Indian Bureau in 1824, the federal government adopted a policy of federal responsibility for the welfare of the Indian. The interpretation of this welfare policy has varied from time to time. During the period when the Indian Bureau was under the Department of War, physical subjugation was the chief interpretation given to Indian welfare. Since the transference of the Indian Bureau to the Department of Interior, a new interpretation of "Indian Welfare" has evolved. In 1946 Brophy, then Commissioner of Indian Affairs, pointed out this change by defining the control exercised by the federal government over Indians as a wardship over certain kinds of Indian property and not over his person. *Regardless of this change in the interpretation of Indian welfare, Indian reservations still provide a form of ethnic segregation and subject Indians to several legal limitations.*

As the legal status of the Indian in the United States is closely tied up with the regulations of the federal government, some knowledge of the program of the federal government is essential. To provide this source of information the following reading by Brophy is presented which outlines the legal status of the Indian in the eyes of the federal government.

[14] 43 *U. S. Statute* 253 (1924).
[15] *Porter v. Hall,* 34 Arizona 308.

THE FEDERAL GOVERNMENT AND THE INDIAN [16]

WILLIAM A. BROPHY

Throughout the country, and particularly in the East, where Indians are a rarity, there are many unfortunate misapprehensions as to the status of our Indian citizens. Please note that word "citizens," for it is important. In 1924, Congress passed a law providing that all Indians born within the Continental United States were American citizens as of that date, and, of course, all Indians born since that time are automatically American citizens. Furthermore, the Supreme Court has held that citizenship is compatible with the wardship which the United States exercises over the Indians, the result being that there is no question whatever as to the Indians' citizenship. . . .

The terms "wards of the Government" and "wardship" also need clarification. They do not mean that the Federal Government can control the actions of an Indian in the sense that a legal guardian can control the actions of a child who is his ward. The term "ward" was first used by Chief Justice Marshall as an analogy—the relationship between the Federal Government and an Indian tribe, he said, was *like* that between a guardian and his ward. Note, however, that it was the various tribes and *not* the individual Indians which occupied a position similar to that of a ward. This distinction is important to keep in mind even today.

The Government has no more control over the comings and goings and everyday activities of an individual Indian than it does over any other individual person. Wardship applies not to the person of an Indian but rather to certain types of his property, particularly land. This arises from the fact that most Indian land today was tribal land to begin with, and the trusteeship which the Government exercised over the tribe and its possessions was extended to the individual when the land was individualized. This means that the tribe or the individual cannot sell or otherwise dispose of the land without the consent of the Secretary of the Interior, who is the official charged with exercising the trust. This same restriction applies to certain funds which are on deposit in the United States Treasury in a trust status and which, in most cases, were derived from the sale of Indian assets. These funds bear interest and both the principal and

[16] William A. Brophy, "Story of the Indian Service." An address delivered before the employees of the Department of the Interior (Aug. 29, 1946). Used by permission of the U. S. Department of the Interior.

interest can be used by the Indians for purposes approved by the Secretary of the Interior. It should also be carefully noted that the Government itself cannot use these funds for any purpose without the approval of the Indians concerned.

The lands and funds which are held in trust are commonly called *restricted*. But some of the Indians also possess *unrestricted* lands and funds, over which the Government has no control, and which they may sell or dispose of at will. And, of course, an Indian may possess both restricted and unrestricted property. For example an Indian who lives on a reservation which is restricted land may also own a lot and house in a neighboring city in the same manner as a non-Indian.

Inasmuch as "wardship" applies to the property rather than to the person of an Indian, it follows that he is free to live and work wherever he may choose, subject only to the restrictions that apply to all of us. Contrary to a widespread misunderstanding, the Government cannot and does not require them to live on reservations. If a Navajo Indian, for instance, decides that he would like to live in Washington or in New York City, he is perfectly free to do so. The reasons why most of them have preferred to stay on the reservations up until now are precisely the same reasons why many rural-born people remain in the communities of their birth. These reasons are in part economic and in part sentimental. During the recent war, however, thousands of Indians left the reservations to enter war work, and many of them will continue to live away from the reservations. We in the Indian Service try to encourage this trend toward outside employment because there is not enough land in the reservations to provide a living for the ever-increasing Indian population.

Keeping in mind the position of the Indian today, let us review briefly the historical development of Indian policy in the United States. While the problem of Indian-non-Indian relationships started with the arrival of the first European settlers, I shall limit my discussion for now to the period since the American Revolution. It was realized by the drafters of the Constitution that they should include some provisions for dealing with the Indian tribes. Thus the Constitution provides that all relations with the Indian tribes and nations are the concern of the Federal Government and not of the individual states. The many treaties entered into by the United States acknowledged the sovereignty of Indian tribes and the possessory rights in the lands which the tribes occupied. However, between 1800 and 1820, a period during which the United States acquired vast areas of new territory from France and Spain, there developed a tendency to deny the sovereignty of Indian tribes and to deal with them by force of arms. This tendency was marked by the establishment in 1824 of an Indian Office as a part of the War Department.

Although the United States continued until 1871 to make treaties with the Indians, most of them were written at the end of a war or under the threat of military action, and they generally contained large cessions of land to the United States. But even then the white settlers were not satisfied, with the result that the treaties were violated and the Indians dispossessed of additional tracts which the treaties had supposedly guaranteed to them.

This harsh treatment of the Indians was the principal cause of the costly and scandalous Indian wars which occurred during most of the 19th century. About 1870, it was estimated that it had cost the Government more than $1,000,000 for every Indian killed. The wars were followed, moreover, by innumerable claims against the United States, many of which have never been adjudicated to this day. I am glad to say, however, that just this month, President Truman signed the Indians Claims Commission Bill, which we believe will go far toward settling these longstanding claims. But more about this Commission later.

As the number and intensity of Indian wars decreased, the Government adopted another policy, more subtle but equally demoralizing, of dispossessing the Indian. This was the Allotment Act of 1887, under which tribal reservations were divided into individual allotments of land. On most reservations where allotment took place, lands not designated for individual ownership were classed as "surplus" and opened for homesteading by non-Indians, resulting in the immediate alienation of some 20,000,000 acres of Indian lands. Thousands of allotments were subsequently bought by white men with varying degrees of fairness to the Indians. This system not only further decreased the Indians' land base, but completely disrupted community and family life, both of which are of great significance in Indian culture. In an effort to assimilate the Indian, the Government suppressed or discouraged his languages, religious ceremonies, arts and crafts, and other traditions of Indian culture.

The allotment policy was accompanied by an increase of white superintendents, farm agents, teachers, and missionaries, who superseded Indian leaders. The Indian Office, which had been transferred from the War Department to the Department of the Interior in 1849, maintained an autocratic rule over the Indians under a constantly increasing but never correlated series of statutes. The conduct of Indian affairs sank to a shameful level—graft among the officials and misery among the Indians were both widespread. Indian religions were forbidden and it was acknowledged that Indians were entitled to the constitutional guarantees of liberty of conscience. The prevailing thought was that death and assimilation would soon obliterate the Indian and that his land holdings should be liquidated.

A few tribes fortunately were able for various reasons to escape the allotment policy. These tribes, located chiefly in the Southwest, have maintained their lands and chosen method of life relatively intact. The difference between their condition today and that of the other reservations is evidence of the folly of the allotment policy.

In the 1920's the people of the United States gradually became aware of the shortcomings of their Indian policy, and two important surveys were made as a basis for improving conditions. These paved the way for the Indian Reorganization Act of 1934, which is the legal basis of the Indian Service policy which has been in effect since that time. The principal provisions of this Act are as follows:

1. Stops the breaking up of Indian reservations and protects the remaining Indian land from further loss.

2. Restores to Indian ownership land which had originally been within reservations and later opened to white homesteaders but which had not actually been homesteaded.

3. Enables tribes to organize themselves for their mutual benefit, to enjoy self-government under Federal guardianship, and to incorporate for business purposes.

4. Establishes an education loan fund to enable gifted Indians to receive advanced education.

5. Establishes a special Civil Service for Indians to facilitate their working in the Indian Service.

6. Authorizes purchases of additional lands for Indians.

7. Establishes a revolving loan fund to provide needed credit for Indian tribes.

It is important to note that acceptance of the Indian Reorganization Act by the Indians was voluntary and was decided in a secret-ballot election held by each tribe. A large majority, but not all of the tribes, decided to organize under the Act and are now operating under their own constitutions.

As an indication of the contribution which the Indians are making to our national life, let me summarize their activities in the war:

The record of the American Indian in World War II is impressive. In the spring of 1945 there were approximately 22,000 Indians in the Army, 2,000 in the Navy, 120 in the Coast Guard, and 720 in the Marine Corps. These figures do not include officers for whom statistics are not available.

Indians were in the fighting on all our battle fronts from Iwo Jima to Salerno. In all theaters they distinguished themselves. The Indian Office has recorded the following awards to Indians: 71 awards of the Air Medal; 51 of the Silver Star; 47 of the Bronze Star;

34 of the Distinguished Flying Cross, and two of the Congressional Medal of Honor. There are undoubtedly many more which have not been recorded. The casualty lists are long. There were many Indians in the prison camps of the Philippines after the fall of Bataan and Corregidor. Pfc. Ira B. Hayes, a full-blood Pima Indian, was one of the six Marines in the famous flag-raising incident on Mount Suribachi at Iwo Jima.

The Indians at home also have a fine record which matches that of their fighting men. More than 40,000 left the reservations during each of the war years to take jobs in ordnance depots, aircraft factories, on the railroads, and in other war industries. The older men, the women, and the children who stayed at home increased their production of food in spite of the lack of help. Indians invested more than $17,000,000 of restricted funds in war bonds, and their individual purchases probably amount to twice that amount.

It is a superb record of which the Indians may well be proud.

Turning now to the Indian Service as it is today, I think that probably no other bureau in the Department, or perhaps even in the whole Federal Government, encompasses such a wide variety of activities as the Indian Office, ranging as they do from health, education and welfare on the one hand to irrigation, road building and construction on the other. For it is our responsibility to provide for the Indians of this country almost all of those services and facilities which are ordinarily provided for the non-Indian population by the Federal, State, and local governments. In many instances, of course, we work with other Federal and State agencies in carrying out our duties, and we certainly could not do it all by ourselves, but the fact remains that we are charged by treaty and legislation with the primary responsibility of all government activity on Indian reservations.

The best way to explain the work of an agency is to describe briefly the work of each division. So let us start out with:

1. *The Medical Division.* The activities of this division fall into three categories—general hospitals, tuberculosis sanatoria, and field medical service. When medical aid was first offered to the Indians, many of them hesitated to accept it principally because it was so unfamiliar. Gradually, however, as they noted the favorable results, many have come to depend upon it. Today the demand for hospital care far exceeds hospital facilities. Indian Service doctors and nurses are working particularly hard on the cure and prevention of tuberculosis and trachoma, to both of which the Indian is peculiarly susceptible. Definite progress is being made against these two diseases, although there is still a long fight ahead. The Indian death rate has been steadily falling as a result of better medical care. Equally

significant is the well-established fact that as the health of a group improves, so does its ability to provide for its own needs and to improve its standard of living. Thus the medical program is basic to the success of the whole Indian Service program of helping the Indians to reestablish their rightful place in the nation.

2. *Education Division.* The Indian Service operates two types of schools for Indian children—day schools, which are located on the reservations and include the elementary grades and some vocational training, and boarding schools, many of them located in towns outside the reservations, which are comparable to high schools. Formerly there were only boarding schools, but about twenty years ago, there began a trend toward day schools in order to let the younger children live with their parents and to permit more children to attend school. Although the results have been more than justified, there has been a limiting factor in the use of day schools. Roads must be built for the school buses which are needed to bring the children in from outlying districts. Roads are, unfortunately, very expensive to build and maintain, and our appropriations for them have not been sufficient to build all that are needed. Therefore, we are now experimenting with the system of providing small dormitories at existing day schools to care for those children who cannot walk or be brought by bus to school each day because of the lack of roads.

It is significant to note that the recent war caused a greater incentive for education on the part of many Indians. Having realized how necessary it is to have training for better jobs, they have taken a new interest in their own education and that of their children.

There are many special problems in Indian education, such as the fact that many of the children can speak only their native tongue when they come to school and must be taught to speak English before they can learn to read and write. Then, also, there is the problem raised by the desire of some children to return to their reservations where vocational training would be most valuable, while others wish to take advanced courses and hence need more courses in the liberal arts. Research is constantly being carried out in an endeavor to improve Indian education.

Wherever possible, we contract with local non-Indian schools to permit the attendance of Indian children. But since in many communities there are no other schools, we must continue to provide this vital service.

3. *Welfare Division.* This division has a variety of functions roughly similar to those of welfare agencies in urban and rural non-Indian communities, in addition to special services which are peculiar to the Indians by reason of their economic condition, mode of living, social customs, etc. The employees of the Welfare Division

take care of child welfare and family case work and assist Indians in presenting their claims to Federal and State agencies such as Social Security and the Army and Navy (for dependents of service men). They assist returning veterans and their families and help Indians obtain employment. This division is also responsible for direct relief to needy and destitute Indians who have no other source of such assistance. There is, on the whole, very little direct relief, and the grants of this nature which are made are pitifully inadequate in these days of high prices.

The Welfare Division likewise handles law and order, which is a complex problem, not because there are many crimes but because the lines between federal, state, and tribal jurisdictions are not clear in all cases. In general, however, tribal courts handle offenses on Indian lands other than ten major crimes, which are subject to Federal jurisdiction. But when an Indian is outside a reservation, he is subject to state law as are other individuals. The chief law and order problems with respect to Indians arise from the Federal prohibition against the sale or gift of liquor to Indians. It is my opinion that Indians should be permitted to buy liquor outside reservations and we are hoping to change the law.

Let us now turn to the Resources Branch of the Indian Service, which includes the Divisions of Forestry and Range Management, Extension, Soil and Moisture Conservation, and Land Acquisition. Although these divisions are obviously interrelated, I shall mention each division as a unit.

4. *Forestry and Range Management.* The fact that the great majority of Indian lands are in either range or forest makes this a very important division of the Indian Service. It has the tremendous responsibility of helping the Indian utilize these resources on a perpetual-yield basis.

Proper range management is no easy task on a reservation such as the Navajo, where the Indians are almost completely dependent upon their livestock. When the first range surveys were made about 12 years ago, it was found that the reservation was more than 100 percent overstocked. The land, which had never been rich, was being overgrazed and consequently eroded so badly that it had long since reached the point of diminishing returns. Therefore, a range-management program was instituted by the tribe with the guidance of the Indian Service range experts. The results of the last decade have been definitely favorable, but much more work lies ahead before the Navajo range land is stabilized. Similar problems exist on every other reservation in the West. Wherever possible, the Indian Service cooperates with the Bureau of Land Management, the Forest Service and other agencies concerned with the conservation of our natural resources. The Indians have no monopoly on critical areas, but they do have some of the worst lands in the United States, because of the unfortunate tendency in the past to relegate them to the lands which no one else wanted.

5. *Extension Division.* Extension work is the name commonly applied to the service extended to Indian farmers. The service is similar to that supplied by County Extension Agents throughout the country and includes advice and guidance on all types of agricultural undertaking. Improvement of farm methods, crop rotation, the use of fertilizers and machinery are but a few of the fields in which the Extension Division works.

This Division is also responsible for the credit system of the Indian Service. Indian farmers like all others need credit facilities. Since they cannot post as collateral any property or land in a trust status, they have more difficulty than non-Indians in obtaining credit from commercial banks. Hence the government has established a revolving credit fund which has been used extensively by the Indians. And I am glad to say that there is an extremely low rate of delinquency—about 3½ percent.

6. *Soil and Moisture Conservation.* This Division is part of a Department wide program of soil and moisture conservation. It is extremely important work which must be maintained and expanded for the protection of these vital resources.

7. *Land Acquisition.* The land acquisition program of the Indian Service has been an integral part of our whole plan of rehabilitation. Inasmuch as the great majority of Indians are dependent on the land, and huge areas had been taken from them, their remaining land base was totally inadequate. Hence an extensive program was undertaken to restore a part of this essential. The lands have been obtained in several different ways. Although the Congress has appropriated some funds for this purpose, most of the money used has been tribal funds held in trust by the United States.

Where land could not be bought, we have had some success in arranging long-term leases from states, railroads, and private individuals. There has also been a large-scale program of land exchange. Those of you who know the Western range, realize that it is not economically sound to utilize small, isolated tracts. Large consolidated areas are needed on which it is profitable to build fences, drill wells, and make other improvements. Consequently, we have helped the Indians work out trades which are advantageous to all parties concerned. Each purchase, lease, or exchange involves a great deal of time-consuming and detailed work. I know of a tract in New Mexico where the title was so complex that several hundred people had to consent before the purchase could be consummated. We are making progress, however, and every acre helps some Indian family support itself.

Lastly we come to the Engineering Branch, which is made up of the Irrigation, Roads, and Construction Divisions. Each of these plays a vital role, which I shall outline very briefly.

8. *Irrigation Division.* On a great many of the Indian reservations, little farming would be possible without irrigation. Indians were irrigating, of course, long before there was any Indian Service. But as systems have been enlarged and the limited supply of water more and more in demand, it has been necessary to construct dams and canals on a large scale. The irrigation engineers of the Indian Service provide the technical plans, supervision, and heavy equipment for those large projects although the labor is performed by the Indians. This service is comparable to that provided by the Bureau of Reclamation on non-Indian projects.

9. *Roads Division.* This division supervises the construction and maintenance of thousands of miles of roads and hundreds of bridges on Indian reservations. These are the life lines without which the other division could not operate. Their importance to our school system has already been brought out. At present, we are building so-called "access" roads over which timber can be hauled to the mills where it will be processed for use in the national housing program. These roads have been requested by the National Housing Authorities and carry a very high priority.

10. *Construction Division.* To carry on its many and varied activities, the Indian Service has several thousand buildings of different types: schools, dormitories, hospitals, offices, employees' quarters, garages, and numerous other structures. An essential adjunct of these are the electricity, water supply, sewage disposal, and telephone systems. The construction and maintenance of such buildings and utilities are the responsibility of our Construction Division. You can well realize what a difficult job it has now, when materials are so scarce and costs so high. Yet the schools and hospitals must operate, and they do operate, thanks to this division.

To complete the picture of the legal status of the Indian in the United States, it is necessary to note the ways by which the federal legal status of the Indian is modified by several of the states. As late or 1945 Armstrong reported that suffrage rights in Idaho, New Mexico, and Washington were denied to Indians because of constitutional provisions forbidding suffrage to Indians not taxed, and in Arizona because of a law denying the ballot to persons under guardianship.[17] However, in 1947 the United States Supreme Court ruled that all states must grant the Indian full privileges of citizenship. A few years earlier Mangum reported laws in North Carolina, North Dakota, and South Dakota that made possible separate schools for Indians.[18] Also, the marriage of white and Indians has been prohibited in Arizona, Georgia, North Carolina, and South Carolina; and Louisiana and Oklahoma prohibited the marriage of Negroes and Indians.[19] Hence, in at least nine states the activities of the Indian have been or are now restricted by law in some way. In 1940 these states were inhabited by more than two-thirds of the Indians residing in the United States. Thus, to the property restrictions of the federal government we must add the suffrage, educational, and marriage restrictions of the several states if we are to have a clear view of the legal status of the Indian in the United States. Because of the present campaign to extend civil rights to all minority groups, many of these restrictions are in the process of being recinded. However, since it is not probable that these prohibitions will be removed very soon in all of the states where they exist, these restrictions must be kept in mind to comprehend the legal status of the Indians in the United States at the present time.

EDUCATIONAL STATUS

Several factors have served to retard the educational status of the Indian in the United States.[20] First and foremost among these was the great cultural variation that existed between early European settlers and the Indian. From the beginning, European settlers attempted, with little success, to indoctrinate the Indian with European culture. *After a voluntary plan of indoctrination failed, forceful attempts were made to "stamp out" the Indian culture and to substitute a European culture.* In carrying out this attempt, Indian schools were patterned after white schools, and Indian children were moved from their homes to boarding schools at six years of age and kept there through adolescence.[21] In these boarding schools the use of the native

[17] O. K. Armstrong, "Set the Indian Free," *Reader's Digest*, Vol. 47, No. 47-52 (August, 1945), p. 49.

[18] Charles S. Mangum, Jr., *The Legal Status of the Negro* (Chapel Hill: University of North Carolina Press, 1940), pp. 83-85.

[19] *Ibid.*, p. 253.

[20] For an intensive treatment of this problem, see Evelyn G. Adams, *American Indian Education* (New York: King's Crown Press, 1946), 122 pp.

[21] John Collier, "United States Indian Administration as a Laboratory of Ethnic Relations," *Social Research*, Vol. 12 (Sept., 1945), p. 271.

language and the teaching of Indian religion were banned. At first
these schools were conducted by missionaries representing several
religious groups. In 1819, with the appropriation of the Civilization
Fund, the federal government started a program leading toward federal responsibility for the education of Indians. The educational
program started by mission schools was continued in the early schools
established by the federal government.

Adams points out that Indians now attend many types of schools.[22]
As reported in Table XXIV, they attend schools that are organized

Table XXIV: SCHOOL ATTENDANCE OF INDIAN CHILDREN 6 TO 18 YEARS OF AGE
BY TYPES OF SCHOOLS AND BY NUMBER AND PER CENT *

Type of School	Number	Per Cent
Public Schools	36,215	34.9
Federal Government Boarding and Day Schools	33,300	32.0
Mission and Private Schools	8,000	7.7
Not Attending School	18,400	17.7
Information not Available	8,055	7.7
Grand Total	103,970	100.0

* *1951 Annual Report of the Secretary of the Interior*, p. 359.

especially for Indians such as the nonreservation boarding schools,
the reservation boarding schools, and day schools that are maintained
by the federal government. Others attend mission schools that have
been established by religious organizations with or without federal
or tribal aid. Still others attend public schools along with children of
other ethnic groups. Most of the schools attended by Indians are supported by the federal government, or the government grants per
capita fees for students attending public, private, or mission schools.
Thus, it appears as though Indian children have an advantage over
some other population groups in so far as educational facilities are
concerned. In addition to their special educational facilities, Indians
may also use the public school facilities that are available to other
children.

Many opportunities are open to Indians for higher and technical
education.[23] Haskell Institute, a government school for Indians in
Lawrence, Kansas, offers work on the college and technical levels.
Many universities in the United States offer special scholarships to
Indians. Several organizations and clubs offer financial aid and
scholarships to Indians who are interested in higher and technical

22 *Ibid.*, pp. 80-84.
23 Adams, *op. cit.*, pp. 82-83.

education. The Indian Reorganization Act of 1934, and several sub-sequent acts by the Federal Legislature, made available a sizable amount for higher and technical education. Also, some federal loans that are reimbursable are available to Indian students. Then, too, in some states all colleges and universities will admit Indians as students. In Oklahoma, where education in many professional and technical areas are closed to Negroes, Indians are admitted to all white colleges and universities.

The number of school years completed by Indians over 25 years of age, as compared with the school years completed by two other population groups, is shown in Table XXV. This table indicates

Table XXV: NUMBER OF SCHOOL YEARS COMPLETED BY ALL POPULATION GROUPS, NATIVE-WHITES AND INDIANS OVER 25 YEARS OF AGE IN THE UNITED STATES BY PER CENTS *

Years of School	All Population Groups	Native White	Indian
None	3.7	1.3	25.2
Elementary			
1-4 years	9.8	6.1	18.3
5 & 6 years	11.4	9.7	15.8
7 & 8 years	34.6	36.0	21.4
High School			
1-3 years	15.0	17.3	9.4
4 years	14.1	16.6	4.9
College			
1-3 years	5.4	6.6	1.9
4 or more years	4.6	5.4	.8
No report	1.4	1.1	2.3

* Sixteenth Census of the United States, *Population* (1940), Vol. II, Part 1, p. 52.

that the Indian has a very low educational status when compared with other population groups. In 1940 more than one-fourth of the Indians over 25 years of age were without any schooling. On the other extreme, only .8 per cent of the Indians had completed four years or more of college work, as compared with 4.6 per cent for all population groups in the United States. Ethnic groups with more than eight years of schooling in percentages were 17 per cent for the Indian and 39.1 per cent for all population groups in the United States. *The percentage of no schooling for the Indian was more than double that of any other population group in the United States, while the percentage with four or more years of college work was much smaller for the Indian than for any other population group.* The small percentage (.8%) with four or more years of college training seems to suggest that very few Indians have pursued higher and professional training.

Two conclusions are evident from the data presented on the educational status of the Indian in the United States: (1) the availability of educational facilities for the Indian is equal to that of most and superior to that of some ethnic groups and (2) Indians have not used and are not using these facilities to advance their educational status. The first conclusion is justifiable, since special Indian schools are available and Indians are also admitted to most of the schools available to the majority ethnic group.

The data presented indicate that the educational status of the Indian was lower than that of other large ethnic groups in the United States. It is recognized that many factors have aided in discouraging the educational advancement of the Indian. Among these factors are: (1) the lack of encouragement by the in-groups as well as the out-groups, (2) restricted occupational opportunities, and (3) the fact that the educational program available has been adapted recently to the interests and needs of the Indian.[24] Regardless of these discouragements, the data presented, and other data that will follow, are sufficient to support the conclusion that the educational status of the Indian is lower than that of any other ethnic group compared in this study.

ECONOMIC STATUS

The Indian is, and has been, from an economic standpoint, perhaps the most mistreated ethnic group in the United States. European settlers took the best land away from the Indian, and at the same time attempted to force him to change the economic system that he had followed for many generations. The extent to which the Indian was deprived of the best land and forced onto worthless land is illustrated by the present condition of the Navajos.[25] The Navajos are now living on a desert or semidesert reservation in Arizona, consisting of around 20 million acres of land. The land on which more than 60,000 Navajos live is unproductive, and could not support more than 5,000 whites.[26] On this unproductive and unbroken land it was

24 *Ibid.*, pp. 84-93.
25 LaFarge, *op. cit.*, p. 10.
26 Collier, *op. cit.*, pp. 286-287. See the statement on the Navajos by Paul A. F. Walter, Jr., *Race and Cultural Relations* (New York: McGraw-Hill Book Company, Inc., 1952), pp. 269-275.

expected that a people inexperienced in competitive agriculture and intensive use of land could develop a self-sufficing economy.[27] Collier indicates that the condition of the Navajos is common among Indian tribes throughout the United States, by pointing out that four fifths of the residual Indian land is unusable or of little value in so far as potential yield is concerned.[28]

Besides taking the best land away from the Indian, many attempts were made to force a complete change of his economic system. Under tribal conditions the Indian lived under an economic system that was more communalistic than anything else. In this economic system individualism was reduced to a minimum and the welfare of the tribe predominated. The allotment Act of 1887 supplemented this economic system with a form of free enterprise based on the individual allotment of land to Indians. According to Brophy, this change was too abrupt and served to demoralize tribal, community, and family life among Indians, all of which were very important factors in their economic system.[29] Thus, the Indian has had many handicaps to overcome in an attempt to become adjusted to the economic system by which he is culturally surrounded in the United States.

At the present time there are three major economic classes among Indians in the United States: (1) those who have acquired a modest degree of wealth in some way, (2) those who live on reservations and are under the guardianship of the federal government, and (3) those who have lost their land after allotment and are now living off reservations. The wealthiest are those who have oil land or good ranches; are business men, politicians, or professional men; or have acquired success as artists, especially as actors. As Strong points out, there are few Indians in this class as compared with the great number who live in extreme poverty.[30] If the 4,000 or more Indians who are employed in various professional and clerical occupations under the Indian Service are included in the first class, it is conservative to estimate that those in this class would not amount to more than 5 per cent of the Indian population in the United States.

The largest number of Indians are included in class 2, those who live on reservations. Almost 60 per cent of all Indians living in the United States are in this class. The income and sources of income

27 A. C. Cooley, "Extension Work Among Indians," *Indians at Work,* Vol. 13 (May-June, 1945), pp. 2-5.
28 Collier, *op. cit.,* p. 273.
29 Brophy, *loc. cit.*
30 Strong, *op. cit.,* p. 144.

of this group, for 1944, are reported in Table XXVI. The earned
income of this group is derived largely from wages and agriculture.
The greater part of the income from wages, in 1944, was earned by
Indians who left reservations in large numbers to engage in occupational activities necessitated by the war.[31] However, before the be-

Table XXVI: INCOME AND MAJOR SOURCES OF INCOME OF INDIANS LIVING ON
RESERVATIONS, 1944 *

Source	Income
Earned Income	
Wages	$22,997,414.00
Agriculture	22,038,111.00
Native products	1,424,632.00
Private business	503,690.00
Arts and crafts	460,088.00
Other	555,966.00
Total earned	47,979,801.00
Unearned Income	30,298,890.00
Total Income	$78,278,691.00

* *Statistical Supplement to the Annual Report of the Commissioner of Indian Affairs*, (June 30, 1945),
p. 82.

ginning of World War II, most of the Indians on reservations were
engaged in agricultural activities, and this "in remote, semi-arid
regions, where the hazards of farming and stockraising are great, and
where distance makes the cost of transportation excessive." [32]

Although the income of Indians on reservations has increased at
an exceedingly rapid rate during the past several years, it is still far
below the income needed if Indians are to increase their economic
status to the level of other ethnic groups in the United States. Cooley,
in reporting on the Blackfoot Reservation in Montana, states that
only 29 per cent of the families had an income of more than $1,000
in 1943, and that one third of the families had a net income of less
than $250 during the same year.[33] The 1945 report of the Commis-
sioner of Indian Affairs, which comments on Indians under the
jurisdiction of Indian agencies, shows that in 1944 the average per
capita income for Indians was around $280.[34] The only logical con-

31 Dover P. Trent, "The Use of Indian Manpower," *Indians at Work*, Vol. 12, pp. 6-9,
(Jan.-Feb., 1945), p. 6.
32 *Ibid.*, p. 9.
33 Cooley, *op. cit.*, p. 5.
34 Commissioner of Indian Affairs, *op. cit.*, see table on pp. 3 and 82.

clusion that can be drawn from the preceding figures is that Indians
living on reservations are living on a very low economic level, an
economic level that is far below that of the other ethnic groups in
the United States.

The Indians in the lowest economic status are "those who have
lost their land through allotment and, not living on federal reservations or belonging to tribes for whom land or money is held in trust
or having trust benefits as a result of treaty agreements, are no longer
wards of the government." [35] Approximately 35 per cent of the Indian
population in the United States is in this class, and are now living
off reservations among the general population. The occupational
activities of Indians off reservations are restricted because of the attitudes of many non-Indians toward Indians, and because their educational level and past occupational experiences have not prepared
them for skilled and semiskilled occupations. The major occupations
open to male Indians off reservations are: seasonal work, especially
in agriculture, and common labor in factories, shipyards, mines,
sawmills, canneries, and railroads. Indian women are usually employed as domestic servants, waitresses, nurses' aids, and in similar
occupations. In these jobs they are in competition with workers of
other ethnic groups who have established themselves in these occupations, and have developed certain skills that aid in making them
superior workers when compared with inexperienced Indians. Hence,
Indians are usually the most marginal of all workers, and, as a result,
they are often the last to be hired and the first to be laid off when
occupational retrenchment is essential.

The preceding discussion is not intended to imply that all Indians
are poverty stricken. Besides those in class 1, there are some who have
advanced their economic status on reservations, and others who
have been successful in competition with other population groups
off reservation. However, available data reports that at least two-
thirds of the Indians in the United States are either landless or own
insufficient land to assure them a standard of living in keeping with
that of other ethnic groups in the United States. Therefore, taking
into consideration that Indians are land poor and that they have not
become adjusted to the economic system of the majority population
group, it seems valid to classify most Indians on the lowest economic
level in the United States.

[35] Strong, *op. cit.*, p. 144.

SUMMARY

The social status of the Indian varies from state to state, and among the different population groups. Indians were rated higher by college students in Oklahoma than by any of the other groups reported on. In Oklahoma, Negro students rated Indians higher than white students, and much higher than they were rated by Negro students in other states. In general, Indians were rated in the lower half by persons responding to the studies cited, but on the upper level of this half. Thus, according to the data cited, the social status of the Indian in the United States is below that of "typical Americans" and that of the white nationality groups, but higher than that of the other colored ethnic and nationality groups in the total population of the United States.

The legal status of the Indian is different from that of any other population group in the United States. It is logical to conclude that his citizenship status is lower than that of other citizens, since it is based on an act of Congress and not the Federal Constitution. In several states his legal status is low because of suffrage, educational, or marriage restrictions. Many Indians are legal wards of the federal government, and these are legally restricted in what is considered one of the most sacred rights of citizens in the United States: the right to own and control property. If consideration is given to the fact that most Indians are living on reservations, and are subjected to reservation restrictions, it is logical to conclude that their present legal status is lower than that of any other population group in the United States with citizenship status.

If the educational status of the Indian is judged by the availability of educational facilities, they are accorded a higher educational status than most of the minority ethnic groups in the United States. They are admitted to the educational institutions of the majority population group, and they have a system of schools financed by the federal government. On the other hand, if educational accomplishments are indicative of the educational status of the Indian, he is now on a lower educational level than any of the ethnic groups in the United States.

Indians are occupied largely in agriculture on some of the poorest land in the nation. Those not engaged in agriculture are forced to depend on common labor or semiskilled occupations for a livelihood because of prejudice or because they lack the education necessary to qualify for professions or skilled occupations. Also, available data show that Indians have a lower per capita income than any other population group in the United States. After considering these facts, practically all authorities on Indian life have concluded that Indians are perhaps on the lowest economic level in the United States.

Thus, in brief, as with other ethnic groups in the United States, the statuses of the Indian vary when evaluated by the standards that are used in this book. The social status of the Indian is below that of white ethnic and nationality groups, but above that of most of the ethnic groups classified as colored; his legal status is below that of any other group that has citizenship status; and his educational and economic statuses are low when compared with the statuses of other ethnic groups in the United States.

PROBLEMS FOR STUDY AND DISCUSSION

1. Explain why it is said that "to understand ethnic relations in the United States it is essential to understand white-Indian relations."

2. List the attitudes that you have acquired concerning the Indian, and evaluate these in keeping with democratic principles.

3. From your knowledge of the Indian population in the United States, list the reasons why you think they are discriminated against by "typical Americans."

4. In this chapter it is suggested that some minority ethnic groups have acquired negative attitudes toward the Indian. Explain why you think this is true.

5. Compare the status of the Indian with that of the other ethnic groups that have been discussed under the following points: (a) social, (b) legal, (c) educational, and (d) economic.

6. Outline the program of the Bureau of Indian Affairs for the Indian, showing the extent to which you agree or disagree with this program.

7. Explain why you think more than 50 per cent of the Indians still remain on Indian reservations.

8. Outline a program that you think would aid in advancing the status of the Indian in the United States.

SELECTED READINGS

ADAMS, E. G., *American Indian Education* (New York: King's Crown Press, 1946).

BROWN, F. J., and ROUCEK, J. S., *One America* (New York: Prentice-Hall, Inc., 1952), pp. 27-32.

COLLIER, J., *The Indians of the Americas* (New York: W. W. Norton and Company, Inc., 1947).

EMBREE, E. R., *Indians of the Americas* (Boston: Houghton Mifflin Company, 1939).

LaFarge, Oliver, Editor, *The Changing Indian* (Norman: The University of Oklahoma Press, 1930).

Linton, R., *Acculturation in Seven American Indian Tribes* (New York: D. Appleton-Century Company, 1940).

Locke, A., and Stern, B. J., Editor, *When Peoples Meet* (New York: Hinds, Hayden and Eldredge, Inc., 1946), pp. 81-85, 158-170, 510-513.

Loram, C. T., and McIllwraith, T. F., Editor, *The North American Indian Today* (Toronto: University of Toronto Press, 1943).

1951 Annual Report of the Secretary of the Interior, "Bureau of Indian Affairs," 1952, pp. 351-382.

Price, A. Grenfell, *White Settlers and Native Peoples* (Cambridge: The University Press, 1950).

Schermerhorn, R. A., *These Our People* (Boston: D. C. Heath and Company 1949), pp. 57-82.

Walter, Paul A. F., Jr., *Race and Culture Relations* (New York: McGraw-Hill Book Company, Inc., 1952), pp. 267-281.

X

Japanese

Introduction

FROM 1636 to around 1860 Japanese were forbidden to go abroad, and those who were abroad at the time this regulation was passed were not allowed to return to Japan. For this reason the Japanese were among the later nationality groups to start migrating to the United States. According to Brown and Roucek the Bureau of Naturalization and Immigration did not include any record of immigration from Japan until 1861.[1] These writers also show that the migration to the United States from Japan was very slow during the latter part of the nineteenth century, and reached its highest numbers during the first two decades of the twentieth century during which time more than 200,000 Japanese came to this country. The passage of the Quota Act of 1924, which included a clause that might be called the Japanese exclusion act, served to reduce the number of Japanese entering the United States to a very small number. Most of those who have entered the United States since 1924 were born in nations other than Japan, or had resided in some other nation a number of years before they immigrated into the United States.

The Japanese in the United States, at the present time, are an ethnic group that has been added to the total population largely during the twentieth century. In 1890 only 2,039 Japanese resided in the United States. This number increased to 24,326 by 1900. The increase continued to 1930 when 138,834 Japanese resided in the United States. As a result of the "Japanese exclusion act," and the emigration of some Japanese to other nations, the number decreased to 126,947 in 1940. Conservative estimates place the present Japanese population in the United States at around 142,000.

[1] F. J. Brown and J. S. Roucek, *One America* (New York: Prentice-Hall, Inc., 1946), see Table I on pages 632-633.

As the Japanese have immigrated to the United States during the past few decades, many people think that most of the Japanese are of foreign birth and are not citizens of the United States. Census data show that in 1940 only 37.3 per cent of the Japanese in the United States were foreign-born, and that 62.7 per cent were native-born citizens of the United States. Further, many of the foreign-born Japanese were not born in Japan, but in one of the Americas or on one of the Pacific Islands. In other words at least 62.7 per cent of the Japanese in the United States were born in the United States, and many others were born in areas far removed from Japan. In most instances these Japanese have been educated in the public schools of the United States, or have had contacts in areas where the cultural activities of the Americas predominate. As a result many of the Japanese in the United States have adopted the principles of United States citizenship that are emphasized in the public schools of the United States.

According to Table XXVII the Japanese population in the United

Table XXVII: JAPANESE POPULATION IN THE UNITED STATES BY STATE *

State	1950	1940
California	84,956	93,717
Washington	3,408	14,565
Oregon	2,102	4,071
Colorado	5,412	2,734
New York	3,893	2,538
43 other states	41,997	9,322
Total	141,768	126,947

* Advance Report prepared for this work by the Bureau of the Census, Oct. 10, 1952.

States in 1950 was a highly concentrated population. Approximately 70 per cent of the population resided in the five states included in the table, 63.8 per cent in the three Pacific Coast states, and more than 59 per cent in the state of California. The other 41,997 Japanese were scattered throughout the United States, with one or more residing in each state. Because of the concentration in a few states many persons in the United States have not had any personal contact with Japanese. However, as conditions resulting from World War II have caused some dispersion of Japanese throughout most of the United States, the 1950 Census shows a definite modification of this concentration. For instance, the three Pacific Coast states all lost a significant number of Japanese. In 1950, Illinois had a Japanese population of 11,646 whereas in 1940 some 43 states, including Illinois, had only

9,322 Japanese. Also, if the more friendly relations that now exist with Japan continue, it is possible that there may be a substantial increase in the number of visitors from Japan. If the dispersion continues and immigration increases it will be of value for all citizens of the United States to have at hand more information concerning this ethnic group. This chapter attempts to provide information concerning the present status of the Japanese in the United States.

SOCIAL STATUS

The social standing or status of persons of Japanse ancestry has fluctuated during the last few decades. If the amount of social distance between members of the majority and the minority groups is interpreted in terms of social status, we find that individuals of Japanese ancestry were rated in twenty-ninth place in 1926 and in thirty-sixth place in 1946 in a list of thirty-six ethnic groups. Dr. Emory S. Bogardus has found that American Japanese tend to be rated a little higher in status than foreign-born Japanese.[2] In some instances the Japanese are rated a little higher than the Chinese by Caucasian evaluators. On the campuses of American universities the impression may be given that the Japanese assimilate American culture at a faster rate than the Chinese. Some Japanese men assume Anglo-Saxon given names with zest. It may be that American evaluators give the Japanese a little more social status than the Chinese because he appears more in the folk mask of an American.

The Richards study of traits ascribed to the Japanese by white and Negro university students is of interest at this point. The combined ratings of these two ethnic groups disclosed the following five traits as representative of the Japanese: (1) are industrious, (2) are good workers, (3) are artistic, (4) are interested in educational advancement, and (5) help to keep wages low. However, an analysis of each of the two ethnic groups will indicate that Negro students ascribed less status to the Japanese than did the white evaluators. In terms of total "plus or minus" items, the whites accorded 17 plus to the Japanese and the Negro only 3 plus. The differential between the white and the Negro reactions to the Japanese may suggest that a minority is most critical of the deviations of another minority. In some instances there may be hypercritical attitudes toward one

2 Emory S. Bogardus, "Changes in Racial Distances," *International Journal of Opinion and Attitude Research*, Vol. I, No. 4 (Dec., 1947), p. 58.

minority, since minorities may seem to lose status collectively. The study by Richards clearly indicates a difference in the white and Negro reactions to the Japanese.[3]

In 1952 Professor George A. Lundberg and Lenore Dickson of the University of Washington completed a study measuring the ethnic preferences of a high school population. The students were asked to name three students they preferred for the following categories: leadership, work, dating, and friendship. As might be expected every ethnic group demonstrated a preference for its own members in each of the four relationships. The researchers found that the non-Jewish whites (the majority group) liked Jews best (or disliked them least), Negroes second, Chinese third, and Japanese least. It was further found that non-Jewish whites were the most chosen group on leadership, work, and dating, but were chosen only moderately frequently on friendship. Interestingly enough, Negroes were second highest in choices of leaders but very little chosen on the other three relations. For our particular purposes in this chapter it was discovered that the Japanese were also disliked, by all groups on leadership, and by all but the Chinese on other questions. Marked antipathy seemed to be revealed between Japanese and Jews, perhaps because both of these ethnic groups place a very high value upon scholastic success. It was also learned that in choosing leaders, work-partners, and dates, the non-Jewish whites showed more prejudice toward Japanese, Jews, and Negroes than these minorities showed toward them. Professor Lundberg and Miss Dickson believe that the Japanese were proportionally least chosen as leaders by all groups, perhaps in part, because they had been away in relocation centers until three years before the time of the study.[4] If the foregoing reason is correct it is a good example of how discrimination (relocation) may promote prejudice.

Cartoonists have often stereotyped the person of Japanese ancestry as an individual with a receding jaw and buckteeth. No doubt the war added much to the prevalence of this stereotyping process. In

[3] E. S. Richards, "Attitudes of College Students in the Southwest Toward Ethnic Groups in the United States," *Sociology and Social Research*, Vol. 35 (Sept.-Oct., 1950), pp. 22-30; and "Attitudes of Negro College Students Toward Ethnic Groups in the United States," a forthcoming publication.

[4] George A. Lundberg and Lenore Dickson, "Selective Association Among Ethnic Groups in a High School Population," *American Sociological Review*, Vol. 17 (Feb., 1952), pp. 23-34. See also the article by the same authors "Further Observations of Interethnic Relations in a High School Population," *American Journal of Sociology* (May, 1952).

order to increase morale of American troops, they were indoctrinated with some of the most absurd stereotypes about the Japanese as an enemy. War has had a tremendous effect upon the thinking processes of both soldiers and civilians. War may easily condone race prejudice. Civilians read in their daily newspapers stories about the "little yellow devils" of the Pacific. One of the chain newspapers described the existence of the "yellow peril." Of course, some newspapers on the Pacific Coast had been describing the worst features of the Japanese for thirty years; thus, war merely gave the press a sanctioned target to depict in despicable terms.

Another factor that aided in lowering the social status of the American Japanese was the tendency of metropolitan newspapers to make no distinction between Japanese as members of an enemy power and American citizens of Japanese ancestry. It was patriotic to call the enemy by such titles as "Nips," "Japs," and "Yellow monkeys." These titles were often used by Americans in describing persons of Japanese ancestry within the United States. The *Los Angeles Times,* a newspaper sensitive to style, often referred to the American Japanese in the following type of headline: "Jap Evacuation Reason Cited by Gen. DeWitt," "DeWitt Raps Biddle Failure to Check Japs," and "Poll Shows How Coast Stands on Japs' Return." In fact the Hearst newspapers seemed to describe the American Japanese as "Nips" and the *Los Angeles Times,* as "Japs."

One of the important factors raising the social status of American Japanese was the magnificent record of the 100th Infantry and the 442nd Combat Team. These two units received favorable publicity in the press during the training period in 1943. The morale of these units, the high percentage of war bonds purchased, and the training record established made good copy for a number of feature stories. However, it was the war record of the 442nd Regimental Combat Team in the European Theater of Operations that offered the final proof of personal patriotism of American Japanese. Colonel Charles W. Pence, wartime Commander of the 442nd Regimental Combat Team, has observed that there never was a problem during the training period. "There were no AWOLS and no disciplinary problems." [5] The record made by the 442nd is "unequalled in the army" and consists of the following: "One Congressional Medal of Honor, 47 distinguished service crosses, 342 silver stars, 810 bronze stars,

[5] *Pacific Citizen* (Sept. 11, 1948), p. 6, official publication of the Japanese American Citizens League.

2,022 purple hearts, and 468 purple heart clusters." [6] Colonel Pence
was of the opinion that a tremendous share of the credit for the fine
comeback which the Nisei have made is undoubtedly due to the
magnificent war record of the 442nd.

The postwar trials of two *Kibei* may detract a little from the record
of the American Japanese in the armed forces. The conviction of
Tomoya Kawakita as a traitor to the United States in October, 1948
is difficult to evaluate at this time. The trial of Mrs. Iva Toguri
d'Aquino (Tokyo Rose) recapitulates the problem of the American-
born Japanese caught in Japan at the outbreak of war. Both of these
"traitors" were on enemy soil, and that fact may offer some balance
to the picture.

Some of the favorable traits of the American Japanese were noted
in the following facts: (1) Juvenile delinquency was almost unheard
of in the Japanese family, (2) unemployment during the depression
was an isolated problem and in most cases the Japanese community
assumed the burden rather than public relief agencies, and (3) the
Japanese adult and crime were not associated in the minds of the
public.

Professor Masuoka in the following reading indicates the status
problem of first- and second-generation Japanese in the United States.
The second-generation Japanese seems to experience many of the
same problems that are common to white immigrants. Masuoka suggests a race relations cycle similar to the one described by Dr. Emory
S. Bogardus. Masuoka presents the different problems that confront
the several generations of Japanese in America because of their
assimilation in the culture.

▌ RACE RELATIONS AND NISEI PROBLEMS

JITSUICHI MASUOKA [7]

Immigration as a political problem in the United States is largely
a thing of the past, but numerous problems arising from it are very
much alive in the present. These problems have been subjected
increasingly to the detached scrutiny of the scientific disciplines.
This study seems to show that in an area where the contacts of
peoples are frequent, cultural change is dynamic. In this dynamic
situation the student of the social sciences finds empirical data which

[6] *Loc. cit.*

[7] *Sociology and Social Research,* Vol. 30, No. 6 (July-Aug., 1946), pp. 452-60. The
footnotes have been omitted. Used by permission of the Journal.

are suggestive of the plasticity of human nature and personality and suggestive also of the possibility of cultural and institutional change. Moreover, in this situation he finds materials rich in human experience that can be subjected to the conceptual framework peculiar to his own discipline. From the restricted point of view of the science of sociology, numerous problems stemming from the contact and association of races can be stated abstractedly in terms of the cycle of race relations.

The cycle of race relations, when viewed sociopsychologically, reduces to a sequence of steps involving the cultural and social adjustments of individuals. Every progression in the cycle is associated, theoretically at least, with expanding areas of common racial participation. There is, in other words, a greater individual freedom to participate in the cultural values of the dominant group. The greater participation in the wider sphere of social life is accompanied by a corresponding transformation in the system of personal and social relationships. Thus the problem of cultural and social adjustment of the once-excluded group becomes more complex as it enters into a wider and more active sphere of society. Everywhere it seems that race relations and cultural and social adjustments are functionally related. This functional relationship is expressed dramatically in the conflict of generations within the immigrant family. This conflict of generations is indicative that the clash of cultures is inherent in widely separated societies and likewise that change is inherent in the very nature of race relations. It is the thesis of this brief paper that the cultural and social problems of the Nisei need to be studied within the wider context of the cycle of race relations.

An understanding of the nature of the immigrant community is a prerequisite for a definitive statement of the Nisei's cultural and social adjustments. For it is in this concrete situation that we can observe and describe realistically the interaction of values and attitudes which are constantly coming from the two divergent social worlds. The system of values that is being introduced and incorporated at any given time in the experience of the Nisei is determined and conditioned by the stages in the cycle of race relations and brings dissimilar peoples into closer contact and association.

The Japanese community, growing as it does in the new milieu in response to the pressing needs of the people, is never a direct replica of the community of origin. For one thing, the transplanted institutions lack their former internal consistency and equilibrium. In the loosely organized community life the immigrant culture loses its traditional organization, and at the same time the customary mode of life loses, in a large measure, the concerted support of the community.

Moreover, the immigrant community is a marginal community. It exists on the periphery of the dominant community, from which the immigrant receives goods, ideas, and other cultural tools and values. To some or to all of these values he cannot remain indifferent for very long if he is to survive effectively in the new environment: they are indispensable to him in making a daily living and for effective execution of his daily activities. The transplanted community is also in contact with the community of its origin and from it the Issei receives goods, ideas, traditional moral values—though progressively less important—and to it he hopes eventually to return. In any event, the fact is that the process of cultural borrowing from the dominant group becomes more important as he resides in the new community for any length of time, especially when he establishes his own family.

The Japanese community has its existence in active interaction with the dominant community *in situ*. In this new community two vast cultural hinterlands interact, and there is a constant cultural diffusion, particularly of the organized systems or institutions. Under such conditions the immigrant society suffers a continuous disorganization. When, for example, new items of foods, goods, modes of greeting and rituals are introduced into immigrant families, these items of the dominant culture initiate and effect in time a complex modification in the traditional mode of life and social institutions of the immigrant. Each article and each activity is incorporated because it is useful to the people, and because it is useful, it wedges itself into the traditional ways of life. Moreover, each new thing is introduced because of aggressively organized efforts on the part of the dominant group, community, and social institutions. With the increasing loss of social and institutional controls, the immigrant has greater opportunities to explore and experiment with the cultural elements of the dominant group.

In the United States the basis of cultural bestowal is relatively broad, and, because of it, the Issei and Nisei accept more readily the cultural values of the dominant group. In other words, there is a relatively small amount of "selective bestowals" of American culture upon the recipients; and, reciprocally, there is a relatively small amount of "selective conservatism" on the part of the latter. But here, as wherever cultural diffusion is in evidence, the process is directed by a definite compulsion by the donor culture and a selective acceptance by the recipients.

The Issei, recruited as he generally is from a peasant society, lacks the necessary cultural equipment and mental orientation—especially the language facilities—to participate fully in the wider sphere of social life of the new community. He restricts his social activities within the narrow confines of the transplanted cultural enclave. Within it, chiefly, he satisfies his basic and social needs and within it he has his own social status.

In his contact and association with members of the wider community, he maintains a symbiotic relationship. His problems of adjustment are nonsocial and are confined largely to economic activities. In addition to these impersonal forces to which he must make a satisfactory adjustment, he finds it increasingly necessary to adjust himself to the prevailing major social institutions of the new community, particularly to the aggressive institutions of the dominant community. The Issei does not enter into and participate in them fully, however; he seldom becomes an integral part of their activities. His inability to participate in them fully keeps him ignorant of their fundamental structures and functions. Thus, the personality of the immigrant remains relatively unaffected in spite of the expanding area of his contacts and associations with the dominant group.

The rate of acculturation of the Issei becomes everywhere more rapid as his community becomes more disorganized; this is in part a function of interaction with the dominant group. Through contact and interaction, the body of conflicting values comes closer and is more readily accessible; a new value emerges in the immigrant community. In this dynamic contact situation, the transplanted formal institutions are first affected. With this modification there is a corresponding change in the attitudes, habits, and sentiments of the participants. The conditions of learning for the Nisei are affected by the disorganization of the old-world institutions, and the conflict of generations is to be expected. Problems of social adjustment, as distinct from those of economic and cultural adjustment, become conscious phenomena among the members of the immigrant family and the community.

The Nisei enjoy greater cultural and social participation in the ways of the dominant group. This person, indigenous to the new community, has in addition to other cultural artifacts and values common to the members of the dominant group, the language facility which the Issei generally lacks. In and through the wider participation which the common language affords, he acquires many of the cultural traits of the dominant group and learns far more adequately than the Issei the structure and functions of the social institutions of the community of his aspiration. However, as he is not born into them but is recruited after he is grown up, his knowledge about the social institutions remains generally superficial: his participation in them lacks the sustaining force of the sentiments peculiar to those born into them. Likewise, he maintains to an amazing degree an impersonal and abstract relationship with the transplanted Japanese institutions. This latter attitude comes about, not so much as a result of his emotional and mental maturity, but as a consequence of his participation in the institutions that are already on their way out. There is a psychological factor of aspiration that accounts further for his superficial knowledge of the transplanted institutions as well as other cultural heritages.

The superficial and shallow cultural basis of the Nisei as compared with the Issei in regard to the old-world social heritages places the former in an advantageous position to adopt the new cultural artifacts, institutions, ideals, beliefs, and attitudes of the dominant group. Moreover, the prestige which the superior culture possesses is a rewarding factor in his learning. As he learns the social heritage of the dominant group, he is rewarded at many points: the school, church, and political and economic institutions of the wider community become more readily accessible to him. He takes on ampler and more varied activities of the wider community in almost direct proportion to his acculturation. This is particularly the case when the dominant community is actively interested in the Americanization of Issei and Nisei or in any program designed to speed up the process of incorporation of the Nisei, who are psychologically inside the dominant community but physically and spatially outside. In the early stages of Americanization even the mediocre individuals among the Nisei are given lucrative jobs. This functions as a further incentive for other Nisei to adopt the superior culture, for it carries with it a kind of guarantee of higher social status within and without his own community.

In the eyes of the dominant group the culture which the Nisei acquires so readily and so eagerly falls short of the community norm. In form his acquired culture is much like that of the nation; in content it is thin and shallow. For instance, he masters with relative ease the grammar of the English language, but his language lacks the idiomatic and other more subtle qualities of that of the American people. The latter takes for granted, understands, and has a peculiar feeling for the very qualities that the former finds so difficult to assimilate. This fact shows clearly the difficulty involved in assimilating those aspects of a culture which are not formal, the very qualities that give to that culture its richness and individuality.

Largely by these intangible aspects of the cultures of both the dominant and the immigrant groups, the assimilation of the Nisei is finally judged and evaluated. In the eyes of the Issei the local-born have very little knowledge of the history of the old-world community. They thus resort to various ways to acquaint the Nisei with the things which they deem vital. The language school, church, immigrant press, and visits to Japan are some of the means used to meet this need. Despite these efforts, things of the old world—artifacts and traditional modes of life—remain pretty much outside the experience of the Nisei. Since his locus of aspiration lies in the community of the dominant group, the Nisei is not concerned with his ignorance of the old-world social heritage. He is, thus, excluded from both groups—from the group of his origin by his own motivation and ignorance and from the group of his aspiration by his cultural and racial differences. Seeking a fuller participation in the dominant society and denied what he has come to regard as rightfully his, the Nisei tends to become psychologically marginal. He may play an active part in the cultural change: he may play a role comparable to that of the nationalistic leader and become keenly interested in the culture of the old world. And yet, here as in the first instance, he becomes a cultural innovator and cultural interpreter with reference to the dominant group. He seeks to create in the latter kindly attitudes toward and appreciation of the alien culture; thus, he seeks to create a new society in which as an individual he has a more satisfactory role to play.

In conclusion, we can state briefly that, owing to the nature of race relations which the Issei encounters, his problem of adjustment is primarily economic and only secondarily cultural. But the Nisei, occupying a marginal position and never fully assimilated into the dominant society, becomes highly conscious of his racial origin; he becomes ever so conscious of the problem of race relations. In spite of this fact he does not fully succeed in mobilizing his group to express united demands and make concerted efforts to influence public opinion. The Nisei group is numerically small and their experience with race conflicts has a shallow history. It is the members of the Sansei who, having been fully acculturated but having been excluded by the dominant group because of their racial differences, really succeed in presenting a united front against exclusion by the dominant group. A genuine race problem arises at this point in the history of race relations.

LEGAL STATUS

Differential legal status accorded to a minority is an objective crystallization of race attitudes. The intent of many laws concerning the Oriental has been to prefer old American stock at the expense of the Asiatic. In some cases these laws have run counter to the expressed ideals of the American democratic society. In the thinking of Charles Morris, legislation that denies equality is responsible for the development of the closed society. Considerable legislation has been passed with the hope of closing the doors of opportunity for the eager Japanese in this country.

As far back as 1890 a movement to stop the emigration of Japanese to the United States achieved considerable momemtum. The Gentlemen's Agreement of 1907 was powerful enough to stop almost all migration of Japanese laborers to the Coastal areas. Then, in 1924 the United States Supreme Court ruled that Japanese Nationals were not eligible for citizenship in the famous case of Toyoto versus the United States. Toyoto came to this country in 1913 and served in the armed forces of the United States during the First World War. A lower court gave him a naturalization certificate which the United States Supreme Court ruled, unanimously should be cancelled. Toyoto based his claim to citizenship on the 1918 Act of Congress which provided that any alien serving honorably in the military forces of the United States be eligible to file a petition for naturalization without the usual proof of five years of residence and filing preliminary intention. However, the United States Supreme Court defined "any alien" to mean a white person or a person of African descent.[8] Hence, the Negro occupied a higher legal status than the person of Japanese ancestry.

The sociological implication of denying citizenship to residents solely on the basis of race affiliation raises the question of the validity of characterizing America as a "melting pot." Migrants might come to our shores, become self-respecting persons, but fail to qualify for citizenship solely because of racial ancestry. *Americans ridiculed the Japanese for their ancestor worship; yet, the United States denied citizenship to these people precisely on the grounds of their ancestors.* The reaction of the press in Japan to this decision is boldly observed as "Americans are as spiteful as snakes and vipers—we do not hesitate to call that government a studied deceiver." [9]

The deliberate omission of the Japanese from the 1924 quota Act was the next blow to the legal status of the Japanese. It is the considered opinion of no less an authority than Professor Samuel E.

---

[8] In the Ozawa case the United States Supreme Court ruled that the Japanese are excluded from naturalization by reason of race. Ozawa had lived here 20 years and had met all of the legal requirements, but the highest court ruled that the naturalization act adopted in 1790 provided that "any alien" being a free white person may be eligible for citizenship. After the civil war, in 1870, the statute was amended to include aliens of African descent. It may be of interest to note that in this respect the Negro occupied a higher legal status than its social status.

[9] *Osoka Mainichi.* See also Carey McWilliams, *Prejudice* (Boston: Little, Brown and Company, 1945), p. 66.

Morison of Harvard University that this act was one of the prime motivators of militarism and the suppression of liberal thought in Japan. In fact, he sees the dawn of the idea of a Pearl Harbor attack in this piece of discriminatory legislation.[10] Charles Evans Hughes, as Secretary of State, wrote to the Chairman of the House Committee on Immigration concerning the 1924 bill when it was pending:

> The practical effect of section 12 (b) is to single out Japanese immigrants for exclusion. The Japanese are a sensitive people, and unquestionably would regard such a legislative enactment as fixing a stigma upon them. I regret that I feel compelled to say that I believe such legislative action would largely undo the work of the Washington Conference on Limitation of Armament. . . . It is useless to argue whether or not such a feeling would be justified; it is quite sufficient to say that it would exist.[11]

President Coolidge attempted to postpone application of the exclusion provision until 1926, anticipating a negotiated treaty with Japan. However, his suggestion was turned down, and the President signed the bill with the following comment:

> In signing this bill which in its main features I heartily approve, I regret the impossibility of severing from it the exclusion provision . . . If the exclusion provision stood alone, I should disapprove it without hesitation if sought in this way at this time.[12]

The Japanese government made a formal protest pointing up the discriminatory features of the 1924 Immigration Act, the American Ambassador in Japan commented that the legislation was a real blow to their natural pride, and the leading newspapers in Japan continued to make vigorous protests. In restrospect was this legislation the spark that inflamed Japanese militarism to define the United States as a potential enemy nation?

In still another area of legal status, namely, property ownership, a somewhat similar story must be repeated. As the twentieth century opened some of the ill feeling against the Chinese was transferred to the Japanese. Inasmuch as the Japanese had been very aggressive in the development of agricultural products and businesses, some of the pioneer American stock felt the growing competition. Former desert lands were turned into rich agricultural areas under the direction

[10] Samuel E. Morison, *Rising Sun in the Pacific* (Boston: Little, Brown and Company, 1948).

[11] Cited in Y. Ichihashi, *Japanese in the United States* (Palo Alto: Stanford University Press, 1932), p. 300, from *Document Relating to the Immigration Act of 1924*, compiled by the Department of Foreign Affairs (Tokyo, Japan), pp. 76-77. Used by permission of the author and the publisher, Stanford University Press.

[12] *Ibid.*, p. 309.

of Japanese farmers. The Japanese used some of the waste lands in Northern California for experimental rice projects. Rice that yielded a profit to the grower could be grown in these areas. McWilliams, a controversial writer on California agriculture, claims that the Japanese pioneered as agriculturists in the Sacramento, San Joaquin, Santa Clara, and the Imperial valleys.[13] Because of long hours of work and the application of their knowledge to agriculture, the Japanese soon had a tremendous control over the following crops: potatoes, flowers, berries, and truck garden vegetables. Attempts thus were made in 1907 to pass discriminatory legislation against the Japanese, but President Theodore Roosevelt would not tolerate such innovations in view of their obvious international implications. However, in 1913 agitation in California resulted in the passage of a measure declaring that persons ineligible for citizenship could hold land only to the extent of existing treaties with Japan and for short periods of lease.[14] The government of Japan lost no time in protesting its passage. President Wilson tried to persuade the California legislature not to pass the measure. In 1920 the measure was amended to delete the section concerned with the period of leases, and a section was added that persons ineligible for citizenship were not to acquire stock in any organization authorized to enjoy real property rights.[15] The aim of this legislation was to deprive the Japanese aliens from purchasing land in California; however, the alien Japanese circumvented this law by purchasing property in the name of their American-born children.

World War II instantly brought to the surface all the past prejudice against the Japanese and initiated a new phase of differential treatment toward these people unique in the history of America. *Japanese ancestry became the test of loyalty to this country, not citizenship or established reputation.* Nationals of Germany and Italy were not segregated as a group; yet, American citizens of Japanese ancestry were forced to sell or store their property and leave the coastal areas under military escort to internment centers.[16]

Regardless of the conclusions of historians and politicians, the Pearl Harbor attack was shocking enough to throw this country into

[13] Carey McWilliams, *Factories in the Fields* (Boston: Little, Brown and Company, 1939), p. 110.
[14] Milton R. Konvitz, *op. cit.*, pp. 158-159.
[15] *Ibid.*, p. 160.
[16] The outstanding work in this connection is by Dorothy S. Thomas and Richard S. Nishimoto, *The Spoilage* (Berkeley: University of California Press, 1946), 388 pp.

war immediately. Whatever interpretation scholars may offer on the background to World War II, the "first shot" by the Japanese turned out to be a major battle blow that proved costly in men and military equipment to the United States.[17] Propaganda experts were quick to point out the nature of the Pearl Harbor attack, coming on a Sunday morning, with no warning, and its terrific impact. The attack served to focus attention of the American people on the Japanese as untrustworthy. To many Americans, Japanese militarists and all persons of Japanese ancestry were the same. However, one of the experts on psychlogical warfare states that the Japanese militarists had to outsmart the home people of Japan by initiating the attack.[18]

War turned the long-standing animosity between Japan and the United States into the logic of hate. On the Pacific Coast this hate for the government of Japan and its people found its closest target in the resident Japanese, whether nationals or citizens. Some of the civilians on the coast believed that "something ought to be done" about the Japanese problem. Some argued that the possibility of sabotage was real. The rumors of sabotage in Hawaii were believed by the mainland residents in spite of the fact that the Federal Bureau of Investigation and the police of Hawaii both denied the charges made against resident Japanese there. Rumors often live long enough to be "facts" of influence regardless of their falsity. Newspaper columnists wrote that the Japanese in California were residing in areas of tremendous strategic importance, such as on the coastal strips, under high voltage lines, near petroleum storage tanks, and as fishermen they had a valuable store of information concerning the coast. Americans of Japanese ancestry were living in these areas solely because of occupational reasons—with the end of World War II many of these Japanese have gone back to these very areas. However, during the war reason seemed to be subordinated to the power of anxiety, and a campaign to evacuate the Japanese developed.

When the Americans of Japanese ancestry had committed no act of sabotage in California, it was ridiculously explained by one of the military leaders that the lack of such sabotage was positive proof of Japanese future intent. In fact, General DeWitt observed in his report made public in January, 1944 that the evacuation of the Japanese

[17] Charles A. Beard, *President Roosevelt and the Coming War*, (New Haven: Yale University Press, 1948). Beard is of the opinion that the Roosevelt administration attempted to maneuver Japan into firing the "first shot."

[18] Paul M. A. Linebarger, *Psychological Warfare* (Washington, D. C.: Infantry Journal Press, 1948), p. 42.

was based on the fear of sabotage and espionage. In this type of social situation innocence is proof of espionage.

With such a background the demand for evacuation followed, in brief, the pattern outlined:

1. December 11, 1941, The Western Defense Command was created and the area declared a theater of war.

2. February 19, 1942, Executive Order No. 9066 signed by President Franklin D. Roosevelt. This order delegated to military commanders the authority to declare military areas, the power to exclude designated persons, and the power to issue leaves.

3. March 2, 1942, Proclamation No. 1 was issued setting up the military areas.

4. March 24, 1942, The Japanese were subjected to the order of exclusion.

5. On May 3, 1942, all persons of Japanese ancestry whether or not citizens of the United States were to be excluded from Military Area No. 1.

6. By June 5, 1942, all persons of Japanese ancestry had been excluded and removed from Military Area No. 1.

7. December 17, 1944, General DeWitt rescinded orders of exclusion.

8. September 4, 1945, loyal Americans of Japanese ancestry were permitted to return to their homes. This order rescinded all orders against the resident Japanese.

Most of the Japanese were sent to assembly centers, then to relocation centers, and many of them were permitted to leave these centers for voluntary work outside of Military Areas No. 1 and 2. McWilliams is of the opinion that General DeWitt was a man of deep prejudice against the Japanese. He probably based his judgment of DeWitt on the following observation made by the General before the House Naval Affairs Subcommittee on April 14, 1943:

A Jap's a Jap. They are a dangerous element, whether loyal or not. There is no way to determine their loyalty. . . . It makes no difference whether he is an American; theoretically he is still a Japanese and you can't change him. . . . You can't change him by giving him a piece of paper.[19]

One of the native patriotic groups in California discussed the following resolution on April 24, 1942, in Los Angeles: "No person of a race ineligible for naturalization shall be a citizen by reason of having been born in the United States, or in any territory, or possession of the United States." Prejudice was moving in the direction of excluding citizenship regardless of native birth in the United States. In restrospect, such a discussion may seem beyond the range of common sense.

Ten relocation centers were established to take care of evacuees.

19 Carey McWilliams, *op. cit.*, p. 149.

These centers resembled military barracks, and as family quarters privacy was placed at a minimum. These camps were located in Utah, Arizona, California, Idaho, Wyoming, Colorado, and Arkansas. Most students of relocation life claim that the War Relocation Authority was motivated by humane principles. A good deal of democratic control was permitted within these areas. Coöperative enterprises were encouraged and permitted the residents to enjoy many items of food and clothing at somewhat reduced prices. Evacuees were fed in large mess halls at a cost of 42 cents per person per day.

One of the interesting implications of relocation life was that prejudiced persons accused the WRA (War-Relocation Authority) of coddling Japanese residents. Congressional investigations were made which determined that the Japanese were being treated fairly, but not given better food than the average civilian or soldier. The "apartments" in which the Japanese tried to maintain family life consisted of a single room 25 by 20 feet.[20] It is difficult to understand how editors on the coast could write of coddling under mass conditions of living.

About 90 per cent of the Japanese adults in the centers were engaged in some useful work. For the work they received cash allotments varying from twelve to nineteen dollars per month. One area of conflict was inevitable, namely, the wide difference paid to a Japanese resident and a civilian employee for the same work. This situation resembled the low pay given enlisted men as teachers in Special Training Battalions and the rather generous amounts given to civilians as teachers. Chagrin is inevitable when one person occupies a status of involuntary inferiority, yet is asked to perform a task calling for specialized training or information. It is not difficult to understand the feelings of inadequacy that must have been aroused in the minds of Japanese physicians, dentists, teachers, nurses, and other professional persons paid in terms of almost a child's allotment.

At the beginning, it was believed that the relocation centers could be used for the duration of the war; however, the problem of manpower and the success of the temporary leave policy stimulated the directors to view the entire program as most temporary. As a result, the centers began to release the men to the fields, to the armed forces, and to the factories. The relocation centers became "way stations" on the eastern trek of many Japanese. About 20,000 Nisei were released

20 *Relocation of Japanese-Americans* (Washington, D. C.: War Relocation Authority, 1943), p. 6.

in 1943 to accept jobs outside the relocation center. Some of the evacuees felt secure in the centers and did not care to leave. In fact, when the war ended and the War Relocation Authority had to close the centers, some of the Japanese residents had become so accommodated to the routine that they did not desire to leave. Perhaps some students of the program might explain such behavior as a manifestation of the loss of social motivation and spirit.

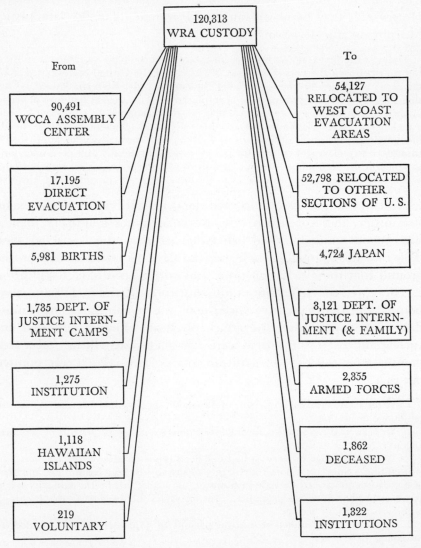

From

To

120,313
WRA CUSTODY

90,491
WCCA ASSEMBLY
CENTER

54,127
RELOCATED TO
WEST COAST
EVACUATION
AREAS

17,195
DIRECT
EVACUATION

52,798 RELOCATED
TO OTHER
SECTIONS OF U. S.

5,981 BIRTHS

4,724 JAPAN

1,735 DEPT. OF
JUSTICE INTERN-
MENT CAMPS

3,121 DEPT. OF
JUSTICE INTERN-
MENT (& FAMILY)

1,275
INSTITUTION

2,355
ARMED FORCES

1,118
HAWAIIAN
ISLANDS

1,862
DECEASED

219
VOLUNTARY

1,322
INSTITUTIONS

* From *The Educated People, A Quantitative Description* (Washington, D. C.: U. S. Government Printing Office, 1946).

The relocation of the Japanese people during the war has been a subject of legal action in the courts of the nation, particularly the United States Supreme Court. The Gordon Hirabayashi case involved a citizen of the United States, a senior at the University of Washington, who violated the curfew imposed on all persons of Japanese ancestry by the military authorities. The United States Supreme Court ruled that the curfew decision by the military authorities was a war measure and that proper delegation of powers existed. However, it may be worth noting the comments of the late Justice Murphy on this decision:

Today is the first time, so far as I am aware, that we have sustained a substantial restriction on the personal liberty of citizens of the United States based upon the accident of race or ancestry. Under the curfew order here challenged no less than 70,000 American citizens have been placed under a special ban and deprived of their liberty because of their particular racial inheritance. In this sense it bears a melancholy resemblance to the treatment accorded to members of the Jewish race in Germany and in other parts of Europe. The result is the creation in this country of two classes of citizens for the purposes of a critical and perilous hour— to sanction discrimination between groups of United States citizens on the basis of ancestry. In my opinion this goes to the very brink of constitutional power.[21]

A second famous case concerned the constitutionality of the exclusion order, the Korematsu case. Korematsu was a nursery man, a high school graduate, who had failed to leave the restricted area. This case was argued by the American Civil Liberties Union on the ground that the evacuation order was without military justification and deprived the defendant of his constitutional rights. His attorneys pointed out that Executive Order 9066 was not initiated until more than two months after the attack on Pearl Harbor, and that the curfew and exclusion orders were not made until three and a half months after the war. In addition to the foregoing, it was pointed out that:

1. After Pearl Harbor no person of Japanese ancestry had been arraigned for espionage or sabotage.
2. In Hawaii there was no internment or mass exclusion of persons of Japanese ancestry.
3. Acts of sabotage on Hawaii had not been reported after Pearl Harbor. The United States Supreme Court voted 6 to 3 to sustain the conviction. The majority of the court interpreted the case in terms of "necessity," while the minority saw it as an example of "social prejudice." Justice Black believed that the exclusion order was necessary because:
1. An uncertain number of disloyal persons of Japanese ancestry resided on the coast.

[21] As quoted by Konvitz, op. cit., p. 249.

2. Since it was impossible to segregate immediately the loyal from the disloyal Japanese, temporary exclusion was necessary.

3. Subsequent to the mass exclusion, about 5,000 Americans of Japanese ancestry refused to sign the unqualified allegiance to the United States.[22] Again Justice Murphy protested. He cited the statement by General DeWitt which referred to the Japanese as disloyal. Justice Murphy seemed to be convinced that prejudice rather than military necessity dominated the plan for exclusion.

A third case, the Endo case, decided on December 18, 1944, centered on the internment of a Japanese American. Miss Endo had been a civil service employee of the State of California and of unquestioned loyalty to this country. She protested internment in a War Relocation Authority Center. The case was decided unanimously in her favor. The Court ruled that she was concededly loyal and that the WRA had no authority to intern such persons. Exclusion from the military area had been constitutionally sound, not internment. Justice Murphy in his opinion observed that the case was another example of the unconstitutional resort to racism inherent in the entire evacuation program.[23]

Another change of legal status concerns the renunciants at Tule Lake Segregation Center. On April 29, 1948, Federal District Judge Louis E. Goodman reinstated the citizenship of 2,300 Nisei renunciants. The judge ruled that these renunciations had been obtained under duress from other nationalist-minded segregees at the Tule Lake Camp. He pointed out that the camp "held disloyal aliens, Americans of Japanese ancestry suspected of disloyalty, and Japanese Americans whose loyalty was not in question at all." [24]

One of the results of the war between this country and Japan had been the abrogation of existing treaties. In the Stockton theater case decided in June, 1948, the California Supreme Court upheld the right of Japanese aliens to lease commercial property. Emil Palermo, operator of the Star theater in Stockton sought to break a ten-year lease held by Stockton Theaters, Inc., a firm owned and operated by Japanese aliens. In the Superior Court of Stockton, Judge Woodward decided in favor of Palermo, and the Stockton Theaters, Inc., was forced to give up the property. However, the case was appealed to the third district court of Sacramento which reversed the decision. Palermo then took the case to the California Supreme Court, which ruled in favor of the Japanese. Since the institution of the case, many

22 *Ibid.,* p. 258.
23 *Ibid.,* p. 273.
24 *Pacific Citizen* (May 1, 1948).

leases drawn up with a Japanese alien participant have carried a special clause referring to the Palermo case. The Stockton Theaters, Inc., initiated court action to sue Palermo for the losses involved.[25]

Another important decision of the United States Supreme Court concerned the California law denying commercial fishing licenses to Japanese and other aliens ineligible for citizenship. The law was declared unconstitutional by a 7 to 2 decision in the Takahashi case. The high court ruled that section 990 of the California Fish and Game Code, enacted in 1945 as a legislative device to keep the Japanese out of commercial fishing, cannot stand because it violates the Fourteenth Amendment, which provides that all persons, whether citizens or aliens, shall enjoy equal protection of the laws of the state in which they abide. The decision affects about five hundred Japanese fishermen. Justice Murphy observed "The statute in question, is but one more manifestation of the anti-Japanese fever which has been evident in California in varying degrees since the turn of the century." However, the sweeping decision in the Takahashi case was somewhat invalidated by the enforcement of certain regulations by the Los Angeles Immigration Office. The immigration officials called attention to the fact that from June, 1945, an alien fisherman must have (1) a departure permit, (2) a passport, and (3) a re-entry permit or border-crossing permit. The "red tape" involved is enough to discourage a Japanese from fishing, in fact, to make it almost impossible for him to comply with the law.[26]

One of the most important pieces of legislation affecting the economic status of the Japanese was signed by President Harry S. Truman on July 2, 1948. The evacuation claims bill was passed fifteen hours before the 80th Congress adjourned. The bill authorizes the Attorney General to settle damage claims of persons of Japanese ancestry for the recovery of a part of their losses incurred as a result of evacuation. Estimates as to the amount of damages to be filed against the government range from $10,000,000 to $100,000,000. Government estimates placed the value of property left behind by Japanese at approximately $200,000,000. The Attorney General is authorized to pay damages up to $2,500 for damage to or loss of property. Awards higher than $2,500 must have the approval of Congress. It has been pointed out that the small claimants will have a difficult time showing proof, whereas the large business owners have kept

25 *Ibid.* (Saturday, June 19, 1948).
26 *Ibid.* (Aug. 14, 1948).

books which indicate inventories and probably losses. It has been pointed out that as little as $10,000,000 might be adequate to fulfill the obligations of the law if it were narrowly interpreted and rigidly administered. If that is done, little more than a "soothing of the national conscience" is achieved. However, if the Japanese evacuees are to be reimbursed for actual income and property losses, at least $350,000,000 is necessary.[27] In the proposed federal budget for the fiscal year beginning July 1, 1951, the Attorney General estimated that the Department of Justice would pay out approximately $450,000 of evacuation claims for the fiscal year ending June 30, 1951. However, the Attorney General's Evacuation Claims Report for the calendar year 1950 showed that for the first half of the fiscal year (1950-51), the Department made awards only amounting to $55,142.98, and paid out only the sum of $26,359.57 for the first half-year period.[28] However, the legislation is positive admission of the differential effect that World War II had upon Japanese aliens and Americans of Japanese ancestry. In summary, an inferior legal status had been imposed on the Japanese with the hope of limiting the success of these people in the economy which is being relaxed in a number of particulars.

On June 27, 1952, the McCarran-Walter Immigration Bill was passed by Congress over President Harry S. Truman's veto and became effective December 27, 1952. This measure, a very controversial one, removes some of the discriminatory features of the 1924 law toward the Japanese. Briefly, the McCarran-Walter legislation accomplishes the following:

1. Pacific area receives a total quota of 2,000 immigrants per year. Quotas of independent islands and trusteeships are 100 each, Japan receives 185.
2. Present bar to the naturalization of the foreign-born Japanese (Issei) has been rescinded. It is estimated that about 85,000 Japanese are now eligible for American citizenship and the ownership of real property is possible in states that attempted to preclude such ownership on the ground of non-citizenship.
3. Present national-origin system of quotas for entry on the basis of ratios of foreign-born to United States population in 1920 is retained.
4. Foreigners married to women who are United States citizens may come into the country without regard to quotas. Service men also are able to bring their foreign-born brides home.[29]

27 Leonard Broom and Ruth Riemer, *Removal and Return* (Berkeley: University of California Press, 1949), pp. 201-3.
28 Japanese American Citizens League Evacuation Claims Status, Monthly Report (Feb., 1951).
29 *New York Times* (June 28, 1952). This newspaper was most critical of the McCarran Bill and termed it as "unfair" and "unwise" because of the retention of the quotas and other "compromise" features.

EDUCATIONAL STATUS

There is little doubt that public education is one of the chief characteristics in the American culture. In some particulars the public schools have been defined as the social elevators to a higher general status in the community. It is worth noting that the Japanese come from a country where illiteracy is almost unknown and status is accorded to the man of letters. *Hence, it may not be surprising to learn that the Japanese excel most of the minority groups in school attendance and the quality of school work assigned.* Reference is made to Table XXVIII, which indicates that both the Japanese natives and

Table XXVIII: NONWHITE MALE POPULATION 25 YEARS OLD AND OVER BY MEDIAN SCHOOL YEARS COMPLETED *

Race	Native	Foreign Born
Negro	5.3	7.6
Indians	5.7	. . .
Chinese	6.2	5.3
Japanese	12.2	8.3

* Sixteenth Census of the United States, *Population* (1940). Characteristics of the nonwhite population by race.

foreign-born males excelled the other population groups by significant differences in the median year of school completed. Also Table XXI in Chapter VIII disclosed that the Japanese had the highest percentage of children 5 to 20 years of age attending school in 1930.

Attempts have been made to measure the intelligence of various ethnic groups; however, the factor of cultural differences has made it almost impossible to account for the variety of scores resulting. One of the most comprehensive surveys concerning the innate abilities of the Japanese was undertaken during 1922-24 by Dr. M. L. Darsie. He used the Army Beta, the Stanford-Binet, and the Stanford Achievement tests on a sample of city and country Japanese. The results of these tests seem to show the influence of cultural experience. In reading, the Japanese when compared to American norms were 14.25 months retarded, 12.5 months retarded in language, in arithmetic 1.75 months retarded, and about 6.0 months retarded in general information. In spelling, the Japanese were about 2.75 months ahead of the Americans.[30] On tests standardized with American children it may not be surprising that the Japanese do not excel.

[30] M. L. Darsie, "The Mental Capacity of American-Born Children," *Comparative Psychological Monographs,* Vol. 3, No. 15 (1926).

There is considerable evidence to support the thesis that the Jap-anese receive higher grades than do other children in school. Dr. Reginald Bell found that in Los Angeles high schools the Japanese, compared with a heterogenous group of Caucasians, Negroes, Chinese, and Mexicans, excelled in securing scholastic grades of "A" at every level, a superiority that is statistically significant at all levels except A12 where the number of Japanese is so few as to make gen-eralizations unsound.[31] Another study on the comparative scholastic achievements of Japanese and American children yields about the same results. George H. Freeman selected the scholastic records of 200 Japanese children and compared them against a random sample of 200 records of American students. The records gave the marks earned from the seventh to the twelfth grade inclusive. It might be pointed out that the study concerned children in the town of Gardena, a community about fifteen miles from Los Angeles. Free-man found that the Japanese, who comprised only 20 per cent of the student body, have been represented by 37 per cent of the stu-dents eligible for the California Scholarship Federation.[32] Election to the California Scholarship Federation is limited to students attend-ing senior high schools and who have received the highest grades in all their academic subjects. Freeman found that the "Japanese re-ceived 11% more A's, 8% more B's, 10% less D's, and 1% less F's than their fellow Americans."[33] There was almost no relationship found between the intelligence quotients and grades received; hence, the Japanese tested lower in intelligence as measured by the instru-ment than American children, but made consistently higher grades. In terms of academic success as measured by grades received, the Japanese excel American children. It appears that the intelligence tests used do not predict academic success with this ethnic group. If achievement is the test of intelligence, then the Japanese children occupy a very high status.

Dr. Edward K. Strong of Stanford believes that the Japanese student may manifest qualities that are pleasing to the teacher and thus receive academic grades in reference to personal qualities. For instance, it may be that the "docility" of the Japanese appears attrac-

[31] Reginald Bell, "Public School Education of Second-Generation Japanese in Cali-fornia" (Stanford: Stanford University Press, 1935), p. 54.

[32] George H. Freeman, "A Comparative Investigation of the School Achievement and Socio-Economic Background of the Japanese-American Students and the White-American Students of Gardena High School" (Los Angeles: University of Southern California, 1938), p. 25. Unpublished Master's Thesis.

[33] *Ibid.*, p. 26.

tive to the teacher; less disciplinary problems may cause the teacher to think of them as hard workers.[34] It has been noted that, as the Japanese child progresses from the seventh to the twelfth grade, his grades or marks decline. Strong believes that the Japanese student body is not so select in the higher grades by comparison with the American student body. Inasmuch as the Japanese place a great value on school attendance, there may be more inferior students in the higher grades. Another explanation of the declining marks of Japanese children as they advance through the grades might be in terms of assimilation. As the older second-generation Japanese child becomes "American," he may value football or being a "regular fellow," which may tend to lower his value of high marks. However, we must not miss the valuable fact that teachers grade the Japanese student in terms of his abilities and personality rather than in terms of any residual race prejudice.

Prior to World War II, the Japanese were criticized for their operation of Japanese-language schools. It was purported that the Japanese children were indoctrinated against the democratic values of this country. Little significant evidence was gathered to support the charge. In reality, these Japanese-language schools were similar to the foreign-language schools of other ethnic groups. About two-thirds of the Nisei attended the language school. It is generally accepted that Nisei enrolled in the language schools at the request of their parents. Some believed that parent and child relationships were thought to be better when communication between the two generations was possible. In some cases a Nisei learned English and did not know Japanese. When he became a business man, he found himself at a disadvantage in dealing with the Issei. The success of these schools was not too significant, inasmuch as the Army had a most difficult time securing American-born Japanese who could serve as interpreters. Several universities on the Pacific Coast offer Japanese-language courses, which are attended by Nisei. It thus appears that the second-generation Japanese tends to be an assimilated American in many particulars.

ECONOMIC STATUS

The marked success of Japanese in business and agriculture has

[34] Edward K. Strong, Jr., *The Second-Generation Japanese Problem* (Palo Alto: Stanford University Press, 1934), p. 197.

been one of the reasons suggested for discrimination against the Japanese. Perhaps no ethnic group has contributed so much in the fields of California in terms of new crops and agricultural methods as the Japanese. The economic success in California of the Japanese in Agriculture certainly initiated the discriminatory legislation passed. While difficult to prove, some of the sympathetic students of the Japanese claim that the real motivation behind the mass evacuation of the Japanese was to eliminate these people as economic competitors. Perhaps the essential point to keep in mind is that the discrimination against these people in economic areas speaks well for their high economic status. A Nisei made the following distinctions: "Mass evacuation of my people was an economic measure, individual segregation of the disloyal Japanese would have been a military precaution. However, given a fair chance we will make a success of our careers in the postwar period.[35]

Prior to evacuation, the Japanese farmed about one-third of the total truck crop acreage of California, and their production of a number of products, including strawberries, snap beans, celery, cauliflower, spinach, and peppers, constituted between 50 to 85 per cent of the total.[36] In California, Oregon, and Washington, Japanese farmers operated 6,118 farms containing 258,074 acres and valued at $72,641,934, or about 2 per cent of the total farming activity. The three counties in which the communities of Los Angeles, Seattle, and Tacoma are located contained about 33 per cent of all the Japanese farms in the three Coast states, and within these counties the Japanese farmers in 1941 accounted for 63 per cent of the truck crop acreage.[37] About 45 per cent of all Japanese gainful workers in 1940 were engaged in agriculture. Over three-fourths of the remainder were employed in various trade and service activities, while only a very small number were engaged in manufacturing and the professions.

Japanese farmers have concentrated on the intensive farming of small areas of land near urban centers. In 1940 the average size of Japanese farms in the Pacific Coast states was 42 acres, as compared with an average of 231 acres for all farms. It is worth noting that of

[35] From a statement of J.T.T., a senior at the University of Southern California.

[36] *Monthly Review*, Federal Reserve Bank of San Francisco (April 1, 1942). The entire issue was devoted to a detailed statement of the economic characteristics and holdings of Japanese on the Coast. The mass evacuation of these people had tremendous economic implications.

[37] *Ibid.*, p. 1.

the 42 acres, 76 per cent was under cultivation in contrast to an average of only 20 per cent for all farm land.

Because of the alien property provision, it is not suprising to find that the Japanese are largely tenants of farms. The 1940 census reveals that of the 6,118 Japanese farm operators in the Pacific Coast states, 1,197 were full owners, 378 were part owners, 261 were managers, and 4,282, or 70 per cent, were tenants. Inasmuch as the Japanese farm rather small areas and have large families, they do not hire much outside help. However, on occasion during the peak harvest period Japanese operators may hire some Filipino and Mexican farmhands. It is, on the other hand, rare to see a Japanese as a farmhand for the Filipino or Mexican operator.

In terms of economic output, the Japanese in California produced about 35 per cent of all truck crops during the years preceding the Second World War. In 1938 the Japanese grew between 75 and 90 per cent of the following market crops: strawberries, snap beans, celery, cucumbers, spinach, and southern tomatoes.[38] It might be recalled that before the war the Japanese were prominent in the commission houses in the large central fruit and vegetable markets of California. In the fruit and vegetable stands he took considerable pride in displaying the products of the field in patterns of beauty. However, this display of fruit had been abandoned with the coming of permanent artificial displays. When the Japanese left the fruit stands in the California markets for relocation centers, their successors lacked the ability to maintain the attractive fruit displays.[39]

In the state of Washington, with the exception of an important concentration in Yakima Valley (78 farms) and a smaller one near Spokane (14 farms), most of the 706 Japanese farms are located west of the Cascade Mountains. Here the Japanese accounted for approximately 30 per cent of the total acreage in fruit and truck crops. In King County, which includes Seattle, the Japanese grew 56 per cent of all truck crops and in Pierce County, which includes the City of Tacoma, they grew almost 39 per cent of such crops. In Oregon over half of the 277 Japanese farms were located in the Portland region. In the very important Gresham area just east of Portland, the Japanese growers accounted for almost 90 per cent of the vegetables grown and about 35 per cent of the berry crop.[40]

[38] *Ibid.,* p. 19.

[39] It is no exaggeration to say that behind an artificial display of oranges a customer may now find turnips.

[40] See *Monthly Review* (April 1, 1942).

The economic impact of relocation of the Japanese may be appreciated by comparing their business stake before and after World War II. The writers found the following changes in Los Angeles upon questioning a number of leading American Japanese. Before the war, there were at least 25 "major" Japanese wholesale houses, that is, produce commission merchants and brokers, controlling about 65 per cent of the wholesale produce business in Los Angeles. Some 150 to 200 smaller businesses or "stalls" were also operated. The Ninth Street Market was almost entirely Japanese at the time of Relocation, with small additional houses established in the Seventh Street Market. At the present time (April, 1953) there are only 4 major houses entirely operated by Japanese and 40 to 50 smaller stalls constituting about 15 per cent of the entire produce business. There is little doubt that relocation has changed the economic status of the American Japanese, but this lower status in this respect seems to be temporary and almost certain to improve.

SUMMARY

The social status of the Japanese as estimated by social distance scales and preference tests seems to cluster in the lowest quartiles of a list of the more widely known ethnic groups in the United States. During World War II the social status of the Japanese dropped, but it may be expected to resume its former status. Foreign-born Japanese have been subjected to a legal status that denied them the opportunity to own property in California, to migrate to this country on a quota basis, and to become American citizens. World War II policies defined the alien and American citizen of Japanese ancestry in the same category, a unique definition. Never before in the history of the American democracy had ethnic affiliation been used as the measure of loyalty. Nevertheless, Americans of Japanese ancestry served in the military service in combat areas, though they were not permitted on the Pacific Coast. From the data available it appears that the Japanese excel in school attendance and in the marks assigned. The educational status of the Japanese ranks high in the elementary and secondary school experiences. His economic status is characterizd by agriculture and small business pursuits. It is doubtful that any other ethnic group has been able to remain so self-sufficient during periods of economic distress as the Japanese.

PROBLEMS FOR STUDY AND DISCUSSION

1. Explain why the Japanese immigrated into the United States largely during the earlier part of the twentieth century.

2. List the states in which the Japanese were concentrated in 1940, and show how this concentration has contributed to the problems of the Japanese in the United States.

3. List at least five attitudes that you have acquired toward the Japanese; and explain whether each was acquired before, during or after World War II.

4. List and explain what you think to be the major problems of the Nisei in the United States as pointed out by Masuoka.

5. Explain how the legal status of the Japanese in the United States differs from that of the Negro in the South and of that of Indians in the United States.

6. Keeping in mind the fact that most of the Japanese are native-born citizens of the United States, explain the social and legal reasons why it was possible to remove them from the Pacific Coast to relocation centers during World War II.

7. In this chapter it is shown that Japanese have attained a higher level of schooling, and usually rank high for grades made in school. Explain why this is true.

8. Compare the economic status of the Japanese with that of the Negro, the Indian, and the Mexican, explaining why the Japanese have attained a higher status than these other minority ethnic groups.

9. Compare the Japanese with the Jew under the following points: (1) social, (2) legal, (3) educational, and (4) economic, showing which of these ethnic groups have attained the highest status in the United States.

SELECTED READINGS

Broom, L., and Riemer, R., *Removal and Return* (Berkeley: The University of California Press, 1949).

Brown, F. J., and Roucek, J. S., *One America* (New York: Prentice-Hall, Inc., 1952), pp. 319-335.

Ichihashi, Y., *Japanese in the United States* (Palo Alto: Stanford University Press, 1932).

Konvitz, M. R., *The Alien and the Asiatic in American Law* (Ithaca: Cornell University Press, 1946), pp. 22-25, 157-170, 241-279.

LaViolette, F. E., *Americans of Japanese Ancestry* (Toronto: Canadian Institute of International Affairs, 1945).

Lundberg, George A., "Inter-Ethnic Attitudes in a High School Population," *American Journal of Sociology*, Vol. 58 (July, 1952), pp. 1-11.

Marden, Charles F., *Minorities in American Society* (New York: American Book Company, 1952), pp. 171-196.

Morgan, J. B., "Attitudes of Students Toward the Japanese," *Journal of Social Psychology*, Vol. 21 (May, 1945), pp. 219-227.

Morison, S. E., *Rising Sun in the Pacific* (Boston: Little, Brown and Company, 1948).

Schermerhorn, R. A., *These Our People* (Boston: D. C. Heath and Company, 1949), pp. 199-224.

Thomas, Dorothy S., Kikuchi, Charles, and Sakoda, James M., *The Salvage* Berkeley: The University of California Press, 1952).

Walter, Paul A. F., Jr., *Race and Cultural Relations* (New York: McGraw-Hill Book Company, Inc., 1952), pp. 360-377.

XI

Chinese

Introduction

ONE OF THE MOST analytic descriptions of the essential characteristics of the Chinese population in the United States has been written by Rose Hum Lee. The Chinese have passed through several periods in the ethnic relations cycle of immigrants; for instance, the period of economic welcome, the period of economic competition, the period of restrictive legislation, and finally, the present period of quiescence. We now turn to the reading by Lee to learn some of the important factors in the demography and immigration difficulties of the Chinese.

THE CHINESE IN THE UNITED STATES [1]

ROSE HUM LEE

An adequate understanding of the population trends of the Chinese in the United States necessitates a consideration of the history of their migration from the middle of the 19th Century to the present. Pertinent, likewise, is a consideration of their distribution within the country over the decades. Are the Chinese like most other ethnic groups concentrated in large cities, or are they rural? If they are not concentrated when did dispersion take place? What will the trend of their future settlement and immigration be? All of these aspects should be treated to enable prediction of future trends.

In analyzing the available data contained in the census reports of the United States, the following main trends of Chinese immigration manifest themselves: (1) the concentration of Chinese during the period immediately following the Gold Rush was in California, and the Rocky Mountain States; (2) the dispersion of the Chinese to

[1] Rose Hum Lee, "Chinese Population Trends in the United States," *The South-western Journal*, Vol. 2, No. 2 (Spring, 1946), pp. 97-104. Used by permission of the Journal.

midwestern and eastern parts of the United States was from 1880 to 1910; and (3) their concentration in metropolitan cities has been in process from 1910 to the present.

However, it must be pointed out that population trends of the Chinese are greatly influenced by several factors. These factors fall under several categories: (1) the conditions in China contributing to their migration; (2) the classes of Chinese nationals permitted entrance into the United States; and, (3) types of occupations engaged in by Chinese Nationals.

Reasons for Migration: In discussing the first category bearing upon the migration of Chinese to America, one needs to analyze the social, political, and economic conditions of China during the 19th Century. China was overrun with Manchus, an ethnic group who had different customs, social organization, and political aims than the Chinese (who are Hans and the largest of the five ethnic groups in China). As conquerors the Manchus had little concern for the welfare of the conquered. The southern Chinese (the Cantonese) were the largest group who escaped their domination. They migrated and settled in the Pacific rim countries: Malaya, Indo-China, Philippines, Hawaii, and America. They arrived here in great numbers to join the European immigrants opening the western frontier. They came to seek economic gains, to alleviate the downtrodden plight of their families at home as well as that of their kinsmen and native villages.

Classes of Chinese Admitted: Much has been written and said about the "types" of Chinese immigrants settling in this country. Without undue repetition, it can be pointed out that those who do migrate are of two extreme types: the lower economic groups, and those of the very elite. This disparity between social classes has caused considerable heartaches to the Chinese elite, who have been continuously regarded as the lower economic groups until their statuses are made known. The American public has stereotyped, rightly or wrongly, the Chinese into three categories: chop suey men, laundrymen, students or officials. Merchants, herb-doctors, curio dealers, clerks, and managers of various establishments have no social classification. This misconception is partly due to the immigration laws permitting Chinese nationals entrance into this country.

When the first Exclusion Act was signed in 1882 (The Burlingame Treaty), it was primarily aimed at the influx of Chinese laborers and the cessation of their immigration in large numbers. Ten years later another Act was signed extending the restriction another decade; by this time the Chinese had become permanently and irrevocably classified as "laborers" by the general American public. Considerable public feeling had accompanied the Exclusion Acts; the country was now rid of undesirable laborers. However, provisions were made to admit certain classes of Chinese whom the United States government considered harmless or beneficial. In the main they include: (1) teachers, ministers, missionaries of religious denominations, newspaper editors, and other public instructors; (2) students; (3) travelers for curiosity or pleasure; (4) merchants and their lawful wives and minor children; (5) government officials, their families, attendants, servants, and employees; (6) Chinese in continuous transit; and (7) bona fide seamen. These latter groups are far outnumbered by the "laboring" groups already resident in this country. It was not until after the Exclusion Act of 1924 that the social composition of the Chinese population became more equalized. However, the presence of the more "elite" does not affect the popular conception that the Chinese in this country are of the lower classes. The very nature of their occupations emphasizes this misconception and no consideration is taken of the fact that an American-born Chinese might also be forced into the same occupations through occupational barriers erected by the dominant community.

Types of Occupations: The Chinese were imported into this country in large numbers during the Gold Rush to supply cheap labor needed in the placer mines in California and the Rocky Mountain regions. Their main function was to perform the "women's work" in mining camps, predominantly male. When the prospecting stage gave way to organized, large-scale mining, the Chinese entered into occupations which offered the least competition to the laboring groups—cooking and laundry work. They have achieved excellent accommodation pursuing these occupations throughout the United States. In no small measure has this contributed to their dispersion; when the steam laundries offered competition, the Chinese settled in large cities where their services were more in demand. There are still many Americans who prefer their washing to be done meticulously by Chinese, and are willing to pay a slightly higher rate than that demanded by the steam laundries. The same parallel can be made of the chop suey and chow mein establishments which have virtually a monopoly on the preparation of these dishes for the American public. While a specialty, these establishments cater to a special group of customers. Hence, the larger the city, the more trade they can expect.

THE PERIOD OF CONCENTRATION

Having considered the three main factors influencing Chinese migration, we can now turn our attention to the character of their settlement within this country.

First Step: As already stated, the Chinese first located in California where opportunities were ripe for work in the placer mining camps. More aggressive immigrants repanned abandoned claims and some grew wealthy through painstakingly separating the gold dust from sand. Between 1850 and 1860, California was the only state which had a Chinese population; there were 34,933 scattered throughout the state. San Francisco, then a young city, had 2,710 Chinese. From 1860 to 1880 gold, silver, lead, copper and other metals were discovered in the Rocky Mountain region; the Chinese began trying their fortunes in all the mining camps there—cooking, washing, repanning abandoned gold mines, cutting wood, working on cattle ranches as well as farms. When the frontier closed in 1880, they began their dispersion to the mid-western and eastern cities of the United States.

Second Step: During this period, the population was highly concentrated in California, Montana, Idaho, Nevada, Colorado, Wyoming, and Utah. As these states attained statehood and the character of their industry changed, the concentration of the Chinese followed suit. During these decades, however, the Chinese population was mainly rural; cities in this region had not developed and the Chinese lived in segregated groups. Many Chinatowns were formed to take care of their needs as immigrants with a different culture and social organization from that of the European immigrants. Their dispersion to the midwest and east was to a great extent heightened by the hostility of the dominant group toward these immigrants who regarded the latter as competitors in a settled economy.

Third Step: By 1880 the Chinese population had increased to 105,465, which, incidentally, was the peak of Chinese immigration. When the Exclusion Act was repealed in the fall of 1943, the annual quota of 105 nationals who may seek admittance into this country was based upon these figures. The demographic distribution by the end of 1880 showed a slight trend toward urban settlement; twenty cities with a population of 100,000 and over had a total Chinese population of 22,925. Cities under 25,000 (including unincorporated villages) had a Chinese population totalling 82,050.

THE PERIOD OF DISPERSION

From 1890 and up through 1910, the Chinese dispersed to the New England, Middle Atlantic, the East and West North Central, West North Central, East and West South Central, and South Atlantic States. The Rocky Mountain and Pacific States began losing their Chinese population. The trend toward concentration in large seaboard metropolitan cities, especially New York, Philadelphia, Boston, Baltimore, Washington, Newark, and Jersey City was evident.

During this period the decline was marked in cities with a native white population of 25,000 population and under. This can be attributed to one of the reasons given in the foregoing paragraphs, viz: that the monopolistic nature of Chinese occupations—laundries and eating establishments—necessitated a large native population to support them. Thus, there was an increase of Chinese population in metropolitan cities.

Before proceeding further, one should ask, "What effect did the Exclusion Act of 1882 and its subsequent extension have upon Chinese immigration? There was a steady decline of population from 1890 and there was a loss of approximately 30,000 in three decades. Many immigrants, who had entered this country as "sojourners" (men who came for economic gain and subsequently returned to their families when their objectives were accomplished), returned to China never to leave again. As Chinese women were restricted, unless wives of merchants, officials, etc. as stated previously, the population did not grow sufficiently to compensate for the loss. The decrease was even more marked by 1920 when the Chinese population figures reached a low of 61,639 for the entire country. It was not until 1930 that the Chinese population showed any increase. Moreover, by this time the American-born Chinese were increasing sufficiently to bring about a more equal distribution of sexes.

During this period of dispersion, the trend toward urbanization was marked. Chinese in cities under 100,000 and above 25,000 were on the decrease, while seventy-three metropolitan cities showed marked increase. As would be expected, the rural population of the Chinese (for cities under 2,500) declined proportionately.

PERIOD OF RECONCENTRATION

From 1920 until the present, the Chinese population has increased approximately 16,000. Sixty-nine per cent of the Chinese now reside in metropolitan communities of 100,000 and over while 25 per cent live in cities under 100,000, and only 8 per cent are rural. The concentration in metropolitan communities, however, shows a wide variation in the size of cities. San Francisco has the largest Chinese population for historical reason—being the area of first urban settlement and because the Chinatown there has the most cohesive social organization, followed closely by New York City. One might pertinently ask, "Is there any relationship between Chinese population and the size of an American city?" An analysis of the available data reveals no positive correlation. For example, San Francisco has a Chinese population of 17,782 and a total population (all races) of approximately 500,000. On the other hand, New York City has approximately 11,500 Chinese inhabitants, while her total population is several million. While Kansas City, Missouri and Kansas City, Kansas have few Chinese residents, whereas their total populations are larger than that of San Francisco.

Cities which show an increase in Chinese population between 1930 and 1940 are: Los Angeles, Seattle, Portland, Oakland, Washington, D.C., New York and Minneapolis. These also show a wide variation between Chinese population and native population. Then, one may ask, "Is there a correlation between geographic location and increase in Chinese population?" An examination of the location of these cities reveals four of them are on the Pacific Coast, two on the Atlantic seaboard, and one in the midwest. Although not thoroughly representative numerically, as far as geographic distribution is concerned, it is pertinent that the Pacific Coast and the East Coast have the largest increases. This increase appears to be due to the location of industries at the beginning of the present decade, as well as the establishment of Chinese government agencies, in those cities. Many Chinese (American and foreign-born) residing in small urban centers, as well as other metropolitan cities before 1940, have been attracted to these locations by new occupational opportunities hithertofore unavailable.

Now that the war has been successfully and victoriously terminated, the question becomes: Is there a likelihood that the Chinese will redisperse to their former homes? From first-hand observation and interviews with many young Chinese, this does not appear likely. Even though they may not find new occupations during this period of reconversion, they appear to have come to the city to stay. The metropolitan cities offer more opportunities for cultural, social, and economic security. If need be, they will re-enter laundries and chop suey establishments, but that they will remain in metropolitan cities seems to be a certainty.

THE FUTURE

There does not seem to be a trend toward a substantial increase of Chinese population in this country. The admittance of 105 Chinese —75 per cent of whom must apply from their respective residence throughout China and 25 per cent from Chinese already in this country will not be sufficient to alter the present trend. Taking away the 25 per cent who are already here, and who are privileged to undergo the process of naturalization, approximately eighty Chinese can enter annually the United States henceforth. This is equivalent to about forty families per year dependent upon the condition that the new immigrants bring their wives and children. This small addition to the Chinese population is not likely to change its composition materially. It is doubtful if these 105 persons will compensate for the "loss" to the existing population—of those who marry outside the race, as men are often tempted to do because of the unequal distribution of the sexes and personal reasons. Many Chinese-American girls marry business men, officials, and students from China; their offspring are lost to the population in this country since their permanent residence is more apt to be in China. Officials, business men, and students return to China once their purpose in this country is accomplished. With these possibilities in mind, it can be concluded that the Chinese population in the future may again show a decline. However, we might expect those remaining in the United States to continue to concentrate in urban areas throughout the nation.

SOCIAL STATUS

In some respects the social status of the Chinese and the Japanese are comparable; however, there have been periodic fluctuations of a minor nature over the last thirty years. The Bogardus social distance scale placed the Chinese in thirty-third place in 1926 and twenty-fifth place in 1946. Thus it appears that the recent war had the effect of changing the respective places of the Chinese and Japanese. Apparently war allies had the effect of reducing social distance. Nevertheless, the Chinese are still accorded a social status by Caucasians that is in the lowest quartile.[2]

Another study indicating the social status of the Chinese was made by Richards in the spring of 1948.[3] It is recalled that this study was based on the evaluations of some 1,672 white university students in the states of Oklahoma, Texas, Arkansas, and Louisiana. The Chinese received the third highest rating as is indicated by Table XXIX.

Richards found that the traits most frequently checked for the Chinese were: (1) possess civic pride, (2) are good workers, (3) are artistic, (4) are loyal and trustworthy, and (5) will coöperate with others. It appears that the items checked most often were favorable personality traits.

In the exploratory study of sixteen ethnic groups, the writers found that the Chinese were rated in ninth place by white students at the

2 Emory S. Bogardus, "Changes in Racial Distance," *International Journal of Opinion and Attitude Research*, Vol. 1, No. 4 (Dec., 1947), p. 58.

3 E. S. Richards, "Attitudes of College Students in the Southwest Toward Ethnic Groups in the United States," *Sociology and Social Research*, Vol. 35 (Sept.-Oct., 1950), pp. 22-30.

University of Oklahoma and in eleventh place by Negro students at Langston University. It is of interest to recall that the Japanese were rated in thirteenth place by white students and fourteenth place by Negro students. This preliminary study suggests a possible shift in opinion toward a more favorable rating of the Chinese; however, the duration of this evaluation cannot be ascertained at this time due to the Korean war.

It is of definite significance to contemporary students of ethnic relations to realize the former attitudes toward the Chinese in the United States. In order to appreciate the importance of the current attitude toward the Chinese, it is necessary to trace briefly some of the expressed attitudes of early Californians, the legislation passed in respect to the Chinese, and the definite effort to restrict the Chinese from the more lucrative occupations.

The exact date of the arrival of the Chinese in the United States is not known, but it is believed to be in the year 1848. Most of the Chinese came from the province of Kwangtung in southeastern China. Canton is the principal city of this province. Three groups of

Table XXIX: SOCIAL STATUS ACCORDED SELECTED ETHNIC GROUPS IN THE UNITED STATES BY 1,672 WHITE UNIVERSITY STUDENTS *

Ethnic Group	Per Cent of Positive Items
Native-born White	86.0
Foreign-born White	78.7
Chinese	70.5
Indian	64.4
Jews	64.3
Filipino	64.2
Japanese	49.7
Negro	40.4
Mexican	38.5

* E. S. Richards listed forty action patterns or traits that might be ascribed to the ethnic groups selected. The evaluators were to select the items that applied to the ethnic group under review. There was an equal number of positive and negative traits. The positiveness and negativeness of each item had been previously established by submitting the list to a group of social scientists.

persons came to America from China: the merchants, who ranked close to the bottom in the social scale in China; the laborers, who appeared industrious, frugal, sober, and alert to learn the ways of the West; the prostitutes, who came to America, since custom forbade Chinese women of respect the opportunity of leaving their homes. Perhaps most of the Chinese men came to America with the happy anticipation of making a great fortune in "gold mountain" and then returning to China.[4] Prostitution was greatly restricted after the passage of the Page Law of 1875 which made it difficult for such women to gain entrance to the United States. *The Chinese came to America because of the combined forces of poverty, civil wars, and the shipmasters' stories and pictures of easy wealth in America.* Additional incentives bringing the Chinese to California were the constant demands for labor in the mines, cheap construction laborers on railroads, and for general labor in the service occupations. While the Central Pacific Railroad officials stated in the beginning that they were against the plan of hiring Chinese, keen competition from the Union Pacific Railroad forced them to hire Chinese not later than 1865. Before the work was completed, there were ten thousand Chinese on the payroll of the Central Pacific. A considerable number of the Chinese were imported direct from China through the contracting companies of San Francisco. Not long afterward the Southern Pacific Lines in California were built almost entirely by Chinese laborers. After 1860 the Chinese were used chiefly as laborers on the railroads, in agriculture, and as domestic servants and in related service occupations. The pioneer miners were perhaps the first in demanding the taxing and later exclusion of the Chinese from the mines.

Professor Robert Cleland describes the early reactions of the Chinese to America and the Californians to them:

Once in California, the Chinese kept almost entirely to themselves, did not understand the white man, had no desire to associate with him, and refused to adopt his customs or manner of life. The Californian on the other hand, saw in the Chinaman only an inferior being, simple in some ways but cannier than a Scot in others, who lived in squalor and stench, spoke an outlandish jargon, worked with patience and industry beyond comprehension, worshipped strange gods, suffered from strange diseases, practiced strange vices, ate strange foods, regarded China as the land of the blessed, thrived under standards of living no white man could endure, administered his own law in his own way through his own agents, without much regard for the officials and statutes of the Sovereign State of California, suffered with helpless stoicism whatever indignities were thrust upon him (partly because he had no vote), and represented but the far flung skirmish line of an army of 400,000,000 beings like unto himself.[5]

Since the Chinese lived in ghettoes, their assimilation of the Western culture was retarded. No doubt a great amount of speculation and many rumors facilitated the stereotyping process of the Chinese

[4] Elmer C. Sanmeyer, *The Anti-Chinese Movement in California*, Vol. 24, No. 3 (Urbana: University of Illinois Studies in the Social Sciences, 1939), p. 13.

[5] Robert Cleland, *A History of California* (New York: The Macmillan Company, 1930), p. 416.

as a unique member of the race of man. *In some cases the white man passed laws restricting the assimilation process; yet, other white men blamed the Chinese for not wanting to learn the Western culture.* For the most part, the early period of the Chinese in the United States was characterized by expediency. He came here on a temporary basis, the industries desired him only for the initial construction period, and the white man, as a permanent resident, demanded that the Chinese leave when the work was completed. Prejudice against the Chinese reflected the many facets of daily living. Perhaps the following list of accusations against the Chinese published in 1876 will give a fair conception of ethnic prejudice and evaluation:

That he is a slave, reduced to the lowest terms of beggarly economy, and is no fit competitor for an American freeman.

That he herds in scores, in small dens, where a white man and wife could hardly breathe, and has none of the wants of a civilized white man.

That he has neither wife nor child, nor expects to have any.

That his sister is a prostitute from instinct, religion, education, and interest, and degrading to all around her.

That the American men, women and children cannot be what free people should be, and compete with such degraded creatures in the labor market.

That wherever they are numerous, as in San Francisco, by a secret machinery of their own, they defy the law, keep up the manners and customs of China, and utterly disregard all the laws of health, decency, and morality.

That they are driving the white population from the state, reducing laboring men to despair, laboring women to prostitution, and boys and girls to hoodlums and convicts.

That the health, wealth, prosperity, and happiness of our State demand their expulsion from our shores.[6]

Much of the social status of the Chinese as a laborer prior to the exclusion legislation of 1882 was due to the conflict of strange customs in a pioneer world. The Chinese men were almost beardless, while the pioneers took a distinct pride in their rugged facial appearance. His oriental clothes seemed too delicate and perhaps a little effeminate compared with the coarse appearing outer garments and boots of the miner. No doubt the failures of the gold miners to make a quick fortune panning gold nuggets along the Sacramento River found their logical scapegoat in the presence of the Chinaman, especially since the pioneers realized that they would have to compete with the Chinese for wages rather than fortunes. An investigation of the social status of the Chinese during the early days in California will disclose a comparison with the ignorant Irish, the canny Scotch, and the unreliable Indians. At that point most of the "foreign" ethnic

6 *Marin Journal* (March 30, 1876). Quoted in Sanmeyer, *op. cit.*, p. 25.

groups might be compared with one another to their mutual loss in status. It is indeed encouraging to observe that there have been distinct changes in the status of many of the ethnic groups. Today, such a comparison would yield only amusement concerning the ethnic convictions of another day. The Chinese illustrate the complexity of comparing different periods of time. Prior to the repeal of exclusion laws, the Chinese occupied a low social status; however, with the termination of legislation of this type, presently to be reviewed, a marked change in the social status was conditioned on the steadily improving social status of the Chinese as a useful and desirable ethnic group in the United States.

Mr. Walter Kong in the following reading indicates what Chinese in this country think of the habit of some Americans to use unfavorable titles for these people. He provides some interesting examples of the "name-calling" device and the damage it does to the social status evaluation of all concerned.

▌ NAME CALLING [7]

WALTER KONG

In considering how to get along with people of another race, the idea of understanding them as the first step immediately comes to mind. For years this truism has been pointed out by all sorts of teachers—from the philosopher down to the discussion group leader. Yet no serious steps seem to have been taken by members of any one race to understand another with which they live.

Half-hearted attempts in that direction now and then are made by individuals who attend lectures or go on organized "tours" of a local Chinatown or a Harlem. But these moves are prompted more by curiosity and pleasure than by the serious purpose of promoting understanding. There is still to be seen a deliberate, large scale effort on the part of any people to get acquainted with neighbors of another race for the express purpose of friendly living together.

The traffic situation offers a clue to interracial relationships. Our annual toll of automobile victims runs into alarming figures. It frequently has been suggested that if drivers would only learn road manners, this shocking total could be markedly reduced. Such disregard of the rights of others as crowding, cutting in, deliberate blocking, are among the chief causes of traffic accidents. The tragedy is not only that so many should have been killed or injured, but that

[7] Walter Kong, "Name Calling," *Survey Graphic,* Vol. 33, No. 6 (June, 1944), pp. 296-304. Used by permission of Survey Associates.

they could have been saved by such a simple thing as the practice
of highway courtesy.

Granting that difference of language and custom are major sources
of misunderstanding between peoples of different races, many
thoughtless little acts of discourtesy tend to widen the gap. Take,
for example, the childish habit of name calling.

CHINESE CONTEMPT

The Chinese still call Westerners Fan Kuai, "Foreign devil." (*Yang
Kuei Tse* in the North.) When European traders first landed in
China, their white skin, reddish hair, and blue eyes caused consterna-
tion among the Chinese. Being seafaring adventurers, these first
comers were as a rule big and rough, insolent in speech and cruel
in conduct to the peaceful inhabitants of China, devils indeed.
Immediately, the Chinese called them Fan Kuai and later the term
was indiscriminately applied to all Westerners.

Of course, the unfamiliar and hence terrifying appearance and
manners of the early traders were not the only reasons the Chinese
called them Fan Kuai. The Chinese were then under the illusion
that the inhabitants of the Central Flowery Kingdom were the only
civilized human beings on earth. Fan Kuai was a term coined to
express a feeling of contempt for the Westerner.

There is no way of telling how many Westerners-travelers or residents in China have been antagonized by this uncomplimentary
epithet and returned to their homeland with a dislike for the Chinese because of it. But one thing is certain, the term has never been
a generator of good will. "The Chinese despise and hate us. They
call us 'foreign devils.' "

This familiar comment overlooks the fact that time and frequent
usage have robbed the words of their original meaning, and today
they carry none of their early contempt. In fact, Fan Kuai, to the
Chinese, has become a harmless synonym for Occidental. However,
that does not soothe a Westerner's feeling nor lessen the offense the
words give.

For some time a silent campaign has been going on among the
Chinese, notably the Christians and the educated, to refer to an
Occidental as Sai Ying (Westerner). Even in intimate circles, out of
the hearing of any Westerner, this practice is encouraged, and to
use Fan Kuai is coming to be regarded as a mark of vulgarity.

AMERICAN SCORN

When the Chinese dubbed Westerners Fan Kuai, they did not
dream that some day they themselves would be called disparaging
names. Self-sufficient and self-satisfied, it did not occur to them that

they or their descendants would migrate to other parts of the world. But the gold rush of the Fifties saw them streaming to the Gold Mountain, their name for California then as now. They had hardly finished their first bowl of rice on American soil when agitation was started against them and the name of "Chink" was hurled at them.

If the term Fan Kuai has caused Westerners much exasperation, its American counterpart has given the Chinese a host of complexes. Whether it was originated by their competitors for jobs, the Irish immigrants, or by native Americans is of little significance. As an insult to the Chinese, it was a huge success. They hated it from the day it was coined; even today they are perturbed when it is thoughtlessly used. They feel the full impact of its belittling scorn and there is no Chinese who does not feel indignation and resentment at the use of this name.

It is a tribute to American good taste that children using it innocently are corrected by parents and teachers. Newspapers and magazines have deleted it wholly from their columns. To his great relief and gratitude, it is only rarely that a Chinese is offended by hearing it today.

WORDS WITH ASSOCIATIONS

Frequently, in pursuing my favorite game of golf, a recalcitrant shot leads me to the wrong fairway. And just as frequently some American friend loudly warns me to clear his line of fire lest I become "a dead Chinaman." I always enjoy the banter and contribute my share of it. But what some of my friends do not know is that I resent this word Chinaman. Most Chinese do, especially those of the educated class from China and, to a certain extent, those born in this country. Each prefers to be called a Chinese.

Comparatively few Caucasian Americans are aware of this preference. It is not unusual to hear professors, ministers, and other well educated persons referring to the Chinese as Chinamen. Unquestionably they would be surprised to learn that the Chinese themselves regard the word Chinaman with disfavor. Indeed, they might well wonder why the Chinese have the feeling when Englishman, Frenchman, and Dutchman are considered by the English, French, and Dutch people, respectively, to be in perfectly good taste.

Are the Chinese absurdly sensitive? Or are there sound reasons for their objection? "I don't call you America-man, so why should you call me Chinaman?" a young Chinese student once protested.

And that is the only explanation that most Chinese are able to formulate. But the real reasons are in the associations of the word. It conjures up many of the humiliations and indignities to which the Chinese were subjected in the years when agitation was running high against them. In those days anyone who had anything to say against the Chinese used the word Chink or Chinaman, and many ugly things were said. These associations with the word still arouse unpleasant and uneasy feelings in the Chinese.

Then there was the song "Chin Chong Chinaman," making fun of the Chinese. I remember several years back when a group of children hailed me with the alliteration as I strolled along the street in the city of Orange, California. Probably they had no more feeling about the jingle than about a Mother Goose rhyme. Yet I cannot deny that they managed to make me feel unnatural and uncomfortable.

To the Chinese, the word "Chinese" denotes refinement and an attitude of friendly respect on the part of the speaker. "Chinaman" gives quite the opposite feeling. In short, a great many Chinese immediately form an unfavorable opinion of any Caucasian they hear using that word. He is suspected, usually without justification, of feeling contempt for the Chinese.

A high school student at present enrolled in a college course in airplane mechanics is thinking of withdrawing because the instructor said to him one day, "Now, little Chinaman, you must learn all you can about the airplane from us here so that you can go back to China and bomb hell out of the Japs." No amount of explanation can convince this boy that the instructor did not mean to insult him.

THE NAME ISN'T CHARLIE

Perhaps even less known is the fact that there is a common English name with which many Caucasian Americans greet the Chinese and for which the latter have violent dislike. That abomination is "Charlie." How the Chinese happen to be so christened no one now knows, but its use is common from Maine to California. "How are you, Charlie?" "What can I do for you Charlie?" "Your countrymen are doing all right, Charlie—they've got those damned Japs on the run now."

Unless it happens actually to be his name, you cannot find an American-born Chinese who does not resent this. Students and educated Chinese from China are no less provoked—they grow hot with suppressed anger when so addressed.

The reasons are clear enough. To be distinguished from the human mass is a matter of great importance to the individual. To ignore that individuality is to strike at something sacred to him. Any person resents being mistaken for another, or greeted with the wrong name by a lapse of memory. To toss at him a casual misnomer is to violate a basic human instinct. Thus, to the Chinese, Charlie seems either a deliberate affront or the unconscious expression of an inner disdain.

Further, such a greeting is contrary to all Chinese etiquette. When addressing a person whose name you do not know—scholar, official, businessman, coolie—Chinese courtesy requires you to call him "teacher," or "uncle," or "Elder brother," which, so used, are approximate equivalents of the English "sir" or "Mister." It is the height of rudeness to omit the salutation.

A LESSON IN MANNERS

I was once in a hurry to catch a ferry from Yaumati to Hong Kong and, unacquainted with the place, asked an old gentleman where the jetty was. Then I ran in the direction he indicated with a nod. For ten minutes I looked for that ferry. Then, to my dismay, I discovered that I had been sent in the wrong direction. It suddenly dawned on me that in my haste I had entirely forgotten to address the old gentleman as "uncle" and he had taken the trouble to teach me a little lesson.

This is not to suggest that in speaking to the Chinese, Caucasian Americans should follow Chinese etiquette and punctuate their speech with honorific titles. It is only to point out that people who place such emphasis on formal greeting necessarily find it difficult to be hailed as Charlie, whatever their names may be.

When a Chinese is called Charlie, he seldom expresses his resentment by violence of either language or gesture. Instead, he shows his displeasure in typically Chinese ways. If the name occurs in conversation, he may assume a less sociable attitude, and find an early excuse to leave the offender. If it is attached to a request for information, he may profess ignorance, pretend deafness, or simply look at the offender in silence.

Obviously, this is not a constructive way for the Chinese to handle the situation. Americans are not mind readers. And they are, in the main, a polite and reasonable people, not afraid to admit mistakes and ready to correct them. And yet the Chinese, as a rule, find it difficult to offer a friendly explanation of this matter.

For several years a small town publisher has been soliciting my firm's advertising and getting it at regular intervals. Our mutual greetings always had been formal and cordial until a few months ago when for some reason he started to call me Charlie. I ignored it the first few times, hiding my resentment. One day I was on the verge of telling him his presence was no longer welcome, but the arrival of a customer stopped me. Clearly, it never occurred to him that calling me Charlie had anything to do with my sudden coldness nor with the withholding of our advertising. The only wise and sensible thing for me to do was to let him know how I felt, and finally I did so. He was both surprised and embarrassed. He apologized and assured me he never would make that mistake again in speaking to me or to anyone of my race.

Had I remained silent, I am sure he would have continued to call me Charlie, and I would have continued to nurse injured feelings. Now our relations, business and personal, are cordial again. Far more important is the likelihood that the publisher will warn his friends against committing his mistake in greeting other Chinese.

For the Chinese, friendly explanations, however troublesome, are vastly better than maintaining silent resentment and then withdrawing to curse offenders in the kitchens of chop suey houses, in the social halls of benevolent associations, around the counters of art stores, or in college dormitories. Frank airing of grievances is a sound way to bring about better understanding between peoples more swiftly and more effectively than exchange-scholarships and professorships.

Americans, in their turn, might examine their own conduct when they meet with a chilly reception from the Chinese. Before loosing the stock criticisms, let them first ask themselves whether they inadvertently called these people Charlie, or some other provocative name, be it in ever so friendly a tone. All too frequently the answer is there.

DAMAGING REPERCUSSIONS

In the search for causes of friction between different races, we are apt to overlook these little provocations. Yet they are not unworthy of attention if one stops to consider their effect on the attitudes of the individuals subjected to them. They tend to strengthen prejudices and false conceptions, and may crystallize into permanent hatred for the race represented by the offender. Often some of these embittered individuals reach places of power and influence. Then their warped attitude may have national or even international importance.

I always feel uneasy when an injured Chinese begins to condemn the Manchu dynasty and the corrupt Chinese officialdom, past and present, for the weakness of China today—the condition to which he attributes some insult tossed at him. For he goes on to hope for the day of a China so strong that no one dare insult the Chinese, no matter where they are. This is not a wholesome attitude. It pictures a barbaric future in which only citizens of a country bristling with tanks and guns will be accorded common courtesy and respect.

That little offenses can become great obstacles in the way of friendship and understanding between two nations is realized by the wartime governments of the United States and Great Britain. Both have taken the trouble to study the social customs of the people to whose countries American and British soldiers are being sent. On the basis of this study, pocket guides are issued to servicemen, telling them in great detail what to do and what not to do in these countries. The purpose is to prevent the innocent commission of small social errors that might have damaging repercussions.

What does this all add up to? Just one thing. That the human being is a very sensitive creature with feelings that are quickly hurt; that every normal individual, whatever his race or creed, values his own individuality; and that any satisfaction gained by belittling him is small, while resulting enmity may reach far.

LEGAL STATUS

One of the unique features concerning the legal status of the Chinese is that the process from marked Legislative exclusion to gradual Legislative inclusion illustrates clearly the evolutionary steps toward an expression of ethnic democracy in the United States. In some respects the changing legal status of an ethnic group is a splendid measuring rod of social distance. Laws assuring equality dramatically portray the lack of great social distance. Perhaps no other ethnic groups affords a better insight into the changing legal patterns of thinking from prejudice to equality than do the Chinese.

As early as 1854 legislation was proposed in California forbidding Chinese from testifying against a white person. While this discriminatory legislation did not pass, a decision in the California State Supreme Court accomplished the same thing. Several other attempts were made to admit Chinese testimony, but were defeated. This prejudicial attitude toward the Chinese was voiced by Pacific Coast senators to a point where these people were denied naturalization rights in 1870.[8]

Prior to 1875 the United States accepted all immigrants desiring to enter this country. In many respects the United States was a frontier democracy in a decadent world. Any person who could lend a hand in the construction of cities and railroads was eagerly sought. In some instances the immigrants were bribed to get them to come to America. However, after the railroads were built across the country, there developed a definite feeling against the "foreigner." It was assumed that the "foreigner" would upset the American standard of

[8] Sanmeyer, *op. cit.*, p. 34.

living. At any rate, legislation was talked about with an earnestness that indicated a strong reservoir of attitudes. In connection with the Chinese, the pattern of immigration legislation was first attempted. It is possible to discern at least four periods of ethnic thinking in regard to the Chinese that are reflected by the following measures: (1) 1848 to 1882—marked by free access to the United States with few exceptions, (2) 1882 to 1903—exclusion of the Chinese in periods of decades, (3) 1903 to 1943—permanent exclusion of the Chinese, and (4) 1943 to the present time represents the application of the quota system for admission and eligibility for naturalization of the Chinese.

In spite of the contribution of the Chinese in the mines, in the construction of railroads, and in the fields, there developed a growing feeling against these people. The Chinese played an important part in the development of our immigration laws. It was not until 1875 that a federal law was passed excluding convicts and prostitutes from entrance to America. A few years later in 1882, Congress passed the first general immigration laws, by which lunatics, idiots, and public charges were excluded from entry. Also in 1882 the Chinese Exclusion Act was passed, which suspended all Chinese immigration for a period of ten years; in 1892 it was renewed for another decade; and in 1903 the suspension was converted into a permanent exclusion.[9] *The only exceptions to the exclusion of Chinese were teachers, merchants, and travelers.* The exclusion of the Chinese marks the beginning of the so-called selective immigration policy, which was based on skin color and national origin.[10] Ten years after the adoption of the Chinese Exclusion Act, the United States Supreme Court ruled on an act passed in 1892 which required that all Chinese laborers resident in the United States at the time of the passage of the act must apply for a certificate of residence. A person who did not apply for such a certificate was deemed subject to arrest. Unless he could prove hardship in not applying for the certificate, he might be deported. One of the provisions of the act was that the Chinese had to prove by the testimony of one *white* person that he was a legal resident in the Unitd States at the time the act was passed. The court observed that the Chinese remain in the United States only "by the

[9] Milton R. Konvitz, *The Alien and the Asiatic in American Law,* (Ithaca: Cornell University Press, 1946), p. 9.

[10] A law of 1888 revoked the reëntry of about 20,000 Chinese, who left the country for a short visit to China. The revoking worked a real hardship on the Chinese, who had property in this country and their wives and children.

license, permission and sufferance of Congress." [11] *It was alleged that one white witness was necessary, inasmuch as the Chinese did not comprehend the meaning of an oath.* It was not too long until the expulsion of persons became one of the principal jobs of the immigration authorities. In fact in the years 1921-1925 there were deported 26,427 persons and in the next ten years 64,123.[12]

Another facet of legal discrimination against the Chinese has been reflected in the passage of legislation depriving aliens of the right to own real property. In the Burlingame Treaty of 1868 the right of Chinese immigration was admitted, but their naturalization as United States citizens denied. The California Constitution in force in 1870 invested foreigners, bona-fide residents of the state, with the same rights in respect to possession and enjoyment of property as citizens might enjoy. However, in 1894 Article I, Section 17, of the California Constitution was amended limiting this right. The amendment provided that foreigners *eligible* to citizenship shall have the same rights in respect to all property other than real estate as native-born citizens. It was this provision that made it possible for the state legislature to enact the Alien Land Law in 1913. Then, in 1920 the people of the State of California passed an initiative measure at the general election, which is California's present law in this connection.[13] This law denied aliens ineligible to citizenship, either individually or through any form of association, the right to own any interest in California other than provided under treaty agreements. Both Washington and Oregon have somewhat similar laws, except that Washington makes the provision against the Oriental less pointed. These laws are objective measures of the effect of ethnic discrimination. Note the following statement by a Caucasian in reference to the Asiatics:

I would rather every foot of California was in its native wilderness than to be cursed by the foot of these yellow invaders, who are a curse to the country, a menace to our institutions, and destructive of every principle of Americanism. I want no aliens, white, red, black or yellow to own a foot of land in the State of California.[14]

Eight states impose restrictions or prohibitions on aliens ineligible for citizenship-taking and holding real estate, namely, Arizona, Cali-

11 See 149 U.S. 698 (1893) Fong Yue Ting v. United States.

12 Konvitz, *op. cit.,* p. 55.

13 Eliot G. Mears, *Resident Orientals on the American Pacific Coast* (Chicago: The University of Chicago Press, 1928), p. 165.

14 Cited by Y. Ichihashi, *Japanese in the United States* (Palo Alto: Stanford University Press, 1932), p. 262. From *The San Francisco Chronicle* (Feb. 3, 1909).

fornia, Idaho, Kansas, Louisiana, Montana, New Mexico, and Oregon. In addition, Minnesota, Missouri, Montana, and Washington impose prohibitions or restrictions on aliens who have not declared their intention to become citizens. Obviously persons ineligible to become citizens could not file declarations of intentions; hence, these statutes affect such inelegible persons in precisely the same way as did the laws of Arizona or California.[15]

The Chinese exclusion laws were repealed on December 17, 1943, with the passage of Public Law 199. The present quota as indicated earlier permits 105 Chinese to enter the United States annually. Several reasons have been advanced accounting for this change in immigration policy, and they are summarized as follows: (1) repeal of the Chinese exclusion laws would silence Japanese propaganda implying that the United States discriminated against all Asiatics, (2) morale of the Chinese soldiers would be increased in their battle with the Japanese, and (3) there is no need to exclude all the Chinese by law, when the present immigration laws permit a quota that accomplishes about the same thing. Each nation on the quota system is permitted a number representing the ratio of its population to the total population in the United States in the year 1920. Hence, the quota discriminates against certain ethnic groups by its base year.[16]

In spite of a few technical discriminations against the Chinese, he has gained certain significant rights with the repeal of the exclusion laws. *He is now eligible for naturalization.* All the laws denying certain aliens the right to own real property in particular states have become null and void in regard to the Chinese who are legal residents of the United States. The value of Public Law 199 to the Chinese is not in the number of Chinese eligible for entry, but in the naturalization right accorded Chinese who are legal residents of the United States. *With the "rescinding" of restrictive covenants in May of 1948, a new page was written in behalf of the people who helped build the railroads, dig the mines, and inaugurate the important practices in agriculture in California.*

15 Konvitz, *op. cit.*, p. 161.
16 Eire is permitted 17,853 persons on the quota, although its population is only 2,953,452. China, on the other hand, is accorded 105 persons as migrants from its total population of 460,000,000. Each country is given a base quota of 100 immigrants.

EDUCATIONAL STATUS

The educational status of the Chinese when compared to the Japanese indicates some rather striking differences in these two Oriental peoples. It is important to remember that many classes of Chinese were prohibited from entering the United States after the year 1882 and that the Japanese have been prohibited from sending laborers to the United States since the year 1907. One of the objective factors that is important in throwing light on the reasons for the educational differences between the Chinese and Japanese is the wider regional distribution of the Chinese throughout the United States. This distribution of Chinese and Japanese is easily observed in Table XXX.

Table XXX: DISTRIBUTION OF THE CHINESE AND JAPANESE IN THE REGIONS OF THE UNITED STATES *

Region	Chinese	Japanese
North Eastern States	28,931	7,438
North Central States	10,646	18,734
The South	10,468	3,055
The West	67,584	112,541
Total	117,629	141,768

* Advance Report prepared for this work by the Bureau of the Census, Oct. 10, 1952.

The early prejudices against the Chinese served to disperse many of the Chinese from the Pacific Coast area to the eastern metropolitan districts. Inasmuch as the Chinese were recruited as laborers, some distinct differences in the educational attainments of the Chinese

Table XXXI: SCHOOL YEARS COMPLETED BY CHINESE AND JAPANESE PERSONS OVER 25 YEARS OF AGE IN THE UNITED STATES *

Chinese	Median Grade Attained	Japanese	Median Grade Attained
Total	5.5	Total	8.7
Male	5.6	Male	8.8
Female	5.0	Female	8.6
Native	6.8	Native	12.2
Male	6.2	Male	12.2
Female	8.6	Female	12.1
Foreign Born	5.0	Foreign Born	8.3
Male	5.3	Male	8.3
Female	1.6	Female	8.1
Urban Total	5.6	Urban Total	9.8
Male	5.6	Male	10.1
Female	5.0	Female	9.3

* Sixteenth Census of the United States, *Population* (1940).

and Japanese might be expected. Differences disclosed in Table XXXI are certainly significant and surprising.

The essential factors that might account for the differential educational status of these two ethnic groups may be stated in terms of immigration entrance periods and changing immigration policies. The Chinese came to America almost half a century prior to the Japanese. Table XXXII indicates the progression of Chinese and

Table XXXII: SELECTED ETHNIC GROUPS IN CALIFORNIA *

Year	Chinese	Japanese	White
1950	58,324	84,956	9,915,173
1940	39,556	93,717	6,596,763
1930	37,361	97,456	5,408,260
1920	28,812	71,952	3,264,711
1910	36,248	41,352	2,259,672
1900	45,753	10,151	1,402,727
1890	72,472	1,147	1,111,833
1880	75,132	86	767,181
1870	49,277	33	499,424
1860	34,933	—	323,177
1850	—	—	91,635

* Seventeenth Census of the United States, *Population* (1950).

Japanese in California. The insignificant number of Japanese in California prior to 1890 may seem unusual when it is realized that there were more Chinese in California in the nineties than at the present time. The unskilled worker was the occupational type of Chinese needed in the pioneer period on the Pacific Coast. The two areas of employment, namely the mines and the railroads, did not demand very much in the way of formal education. By the time the Japanese began to migrate to this country in significant numbers, the policy of selective immigration had been initiated in the Gentlemen's Agreement of 1907 between the United States and Japan. The chief provision of this agreement made its almost impossible for an unskilled worker to enter this country from Japan. The public schools of Japan and the growing industrialization of the island empire may have developed more interest in public school education than was the case in China. *However, the Chinese need not suffer by a comparison with the Japanese inasmuch as the native Japanese rank first in the median number of grades completed in school among all the population groups surveyed in the 1940 census.*

ECONOMIC STATUS

On several occasions the use of legislation has been cited as a device to limit the economic status of an ethnic group. The Chinese have been the target of such economic discrimination for a long time, especially in California. It has been the aim of the most aggressive pressure groups to remove the economic rungs from the ladder to success. Hence, the more profitable occupations associated with certain businesses and agriculture have been almost closed to the Chinese by arbitrary legislation on the state level.

It will be noted that in Table XXXIII there are manifest some

Table XXXIII: OCCUPATIONAL STATUS OF CHINESE, JAPANESE, AND THE GENERAL MALE POPULATION 14 YEARS OF AGE AND OVER BY MAJOR SOURCE OF EMPLOYMENT IN THE UNITED STATES *

Occupation	Chinese Per Cent	Japanese Per Cent	General Population Per Cent
Professionals	1.5	3.8	4.4
Semiprofessionals	1.1	1.2	1.1
Farmers & Farm Managers	0.3	5.0	14.7
Proprietors & Managers	20.1	21.6	9.8
Clerical Workers	10.4	15.5	12.8
Craftsmen & Foremen	1.4	3.6	14.5
Operatives & kindred workers	24.0	8.2	18.2
Domestic Service workers	5.3	6.9	0.4
Service workers except domestics	32.5	10.8	6.5
Farm Laborers	0.6	5.7	5.4
Farm Laborers unpaid	.0	1.5	2.8
Laborers except farm	1.6	16.2	8.7

* Sixteenth Census of the United States, *The Labor Force* (1940). "Not reported" categories excluded from the above table.

interesting occupational patterns of Chinese and Japanese males compared with the general population. In 1940 Chinese males were most likely to be classified in the following work categories: proprietors and managers, operatives, and service workers. It is important to note that the Chinese had been discouraged from agricultural callings by the forces of prejudice and discriminatory legislation. The Japanese manifest a greater spread in the range of occupations classified by the Bureau of the Census than the Chinese. The evacuation of the Japanese population from the Pacific Coast, during World War II, may have upset the basic pattern outlined in the table cited. Table XXXIII also discloses that the Chinese and Japanese differ in their occupational distributions from the general United States male working population particularly in reference to farmers, industrial workers, and domestic service employees. Somewhat similar patterns for the three population groups may be observed in the professions, the semi-professions, and the clerical jobs. It may be of some interest to note that in the proprietor and manager categories the Chinese and Japanese excel the distribution of the general population by more than 10 per cent.

The occupational patterns of Chinese and Japanese females are compared with the general population in Table XXXIV. The Chi-

Table XXXIV: OCCUPATIONAL STATUS OF CHINESE, JAPANESE, AND THE GENERAL FEMALE POPULATION 14 YEARS OF AGE AND OVER BY MAJOR SOURCE OF EMPLOYMENT IN THE UNITED STATES *

Occupation	Chinese Per Cent	Japanese Per Cent	General Population Per Cent
Professionals	5.9	4.3	12.3
Semiprofessionals	1.5	0.6	0.9
Farmers & Farm Managers	0.1	1.0	1.4
Proprietors & Managers	8.8	9.3	3.8
Clerical Workers	25.4	22.2	28.3
Craftsmen & Foremen	0.3	0.8	1.0
Operatives & kindred workers	27.5	12.9	18.4
Domestic Service workers	9.4	23.1	17.7
Service workers except domestics	20.2	15.2	11.3
Farm Laborers	.0	3.2	0.9
Farm Laborers unpaid	.0	5.9	2.0
Laborers except farm	0.9	1.5	0.9

* Sixteenth Census of the United States, *The Labor Force* (1940). "Not reported" categories excluded from the above table.

nese women represented in occupations appear to be better distributed in the professional, clerical, and operative occupations than is the case of the Japanese women. However, the Japanese women appear to afford a greater spread in all the occupational callings than the Chinese. When the Chinese and Japanese women are compared with the general female population of the United States, they are under-represented in the professional and clerical jobs. Chinese women in the operative jobs excel both the Japanese women and the general female population. *Jobs offering high status are not so well represented by Chinese and Japanese women as the general distribution for the United States population of this sex.* Only about one-third as many Chinese female workers were enumerated in the 1940 census as Japanese females. The sex ratio of the Chinese still reflects the characteristics usually associated with a pioneer ethnic group. In the pioneer setting or region the males usually predominate, and as the community becomes more stabilized the ratio of males to females approaches a balance. In spite of the fact that the Japanese are comparatively recent migrants to the United States compared to the Chinese, the sex ratio of the Japanese reflects a somewhat stabilized population. In 1940 there were 57,389 Chinese males to 20,115 Chinese females, whereas there were 71,967 Japanese males to 54,980 Japanese females.

Some of the reasons why the Chinese are found in the categories enumerated in the tables cited can be listed: Chinese men were taxed as miners, and hence their sparse representation in similar callings; the alien land laws made agriculture a most difficult occupation to pursue; and many of the professional callings were restricted by stimulations that foreigners may not acquire licenses. As the Chinese were driven into the cities with the closing of employment on railroads, in the mines, and on the farms, the urban areas attempted to discriminate against these people. The case of Yick Wo in San Francisco is one of the most striking examples of applied discrimination by a community on an ethnic group. In the eighties, the City of San Francisco passed an ordinance requiring that operators of laundries housed in wooden buildings must purchase a license while laundries in brick buildings need not. Presumably the license was a fire protection device, but upon investigation it was found that the City had issued eighty licenses and all to white applicants with only one exception. Some two hundred Chinese laundries were denied licenses. However, Yick Wo continued to operate his laundry without the necessary license, but made every effort to observe the fire protection cautions. The City of San Francisco arrested Yick Wo and about 150 other Chinese laundry operators for violation of the license provision. The United States Supreme Court upheld Yick Wo and his fellow Chinese laundry operators. Mr. Justice Mathews pointed out that the San Francisco ordinance amounted to unjust and illegal discrimination between persons in similar circumstances.[17]

Inasmuch as the foreign-born Chinese, until very recently, might not become a citizen of the United States, numerous occupations were permanently excluded from their interests. Hence, in California as an example, the Chinese alien might not become a lawyer, collection agent, private detective, domestic fish breeder, horse racetrack operator, liquor dealer, pilot of a boat, or a teacher.[18] Native-born Chinese,

[17] Konvitz, *op. cit.*, p. 173.

[18] *Ibid.*, p. 190. Students may be interested in studying the occupations denied to aliens; for this purpose read pp. 190-210.

while eligible to become professional persons, find great difficulty in securing employment after the completion of academic work. Medical and dental schools may use the quota plan to limit the number of Chinese, but so few Chinese apply that it never becomes an issue. The following comment by a placement official of a large public university in the West may give a realistic summary to this problem:

Now and then we have qualified Chinese graduates as prospective teachers, business managers, and chemists. It is very discouraging to the young man or woman of Chinese ancestry to realize that he or she qualifies for the position on such objective requirements as adequate training, superior academic marks, and strong letters of recommendation, but fails on the one score of race—an item beyond the control of the applicant.[19]

Some persons may suggest fair employment practices as the only way to assure that qualified minorities have an opportunity to secure positions in keeping with training and ability. Such legislation would probably help, but it would not change some of the attitudes that employers command, and indirect methods may be utilized to maintain discrimination.

One of the interesting occupational characteristics of the Chinese has been high employment even during periods of economic depression. The study by Neal C. Perry disclosed that, through personal interviews with thirty-seven of the sixty-five Chinese alumni of the high schools of Fresno, all were employed. He found that 85 per cent of the Chinese graduates were native born. There were about three male graduates for every two female graduates. About half the Chinese continued to live in districts described as "old Chinatown," and about 60 per cent of the graduates were employed by Chinese employees. Very few of the Chinese high school graduates were in business or had become qualified professional workers, perhaps less than 5 per cent.[20]

In the new Los Angeles Chinatown, Dr. Wen-Hui Chung Chen found that the community had passed from a cultural area to an *artificial* cultural area. The new Chinatown had been designed as a tourist attraction where Chinese food and art pieces might be purchased. Instead of a community where Chinese live the new community has become a place where Chinese drive their automobiles to

19 From a personal conversation with the placement officer.
20 Neal C. Perry, "An Investigation of Certain Aspects of the Social, Economic, and Educational Status of Second-Generation Chinese and Japanese Graduates of the High Schools of Fresno, California" (University of Southern California, 1938), p. 32. Unpublished Master's Thesis.

their respective places of business. These Americanized Chinese are to a large degree "selling" Chinese atmosphere, but "living" as other Americans.[21]

There is no question that the Chinese-Americans have made remarkable progress since the 1870's. In many instances occupational restrictions are gradually beginning to decrease, relaxation of housing restrictions has made possible emigration from the old Chinatowns, and there is some evidence of an increasing interest in the social and political events of the city. Finally, the Chinese have come a long way since the "cheap-labor-discriminatory-days" of the 1870's, when the slogan was "The Chinese must go."[22]

SUMMARY

The social status of the Chinese is probably in the lowest quartile of the usual ethnic groups included in social distance studies; however, the Richards study would indicate that the Chinese are considered to have many favorable traits. Legal status of the bona-fide Chinese residents of the United States is no different from the majority group since 1943. About the only legal status that is at some variance with the majority group is perhaps found in the case of the restrictive covenants; and such documents are private agreements and not legal expressions in the strict sense. Educational status ranks a little lower than the majority group, but the differences may not be very permanent. Economic status is reflected as moderate success, with the realization that the principal occupational callings of the Chinese tend to be in the low income brackets, especially the service jobs.

PROBLEMS FOR STUDY AND DISCUSSION

1. List and explain reasons why the Chinese population in the United States is not as concentrated as the Japanese population.

2. Explain why the Chinese population is largely an urban population.

3. List at least five attitudes that you have acquired toward the Chinese. Compare these attitudes with those that you have acquired toward the Japanese and try to account for any differences that might exist.

[21] Wen-Hui Chung Chen, "Changing Sociocultural Patterns of the Chinese Community in Los Angeles" (University of Southern California, 1952), chap. 6. Unpublished Doctor's Thesis.

[22] Robert Lee, "Acculturation of Chinese Americans," *Sociology and Social Research,* Vol. 36 (May-June, 1952), pp. 319-322.

4. Discuss your attitudes toward the Chinese showing whether they are in keeping with the attitudes toward the Chinese during the latter half of the nineteenth century or the present attitudes toward the Chinese.

5. Compare the legal status of the Chinese with that of the Negro under the following points: (1) admittance into the United States, (2) citizenship in the United States, and (3) right to own property.

6. Compare the educational status of the Chinese with that of the Japanese, and give possible reasons for the differences that exist.

7. List the major occupations in which the Chinese are usually employed, and point out whether these occupations suggest a high or low economic status.

8. List and discuss some of the major problems confronting Chinese youth in the United States.

9. Discuss the ethnic groups that have been presented pointing out the variations that exist in each of the following status areas: social, legal, educational, and economic.

SELECTED READINGS

BROWN, F. J., and ROUCEK, J. S., *One America* (New York: Prentice-Hall, Inc., 1952), pp. 309-319.

KEIM, M. L., "The Chinese as Portrayed in the Works of Bret Harte: A Study of Race Relations," *Sociology and Social Research,* Vol. 25 (May-June, 1941), pp. 441-450.

KONVITZ, M. R., *The Alien and the Asiatic in American Law* (Ithaca: Cornell University Press, 1946), pp. 1-22, 37-59.

LEE, Robert, "Acculturation of Chinese Americans," *Sociology and Social Research* (May-June, 1952), Vol. 36, pp. 319-322.

MARDEN, Charles F., *Minorities in American Society* (New York: American Book Company, 1952), pp. 155-196.

MCWILLIAMS, C., *Brothers Under the Skin* (Boston: Little, Brown and Company, 1943).

MEARS, E. G., *Resident Orientals on the American Pacific Coast* (Chicago: University of Chicago Press, 1928).

WALTER, Paul A. F., Jr., *Race and Culture Relations* (New York: McGraw-Hill Book Company, Inc., 1952), pp. 360-376.

ZELIGS, R., "Influencing Children's Attitudes Toward the Chinese," *Sociology and Social Research,* Vol. 26 (Nov.-Dec., 1942), pp. 126-138.

XII

European Immigrants

Introduction

A STUDY OF ethnic relations would not be complete without giving
some consideration to the status of European immigrants in the
United States. It is recognized that European immigrants are of
the same basic racial group—as biologically defined—as members
of the majority racial group, but they are members of nationality and
cultural groups that are socially defined as different from native-born
whites in the United States. In Chapter I it was pointed out that all
groups—racial, national, or cultural—that differ in any marked way
from "typical Americans" are considered as members of out-groups,
and are assigned a general status that is comparable to that of an
ethnic group. Further, it was pointed out that many differences were
accredited to European immigrants when they are compared with
native-born whites in the United States. Among the differences
accredited to European immigrants are differences in physical appearance, cultural standards, family life, standards of living, religious
life, and occupational outlook. These and other differences, have
been used as criteria for classifying European immigrants in groups
that are considered as ethnically different from native-born whites in
the United States.

For a number of years European immigrants have been divided
into three major groups in literature and by administrative agencies
in the United States: (1) old immigrants, (2) new immigrants, and
(3) aliens. In 1925 Fairchild reported that the Immigration Commission had given its official sanction to a two-fold classification of
European immigrants: old immigrants and new immigrants.[1] This
grouping of European immigrants has been stressed to such an extent

[1] Henry P. Fairchild, *Immigration* (New York: The Macmillan Company, rev. ed.
1925), pp. 132-133.

in the works of various writers that it is now accepted as the major groups into which European immigrants in the United States should be classified. The old immigrants are distinguished by three characteristics: (1) they have emigrated from western and northern Europe, (2) they are from the European nations that are responsible for the first immigrations into the United States or the territory now included in the United States, and (3) they have provided the ancestors for approximately three-fourths of the present population of the United States. Brown and Roucek include the following national groups among the old immigrants: British, Irish, Norwegian, Swedish, Danish, Dutch, Belgian, French, German, and Swiss.[2]

New immigrants are also defined by three chief characteristics: (1) they are from the southern and eastern parts of Europe, (2) they started immigrating into the United States in large numbers since 1880, and (3) they possess many cultural traits and complexes that vary greatly from those of "typical Americans." *The new immigrants not only possess cultural differences but these cultural differences are usually continued by the first generation, and serve to make at least the second generation a cultural hybrid group.* Among the new immigrants are the nationals from Russia, Poland, Czechoslovakia, Italy, Portugal, Spain, Greece, and the Balkan nations.[3]

The third major classification of foreign-born whites is that of aliens. This group includes members from both the old and the new immigrant groups. White aliens are those foreign-born whites who reside in the United States, but still maintain citizenship with some foreign nation, or who have failed to acquire or apply for citizenship in the United States for some reason.

Thus, foreign-born whites in the United States are classified into three major groups: (1) old immigrants, (2) new immigrants, and (3) aliens. The general status of these groups varies from that of native-born whites in many ways. However since new immigrants are more "different" in regard to social, economic, educational, and cultural characteristics, they are usually accorded a lower status than old immigrants. Also, because of the legal restriction that white aliens are confronted with, they have still a much different general status in the United States than any other white ethnic group.

Size of Population. In 1950 at least 10,161,168 foreign-born whites

2 F. J. Brown and J. S. Roucek, *One America* (New York: Prentice-Hall, Inc., 1945), p. 13.
3 *Ibid.,* pp. 13-14.

resided in the United States. This number had migrated to the United States from all continents, and from practically all established nations. As shown in Table XXXV, the majority of white immigrants

TABLE XXXV: FOREIGN–BORN WHITE POPULATION IN U. S. BY AREA OF BIRTH *

Area	Number	Per Cent of Total
New Immigrants (Europe)	5,637,301	49.4
Old Immigrants (Europe)	4,063,443	35.6
From Americas	1,509,855	13.2
From Asia	149,909	1.3
All other	58,630	.5
Total	11,419,138	100.0

* Sixteenth Census of the United States, *Population* (1940), Second Series, pp. 36-37. European immigrants are classified as old and new in keeping with the outline in F. J. Brown and J. S. Roucek, *One America* (New York: Prentice-Hall, Inc., 1945), pp. 13-14. Note that in the decade 1940 to 1950 the foreign-born white population decreased by 1,257,970.

in the United States (85 per cent) are from European nations. More than 49 per cent of all white immigrants, or 58.1 per cent of all white immigrants from Europe are from the nations that are classified as new immigrants. Thus, new immigrants predominate in the foreign-born European population now living in the United States. *It is recognized that foreign-born status is a temporary status and that the offspring of these European immigrants will be native-born citizens and lose their foreign-born status.* However, as the offspring of white immigrants are merged into the native-born population other foreign borns will arrive to take their places. Although, in keeping with present immigration laws the foreign-born population will decrease, the number will still be large enough for foreign-born whites to be a problem in understanding ethnic relations in the United States for several decades. This is the case since some of the future immigrants will be new immigrants, and many will remain, or will be forced to remain as aliens.

Table XXXVI: CITIZENSHIP STATUS OF THE FOREIGN–BORN WHITE POPULATION IN U. S.*

Status	Number	Per Cent
Naturalized	7,250,252	63.5
No papers	2,429,325	21.3
First papers	914,489	8.0
Citizenship not reported	825,072	7.2
Total	11,419,138	100.0

* Sixteenth Census of the United States, *Population* (1940), Second Series, p. 24.

The foreign-born white population is classified according to citizenship status in Table XXXVI. In 1940, 63.5 per cent of the white immigrants had been naturalized, 21.3 per cent were reported as aliens, 8 per cent had received their first papers, and the citizenship status of 7.2 per cent was not reported. In other words 36.5 per cent of the foreign-born whites in the United States were not citizens in 1940, and at least 21.3 per cent had not initiated the first step required in the process of becoming naturalized.

Distribution of Foreign-Born White Population

The distribution of the foreign-born white population by states is presented in Table XXXVII. According to this table the major con-

Table XXXVII: FOREIGN–BORN WHITES IN THE UNITED STATES BY STATES *

State	Number	Per Cent of Total Population
New York	2,853,530	21.2
Pennsylvania	973,260	9.8
Illinois	969,373	12.3
California	870,893	12.6
Massachusetts	848,852	19.7
New Jersey	695,810	16.7
Michigan	683,030	13.0
Ohio	519,266	7.5
Connecticut	327,941	19.2
Minnesota	294,904	10.6
Wisconsin	288,774	9.2
Texas	234,388	3.7
Washington	203,163	11.7
Rhode Island	137,784	19.3
Iowa	117,245	4.6
Missouri	114,125	3.0
Indiana	110,631	3.2
All other states (31)	1,176,169	10.3
Total	11,419,138	

* Sixteenth Census of the United States, *Population* (1940), Second Series, p. 46.

centration of the foreign-born white population is in the North, with 82.1 per cent residing in this region. Only three states outside the North are included in the seventeen states in which 100,000 or more foreign-born whites resided in 1940: California, Texas, and Washington. A better illustration of the concentration of foreign-born whites in the North is indicated by considering the proportion of foreign-born whites to the total population. Around one-fifth of the total population in New York, Massachusetts, Rhode Island, and

Connecticut is of foreign-born white origin. New Jersey is the only other state in which 15 per cent or more of the total population is foreign born. Therefore, the five states in which foreign-born whites constitute 15 per cent or more of the total population are states that adjoin each other, and more than 40 per cent of the foreign-born whites reside in these five states. *Thus, there are three major concentrations of minority ethnic population groups in the United States: Negroes in the South, Orientals in the West, and foreign-born whites in the North.* The interesting fact to note is that the major concentration areas for minority ethnic groups vary to such an extent that most states are relieved from a complex ethnic problem in so far as the concentration is concerned. The two states in which we do find a considerable number of members of several minority ethnic groups are California and New York. An analysis of the 1950 census statistics discloses that the concentration of the foreign-born whites remains in the North; however, California and Texas show a slight increase in foreign-born population.

The rural-urban distribution of foreign-born whites is presented in Table XXXVIII. This table shows that 80 per cent of the popula-

Table XXXVIII: RURAL–URBAN DISTRIBUTION OF THE FOREIGN-BORN WHITE POPULATION IN THE UNITED STATES *

Area	Number	Per Cent
Urban	9,134,318	80.0
Rural-nonfarm	1,371,206	12.0
Rural-farm	913,614	8.0
Total	11,419,138	100.0

* Sixteenth Census of the United States, *Population* (1940), Second Series, p. 36.

tion is urban, 12 per cent rural-nonfarm, and 8 per cent farm. The preceding percentages point out two conclusions for foreign-born whites in the United States: (1) they are in most instances urban dwellers, and (2) those residing in rural areas are not engaged in agricultural activities.

SOCIAL STATUS

It is difficult to discuss the social status of European immigrants in the United States because of the varied and complex background of this population. However, it is suggested by several writers that there is some differentiation in the social status of European immigrants when their social status is compared with that of native-born whites in the United States.[4] This differentiation in social status is directed toward old and new immigrants, but is more intense in the direction of new immigrants. As with Negroes and other minority ethnic groups this differentiation serves to discriminate against minority ethnic groups, and to encourage the voluntary segregation of these groups. This voluntary segregation, on the part of European immigrants in the United States, seems to be illustrated in the following ways: (1) cultural continuation, (2) nationality communities, (3) intermarriage among nationality groups, and (4) nationality organizations established to work for the welfare of specific nationality groups.

One of the early arguments used against the continuation of the immigration of foreign-born whites to the United States was the cultural differences among these groups and native-born whites. This argument was centered largely around religious differences among old immigrants, and was directed, during the latter part of the nineteenth century, toward Irish and German immigrants, many of whom were members of the Catholic Church. It was argued, by Protestant Americans, that these immigrants were establishing Catholic communities and that these communities would be used as centers from which Catholics would attempt to diffuse their influence throughout the United States.[5] At a later date, when immigrants from southern and eastern Europe arrived, this argument was intensified as most of these immigrants were from Catholic nations. This argument probably reached its highest point in the United States in 1928 when many southern states voted against Alfred Smith for President of the United States since he was a member of the Catholic Church. It is also interesting to note that the Ku Klux Klan has been more anti-Catholic and anti-immigrant than anti-Negro.[6]

[4] See the following books for discussions on this point: H. E. Barnes, *Society in Transition* (New York: Prentice-Hall, Inc., 1939), pp. 271-297; F. J. Brown and J. S. Roucek, *One America* (New York: Prentice-Hall, Inc., 1945), pp. 431-538; M. R. Davie, *World Immigration* (New York: The Macmillan Company, 1936), pp. 84-92, 183-188; H. P. Fairchild, *Immigration* (New York: The Macmillan Company, 1925), pp. 166-368; P. H. Landis, *Population Problems* (New York: American Book Company, 1948), pp. 402-413; R. A. Schermerhorn, *These Our Peoples* (Boston: D. C. Heath and Company, 1949), pp. 227-373; W. F. Willcox, *Studies in American Demography* (Ithaca: Cornell University Press, 1940), pp. 159-175.

[5] George M. Stephenson, *A History of American Immigration: 1820-1924* (Boston: Ginn and Company, 1926), pp. 100 ff.

[6] Davie, *op. cit.,* pp. 184-188.

There is a tendency for European immigrants of the various nations to concentrate in national communities in the United States. These national communities are found in most of the cities in which European immigrants reside in large numbers. Immigrant communities are found largely among the first generation of foreign-born whites, and result in most instances from two social conditions: (1) the desire on the part of foreign-born whites to live near others with a similar cultural background so as to avoid discrimination based on cultural differences; or (2) the similar economic status of foreign-born whites, which serves to restrict them to the same communities. *These differences aid in bringing about voluntary segregation which in turn helps to continue the discrimination against foreign-born whites that was originally based on cultural differences.* By the continuation of this process cultural differences serve to promote social discrimination against foreign-born whites.

Voluntary segregation, as illustrated by intramarriage among European national groups, is shown by Kiser.[7] In the paper by Kiser it is shown that there is a tendency for foreign-born whites to marry foreign-born whites of the same national group. That this tendency is stronger among new immigrants than old immigrants is illustrated by the fact that the percentages for intramarriage among nationals from the new immigration nations are much higher than those for nationals from the old immigration nations.[8] However, as there is a tendency for residential propinquity to influence marriage selection, in many instances,[9] it is logical to assume that much of the intramarriage among foreign-born white national groups has resulted from residential nearness. Thus there is a process in operation to continue social segregation among foreign-born whites. As there are cultural differences, the first generation tends to live in segregated communities that are voluntarily selected, and because they live close together they often marry among themselves. This process serves to continue social segregation and social selection among foreign-born whites in the United States.

The extent to which voluntary social segregation exists among foreign-born whites is also illustrated by the many organizations that

[7] Clyde V. Kiser, "Cultural Pluralism," *The Annals of the American Academy of Political and Social Science,* Vol. 262 (March, 1949), pp. 126-128.

[8] *Ibid.,* p. 127.

[9] Ray H. Abrams, "Residential Propinquity As a Factor in Marriage Selection: Fifty Year Trends in Philadelphia," *American Sociological Review,* Vol. 8 (June, 1943), pp. 288-294.

have been established by nationality groups.[10] Brown and Roucek report that 155 organizations—with 31,990 branches, and 2,883,541 members—have been established by nationality groups in the United States.[11] These organizations have been established to serve nationality groups in many ways: socially, recreationally, culturally, educationally, and from the standpoint of general welfare. The existence of these nationality organizations is indicative of one of two conditions: (1) that foreign nationality groups desire social segregation for one or several reasons, or (2) that they have been discriminated against in other organizations and establish their own organizations in an attempt to avoid discrimination. Although it is impossible to state the exact reason for the establishment of these organizations, it is a fact that they do contribute to the social segregation of foreign-born whites, and to continue this process in the United States. Further, it is debatable whether or not these organizations contribute to the assimilation of foreign-born whites in the United States. However, Chyz and Lewis, after discussing the pros and cons of these organizations in the assimilation process, conclude that they are of more aid than hindrance in the assimilation of foreign-born whites in the United States.[12]

The rankings of various ethnic groups in the United States, as determined by a social distance scale, have been reported by Bogardus for two periods: 1926 and 1946.[13] These rankings are presented in Table XXXIX, and represent the rankings of various white nationality groups as measured by the social distance scale of Bogardus. The numbers in the table represent the rank numbers of various white population groups among a total of thirty-six ethnic, cultural, and nationality groups in the United States. According to this table, especially the rankings in 1946, as the English ranked first in 1926, the general rankings of whites in the United States are: native whites, Canadians, old immigrants, and new immigrants. In 1926 the English ranked above native whites, but this nationality group was reduced to third place in 1946. For both periods new immigrants ranked below native whites, Canadians, and old immigrants, but above the other

10 Y. J. Chyz and R. Lewis, "Agencies Organized by Nationality Groups in the United States," *Annals of the American Academy of Political and Social Science,* Vol. 262 (March, 1949), pp. 148-158; and F. J. Brown and J. S. Roucek, *One America* (New York: Prentice-Hall, Inc., 1945), pp. 392-399.

11 *Ibid.,* p. 650.

12 *Ibid.,* pp. 157-158.

13 Emory S. Bogardus, "Changes in Racial Distances," *International Journal of Opinion and Attitude Research* (Vol. 1, Dec., 1947), p. 58.

ethnic groups residing in the United States. In 1946 native whites were in first place, Canadians in second place, third to eleventh places were occupied by old immigrants, the next eleven places by new immigrants, and the last fourteen places by Asiatics or ethnic groups not commonly classified as whites. The following ethnic groups ranked below all whites in 1946: Jews, Indians, Chinese, Mexicans, Syrians, Filipinos, Turks, Koreans, Negroes, and Japanese in the order listed.

Table XXXIX: RACIAL DISTANCE RANKS OF WHITE NATIONALITY GROUPS IN THE UNITED STATES: 1926 AND 1946 *

Nationality Group	Rank in 1926	Rank in 1946
Native-born whites	2	1
Canadians	3	2
Old immigrants	1-4-5-6-7-8-9	3-4-5-6-7-8-9
	10-11	10-11
New immigrants	12-13-14-15-16	12-13-14-15-16
	17-18-19-20-23	17-18-19-20-21
	24	22

* Rank numbers are compiled from Emory S. Bogardus, "Changes in Racial Distances," *International Journal of Opinion and Attitude Research,* Vol. I (Dec., 1947), p. 58.

The study by Bogardus indicates a definite social stratification of whites in the United States, with new immigrants on the lowest social level among whites. However, all whites ranked above members of other ethnic, cultural, and racial groups. Thus, it seems logical to conclude that, according to the study reported on, the social status of foreign-born whites is below that of native-born whites, but above that of the other ethnic groups in the United States.

An analysis of the social status of European immigrants is presented by Brown and Roucek in the following reading. In this statement the writers compare the problems of European immigrants with that of other minority ethnic groups, giving special emphasis to a comparison of the problems of European immigrants and the Negro. It should be noted that both ethnic groups are confronted with some of the same problems. This fact suggests that the problems of minority ethnic groups in the United States are similar in nature. Thus, if ethnic relations are to be improved, there is a need for concerted action among all minority ethnic groups for improvement.

▌ THE PROBLEM OF THE NEGRO AND EUROPEAN IMMIGRANT MINORITIES[14]

JOSEPH S. ROUCEK AND FRANCIS J. BROWN

Contrary to the popular conception, there are no Czechoslovaks, or Poles, or other immigrant groups living in America, characterized by definite and singular characteristics applicable to each member of such groups. What we really have are immigrant groups whose cultures are, at best, marginal cultures. On the one hand, they incorporate in varying degrees, the culture patterns of the home countries of the immigrants, modified by the impacts of different aspects of "American" culture; and, on the other hand, they modify to a certain extent, the "American" culture patterns within which they exist. Furthermore, it is impossible to speak about such immigrant groups in terms of their collective names ("Germans," "Yugoslavs") without making an additional error, for every immigrant group is again subdivided into numerous other socially stratified classes and castes, disintegrated and frequently warring with each other in terms of their differences.

. . . . . .

PROBLEMS OF THE NEGRO AND THE IMMIGRANT

It may seem very strange, but from the viewpoint of the attitude of mind known as "happiness," every comparison that one can make between the Negro and the immigrant would indicate that the Negro faces in America a set of problems, some of them peculiar to him alone, but not so different on the whole from those facing the immigrant and his children. If it is true that the Negro can be more or less easily identified on account of his "color" and therefore cannot escape so easily the status assigned to him by his racial heritage, then the fact remains that the hope that he will succeed in climbing up the ladder of social mobility is not as great as that of the average immigrant. In other words, in spite of all the constitutional and legal provisions in the United States the Negro knows that certain ranks in the social scale are closed to him and hence he does not have to face the psychological sense of frustration which often agitates the average immigrant who has been misled by the shop-worn slogans of "equality," "opportunity," etc., which in actual practice and from the standpoint of the economic and social conditions of

14 Roucek, Joseph S. and Francis J. Brown, "The Problem of the Negro and European Immigrant Minorities: Some Comparisons and Contrasts." *The Journal of Negro Education*, Vol. 3 (Washington, D. C.: The Bureau of Educational Research, Howard University, July, 1939), pp. 299-312. Used by permission of the Journal.

the country in most cases are little more than a fiction. It cannot be denied that many sons of the Old World have succeeded in various spheres of human endeavor in America and have reached the symbols of economic success to the extent which is no more offered elsewhere. But it must be also noted that we know very little about the millions of forgotten small men whose high hopes have been buried under the severe strain of social maladjustment and economic strivings, and who, when dying, were consoling their last hours with vivid pictures of the green fields of their homelands which they had never had a chance to re-visit, as had some of their better known and more fortunate friends. Many have learned to love their newly adopted land, and one feels sorry for them if they have not. But others could not love it very much when that land was nothing for them but a row of houses in a mining or steel town, with soot covering everything living and dead; and heavy, relentless work when available, and many months, if not years, of enforced idleness when not available. To be fair, those at the bottom of the social scale performed only similar tasks that are the tasks most frequently assigned to the Negro. But the latter has no longing for his country somewhere in the Old World; he is the native of the country and consequently he does not suffer as severe mental conflicts as his immigrant neighbors. There is simply the difference of the conditioning processes of the childhood days and the earliest memories which make a subtle but extremely important difference in the mental outlooks of these two types of our minority groups.

The Negro, therefore, is more of an integrated group in America's culture pattern, although so inseparable from it that there is no way of drawing lines demarking it from the "white man's" pattern. The same thing applies to the immigrant. But there is, in many cases, a somewhat greater sense of self-confidence in the Negro, since he is born into the culture pattern of this country and since, therefore, adaptation to its various conflicts is much easier. The difference can be illustrated by the famous last words: "If you don't like it over here, why don't you go back to the old country?" Can anybody tell that to the colored man?

Parallel to this nuance of psychological reaction is the problem of the second generation, which takes on a much more definite form in the case of the immigrant.

The Negro, one can generalize, does not fully escape, of course, the problem of the second generation. Like any other minority group, he has to face the conflicts arising from the urban-rural relationships, and the conflicts which are based on the attempts of the more determined and aggressive individuals to reduce the effects of the high degree of Negro "visibility" in social relations, or even to reduce the "visibility" itself. But, basically, these processes take place within one large "American" culture, within which the Negro culture (if such a term can be used at all) is already inseparably integrated. The other minority groups, and particularly the more recent immigrants, face their second-generation problem with a much more marked degree of difficulty, because, quite often the resulting clashes of values are well-nigh prone to break the family ties, as shown in the classic study of W. I. Thomas and Florian Znaniecki, *The Polish Peasant in Europe and America*. The latest manifestation of such difficulties has been the increasing pro-Nazi and pro-fascist propaganda, directed from Europe, and the growing number of anti-Semitics in the United States. We doubt, however, that this wave will rise very high. We have had them before—notably in the early twenties when the Ku Klux Klan set out to put down both the Catholics and the Jews, but presently folded up. Its ghost goes mumbling along, with a recent revival of interest. The effects of such propaganda on the American-born Jews, Germans and Italians are psychologically more damaging than it appears on the surface. To be a Jew, born in America, and to have some physical characteristic which gives a "Jew-baiter" a chance at some form of attack is bound to produce undesirable reactions, and particularly the resentment of the generation of which it is a member of a despised and hated race.

.   .   .   .

The seriousness of the problem of the "second-generation" ranges, in various forms, from the already well-assimilated immigrant groups, which are hardly aware of this problem because of the long period of time spent in America, to the most serious aspect of it offered by the most recent immigrants and the groups characterized by some degree of physical "visibility," such as American-born Chinese, Japanese, Indians and Mexicans. The latter come nearest to the problems faced by the Negro, because of the various forms of the "visibility," although their problem loses some of its seriousness in proportion to their numbers, the regions they live in, and the role of classes assigned to them as nationalities in the American social structure on the basis of their work, and the vigor with which they aim to rise in the social scale. But, whatever is the case, it seems that their problems are psychologically more damaging to them than to the Negro, because there are always the visions and emotional pulls and pushes of the "Old Country." These are always transferred by the families to their American-born offsprings, even if only in the form of resentment, which culminate in the efforts of the Chinese or Japanese American-born individuals, educated in American schools, to escape the prejudices against their "visibility" by seeking occupations either in the communities of their nationals in this country, or in the countries of their parents. Consequently, they frequently fail to fit in anywhere. They have been "Americanized" by education, but by their looks, they remain "Chinese" or "Japanese" in the eyes of the average American and outsiders, as well as in the Chinese or Japanese settlements or in China or Japan. The lighter Mexican can escape such handicaps to some degree, and especially more than darker Mexicans. At any rate, the prejudice of other workingmen tends to prevent him from rising beyond a certain point. Thus Mexicans frequently try to pass for Spanish, and Negroes for Mexicans, in order to get employment, and the very attempts demonstrate that they can be successful in this respect. But the Chinese or Japanese have no chance to escape their facial appearance. Here they face nearly exactly the same situation as the Negro, as a class and caste, although the latter is more favored, since he can fall back upon his group which offers him some sort of refuge already with its considerable large numbers composing it.

Furthermore, the Negro has been assigned his definite place in our social ladder. And what is even more important he has developed the art of adjustment and the rules of the game of social relations, to the degree achieved by no other minority group, simply because of the trial-and-error method going back to the days when the first Negro was imported here. The other minorities on the other hand, do not have the benefits of such a comparatively well-developed pattern. The fundamental problem of the immigrant is that of escaping the most undesirable and irritating characteristics which design him as a "Greenhorn" on his arrival here. The subsequent transitional period, characterized by considerable resentment, bewilderment, the lack of well-accepted rules of etiquette and bargaining devices, is an individual experience which does not fit any established pattern of collective adjustment, except in terms of the individual's willingness and ability to accept, even if not fully, the most valued points of the dominant culture pattern. The Negro can escape this conflict in most cases, because he can develop his personality within his own (shall we say: American-Negro?) culture values and as a minority group well-adjusted to the culture conflicts by the tried-out experiences as a former slave and now a caste.

This process has its repercussions in the family life of the immigrant as contrasted to that of the Negro. The highly organized patriarchal family of many immigrants has suffered considerably during the depression by the changes of the roles assigned to the various members, or by the loss of the original hierarchical line-up on account of the depression and its subsequent economic and social stress. The most glaring example is possibly the loss of the traditional authority of the head of the house as an unemployed burden of his family, supported, let us say, by an American-born daughter. Whether the head of the family tries to escape the intolerable situation by drunkenness, by brutal domineering, or by joining some "radical" movement appealing to his nationalistic or class sympathies does not matter. What matters, however, is the disorganization of such family life, the effects of which are not so marked in the Negro families.

.   .   .   .

In politics, the manipulation of the votes of a minority group is one of the best known political devices utilized by those who can appeal to the various minorities by the promises of some favors or by the use of various ideologies and symbols dear to such groups or can simply collect such votes because of their ignorance and low social and economic standards. If we generalize again, the Negro has developed, on the whole, his political traditions, mostly of the non-participating kind (especially in the South). Wherever he has settled in large numbers in Northern cities, he has replaced the immigrant, in every big city, in the machine politics as the group needing to get favors in return for the vote and as the material easily controlled by the politician.

For the Negro, as well as for the immigrant, particularly in our cities, where immigrant and Negro adaptation has been most difficult, the party and the political club have frequently been the gateways through which the immigrant entered into the activities of the community. The immigrant has in most cases passed an apprentice position in one of the established parties and even the latest arrivals have learned not only the new language, even if not perfectly, but also the subtleties of our political institutions. Fundamental among the factors which determine party choice by the immigrant nationality groups are the cultural links of the group with the symbols or the issues of the party contest. The importance of this factor is revealed most sharply in the influence of the slavery question upon party allegiances of most immigrant groups in the period when the pattern of immigrant relationships to our party system was being formed. The first large immigrant group to arrive after the formation of our party system was the Irish. Their first and last allegiance was to the Democratic party; but the confirmation of that allegiance in a period when slavery was forcing a reorganization of the party system flowed from their fear of the Negro as a labor competitor. Upon the German group, free from the competitive fears of the Irish, the slavery issue had a more pronounced effect. The Scandi-

navian immigrants, arriving in the United States while the anti-
slavery program of the Republican party was at its height, was
drawn into that party; the primary factor in this allegiance was the
Scandinavian hostility to slave labor. Nativism has also at times
influenced party choice by the immigrant groups. When religious
differences are added to party nativism an almost impassable barrier
is erected between the immigrant and the party. Temperance and
prohibition are party issues which have also influenced immigrant
allegiances. In fact, all the nationality groups who do not share in
the Puritan tradition (and the Scandinavians are almost the only
ones who do share it) have had an additional reason for an alliance
with the Democratic party. The foreign policy advocated by each
of the major parties has been an important influence in determining
immigrant affiliation; thus the Democratic party lost its considerable
German following as an aftermath of its war policy from 1917 to
1920, but gained the votes of the Czechs, Slovaks, Poles, and Yugoslavs, who welcomed Wilson's doctrine of self-determination. Today,
however, "the general tendency has been for the immigrants to
associate with the ruling organization of neighborhood or region,"
and in that respect the immigrant and the Negro do not differ much,
and particularly since the depression and the ability of the Democratic party to command large sums of money for relief. But under
more normal conditions, the minority party, under the necessity of
adding to its strength, will listen with more attention to the pleas
of submerged groups and the immigrant groups will gravitate toward
it. The affinity between minority party and immigrant groups in the
urban areas quite frequently transforms the minority into a majority
party, and immigrant and Negro allegiance is not lost by the tri-
umph. But later both groups are very likely to be wooed more de-
terminedly by the opposition. The large and frequently decisive
vote cast by the Negro and immigrant groups is too important a
prize to be neglected by ambitious and realistic party leaders. Particularly in doubtful areas, overtures from the competing party
organizations may become so generous that both groups are given
opportunities to bargain for "recognition," usually taking the form
(in the industrial states from Massachusetts to Illinois) of a proportionate distribution of the patronage of the party and the "balanced"
ticket on which nominations are carefully distributed between the
various minorities.

Two main forces serve frequently to modify the allegiance of the
minority groups. The economic motive will slowly overcome an
incompatible nationality loyalty. Thus, the Scandinavian groups,
characterized by an early and long-continued allegiance to Republicanism, have progressed in the last half century from insurgency to

independency (as in the Progressive party of Wisconsin and the Farmer-Labor party of Minnesota) or Democratic allegiance, as the Democratic interests of the upper Mississippi and the Northwest deviated from the Republican formula. The revolt from Republicanism by the Italian and Slavic voters of the Pennsylvania mining and industrial centers in 1935 demonstrated a similar modification of immigrant party behavior by economic factors.

The second prominent factor in the modification of established immigrant party loyalties is the rise of native-born leaders of the group. This is particularly important in groups whose foreign-born members are separated by a language barrier from full participation in the party system. It has been the native-born leaders who have led the transfer in party allegiance of Scandinavian voters and, more recently, the Slavic and Italian groups, and it has been also the Negro leader whose leadership in the Northern urban areas is being recognized more and more. In New York, for instance, by 1929, the Negroes had reached the point where they felt entitled to self-government in the Nineteenth Assembly District Republican Club of Manhattan. "They threw out the Jewish leader who had, up to that time, served them as assemblyman as well, and substituted a *colored man* of considerable ability."

One additional point deserves our attention. Contrary to the popular conception, it is seldom possible to unite all the Negro, or the Czech, the Polish, and other votes in certain areas. Such occurrences happen occasionally but are more the exception than the rule, because not only are all minorities subdivided into all kinds of subgroups—as we have already indicated—but also suffer in this respect from their very minority status. Those asking for favors are always prone to have less self-confidence than those granting it, and hence one of the favorite tricks of the politician is to break up the growing opposition, based upon minority status, by granting a few favors to the more outstanding leaders. An additional difficulty marked especially in the more recent immigrants, is the tendency to oppose the immigrant leaders who receive favors of the local political bosses. Since the minority group had such a difficult time in gaining recognition, the more ambitious members are usually unwilling to have the more favored ones enjoy the fruits of their labors too long.

$$\cdot \quad \cdot \quad \cdot \quad \cdot \quad \cdot \quad \cdot \quad \cdot$$

SOME COMPARISONS BETWEEN AMERICAN AND EUROPEAN MINORITIES

Since America has been almost entirely on the receiving end of the line of immigrants, the existence of numerous racial and national minorities in the United States is not only of importance to America but also to the countries whence these minorities have come. The attention paid by various European governments, to their American branches depends, on the whole, on the importance which the emigration plays in reference to the internal and international position of the nation concerned and, in addition, on the influence which the United States exerts, or might exert, on the course of international events of the state concerned. Beginning approximately in 1880 the immigrants began arriving in varying numbers reaching the maximum in 1914, largely from Eastern and Southern Europe. This forced their respective governments to be interested in their nationals in America. The best example of the realization of the international importance of the United States comprised the steps taken by Germany and Austria before and after the entrance of America into the World War. In fact, the World War was utilized by all the immigrant groups of the countries in the death grapple for carrying on their activities on behalf of their nationalistic causes—Czechoslovaks, Poles, Latvians, Lithuanians, Estonians, Finns, Yugoslavs, Russians, and others.

The relationship of various American minorities to America's foreign policies has, in fact, always been of great importance even in the time of peace. America, being the haven of refuge for various social and political malcontents, has also been the place whence these various individuals and their organizations have directed their efforts either to help the lot of the proponents of their cause at home or to help the struggle against their opponents. The Irish Sinn Feiners, for instance, were supported by the American Irish, and De Valera was born in New York. Karlis Ulmanis, the head of the present government in Latvia, was implicated in the revolutionary movement in 1905 and had to remain in America from 1907-1913. Faik Bey Konitza, an Albanian leader against the Turks, came to America in 1908, and strengthened the smouldering Albanian nationalistic spirit by forming the Pan-Albanian Federation of America, which loaned a considerable sum of money to Zog after the World War. The ever-troublesome Macedonian movement has been receiving its financial and moral support since the first Macedonians emigrated to America at the turn of the nineteenth century; their Central Committee of the Macedonian Political Organization of the United States and Canada (20 South West Street, Indianapolis, Indiana) still carries on its vociferous activities. The problem of Jews in other parts of the world has been continually in the center of attention of American Jews.

· · · · · ·

LEGAL STATUS

From a legal standpoint European immigrants in the United States can be divided into four groups: (1) those who have entered the United States illegally, (2) those who have entered legally but have not applied for citizenship—aliens, (3) those who have filed their first papers for citizenship—declarants, and (4) those who have been naturalized and are now citizens of the United States. The first group is without legal status and are deported as they are detected. Members of the fourth group, having acquired citizenship, have the same legal status of other white citizens of the United States unless they are denaturalized.[15] This leaves groups two and three as the groups with a legal status that differs from that of other whites in the United States. To understand clearly the legal status of these groups it is essential to know some of the following groups of laws: (1) laws concerned with entrance into the United States, (2) laws regulating the naturalization process, and (3) laws restricting the status of aliens in the United States.

Entrance Laws

To be eligible for legal entrance into the United States, as permanent residents, all foreign-born people must be able to qualify in keeping with a number of restrictions. The major entrance qualifications that all foreign-born people must measure up to are:

1. They must be educationally, mentally, and physically sound.
2. They must not possess traits or habits that might result in their becoming public charges at the time of entrance.
3. They must not be afflicted with dangerous or contagious diseases.
4. They must be mentally, morally, and physically capable of earning a living.
5. They must not be anarchists or persons who believe in or advocate the overthrow by force or violence of the government of the United States.
6. They must not be contract laborers or persons encouraged to migrate to the United States by offers or promises of employment.
7. They must be able to leave their own nations on their own free will, and with the approval of the officials of their nations.
8. Since December 23, 1952, when the McCarran-Walter immigration law went into effect, they must not be or have been Communists or intend to commit any "immoral sexual act."

The restrictions listed indicate that all foreign-born whites must be classed as average or above average in their own nations before they are eligible for legal entrance into the United States.

[15] Milton R. Konvitz, *The Alien and the Asiatic in American Law* (Ithaca, N. Y.: Cornell University Press, 1946), pp. 117-147.

According to the immigration laws of the United States there are two major principles governing the immigration of eligible whites into the United States. These laws are based on the source of immigration. *Whites from the Americas who can qualify are freely admitted, while whites from European nations are restricted by numbers.*[16] The Immigration Act of 1924, which went into effect after July 1, 1927, provided for an annual minimum quota of 150,000 immigrants from foreign countries. The quota of 150,000 per year is apportioned among the various nations in keeping with their contributions to the population of the United States in 1920, with the provision that at least 100 persons would be admitted from each eligible country per year. As an example, if 15 per cent of the population of the United States was of German origin in 1920, 15 per cent of the quota of 150,000 would be admitted from Germany each year. This same principle is used in determining the number of immigrants that will be admitted from other foreign nations, with 100 being the minimum number. As old immigrants predominated in 1920 the immigration quota system has served as a means of legally discriminating against new immigrants. In keeping with this law 82 per cent of the European immigrants admitted into the United States are from nations that are classified as old immigrants. Or, the quota system serves to provide a form of legal discrimination against the entrance of new immigrants into the United States.

Naturalization

After entrance into the United States foreign-born whites must fulfill certain legal requirements before they are eligible for citizenship. The major legal requirements that they must fulfill are:

1. They must be lawfully admitted to the United States for permanent residence.
2. They must apply for citizenship (first papers), and fulfill the legal and economic qualifications essential for this step.
3. If not exempted otherwise they must reside in the United States for at least five years.
4. If physically able they must be able to speak and write English.
5. They must have a fair knowledge and understanding of the form of government in the United States, and the fundamental principles of the Federal Constitution.

16 See Maurice R. Davie, *World Immigration: With Special Reference to the United States* (New York: Macmillan Company, 1936), pp. 367-385 for a discussion of the immigration policy of the United States.

6. They must be of good moral character, acknowledge allegiance to the Federal Constitution, and be able to prove that they are well disposed to the good order and happiness of the United States.

7. They must have two witnesses who are citizens of the United States who will approve their character, residence, loyalty, and other qualifications.

Foreign-born whites do not only enter the United States under a number of restrictions, but they must live in keeping with many other restrictions before they are eligible for citizenship. Further, after becoming citizens there are many conditions under which they might lose this citizenship or be denaturalized.[17]

Aliens

From a legal standpoint the most precarious position of all ethnic groups in the United States is that of aliens. As most of the aliens in the United States are foreign-born whites, the laws directed toward aliens are applicable to foreign-born whites more than to any other ethnic group. Although white aliens can become citizens after fulfilling many requirements and residing in the United States for five years, there will be a large number of white aliens in the United States as long as the present immigration and naturalization laws are in operation. Thus, from a temporary standpoint white aliens are faced with many legal restrictions. *In fact, aliens are the most legally restricted group in the United States.* The major legal restrictions confronting white aliens are concerned with: (1) the right to own and will property, and (2) the right of aliens to work.

Aliens are restricted in their right to own and will property in several of the states in the United States. In some states the right of aliens to acquire land is restricted to a certain quantity of land. In other states aliens are not secure in their right to acquire property by a will or deed, in that by action of the state they might be divested of the title to such property.[18] Although laws of this nature are passing out rapidly, it should be noted that at an earlier date most of the states had laws restricting the property rights of aliens in some way, and that some of these restrictive laws still remain in a number of the states.

There are many restrictions on the right of aliens to work. It is probable that they are restricted more in this area than in any other area. They are deprived of the right to work on public works projects

17 See Milton R. Konvitz, *The Alien and the Asiatic in American Law* (Ithaca: Cornell University Press, 1946), pp. 117-147.

18 *Ibid.*, pp. 148-153.

by the laws of many states, and these restrictions have been supported by several judicial decisions.[19] Further, aliens are denied the legal right of engaging in many professions and occupations in all of the states of the United States. The number of occupations in which they cannot engage ranges from four in Maryland and Indiana to twenty-seven in New York.[20] *Altogether aliens are denied the right to engage in more than sixty occupations in the states in the United States.* The leading occupations in which they are restricted, and the number of states (including the District of Columbia) in which these restrictions are legal are as follows: attorney in all, certified public accountant in 47, manufacture or sale of liquor in 39, dentist in 26, physician in 25, architect in 22, pharmacist in 22, optometrist in 18, teacher in 18, embalmer in 17, engineer in 14, mine employee in 14, and registered nurse in 12.[21] These occupations include many of the occupations that are accorded a high social status, and in which the monetary returns are on the higher level.

Thus, foreign-born whites in the United States have three possible legal statuses: (1) that of other citizens if they have been naturalized, (2) that of declarants if they have filed their first papers, and (3) that of aliens. As citizens they have the same legal rights as other citizens, but they can be denaturalized under certain conditions, which denotes a lack of security in so far as citizenship is concerned. As declarants they are denied many rights, even the right to engage in many occupations. *As aliens they have the lowest legal status possible in the United States.* In general it is logical to conclude that the legal status of European immigrants is far below that of native-born whites as well as that of other ethnic groups who are natives of the United States.

[19] *Ibid.*, pp. 181-189.

[20] See *Ibid.*, pp. 190-211, for an analysis of the occupations in which aliens and declarants are restricted in the various states in the United States.

[21] *Ibid.*, pp. 210-211. To give balance to this interpretation it might be worth noting that in Europe many persons could not enter certain occupations because of rigid apprentice systems, not because of legal restrictions. This may be illustrated by an example found in a study of refugees in Los Angeles. While in Europe a refugee always wanted to become a bookseller, but could not enter this work because of the lack of proper apprentice training. When he came to Los Angeles all he had to do was to join the bookseller's association and pay the city license. There is considerable occupational mobility among the refugees, though most of the refugees lost occupational status in coming to the United States yet their standard of living here is reported to be higher. There are many facets to a comprehensive interpretation of the status of refugees. See the study by Anton Lourié, "Some Aspects of Social Adjustment of Jewish Refugees in Los Angeles" (University of Southern California, August, 1952), Unpublished Master's Thesis.

EDUCATIONAL STATUS

In legal theory European immigrants can make use of the same educational facilities as native whites. However, in practice two conditions serve to modify this principle for European immigrants as well as for the children of foreign born whites who are born in the United States. The first of these conditions is that foreign-born whites usually live in national communities in cities because of several cultural, economic, or social reasons. As with other minority ethnic groups the areas in which they live are areas in the process of transition. The houses in these areas, as well as the schools, are in a state of deterioration. Because of the transitory nature of these areas school boards are slow in providing new buildings, or new educational and recreational facilities that are considered as permanent equipment. Thus, although the same educational facilities are available to native whites and the children of foreign-born whites, the location of national communities serves to restrict foreign-born whites or the children of foreign-born whites in the use of many of these facilities.

The second factor that serves to prevent the complete educational integration of the children of foreign-born whites is the belief among many educators that these children need a special type of education. Those who hold this view emphasize the point that in the education of children much consideration should be given to the language and cultural background of their parents.[22] In keeping with this view an attempt is made in many schools to group children in keeping with their language and cultural background, where the number of class sections makes this possible. In other words the location of national communities and the belief in the need for a special kind of education for children of foreign-born whites have served to separate foreign-born whites from the main stream of education in many cities in the United States. Further, these same reasons have been used in many instances to deprive children of foreign-born whites of many of the educational facilities that are available for native whites.

However, the educational problems among foreign-born whites in the United States are largely adult problems. This is true because only 2.2 per cent of the foreign-born white population was under 20 years of age in 1940.[23] Thus, to understand the educational status of foreign-born whites it is essential to give consideration to the levels

22 See Brown and Roucek, *op. cit.,* pp. 496-506 for a discussion on this point.
23 Sixteenth Census of the United States, *Population,* Vol. IV, Part 1, p. 3.

of education that have been attained by adults in this group as compared with the levels attained by other ethnic groups. This is shown for four of the major ethnic groups in the United States, for persons 25 years old and over, in 1940 in Table XL. According to this table only one ethnic group—Indian—has a larger percentage for no years

Table XL: SCHOOL YEARS COMPLETED BY PERSONS 25 YEARS OF AGE AND OVER BY MAJOR ETHNIC GROUPS IN THE UNITED STATES *

Years of School Completed	Per Cent for Ethnic Groups			
	Foreign-born Whites	Native Whites	Negro	Indian
None	12.2	1.3	10.0	25.2
1-4 years	16.1	6.1	31.3	18.3
5-8 years	50.7	45.6	41.3	37.2
1-3 years high school	6.9	17.3	8.5	9.4
4 years high school	7.4	16.6	4.1	4.9
1-3 years college	1.9	6.6	1.8	1.9
4 years college or more	2.3	5.4	1.2	.8
Not reported	2.5	1.1	1.8	2.3
Average years completed	7.3	8.8	5.7	5.7

* Sixteenth Census of the United States, *Population* (1940), Vol. 2, Part 1, p. 52.

of school completed. For four years of high school completed, the proportion for foreign-born whites is much larger than that for two of the ethnic groups—Indian and Negro—but less than one-half of that for native whites. The same is true for the proportion of foreign-born whites who have completed four years or more of college, when this proportion is compared with that for the other ethnic groups included in the table. The only logical conclusion that can be deducted from the data in this table is that the educational status of foreign-born whites is above that of most minority ethnic groups in the United States, but far below that of native whites.

ECONOMIC STATUS

Although many factors have been responsible for the immigration of foreign-born whites to the United States—religious, political, social, and economic—it is the consensus that the economic motive has been the major factor, in recent years, that caused persons to leave their native nations and seek a new home in the United States. Many of the early immigrants succeeded in attaining the economic advancement that they sought, but during the last fifty years many conditions have served to restrict the economic opportunities for foreign-born whites. Among these have been: the lack of free homestead land, legal occupational restrictions, the increased use of machinery, the fight of native workers against foreign-born workers, the depression of the 1930's, and the increased need for workers to be able to read the English language.

There is still a scarcity of data concerned with the economic status of foreign-born whites in the United States although they have been a part of the economic system for many years. The data that are available deal largely with the following points: (1) the occupational distribution of foreign-born workers, and (2) the reaction of native-born workers toward foreign-born workers.[24] As late arrivals on the American economic scene foreign-born whites are marginal workers, and as marginal workers they are forced to accept the occupations that are least desired by native-born workers. In discussing the occupations available under this condition Owen shows that foreign-born workers are forced to occupy "more than their proportionate share of the monotonous, disagreeable, and oftentimes hazardous occupations."[25]

The major occupations in which foreign-born whites are engaged are manufacturing and mechanical industries, trade, and service occupations, in the order listed. Between 40 and 50 per cent are engaged in manufacturing and mechanical industries. In these industries they are usually engaged in the heavy occupations: those requiring the most physical exertion, that involve the greatest amount of danger, and are least desired by native-born workers. Those engaged in trade are usually owners or operators of small one man or family businesses. Those in service occupations are in most instances engaged in domestic and personal service. In other words, foreign-born whites are usually engaged in common or semi-skilled occupations. These are occupations that carry with them a low social status, and because of the low social status the wages paid in these occupations are on the lowest economic level.

Foreign-born workers in the United States are confronted with a large degree of antagonism from native-born workers. Native-born

[24] For discussions of the status of foreign-born wage-earners see the following: Carroll R. Daugherty, *Labor Problems in American Industry* (New York: Houghton Mifflin Co., 1941), pp. 242-247; W. L. Owen, *Labor Problems* (New York: The Ronald Press Company, Inc., 1946), pp. 69-76; Harry E. Barnes, *Society in Transition* (New York: Prentice-Hall, Inc., 1939), pp. 271-276; Lois MacDonald, *Labor Problems and the American Scene* (New York: Harper and Brothers, 1938), pp. 234-240.

[25] *Ibid.*, pp. 73-74.

workers accuse foreign-born white workers of many charges that contribute to this antagonism. Among these charges are that: (1) they work for lower wages and under inferior conditions,[26] (2) they lower the wage level and standard of living of native-white workers,[27] (3) they are used by employers to continue a state of labor unrest,[28] and (4) they are responsible for many pathological conditions in cities that contribute to labor inefficiency and serve to cause them to be poor employment risk.[29] Whether these charges are true or not they serve to retard the economic advancement of foreign-born white workers and to hold them on a low economic level.

The desire for upward occupational mobility tends to increase the antagonism of native-born workers toward foreign-born workers. It was pointed out previously that foreign-born workers are forced to accept the least desirable and marginal occupations. As long as they remain content in these occupations conditions will be orderly. However, as most foreign born workers are seeking economic advancement they strive to attain occupations that are higher on the occupational ladder. In doing this they come into occupational competition with native-born workers. This competition not only serves to increase the antagonism between native-born and foreign-born workers, but also to increase the occupational instability of foreign-born workers. Their occupational instability is increased as they strive for higher occupations because they are the last employed in these occupations, and when retrenchment is needed the principle of seniority dictates that they will be the first to be discharged.

The available data point out that foreign-born whites in the United States are usually engaged in common or semi-skilled occupations. In these occupations they come into competition with the lower level of native whites and with other minority ethnic groups. In this competition they are at a disadvantage because of the recency of their entrance into these occupations, and because of the antagonism from native-born whites. However, because of immigration selectivity many foreign-born whites are superior in training and experience to many members of other minority ethnic groups in the United States. This superior training and experience may make it possible for them to qualify for higher occupational positions than members of other

---

[26] Daugherty, *op. cit.*, pp. 245-247.
[27] *Loc. cit.*
[28] MacDonald, *op. cit.*, pp. 237-238.
[29] Barnes, *op. cit.*, pp. 276-279.

minority ethnic groups. Yet, because of the antagonism of native-white workers they are often denied the opportunity to enter many occupations that pay high wages. These facts suggest that foreign-born whites occupy an economic position that is above that of many members of minority ethnic groups but below that of native-born whites in the United States.

SUMMARY

To understand the general status of European immigrants in the United States it is essential to keep in mind the fact that there are differences in the statuses of old immigrants and new immigrants. For each status considered in this volume old immigrants are on a higher level than new immigrants. The status of European immigrants tends to vary in keeping with the extent that they are culturally different from native born whites. Those with a cultural background similar to that of native whites tend to approach the general status of native whites. On the other hand, *European immigrants who are culturally backward, as measured by the American standard, are forced to accept a low status, the lowest possible in many of the cities in which they reside.*

From the standpoint of the specific statuses used in this study the social status of European immigrants is above that of most colored ethnic groups in the United States, but below that of native-born whites. Legally, European immigrants have the lowest possible status until they are naturalized, and after naturalization they are not secure in their citizenship since they can be denaturalized under several conditions. The educational status of European immigrants is higher than that of most minority ethnic groups, but far below that of native whites. The economic status of European immigrants is on a level with or above that of other minority ethnic groups, but also far below that of native-born whites in the United States.

PROBLEMS FOR STUDY AND DISCUSSION

1. List and compare the characteristics of the three major groups into which foreign-born whites in the United States are classified.

2. List the five states in which the largest numbers of foreign-born whites reside, and the five states in which they represent the largest proportions of the population. Give reasons why you think they are residing in these states.

3. List five of the attitudes that you have acquired toward European immigrants, and compare these with the attitudes that you have acquired toward the other ethnic groups included in this book.

4. List and explain the reasons why European immigrants usually voluntarily segregate themselves from other ethnic groups.

5. List and discuss some of the problems that European immigrants are confronted with in the United States. Compare these problems with those confronted by other minority ethnic groups.

6. List and evaluate the major principles included in the present immigration laws in the United States.

7. Outline and explain the steps involved in the naturalization procedure in the United States.

8. List several of the occupations and professions in which aliens cannot engage. Explain why you think they are denied the right to engage in these occupations and professions.

9. Explain why you think the educational level of foreign-born whites is higher than of other minority ethnic groups.

SELECTED READINGS

ADAMIC, Louis, *A Nation of Nations* (New York: Harper and Brothers, 1944).

BERNARD, Williams S., et al. *American Immigration Policy* (New York: Harper and Brothers, 1950).

BROWN, F. J., and ROUCEK, J. S., *One America* (New York: Prentice-Hall, Inc., 1952), pp. 45-376.

FAIRCHILD, H. P., *Immigrants Background* (New York: John Wiley and Sons, Inc., 1937).

KONVITZ, M. R., *The Alien and the Asiatic in American Law* (Ithaca: Cornell University Press, 1946), pp. 29-37, 59-78, 97-110, 117-147.

MARDEN, Charles F., *Minorities in American Society* (New York: American Book Company, 1952), pp. 71-128.

PARK, R. E., *Old World Traits Transplanted* (New York: Harper and Brothers, 1921).

SCHERMERHORN, R. A., *These Our People* (Boston: D. C. Heath and Company, Inc., 1949), pp. 227-373.

SEABROOK, William, *These Foreigners* (New York: Harcourt, Brace and Company, Inc., 1944).

WALTER, Paul A. F., Jr., *Race and Culture Relations* (New York: McGraw-Hill Book Company, Inc., 1952), pp. 377-397.

YOUNG, D., *American Minority Peoples* (New York: Harper and Brothers, 1932), pp. 227-388.

III

IMPROVING ETHNIC RELATIONS

XIII
Research in Ethnic Relations

Introduction

IT IS THE CONSENSUS among students of ethnic relations that two types
of programs are essential in the improvement of these relationships:
(1) intensive and extensive programs of research in ethnic relations,
and (2) organized action programs that will work for the betterment
of ethnic relations. As will be pointed out in the next two chapters,
research and action programs should go along together and should
work hand in hand. It is recognized that in the past more emphasis
has been placed on action programs than on research. In other words,
the organized action programs of the past have been based more on
the personal wishes and whims of one, or several, leaders than upon
the findings of scientific research. This fact has probably contributed
to the failure of many of these organizations to accomplish their
stated objectives. As expressed in some of the readings to follow, it is
believed that ethnic research should precede most organized action
programs. It is for this reason that ethnic research is presented prior
to organized action programs in this book.

Research programs provide the scientific and systematized data that
can be used in planning and directing organized action programs.
As will be illustrated, research programs should be both intensive
and extensive in nature if they are to be of significant value in directing the improvement of ethnic relations. Ethnic research should provide systematized information on: (1) a better understanding of the
present ethnic relations picture, (2) the factors that have contributed
to the development of negative ethnic relations, (3) methods by which
ethnic relations may be improved, (4) the techniques that are most
successful in reducing prejudiced and antagonistic attitudes, and
(5) an evaluation of the present organized action programs for the
purpose of determining the advantages and disadvantages in each of

these programs. Selected readings are presented to analyze how research may contribute to an understanding of the above ethnic patterns, problems, and relationships.

Four readings have been selected to illustrate the need for research in ethnic relations, to point out some of the areas that should engage research interest, to ascertain some of the methods that may be used in conducting ethnic relations research, and to suggest a possible organization for the directing of ethnic research. The first reading by House, is centered on methods in the study of ethnic relations. The second reading by Weaver is concerned with the need for a study of Negro-white relations, with emphasis on the economic area of life. In the reading by Clinchy, special emphasis is placed on the organization for research, and how research and action programs should work in coöperation if the best results are to be expected in the improvement of ethnic relations. A detailed analysis is made of the possible areas in which ethnic relations research should be directed in the final reading by Williams.

▌ VIEWPOINTS AND METHODS IN THE STUDY OF RACE RELATIONS[1]

FLOYD N. HOUSE

Some thirty-two years ago, in summing up the findings of his study of the teaching of sociology in American institutions, Frank L. Tolman made certain provocative statements, which have been quoted occasionally by later writers, but which have never been seriously challenged. Among other things he said:

Sociology must define itself either as a body of doctrine, as a point of view, or as a method of research. It has tried to define itself as a body of doctrine, and it has failed in the attempt. If it is merely a point of view, it cannot be separated from the matter in discussion and must subordinate itself to the various social sciences. It has yet made no serious attempt to develop itself as a method of research, and must develop itself on these lines and show its fruitfulness before it can command consideration at the bar of science.

As a concise commentary on the status of sociology as an academic discipline in 1902, these sentences are not inaptly framed; and it may be that they describe fairly well the state of affairs in 1934. As regards their implications concerning the nature of science, and the boundary lines dividing the various sciences from each other,

[1] *American Journal of Sociology*, Vol. 40 (Jan., 1935), pp. 440-452. Used by permission of The University of Chicago Press.

Mr. Tolman's propositions are open to serious criticism. It may be possible to make such a critique the point of departure for a brief survey of some aspects of the study of race relations.

Tolman seems to imply by his statements that "body of doctrine," "point of view," and "method of research" are mutually exclusive categories, or at any rate that they can be defined as such. If by a body of doctrine is meant a set of ethical evaluations or moral precepts, or some mystical and unverifiable account of the ultimate essences of things, then nothing could be further from a method of scientific research. If, on the other hand, by "body of doctrine" we understand a description, in more or less generalized and abstract terms, of the working of certain observable phenomena, then our body of doctrine is much the same thing as a system of scientific hypotheses. It can presumably be verified, corrected, or rejected in the light of further observations; and, meanwhile, it serves to direct our studies. It defines, in other words, a point of view from which we may carry on further investigations of the matter in question. This is equivalent to saying that our body of doctrine determines, in a very real sense, a method of research—that method, namely, which consists in gathering such additional data as will be needed to show whether our doctrine is correct or not.

Looking at the matter in this light, one can say that the history of the study of race since the beginnings of recorded history is a story of changes in doctrines; that is, ideas of race and race relations, of changes in points of view toward problems of race, and, eventually, of changes in methods of study or research. So far as the Western world is concerned, men's ideas of race seem to have passed through five phases, each having been predominant in a certain period. We may call these phases the naively ethnocentric, religio-ethical, taxonomic, cultural, and sociological phases.

No doubt there was a stage in human social development so simple and so free from travel or communication that it was characterized by no idea of race at all. Various ethnological and historical documents show, however, that, when the curtain of history lifts, each human race or nationality typically has some contacts with groups of people who are different from its own members. In this quasi-primitive stage in cultural evolution, the predominant reaction to contact with an alien people was naively ethnocentric. The differences between one's own people and the "others" seemed patent; aliens were considered to be either a little more than human or a little less than human, according to the failure or success of early attempts to exploit them for the purposes of the in-group. (The classical distinction between Greeks and "barbarians" illustrates this conception of race sufficiently well; and Aristotle's familiar argument that barbarians are slaves by nature suggests something of the motivation underlying the doctrine.) Study of race or of race relations in this stage of things hardly proceeded beyond a simple enumeration of the traits—sometimes quite mythical—by which the aliens differed from the members of the in-group.

By the third or fourth century of our era, the stoic philosophy and the Christian doctrine of the common fatherhood of God, with its implications that all men are brothers, had sufficed to give a new direction to reflective thought concerning the subject of race. There is a period of some twelve or thirteen centuries in European history in which practically no literature dealing systematically with the subject of race was produced. Apparently, in the face of the doctrine of Christian brotherhood, inquiry into race differences would have been thought impious or heretical. To be sure, a substitute for the concept of race was eventually found in the distinctions which were made between believers and infidels, and between believers and heathen. These distinctions afforded a basis for the rationalization of a great many practical discriminations and exploitations; it seems to have been by such lines of reasoning that Negro slavery was justified in an early period of modern history. Nevertheless, so long as it was a generally accepted religious dogma that all men are brothers, neither race differences nor race relations could very well become the object of disinterested study.

It was perhaps as one aspect of the general emancipation of thought and action from the control of the church that, in early modern times, certain writers undertook a fresh consideration of some of the practical and concrete implications of the differences between races and nationalities. Montesquieu discussed the topic in a rather matter-of-fact way and his attitude was characteristic of much else that was being said and written at the time. It does not seem, however, that the new intellectual freedom and activity gave rise to any particularly new conception of race or of race relations for some time. The publication and general acceptance of Linnaeus' scheme for the classification of plant and animal species may be regarded as the starting-point for a phase in the study of race that may be termed taxonomic. Various efforts were made to work out a neat and comprehensive clasisfication of the races of mankind, and these classifications, like the religious and racial distinctions of earlier epochs, served as the point of departure for elaborate reasonings in support of discriminations and exploitations.

This procedure of classification, together with subsequently developed but closely related techniques for the measurement of racial traits, has continued to occupy the attention of students down to the present day. Ever since the time it first appeared as a form of modern scientific inquiry, taxonomy has exercised a certain fascination over the students of biology and related sciences. The collection and classification of data seem to yield in greater measure than almost any other form of scientific investigation the thrills of discovery, while at the same time it is a procedure which apparently conforms thoroughly to the scientific criterion of objectivity. In the latter respect, the method of classification, accompanied and re-enforced by a vast labor of measurement of race traits of physique and behavior, has been such as to command itself particularly to those interested in human race problems. What could be more disinterested, fair, and impartial than the careful, systematic measurement of race traits? (Of course this work has been done, up to now, mainly by representatives of the white or Caucasian race, and they have doubtless found the results of their labors none the less gratifying for the fact that, on the whole, these results have been such as to support the pretensions of the white race to supremacy over the colored peoples.) The findings of physical measurements may be somewhat ambiguous and difficult to interpret clearly as regards their bearing on the question of the relative superiority of one race over another. Measurements of skulls, however, which presumably correlate positively with mental capacity, show a consistent advantage to the white, as compared with the Negro, race or races. And when we turn to the newer schemes for the direct measurement of mental traits, in other words, measurement of performance of tasks presumably requiring intelligence and imagination for their successful execution, the findings are equally gratifying to white investigators. White subjects chosen at random from a given locality or milieu have invariably made better average scores than Negro subjects from the same milieu.

So consistent and satisfactory do the results of this general class of investigations seem to many students to be, that one can notice in much of the recent literature bearing on the problems of race and race relations a marked tendency to proceed on the assumption that these measurements and classifications are the only conceivable, or the only necessary and thoroughly valid, method of research into these problems. The doctrine or scientific hypothesis involved is that the races of man differ from each other on the average in capacities of the kind that are of most significance in human social life, and that the relationships of subordination and dominance, and the like, which exist between racial groups in the modern world, are to be interpreted as the natural and inevitable outcome of differences in average hereditary capacity between the members of the different races. These propositions clearly define a corresponding viewpoint and method for the study of race and race relations.

Within the past two or three decades, however, two or three pertinent criticisms of the theory and method just described have been
put forth. In the first place, it is pointed out that the measurements
of any particular trait or performance of members of a racial group
are distributed through a rather wide range, which can be represented by some variant of the well-known bell-shaped probability
curve; and that the measurements of the same trait of members of
another comparable, racial group can be represented by a similar
curve, which will, no doubt, have a different mode and median from
the first, but which will also overlap it considerably. A few measurements of members of the inferior group may even lie well above the
mode or average for the superior group. This fact, it is contended
by some critics, has implications which should not be obscured by
the difference in average. At any rate they tend to weaken the reasoning which is put forth to support or justify the categoric exclusion
of members of one group from opportunities or privileges extended
to the other.

A second criticism of the findings or conclusions usually drawn
from the results of comparative measurements of members of different racial groups concerns the interpretation of the results of mental
tests. It is pointed out that, even within the bodies of statistics compiled from such texts, there can be found support for the theory
that the performance is affected by education and other forces of
environment. The scores made by northern Negroes on mental tests
are, for example, distinctly better than those made by southern
Negroes; and in some instances, the performance of northern
Negroes on mental tests has averaged better than that of groups of
southern whites. On the basis of such facts and analyses, the hypothesis has been formulated that mental tests measure primarily cultural
differences, and that there is no reliable technique for eliminating
the effect of culture and education from the gross data secured by
mental tests. It is also pointed out that different racial groups from
the same locality do not necessarily have the same environment, in
the sense in which environment is equivalent to opportunity for
mental development. If "intelligence" be defined as that which is
measured by intelligence tests, then according to the line of reasoning now under consideration, intelligence is the result of education,
of home conditions including education of parents, and of various
other factors including influences which are generated by the interracial situation itself. The findings of mental tests and statistics of
retardation in school alike seem to show that Negro children compare more favorably with white children at early ages than at more
advanced ages. It was formerly the fashion in academic circles to
account for this difference by the theory that the mental develop-

ment of Negro children is arrested at an early age by the closing of the sutures of the skull, but this explanation is now quite generally regarded as fantastic; and it has been suggested that the relatively inferior performance of Negro children in their later school years may be due, in part, at least, to the sense of hopelessness regarding opportunities for making use of their education.

It would be worth while to review at much greater length the possibilities and limitations of the general viewpoint and method for the study of race and race relations which proceeds from the hypothesis that race relations are necessarily and permanently conditioned by race differences which can be measured, were not the subject already familiar to all students. The foregoing brief summary of some of the criticisms of the doctrine which are being made today will perhaps be sufficient to serve as a point of departure for the examination of two other general viewpoints and methods of research in race relations, the cultural and what we may call the sociological.

It was perhaps no more than a natural result of the differentiation of sociology from the older social sciences that was manifested in the interest which early sociologists displayed in the subject of race. The writings of Ludwig Gumplowicz, one of the recognized pioneers of modern sociology, were largely centered in a theory of race relations; and the writings of Gumplowicz had, in turn, a considerable influence over many other early students and teachers of sociology. To Gumplowicz the concept of race appeared as a simple and natural one, needing no particular analysis. "Heterogeneous ethnic elements" in the total population of the earth were for him among the primary data of social science. After his day, however, the development of sociological thought and research fell under the influence of other men, who started from somewhat different assumptions. Tarde and Durkheim, Maine and Bagehot, W. H. R. Rivers and his associates, and many others contributed to the formation of a body of social theory which placed much emphasis on culture, and relatively little on the biological concept of race. Little by little the idea gained ground that the obvious and important differences between nationalities, once too lightly assumed to be due to racial heredity, were primarily cultural differences. During the latter part of the nineteenth century and the early part of our own, a great volume of information concerning the customs and institutions of different peoples was accumulated in the hands of ethnologists and made available to other scholars. These were among the reasons why the comparative study of culture began to be regarded by sociologists and anthropologists as a fruitful method of research in the problems of race, or those which had been so classified.

Culture traits are by definition acquired traits. They are customs and beliefs which have been formed in the course of experience and interaction with a given environment or sequence of environments; and they are passed along from one generation to another, or spread from one group to another, by processes of learning and inculcation, which leave the characters of the germ plasm quite unchanged. So soon as the study of race began to be conceived as a task of systematic inventory and description of the customs of racial groups, the door was opened for the entrance of a quite different set of doctrines of race and race relations. It began to be felt that nationality, which is admittedly a matter of customs, language, and group-consciousness, is possibly more important than race. This point of view was strengthened by the gradual discovery of evidence tending to show that there are no pure races of human beings. In treatises and journal articles by distinguished authors it was shown that the significant differences between the so-called "races" might be chiefly cultural differences, and that the relations and interactions of two nationality groups, not racially distinguishable from each other, were much the same as the interactions of two races. In recent years these ideas have become widely current among scholars and scientists, and have in turn done much to strengthen the belief that the careful study of the cultural heritages of the groups in question is a practical method of studying the social problems of race. It is seen that even interracial attitudes may be matters of custom and tradition in the racial groups concerned. Who can deny, for example, that southern white attitudes toward Negroes, in the United States are determined largely by southern white tradition, and are by no means the innate, "instinctive" reactions they are often supposed to be?

The greatest practical significance of the introduction of the concept of culture into the theory of race is, of course, the implied ease of modification of race differences, or what are popularly supposed to be race differences. Race differences, in the strict biological sense of the term, are no doubt very persistent, though it has been pointed out that, in cases where some set of circumstances leads to a great deal of interbreeding between two races, a group may have its racial character, strictly so-called, considerably modified while its culture remains relatively stable. So long as a race remains relatively distinct and set apart by conspicuous physical marks such as color, however, the behavior traits or tendencies which the members of that group have in common by virtue of their biological heritage will presumably remain nearly constant. But if the principal behavior traits by which they differ at a given time from peoples or groups around them are not racial in the proper sense of the term, but cultural, these traits may change rather rapidly, by means of education, communication, and other forms of contact with other peoples. The perception of these possibilities being widely diffused today, it is not surprising that much of the energy which has been devoted to the study of race and race relations has been concentrated on the facts of culture and cultural progress in given race groups.

The point of view and corresponding method for the study of race problems which has been most recently developed of all is that which is suggested by the now familiar phrases, "race prejudice," "racial attitudes," and "race relations." Commonplace though the idea is to us today, it does not appear that anyone thought of making the interrelations of racial groups the object of direct critical study until quite late in the history of social science. For centuries inquiry and discussion focused themselves on race traits, inherent or acquired, and race differences. The relative positions of racial groups in a more inclusive social order, the attitudes of members of different races toward each other, and their common ways of dealing with each other were assumed to be the natural and obvious outcome of the differences between the races in traits, be they instincts, capacities, emotions, intelligence quotients, or what not. With the shift in attention in social science from social structure to social process and interaction, however, it began to appear to some students that the relationship of race groups, like the relationships of individuals and other kinds of groups, is a dynamic one; and that the relationships of races take form and are changed in the course of experience in living together. Gumplowicz had said, to be sure, that there are two essential factors in every natural process, heterogeneous elements and their reciprocal interaction. But while he regarded the racial groups of mankind as the "heterogeneous ethnic elements" of fundamental importance in the social process, he thought the principle of their interaction might be very simply stated, in the following formula: "Every stronger ethnic or social group strives to subjugate or make serviceable to its purposes every weaker element which exists or may come within the field of its influence." We now begin to perceive that the interaction of races is no more than barely adumbrated in this formula. The thesis of Gumplowicz is in effect a theory of competition, and Ray Stannard Baker found, in his brilliant exploratory study of the relations of Negroes and whites in the Southern states, that competition is indeed very fundamental to the whole pattern which is called "the color line." At about the same time Jean Finot suggested by the title of well-known volume, even if he did not develop the proposition, that "race prejudice" is something to be studied and explained. Baker showed that the color line is a shifting evolving thing, rather than the stable and absolute distinction it has been commonly supposed to be. His thought was that the color line shifts with changes in the competitive situation. It remained for Robert E. Park to suggest that there may be a typical "cycle" or sequence in the changes of relations between two races after their first contact.

Today, therefore, we are beginning to agree that our most important problem for social research with reference to race is not race traits nor race differences, and that even the realistic problem of culture traits and culture differences between racial groups may gain in meaning when studied in connection with some inquiry into race relations and their changes. This newer point of view is now represented by several substantial volumes, of which Professor Reuter's *The American Race Problem* and Charles S. Johnson's *The Negro in American Civilization* are outstanding examples.

To point out the importance and extent of the shift in interest and in research emphasis from the study of race traits and race differences to the study of race relations is, of course, only to lay the foundation for a consideration of methods of study in the more specific sense of the term. Even if we consider that we have proved that race relations can be studied objectively, and that research along such lines is the most fruitful approach to race problems at the present time, it remains to be determined by what procedures or what specific lines of inquiry race relations can be studied. As a matter of fact, a number of procedures are beginning to take shape.

(1) Doubtless interracial competition is the most fundamental form of racial interaction. The competition of races or racial groups can be studied by investigating occupations, wealth and income, and the distribution of racial groups in space, locally and regionally. What is particularly relevant, however, is the measurement of the changes that are taking place or have taken place in these matters.

(2) Demographic studies throw some light on questions of racial competition; they reveal the course of that competition in its most elemental aspects. Demographic studies are characterized also by the relative ease with which satisfactory objectivity can be attained in them. These are probably among the reasons for the sustained interest in demographic studies relating to problems of race.

(3) Practical problems of race relations tend to assume a political, administrative, or legal form. Careful descriptions of administrative and legislative acts affecting race relations in a given situation, accompanied by some account of the situation, analysis of the issues, and disinterested discussion of the probable effects of alternative policies if put in effect, may be expected to add their quota to our understanding of the underlying forces and processes involved. Inquiry which starts from a particular practical problem has some

presumption of realism in its favor, though it will not necessarily be free from bias. Such a discussion may beg some of the questions involved in a most plausible fashion. No doubt the most valuable sort of a study which might be termed political, legal, or administrative, would be one which would analyze carefully the effects of a policy which had been put into effect some time in the past.

(4) It can be said of race relations as of many other phases of social organization and social interaction that, humanly speaking, the psychological aspects are the most important ones. The biological and economic aspects of an interracial situation may be most fundamental, but it is the beliefs, attitudes, and sentiments of those involved which more directly determine what happens. It is beliefs and sentiments that give meaning and value to race relations, as to all social relations. We may congratulate ourselves, therefore, on the efforts which are being made to study the sentiments, attitudes, and prejudices which enter into the relations and interactions of racial groups. Such works as Moton's *What the Negro Thinks*, James Weldon Johnson's *Autobiography of an Ex-Colored Man*, and a number of other books, ostensibly fiction, by Negro authors, help to define interracial situations and afford hypotheses which someone may be able to verify or modify by more objective studies. The members of one race may be able to define and describe their attitudes toward the members of another race, by some procedure of self-analysis, but to arrive at a complete explanation of the process of the interaction of two racial groups we must have reliable knowledge of the attitudes of members of both races. Incidentally, it may be the source of some surprise to notice that we have practically no writings by white authors describing the attitudes of white people toward the colored races as vividly as some of the books alluded to describe "what the Negro thinks." Apparently this lack indicates a need for one type of research in race relations.

(5) One of the most promising of all the research devices which have been invented so far for the study of race relations is the introspective recapture of individuals' experiences which have shaped the attitudes toward members of another race, and, perhaps by reflection, one's attitudes toward one's own race. An interesting fact in this connection, or what appears to be a fact, is that members of a dominant race are not race-conscious to the same extent or in the same way as are many of the members of a subject or subordinated racial group. This difference has never been extensively investigated or discussed. It appears that, under some circumstances, the race-consciousness developed by subordination may eventually become an asset to the subordinated race, a source of strength in interracial

competition, but this, too, remains to be studied. Quite clearly, to be subordinated as a racial group is no guarantee of future dominance or equality.

One research procedure which can be very useful in the present stage of development of our knowledge of race relations is the survey. When a series of potential research problems are as poorly defined as those of race relations still admittedly are, something is gained by a systematic canvass of existing knowledge and theories, and a mapping out of the subject or field in such a way as will reveal further possibilities of study.

One serious difficulty which interferes with the successful study of race relations is the bias or prejudice, from which the one undertaking such study is rarely free. Even more strikingly is it true that those whom the student will wish to use as sources of information will rarely be free from bias in their report of their experience or knowledge. Race relations is in the nature of things a controversial subject, toward which the social scientist can achieve a detached attitude only with difficulty. To be sure he may, in the measure of his ability, be able to give objectivity to his data by defining the viewpoints and attitudes of his informants, i.e., by taking into account in the interpretation of evidence the situations to which his informants were responding. It is also, however, some gain in objectivity to have suggestive theories and generalizations concerning supposed facts clearly formulated. That which has been clearly stated as theory or hypothesis may then be susceptible of inductive verification or modification. It may well be, therefore, that much of the study and publication which has already been carried on in the field of race relations will bear its richest fruits indirectly, as a further result of research still to be done.

❚ A NEEDED PROGRAM OF RESEARCH IN RACE RELATIONS [2]

ROBERT C. WEAVER

. . . .

I

We know much about the causes of prejudice. We know how the color-caste system has arisen in the United States, and we know the institutions that give expression to our race prejudices. Better than ever before, we appreciate the intensity of color chauvinism, and many of us are worried. Yet, action to correct the situation has not

[2] Robert C. Weaver, "A Needed Program of Research in Race Relations and Associated Problems," *Journal of Negro Education*, Vol. 16 (Spring, 1947), pp. 130-135. Used by permission of the Journal.

kept abreast of knowledge. This is not due to a lack of organizations
concerned with making democracy real. It is due rather to the fact
that the majority of Americans are not yet convinced that the *status
quo* in race relations has to be changed. At the same time, so much
of the attention of the social scientists has been devoted to describing and measuring that there is a dearth of information supplying
information for dramatizing the necessity of erasing the color line.

It has often been observed that discrimination against ethnic
groups is expensive in a democracy. Recently, we have been told,
and convincingly, too, that segregation inevitably leads to discrimination—there is no such thing as separate but equal facilities for
minorities. Yet, little has been done to indicate the costs in dollars
and cents of racial segregation in America. This is in striking contrast to the rather full accounts of the forms discrimination and
segregation take and how they evolve. In the United States today, it
is possible for an economic and social institution to persist long after
it has been proved to be morally wrong; its longevity is usually much
shorter when it has been established that it costs citizens additional
and unnecessary outlays of money.

The institutions and agencies concerned with modifying the color-
caste system rightly resort to lobbying for and against legislation.
They know that prejudice cannot be legislated away, but they also
realize that laws can and do effect and create institutions and conditions which either encourage or discourage group discrimination.
They realize that the direction and quality of administration are no
less important than the content of laws. Effective analyses of pending legislation and administrative actions require prompt and intelligent evaluation of proposed laws in light of the contents of the
specific legislation and the economic and social milieu in which they
will operate, as well as constant observation of administrative practices. Such analyses require the attention of competent social scientists and lawyers.

Since the problems that face minorities with stark and persistent
reality are often economic, there is need for directed research in the
economic aspects of minority living. At the same time, the trend
toward government regulation, participation, and planning in economic matters suggests the importance of legislative and administrative research.

The areas of specialization are inherent in the economic plight of
minorities. Employment opportunities, union relations and housing
seem now, as always, to have priority. Of the three, housing is perhaps of the greatest immediacy. This is true for several reasons:
America is considering action to rehouse its people, and at the same
time, the concentration of minorities in restricted areas injects the

matter of residential segregation into all discussions of postwar housing. Despite these facts, there is little sound research into the inevitable inconsistency between residential segregation and the flexibility in land use that city planning and effective urban rehabilitation demand. Nor have we analyzed the economic costs of ghettos in modern American cities. Although we do have fragmentary data on the strain on tax funds which a dual system of education extracts, nowhere have the materials been brought together and presented in the larger setting of the economic costs of segregation in all forms of public facilities.

II

This proposal is concerned primarily, although not exclusively, with research which reflects the economic aspects of the position of minorities in our society. It is believed that the problems of minorities are among the most pressing in the nation today and that it is possible to do outstanding work of a scholarly nature incident to them. It must be remembered, however, that these peculiar problems are usually part and parcel of the large social and economic issues which affect the total population. Consequently, a program of research which is concerned primarily with minority groups would, of necessity, include probing into broader issues.

To date, there has been no consistent research into the economic problems affecting Negroes. W. E. B. DuBois, in the Atlanta University Publications, began such a program at the turn of the century. In less than ten years the project had folded up. Then there was a long period when little was produced, save an occasional valuable study such as Phillips' *American Negro Slavery,* Feldman's *Racial Factors in American Industry,* Herbst's *The Negro in the Slaughtering and Meat Packing Industry in Chicago,* and Reid's *Negro Membership in American Labor Unions.* In 1931, Abram L. Harris and Sterling Spero prepared *The Black Worker,* the first penetrating study of Negro labor (and incidentally, of the whole economic problem facing colored Americans). Cayton and Mitchell projected this initial study in their book on *Black Workers and the New Unions;* this latter volume was primarily a report of current developments rather than an analysis of the black man's problem of earning a living. As a part of the Myrdal research, Richard Sterner produced *The Negro's Share,* a study which suffered from its almost complete reliance upon statistical materials. Myrdal's *An American Dilemma* was weak in those sections dealing with recent economic changes; it is an incomplete analysis since its date of publication precluded descriptions of the changes occasioned by World War II, and the author's emphasis upon the moral dilemma led him to neglect and under-emphasize economic factors. In 1944, Herbert Northrup published *Organized Labor and the Negro*. Most recently, Drake and Cayton have produced an excellent volume, *Black Metropolis*. This study of Chicago's South Side, like *An American Dilemma,* is weakest in its discussions of current economic problems. The present writer in *Negro Labor: A National Problem* has attempted to present the experience of Negro labor during World War II and the prospects for the future in the background of the general economic developments of the periods concerned. Brailsford Brazeal in *The Brotherhood of Sleeping Car Porters* has set forth fully the growth and activities of the Brotherhood, and he and others are working on histories of the FEPC.

In addition to the books mentioned above, other volumes of a specialized nature have appeared, but in the present writer's opinion they are so limited in scope or so unsatisfactory in execution as to add little to our knowledge of the basic economic issues. Especially noteworthy is the lack of any competent analysis of the housing problems of minority groups. There has been a limited amount of periodical literature on housing and on the broader economic issues facing minorities. Some of it has been in government publications such as the *Monthly Labor Review* and in Negro journals such as *The Journal of Negro Education, Phylon, Opportunity,* and *The Crisis*. During the last decade periodicals devoted exclusively to economic subjects have welcomed articles on the Negro. Most of the recent contributions in these journals have come from the pens of a few writers including Lloyd Bailer, Herman Feldman, Lester B. Granger, Herbert Northrup, and the present writer.

The situation in Economics is in striking contrast to that in History and Sociology. The work of the Association for the Study of Negro Life and History has stimulated research on subjects of Negro History. In Sociology the situation is even more encouraging. There are numerous first-class books on sociological problems involving minorities in general and Negroes in particular. The periodical literature in this field is voluminous, and much of it is of high calibre. Also, there is a relatively large number of outstanding sociologists who are constantly adding significant contributions to this branch of our knowledge.

The greatest need at the present time is for a series of well-planned studies on the economic problems facing minorities—with special reference to Negro-union relationships, shelter and health. Emphasis upon Negro-labor relations is most important. Research in this area would fill a serious void in our knowledge of contemporary problems and serve to bring Negro labor officials (and white labor officials) into closer contact with those working in the social sciences.

The center producing such research would, ultimately, become a place where current problems would be discussed. It might become an instrument for stimulating action through supplying analyses of unquestionable soundness and validity.

Two new programs of social welfare in America offer a challenge and a source of potential benefit for minorities. They are government's concern about supplying housing for all and the proposals for health insurance. Housing for colored minorities in America has many peculiar features. Residential segregation, for example, is fundamental. Its analysis, studies of the effect of minority groups' occupancy upon property values, and the cost of home ownership to Negroes have received but little attention. Yet they are basic to any rational approach to the housing problem in our urban centers. Medical economics is another important area for investigation. For a group made up predominantly of low and uncertain income recipients, the cost and mode of paying for medical and dental care establish limits upon the quantity and quality of this service. Institutions which are training professional men and women, too, are greatly handicapped by the paucity of information in this field and their failure to acquaint their students with an understanding of medical economics.

As has been suggested above, government will play an increasing role in the economic life of the nation. Already this circumstance has been reflected in the programs of national Negro organizations. The NAACP, the Urban League, the American Council on Race Relations, the AKA sorority, certain church and labor groups, to mention but a few, are analyzing proposed legislation in light of its effects upon minorities, appearing before congressional committees, conferring with federal agencies, and observing the operation of government programs. These agencies, however, are primarily action groups; most of them have few facilities for conducting research. Today they are forced to carry on such research; the result is duplication of effort (with already woefully inadequate staffs), a great amount of last minute preparation, and occasional quick decisions. Seldom do they have the means for analyzing administrative practices prior to a major scandal or some gross malpractice.

The obvious need is for a research program which could analyze pending legislation, conduct systematic surveys of governmental programs and develop proposals for improving both. Factual materials are woefully inadequate at the present time. Nor do we have a body of assembled background materials relative to these important developments. Research to supply these deficiencies would fill a serious void and find ready use in the activities of a score of existing agencies. It would also be useful as source material for sound public information.

III

The major emphasis of the program should be upon economic research. Specific projects, would of course, be determined in light of current developments, detailed discussions, and an evaluation of available data and publications. There are, however, certain obvious gaps in existing materials which indicate some desirable areas of investigation. They are as follows:

I. General Economic Problems
   A. Analyses of changes in racial occupational patterns in industrial employment
   B. Problems of labor displacement incident to the mechanization of Southern agriculture
   C. Experiences of the minority group worker in industrial ghost towns

II. Negro-Union Relations
   A. Extent and experience of Negroes in industrial unions
   B. Minority groups and union seniority
   C. Experience of Negro workers in unions which issued work permits during the war
   D. Influence of Railroad Brotherhoods on Negro employment in railroads

III. Special Areas
   A. The economic costs of racial segregation
   B. Negro occupancy and property values
   C. The economic bases and costs of race restrictive housing covenants
   D. The cost of home ownership for Negroes
   E. The cost of medical care to Negroes
   F. Economic requirements for greater medical care to minorities

IV. Administration of Federal Programs
   A. Racial policies and their results under the New Deal and during World War II
   B. Background materials incident to new legislation
   C. Administration of social legislation

This is neither a complete nor an inflexible program. It is presented as indicative of the type of projects which should be carried on. Some of the elements are long-range projects which should result in books; others are short-run and would yield articles which, in some instances, would subsequently be supplemented with other materials to make up books. Materials assembled under the topics listed in Section IV, obviously, would be of value only if promptly executed and circulated; they would be mimeographed.

The success of the Social Science Departments at the University of Chicago and later at Fisk University in stimulating research in Sociology, in encouraging the development of competent sociologists interested in minority problems and in producing worthwhile research is the best indication of the possibilities in a related field. The interest in economic problems involving minorities and the need for research incident to them today is even greater than were the interest and needs in the field of Sociology at the time the Department of Social Science was established at Fisk University. In light of this fact, it is reasonable to assume that with a sound program, responsible sponsorship, and capable direction, the proposed research program could and would receive financial support.

This research program, because of its nature and the trend of the times, could not only influence thinking but could also make a real contribution toward lending guidance to action programs which are evolving and which will continue to develop. Research in economic, legislative and administrative problems affecting minorities would, if well done, become a service function. Its real worth would be reflected by the extent to which it developed factual material, intelligently analyzed problems and inspired other agencies and individuals to undertake related research. Resulting materials would do much to provide factual data to encourage solution of the American dilemma.

▌ RESEARCH IN INTERGROUP RELATIONS [3]

EVERETT R. CLINCHY

What are attitudes, prejudices, ideas about other groups? Where do they come from, how do they start? What modifies them? To what extent can they be controlled, moderated or outmoded? How can social changes in intergroup relations be brought about? These are the problems of research. Dissecting the nature of attitudes reveals whatever irrationality resides in them, and also their genesis. Prejudiced individuals were asked what they thought of the Uranians and Wallonians: they felt the same prejudices against those non-existent peoples that they had toward their unlike, real neighbors. Anti-Semites considered Jews both exclusive and intrusive—but how could they be both?

[3] Everett R. Clinchy, *Research and Education in Intergroup Relations* (New York: The Louis J. and Mary E. Horowitz Foundation, Inc., 1948), pp. 9-13. Used by permission of the Foundation.

When considering what to do about prejudice and conflict we must keep in mind that action programs should not wait for research. In turn action, which is the engineering phase, should follow a research design. Results of programs in many areas should then be evaluated but work must not stop there. Helpful information must be used in further experimentation.

Research can be discussed under three categories. Each complements the other: fundamental research, evaluation of action programs, and research strategy.

Fundamental Research

Too much wishful thinking among conductors of action programs leads to a neglect of the fundamental factors in intergroup relations. There are basic needs of knowledge which scientists now lack. Here are some illustrations:

To understand pathological conditions in society by setting up studies in conflict and aggression; to analyze the problems of majority as well as minority groups; to discover the roles opposition, tension and cultural competition in society; to find out how attitudes develop in an individual against the background of his culture, and the larger community.

Another fundamental research need is to use projective techniques to get at the basic drives underlying human behavior, and which shape the "personality" of cultures. Personality differences in primitive people offer opportunity for such study. But every American community affords a laboratory for it, too.

The culture personality of Catholicism, Judaism and Protestantism can be accounted for by studies bridging science, philosophy and religion. This research in the fundaments of contemporary culture will get at the basic differences between Jews, Protestants and Catholics. It will also describe what American civilization and present-day world influences are doing to these differences.

Fundamental research includes such fields as the study of early childhood experiences as a factor in later prejudices and conflicts. Psychologists at the University of California have conducted wide studies, even going into prisons to seek a correlation between types of crime and prejudice. Reasons for attitudes have been sought among returning G.I.'s. Here it was found that economic status had a direct bearing on intolerance. Those who were better off economically than before the war—to the tune of $1,500 in yearly income— were less prejudiced than those worse off. The veteran whose income had increased more than $1,500 was as prejudiced, however, as the one who had not moved ahead at all. Case records of individuals were followed from birth but here the experimenters met a blank wall in their effort to determine attitude development. Planned genetic studies, with control groups, are needed.

Recent experimentation has opened up whole new fields for research in human behavior. Case histories of psychoanalytic patients among minority groups as well as among prejudiced members of majority groups were suggested. Deliberate efforts in the laboratory to convert intolerant people would be a way to check on basic mechanisms as well as techniques for resolving conflicts between groups. More case studies of how individuals with little or no unfair prejudices were set free from the garden-variety of hostility infections would be helpful.

The value of broad opinion surveys in fundamental research were open to question. Often they are superficial and misleading because sub-groups questioned—occupation, age, income groups—are usually small. Intensive area sampling in specific communities reveals trends in a more reliable fashion. In fact, there is a great need for more work in all phases on the intensive level of research.

New patterns of research are called for. Little is known of the actual results of legislation such as fair employment practice laws. Moreover, technique results, the use of motion pictures, posters and others, need to be checked. Otherwise efforts are mere chance programs, like arrows shot into the air.

What are the basic methods to be used in preventing aggression? Individuals must be helped to channelize aggression into more acceptable paths. A prejudiced individual, whose attention has been effectively drawn to the causes of his feeling, may even turn his unfulfilled aggression into combating prejudice and become an able intergroup worker! This requires the use of insight, and devious forms of demonstration.

Again, there is the exciting problem of the uses of cultural pluralism, about which too little is known. In what ways, and with what effects, do associations of diverse culture lead to growth: Does the presence of unique groups stimulate to progress? Are some degrees of tension and competition inescapable, if the necessary struggle is to be achieved,—the outward struggle for material prosperity, and inward struggle for moral and intellectual growth?

A contemporary playwright, Maxwell Anderson, has said (if we may be permitted to paraphrase his point) that Western Civilization's laws and institutions, its cities and towns which stand gloriously against the sky and seem so strong and durable, are blown into these shapes by a spirit which inhabits,—blown like a bubble—and will subside again when the spirit is withdrawn. As long as the people keep their faith, that faith will keep the nation. When people cease to believe only a little while, the high roofs take rain and the walls sink to the ground. Perhaps the most fundamental thinking of all which foundations should encourage lies in the fields of philosophy and religion. From these areas can come, not immediately but gradually, the sources of faith needed if men are to use their knowledge wisely and to will the good for all their fellows.

From all such work basic fundamentals of human behavior are emerging. Only when they have been clearly defined, only when "typologies of prejudice" and positive principles of love translated as understanding, have been established, can work toward easing conflicts progress smoothly and effectively.

Translating Research Into Action

One serious shortcoming in intergroup work is clear. This has to do with carrying the results of scientific study into the promotional field. Fundamental research is progressing, much more is needed, but a good start has been made. The next problem is how to make the findings of researchers available to the field workers, who are often operating with enthusiasm but without adequate knowledge of the whys and wherefores of their endeavor. Action programs should be based on up-to-the-minute reports from the laboratory.

One way to combine action and research effectively would be to select forty or so communities, with all kinds of regional and other variations, and turn them into experimental laboratories for action programs. Now there are from ten to twenty school-community projects for which there are considerable data. Foundation support should be given to projects in carefully selected communities which would be directed by competent resident "insiders" rather than a researcher from outside who might not be aware of community patterns. These various community directors would be supplied latest research organizations to discuss comparisons of their projects and techniques used.

Social scientists often tend to write for each other, rather than for a wider market. Valuable biological, anthropological, psychological, sociological and historical research stays on the library shelves and never gets to the people who need it most—the men and women who give much of their daily lives to improvement human relations. In other fields this gap between fact and act is bridged by adequate training. The technologist works side by side with the physical scientist. These days the government official goes to school to learn public administration and is expected to keep abreast of the public law and government theorists. This rift between the social scientist and the practitioner could be filled by a body which would translate fundamental research efforts for the benefit of program leaders.

A Strategy Board

The discussion of Research, and indeed of Education and Community Programs, has revealed the need for intergroup study, and a fund of enthusiasm on the part of promotional workers, educators, and researchers to develop the field of intercultural relations. It also underscores the fact that cohesion is lacking on the part of hundreds of community groups and schools with plans for warfare on prejudice and conflict. Atomic weapons for war and peace are surely no more important to the American people than disruption among groups at home. And yet atomic researchers have a central strategy board to direct their efforts, with all forces,—universities, factories and government—combining as a team in a gigantic effort to promote physical perfection in their field.

Why not a similar plan for perfecting the weapons against hate and intolerance at home? Such direction of intergroup needs, knowledge, and strategy is now required. The primary problem mankind faces today is to rationalize human relations. Failure may result in blowing all civilization to pieces. Clearly, the tested devices which have done so much to advance physical science and technological gains should be applied to human relations.

Much research is wasteful and luxurious because it is never used. It must be turned into applicable information for group workers. Organizations in inter-group work are multiple, their personnel and functions often overlap, even within one community. We need a more systematic, sustained arrangement deliberately planned to bring certain essential elements to intergroup relations.

A central planning board could have for its members representatives of the various social science faculties, education, government administration, religion, labor and industry representatives, and human relations professionals. Since comparative and action research must be taken seriously, team planning with policy makers, practitioners and consumers participating is necessary. The board could be supplemented by a large advisory panel of consultants. For each profession represented on the board, or "core group," there would be ten or so members of the same profession on the panel, representing various fields within the profession, different regions of the country and both urban and rural areas. Thus for any given problem a group of specialists could be selected from the panel to supplement discussion and action by the core groups.

Active intergroup workers could play a large part in the planning of the board of strategists. They could supply the organization with details of their practical experience, they could submit ideas for projects and have them checked by the board. They could request projects and programs to be carried out in their areas.

The panel of experts might move into a larger area and combine research efforts with experimentation. Since insufficient basic experiments are being carried out, and action programs are not sufficiently supplemented with research checks and balances, and since the new demands of circumstances in One World in an Atomic Age are so pressing, a necessary integration and speed-up in social change can be served by such wide activity.

The question of administering the group presents a knotty problem. Capable people to staff the board of strategy are already busy on full-time jobs. Two suggestions might overcome this difficulty. One, that there should be a permanent secretary with full time to bring important matters to the attention of the rest of the group. Two, a rotation scheme could be used, whereby the secretary as well as six outstanding people serving with half salary and travel money, would be replaced each year.

The character of the board must be preserved as a "service" group and not a "membership" group. Nor should it be a functioning body which would compete with existing promotion agencies. If there are a hundred national or regional organizations engaged in action programs now, in addition to schools, churches, and civic institutions active along intergroup educational lines, there is no need of another group in this field. It would be the combined effort of individuals from many different groups, and the work done would not be identified with any particular organization.

An additional function of the planning board would be to implement the suggestion made earlier that the work of social scientists must be translated for the benefit of action program leaders. It could farm out experimental programs to chapters of the International Council of Christians and Jews. It could abstract articles in journals, issue reports on books and research material as they are prepared by the social scientists. It could establish liaison with UNESCO and thereby be related to research and education on a world scale. It could cooperate with writers and book publishing houses. It could integrate work of many foundations desiring to work in this field.

Two aspects of the strategy group apply to universities. One is that the known facts about intergroup relations must be collected from scholarly sources and the other that the universities' research work must be coordinated with each other. At the moment they are pulling in different directions. Institutions must be enlisted in a coordinated program of research. Certainly a "Strategy Board" could serve here.

▌ POSSIBILITIES FOR RESEARCH [4]

ROBIN M. WILLIAMS, JR.

Possible Projects

So much has already been said in this report about the urgent problems which call for further intensive research that a detailed listing of possible studies is hardly necessary. In this field, as in many others, the social scientist or the practitioner is not plagued by any lack of important hypotheses; the difficulty is rather that of deciding among multiple possibilities. Yet there is some value in giving a few concrete illustrations of the types of studies which might be initiated to test certain hypotheses previously outlined. To try to specify a complete study design in each case would be not only impracticable, but would be likely to defeat its own ends as well. Worth-while research on the problems of central interest is not routine, but a flexible and inventive process. Any concrete designs outlined in advance are likely to be out of date or inappropriate in other times and circumstances. At this place accordingly, we shall simply list a limited number of diversified projects as representative of the much larger range of fruitful studies awaiting social scientists in this field. Some of these projects will then be used to illustrate feasible study designs in the second section of this chapter.

An appropriate alternative would have been to list studies which should not be made. The number of relatively trivial studies which give static descriptions of unimportant phenomena concerning restricted and atypical populations is already more than sufficient. This is especially true of some types of attitude or opinion studies. Neither science nor social practice is likely to be well served, for example, by indiscriminate "polling" of school and college classes with ambiguous instruments and inadequate hypotheses. Similarly, we can well do without some of the elaborate correlational studies whose strained ex post facto interpretations have done little to increase casual understanding. Research energy needs to be more sharply focussed, and there is some meaning in the assertion that the quality of studies in this field is presently more important than the quantity.

There is nothing in the facts or logic of the situation to prevent excellent scientific work of great practical importance from being done within the decade. The design of good research does not differ in principle from that in any other social field; important problems

---

4 Robin M. Williams, Jr., *The Reduction of Intergroup Tensions,* Bulletin 57 (New York: Social Science Research Council, 1947), pp. 78-89. Used by permission of the author and the Council.

abound and can be studied; there is a growing demand for usable results; considerable progress in research methods and in the guiding sociological and psychological theory is evident. Given the will to undertake the necessary laborious and continuing studies and the requisite funds, advances of the first order are within reach.

The subsequent list of possible types of studies follows in the main the grouping of hypotheses in Chapter III. Many of the projects suggested are designed to throw light on the effects of specific programs of purposive action; the programs to be observed and tested, in nearly every conceivable instance, will constitute only one set of factors in a complex social situation. *It is therefore of crucial importance that research appraisals of action programs be sensitive to wider, unplanned, or "accidental" factors which may influence the behavior under observation.* A program of education on intergroup relations undertaken in a period of low social tension and good and improving economic conditions may be associated with a measurable and important decrease in intergroup hostility. There can be no a priori guarantee of the same results in a period of severe economic deprivation. The effects of a program which actually increases intergroup cooperation may be completely obscured by the effects of concurrent political agitation. Examples of this kind could be listed in profusion. There is no rule for anticipating the extraneous influences which may appear in any particular situation; but one can be continually alert to such disturbing factors, and they must always be taken into account in the evaluation of specific programs.

I. *General Studies: Historical, Comparative, Genetic*

1. *Comparative historical analysis of internal disturbances, either for the United States alone or on an international basis*

Much work along this line has already been done, but the possibilities for analysis of recurrent causal factors have not been exhausted. There is evidence that there are common factors in many seemingly diverse varieties of mass violence. The constant and variable factors and their interrelations may be further illuminated by a broad but intensive comparison of a series of such events as riots, lynchings, mobs, strikes with violence, insurrections, revolts, and rebellions.

This type of study requires high competence and entails a considerable measure of interdisciplinary cooperation. The contributions of historians, sociologists, psychologists, economists, and political scientists should be utilized. The main potential values of such a study appear to be three: (1) further clarification of uniformities as a basis for prediction in future situations; (2) additional perspective as to prevalence and range of variation of internal group conflicts; (3) indications as to the consequences of various "control measures" which have been put into practice in past situations.

2. *Comparative historical analysis of political anti-minority movements in the United States*

Much of the comment concerning Project 1 is applicable. Countermovements and factors associated with the disintegration of antiminority movements might receive special attention.

3. *Functional analysis of control and displacement of aggression in non-literate societies: a cross-cultural study*

Materials for such a study can be found in the works of anthropologists, and a systematic source of data of wide scope is available in the Cross-Cultural Survey at Yale University. The finding probably would not have a great many immediate implications for specific action. Judging from work already available, however, it is likely that we would gain further worth-while knowledge of the factors in the *total* aggression-balance of social systems, and of the range of specific control mechanisms.

4. *Patterns of prejudice interrelations within the individual personality*

To what extent and in what ways are prejudiced people prejudiced *in general* or only in relation to specific objects? Does removal of a particular scapegoat only result in fixation upon another? Are the resultants different with different basic personality structures, and why or why not? A whole series of studies are suggested by the questions which arise in connection with this topic. Methods of investigation will have to include both clinical and mass-testing approaches.

5. *Continuing study of intergroup developments accompanying large-scale action programs not ostensibly dealing with intergroup relations*

This is a general type of study rather than a specific one. Studies of this kind are certainly difficult to design and execute, but the importance of the subject warrants exploratory work in a variety of situations. It is especially important in the applications of many governmental programs to local communities. Thus, for example, the commodity-control referenda of the Agricultural Adjustment Administration resulted in large numbers of Negro farmers voting on the programs. How extensive was this voting, and how did it vary in different areas and communities? What were the factors in acceptance? What were the reactions of whites and Negroes, initially and later? Did the innovation have any transfer-quality for other situations? Another pertinent example is provided by the programs of the Tennessee Valley Authority. Directly and indirectly the TVA is having tremendous influence on the economy and social structure of a large area of the southeastern states. What connections are there, if any, between this influence and any changes in the patterns of race relations in the region? For example, how have hiring, training, and upgrading of Negro workers affected relations of white and Negro workers? Where local customs were breached, as they certainly were in some instances, what techniques were used and with what apparent results? Large-scale unionization in industry, with its emphasis on solidarity of interests among workers of various groups, provides a third illustration.

6. *Analysis of influences inculcating group prejudice in children*

Specific studies in this area can begin from several well-established generalizations, e.g., (1) prejudices are learned and therefore must be "taught"; (2) prejudices are often established at an early age (under 6 years); (3) early prejudices are generalized aversions with little specific content; only later are they differentiated and rationalized; (4) prejudices can be developed in the absence of direct personal contact with the disliked groups; (5) specific rewards and penalties are invoked by prejudiced elders to teach children their prejudices. There is need for detailed study of the dynamic process by which intergroup attitudes are established using direct observation and intensive interviewing. Careful comparative study of the *specific* behaviors of relatively prejudiced vs. unprejudiced parents and teachers should be especially rewarding.

7. *Effects of a total intergroup program upon a given community*

This project would depend upon the cooperation of a local community and a national agency equipped to carry out a comprehensive local program. Probably the best locale would be a city of 25,000 to 50,000 population, containing several ethnic or racial groups, and sufficiently "typical" in industry and social structure to permit comparison with similar cities. The basic idea would be to test the over-all effects of an integrated program designed to improve intergroup relations. The specific content of the program would be worked out by the responsible parties involved in consultation with such outside advisers and experts as seemed desirable, but presumably would include educational efforts, development of intergroup activities and organizations, changes in housing and recreational situations, efforts to change employment practices, and so on. Prior to the initiation of the program, a reasonably comparable city or cities would be selected. All the communities chosen would be surveyed at the same time to secure a comprehensive initial picture of intergroup attitudes and behaviors. After a period of, say, one year during which one community participated in the program and the others did not, a re-survey would be carried out to determine the effects of the program. It is also essential that such a study provide for intensive observation in the communities throughout the experimental period.

This is a large-scale, expensive study and it would require careful planning, a skilled staff, and close coordination of research with action and of extra-local with local groups. If properly done, however, it would give a far more dependable basis than has hitherto existed for appraising the changes which can be achieved by such a program.

8. *Comparative studies of values and behaviors of various racial, ethnic, or religious groups*

In Chapter III it was indicated that certain varieties of intergroup hostility rest *in part* upon real differences in typical systems of belief and behavior in the respective social groups. A large part of the evidence as to group similarities and differences, however, is fragmentary and impressionistic. To fill the existing gaps in knowledge would require a complex and extensive research program, but much can be added by strategic studies of the more important groups. For the purposes envisaged here these studies should not be broad general descriptions, but should be focused on specific items of difference and commonality between groups exhibiting symptoms of tension. In specific areas are there identifiable characteristics which typically, or in particular sub-groups, differentiate Negroes and whites, "old Yankees" and French-Canadian stocks, Jews and Gentiles, Catholics and Baptists, and so on? To what extent do the characteristics objectively determined by research correspond with each group's picture of itself and of the other group? To what extent and in what ways do the self-other conceptions derive from social defiinitions which are potentially subject to reformulation in terms less productive of hostility?

Of the important groups in the United States, the Negroes have been most adequately studied from this point of view. The least satisfactory body of evidence is that relating to religious groups.

The suggested studies would have practical significance mainly for propaganda and education programs. Research can help by (1) defining the strategic limits beyond which it is probably unwise to stress group similarities; (2) providing objective data to demonstrate internal differentiation of minorities, and to reveal discrepancies between observed characteristics and popular stereotypes; (3) identifying items of seeming difference which can be redefined as congruent; (4) inventorying important common values and behavior patterns which may not be widely known.

9. Basic survey of areas of intergroup tension

Many specific research and action projects would be facilitated by a "reconnaissance" survey to locate the specific points of intergroup contact and friction, area by area and center by center. Such a survey was proposed in 1944 in these terms:

In order to get an over-all view of the critical points of group conflict, one research project might undertake to plot the major area or places in the country where racial, religious, and other group differences become highly acute. This might be a continuing survey or register of data kept at one central place ... This body of material would, in turn, provide a basis for more intensive analysis of both institutional and individual causation of prejudice in the particular areas: industry, business, education, and so on.

10. Inventory of approaches and techniques in intergroup relations

With all the numerous and varied intergroup programs which have been operating for years in the United States, one still searches in vain for a systematic account of specific action approaches. Published accounts are in such general terms that only persons already familiar with the situations described can visualize exactly what was done. There is immediate need for a systematic, concrete, and detailed inventory of the actual events usually connoted by such terms as "educating," "organizing," "persuading," and the like.

This reconnaissance project could be undertaken on a national scale over a period of years. A suitable sponsor might well be a national action agency with a legitimate concern in promoting the interchange of valuable experiences among organizations working on intergroup problems. The type of information necessary could not be adequately obtained by widely circulated questionnaires or other extensive survey methods. It would probably require persistent and intensive interviewing by experts and detailed observation in the field.

PROBLEMS FOR STUDY AND DISCUSSION

1. It is consensus that research has played only a small part in determining the ethnic relations patterns now existing in the United States. Give reasons why you think this condition to be true or false.

2. Point out and discuss several reasons why research is important if we are to understand and improve ethnic relations in the United States.

3. From the many possible reasearch problems in ethnic relations that are suggested by Williams, select and outline a project that you would like to study.

4. Make a list of the problems in ethnic relations that you think need to be studied in your home community.

5. Keeping in mind the research project that you have selected in problem 3, discuss the methods and procedures that you would use in carrying out this research project.

6. Outline and discuss a form of organization that you would suggest for studying ethnic relations in your local community.

7. Explain each of what Professor House considers as the five phases through which men's ideas of race seem to have passed.

SELECTED READINGS

LIPPITT, R., and RADKE, M., "New Trends in the Investigation of Prejudice," *The Annals of the American Academy of Political and Social Sciences*, Vol. 244 (March, 1946), pp. 167-176.

MASUOKA, Jitsuichi, "Can Progress in Race Relations Be Measured?" *Social Forces*, Vol. 25 (March, 1946), pp. 211-217.

SMITH, F. Tredwell, *An Experiment in Modifying Attitudes* (New York: Teachers College, Columbia University), 1943.

WILLIAMS, Robin M., Jr., *The Reduction of Intergroup Tensions* (New York: Social Science Research Council, 1947).

YOUNG, Donald, *Research Memorandum on Minority Peoples in the Depression* (New York: Social Science Research Council, 1937).

XIV

Selected Programs for Improving Ethnic Relations

Introduction

MANY PROGRAMS have been advanced and organized for the purpose of improving ethnic relations in the United States. These programs have been directed into many areas of social life, and various approaches and techniques have been used by those responsible for these programs. The number of organized programs is so large that it is impossible to give space to the programs of all such organizations. However, persons interested in ethnic relations should be familiar with some of these programs, at least from a general standpoint. Thus, several readings will be presented in this chapter in order to point out some of the approaches and techniques that have been used by organizations that have been working for the improvement of ethnic relations in the United States. It is believed that knowledge of past programs may be of value in pointing out some of the approaches and techniques that might be used in the future.

Two types of readings have been selected for this chapter. The first type is a reading, by June Blythe, that provides a general view of the many organizations at work attempting to improve ethnic relations, and discusses the techniques used by some of these organizations. The other readings were selected to illustrate some of the approaches and techniques that have been used or suggested as means by which ethnic, and other intergroup relations, might be improved. The reading by Doyle is concerned with the program of the National Conference of Christians and Jews. Reddick in his selection points out some of the ways by which organizations have failed in their attempts to improve ethnic relations, and some of the reasons for these failures. The reading by Bogardus gives an analysis of the inter-

347

cultural program, and points out how it might be used in the acculturation process of the many minority groups living in the United States at the present time.

▌ CAN PUBLIC RELATIONS HELP
REDUCE PREJUDICE?[1]

JUNE BLYTHE

If public relations, as Dr. Lee has defined it, is "adjusting the relationships of a subject with its publics," then the 700-odd organizations concerned with how Americans of various ethnic origins get along together face one of the most challenging public relations problems of our day.

For the "subject"—whether we consider it to be these organizations and their specific programs, or the total issue of the disadvantaged status of America's minority groups—affects "relationships" rooted deep in the structure of our society and in the personality of society's every member.

Public relations to improve racial and cultural, or intergroup, relations attempts to influence the attitudes and behavior of strategic publics toward action for, or at least acceptance of, full democracy for ethnic minorities. But attitudes and behavior are influenced, if not determined, by prejudices which have become part of our way of life. And the concept of full democracy is subverted not only by custom but by law.

In short, the organizations working toward democratic ethnic relations are attempting to move people in directions opposite to both their personal prejudices and the approved social patterns, and *without* that handy tool of commercial or general public relations, the self-evident reward.

This effort deserves examination, for it has implications for public relations as a whole. The physician's or psychiatrist's interest in pathology leads to knowledge about how to keep people well. Similarly, public relations around inter-group problems is stimulating more sober analysis of public relations *per se,* and increased consideration of that larger problem, the communication of ideas— of not merely the fact, but "the truth about the fact."

Moreover, the effort to improve inter-group relations, if effective, can enhance such other efforts as those to promote democracy in the world and those to strengthen it here at home. As Marshall Field

1 *Public Opinion Quarterly,* Vol. 2, No. 3 (Fall, 1947), pp. 342-360. Used by permission of the author and the Quarterly.

has said, "The larger public relations problem is not merely to pub-
licize the point of view or the program of our particular inter-group
organizations. It is to mobilize and make articulate public support
for a better way of life."

GENERAL VERSUS INTER-GROUP PUBLIC RELATIONS

A brief comparison of the factors affecting general or commercial
public relations with those affecting inter-group public relations
will illustrate this challenge and set the stage for an appraisal of
current inter-group public relations techniques and concepts.

Favorable "Climate" for General Public Relations. The climate
for general public relations, in terms of its goals, is favorable. Those
goals, fundamentally and for most clients, are concerned with sales
promotion. The public relations counsel serves as a kind of master
mind who coordinates the complexities of publicity, advertising,
public opinion analysis, political science and community organization toward the sale of whatever his client has to offer.

Sales resistance proceeds largely from the competition of other
similar or related offerings. Or the resistance may be merely that
necessitated by the time required for a particular public to make
a choice—like the vacationist's choice of plane, train, or auto travel.

General public relations takes advantage of known cultural
realities, such as the social approval of conspicuous consumption
and the desire to maintain or raise social status. The specific appeals based on snobbishness, sex, fear, and the like have been
chronicled by others and need no repetition here. Nowhere do these
appeals conflict with the culture.

Perhaps the closest that general public relations has come to an
attempt to move people in opposition to accepted patterns was
during the war. To return to our transportation example, much
effort from many sources was focused on appeals to the travelling
public to stay at home. The success of this campaign is best known
to public relations counsellors themselves, who were often drafted
to "pull strings" for clients' reservations. In the absence of legal
regulation, the travelling public simply refused to take seriously
appeals to its patriotism.

In addition to cultural *acceptability,* the goals of general public
relations are supported by formal and informal social institutions
and by the total flow of the communications media. The preoccupa-
tion of our statutes and legal practice with property rights is a
matter of record. Our clubs and societies, whether dedicated to
pleasure or professional advancement, enhance the goal of economic
success and the practice of symbolic spending. Our personnel prac-

tices reward the individual who belongs to the "right" club, lives in the "right" neighborhood and drives the "right" class of car.

Logically, our communications media reflect and support these goals. The butts of our jokes include not only ethnic minorities and the physically handicapped, like the deaf and the stutterer. Also considered fair targets for ridicule are the hungry, the shabby, the non-conformists, the intellectuals—all who depart from the overwhelming American self-stereotype of commercial success, from which all other gratifications are made to flow.

Unfavorable "Climate" for Inter-group Public Relations. By contrast, the climate for ethnic public relations, at first glance, looks grim. Ethnic prejudice is an integral part of our culture. Helen V. McLean, reporting the results of a study of racial conflicts conducted by the Chicago Institute for Psychoanalysis, has written:

> . . . 'to our own society or culture the most significant and self-evident fact about race prejudice is that it is socially sanctioned and learned. It is a ready-made and culturally normal outlet for at least mild forms of hostility, fear, and superiority.' In other words, there is a quantum of racial prejudice which is acceptable in even a democratic society. Like many other affects, such as envy or hate, a certain quantity of racial prejudice is the norm. It is in the emotional air which we breathe from earliest childhood. . . .

The fact that prejudice is socially approved makes of it a ready device for use by both the individual and the group. Traits like greed or laziness which we fear may exist in ourselves can be conveniently projected onto members of one or more minorities. Or traits we secretly desire but are ashamed to admit, like sexual freedom or ruthless ambition, can be ascribed to minorities. There are many explanations for the varying degrees and manifestations of prejudice, but common to all of them is the conclusion that prejudice is *functional,* that is serves a purpose, however irrational, in the common need we each feel to justify ourselves.

Our social institutions not only encourage this functional use of prejudice; they make it next to impossible to behave in an unprejudiced manner. Where minorities are not segregated or discriminated against by law, the informal codes, or mores, achieve virtually the same end. Quota systems in schools, race-restrictive real estate covenants, admission rules for certain clubs and labor unions, and the like, all operate to impose upon class distinctions a caste-like system based on ethnic origin.

Here again, the communications media faithfully reflect and support the commonly-held "caste" concepts. Minorities, including nationality groups, are either stereotyped, ignored, or misrepresented. The Writers' War Board declared that "writers of the United States because of the habitual employment of 'stock characters' were unconsciously fostering and encouraging group prejudice." The Board found the stage and the novel first among the media in opportunity for "presenting minority characters sympathetically and honestly." In films, radio, comic cartoons, the press, advertising copy, and short stories, the Board found little to choose among the sins of stereotyping, misrepresentation, or omission by virtue of reliance on "snob appeal." L. D. Reddick, in a study of what he regards as the principal media—films, radio, press, and libraries—has listed nineteen common stereotypes of the Negro alone, many of them mutually contradictory. On those occasions when, prodded by war agencies or private organizations, the mass media have undertaken to do their bit toward ethnic democracy, they have produced most often a mixture of sentimental appeals and vague good-will. There are notable exceptions—but they remain exceptions.

The most important difference, then, between general and ethnic public relations is that of *direction*. General public relations can be said to move mainly in a direction conforming to prevalent attitudes, customs, and institutions. It is concerned chiefly with promoting a given choice among approved or accepted patterns. Further, it holds up as rewards the attainment of goals actively sought in our culture.

Public relations to improve inter-group relations moves largely in opposition to the main body of attitudes, customs, and institutions, and challenges the usefulness of prejudice to the individual and group. It offers the less immediate rewards of a more rational and healthy society.

As Gunnar Myrdal has hypothesized in his exhaustive study of race relations, *An American Dilemma,* the chief sanctions against prejudice and discrimination in our society—or the factors *favorable* to inter-group public relations—are *moral* sanctions. These include such concepts as the "equality of all men" found in religion and the American Constitution, and the "fair play" tradition in the field of sports. Obviously, these moral sanctions can operate in inter-group relations only as forcefully as they operate in the society as a whole.

TECHNIQUES USED BY INTER-GROUP ORGANIZATIONS

Working in a climate at best unfavorable and at worst actively hostile, the inter-group organizations might have been expected at least to take full advantage of existing techniques, and to have developed new and ingenious public relations methods. However, a survey of the mass media techniques in current use reveals a quite different picture.

Based on a ten-page write-in questionnaire, the survey requested detailed information on media employed and audiences reached during the nine-month period from September 1, 1945, to June 1, 1946. Insofar as possible, exact statistics were gathered. The questionnaire went to all known organizations in the field, including race relations divisions or sub-committees of national organizations outside the field, like the Federal Council of Churches and the Congress of Industrial Organizations.

The returns provided an adequate cross-section of the various types and sizes of organizations—small-town or neighborhood volunteer groups, citizens' committees, official mayors' and governors' race relations commissions, regional organizations like the Southern Regional Council, and national agencies like the American Jewish Committee and the National Association for the Advancement of Colored People. The returns held the same proportion of national groups to those of regional, state, or local scope as is found in the country as a whole, or roughly one to three.

Utilization of Media. The study revealed that the most widely-used media are pamphlets and public speakers, with about half of all organizations regularly using both. The majority of respondents also reported use of the general press and production of their own periodicals, news-letters, and direct mailings. But these latter media were used so sporadically as to make their statistical weight (based on the number of organizations employing them) misleading.

The least used media were radio and films. Of all respondents, 38 per cent produced their own radio scripts, mainly speeches, forums, or spot announcements, and 11 per cent produced transcriptions. Only 6 per cent produced films, and 21 per cent exhibited, distributed, or otherwise promoted the use of films.

Advertising was not included in the survey, since it is used so rarely as to be statistically unimportant.

The breakdown of national organizations as against regional, state, and local reveals that 80 per cent of the national groups produce their own pamphlets, while only 30 per cent of the local groups do so. The four largest national producers were responsible for six-and-a-half million pieces, or 90 per cent of all production for all groups during the period of study. Other national groups produced 6 per cent of the total output, while local groups produced only 4 per cent.

Periodicals, newsletters, and direct mail go primarily to members, financial supporters, or other constituents of the issuing organizations.

Of the 70 per cent of the national groups seeking press, radio, or magazine publicity, less than half reported servicing the wire news associations, only one-third serviced radio news desks, and only one-fourth attempted magazine planting. Of the 60 per cent of local groups issuing publicity, less than half serviced their local dailies and only 16 per cent their local radio stations. A handful of national agencies made some attempt to service the foreign language, labor, and trade press, and only one reported servicing the rural press.

Use of lecturers and public speakers was reported by 38 per cent of the national groups and 49 per cent of the local. For this medium, as well as for the distribution of printed materials, the survey attempted to determine the types of audiences reached. For both media, over half the organizations used them to reach the fields of religion and education. Libraries, social agencies, labor unions, government officials, and men's and women's clubs followed in that order, with rapidly falling percentages down to a total of 6 per cent for all other types of audiences.

Only one agency, the National Institute of Social Relations, reported consistent use of the small-group-discussion technique. The Institute's director, Julius Schreiber, is adapting Army discussion group methods to current problems, including race relations, in several medium-size communities. It should be stated, although not reported in the survey, that the Commission on Community Inter-relations of the American Jewish Congress is experimenting with discussion methods as a form of group therapy. Also, the Young Women's Christian Association, by virtue of the non-discrimination policy in many of its branches, brings together young people of various ethnic origins in sustained, small-group activities.

Indirect Use of Media. Much effort also goes into attempts to influence opinion through group leaders and organizations in other fields. Public officials or figures are induced to issue statements, serve as chairmen of drives, or at least admit that the condition of minorities is less than could be desired. President Truman, Eric Johnston, Philip Murray, William Green, Kate Smith—all are on record. In fact, it would be hard to find a public figure other than a poll-tax politician who has not at some time or other, at the behest of an inter-group organization, stated publicly that Americans ought to treat each other like Americans.

Organizations are induced to pass resolutions, or even to take internal steps to modify their own practices. For example, the Federal Council of Churches in 1946 adopted a resolution urging that the congregations of its affiliated denominations be opened up to minorities, and many denominations have followed suit with resolutions of their own.

Another kind of public relations benefit accrues to the inter-group agencies through the independent action of such organizations as labor unions. The success of the National Maritime Union in placing a Negro captain on a war-time Victory ship with a mixed crew, to the accompaniment of plentiful publicity, did much to dramatize the issue of fair employment.

Aid-to-action Techniques. Finally, there are a variety of activities for which the inter-group agencies provide public relations aid. Of these, the most widely used are pressure for legislation, cooperation with existing institutions, and the so-called "defense" activities.

Pressure for legislative and political safeguards for minorities is relentless and never-ending. For example, notwithstanding the defeat of a federal fair employment bill, seven state laws and three municipal ordinances have been pushed through.

Cooperation with such institutions as schools, social agencies, and government departments most often take the form of supplying educational materials, conducting in-service training courses in race relations, and giving advice on personnel practices. For example, the Bureau for Intercultural Education was established for the express purpose of working with school systems. Several other organizations have developed cooperatively an in-service training course for police officers. Social workers and city and county employees are additional categories with whom this technique has been used.

"Defense" activities range from the militant legal defense conducted by the N.A.A.C.P. in the now-famous Columbia, Tenn., trials to the quiet persistence with which the Anti-Defamation League follows and documents the movements of native fascists.

Although this summary of techniques is not all-inclusive, it will serve to illustrate those most widely used and to provide a background for consideration of the basic assumptions and content which the techniques implement.

ASSUMPTIONS AND CONTENT OF INTER-GROUP PROGRAMS

Until recently, no systematic attempt had been made to ascertain and analyze the basic assumptions of inter-group organizations, although programs, and, therefore, public relations efforts, obviously proceed from such, premises. In a study recently prepared for the Social Research Council, Robin M. Williams, Jr., describes three common basic assumptions, as follows:

1. That organized purposive effort can exert an appreciable degree of control over behavior in inter-group relations.

2. That the final goal is either (a) complete acculturation of racial, ethnic, or religious groups to one homogeneous set of beliefs

and patterns, i.e., the "melting-pot"; (b) a "mosaic" society with separate groups retaining cultural characteristics but maintaining harmonious contact; or (c) "cultural pluralism," with extensive interaction among groups retaining some distinctiveness.

3. That action programs should (or should not) emphasize the achievement of gains as against the avoidance of possible conflict or opposition (here, as with 2, the assumption varies with the organization).

Williams then lists "working hypotheses" based on the above premises. The hypotheses most widely-held, and therefore most influential on public relations content are:

1. That facts will eliminate or at least diminish prejudice. This belief leads to expending vast promotional energy on such pamphlets as "The Races of Mankind" and "Sense and Nonsense About Race." The theory seems to be that since prejudice is at variance with anthropological fact, the prejudice will yield when confronted by the fact. Not only in pamphlets, but in all the public relations techniques previously described, emphasis on factual argument against prejudice and discrimination is recurrent.

2. That programs should or must be directed toward either (a) a direct change in attitudes, or (b) a change in those situational factors which are believed to produce existing attitudes and behavior.

Williams points out that few agencies hold exclusively to either variation of this assumption. But certain agencies lean heavily on (a), as evidenced by the enormous flow of materials appealing to "brotherhood," "patriotism," desire for "law and order," and even to "democracy" itself.

The agencies which hold (b) as their most important hypothesis are likely to direct their energies at such action programs, with accompanying public relations, as the drive to equalize salaries between white and Negro teachers in the South, and fight against race-restrictive real estate covenants. But here, too, the specific public relations campaign around such an issue is more apt than not to base its appeals on the same concepts of "brotherhood" and "justice" as are employed by groups holding with (a).

3. That contact brings friendliness, together with the resultant belief that inter-group associations bring changed behavior which carries over into usual, day-to-day activities.

This belief motivates the earnest teacher who conducts her white pupils through Harlem; the ministers who exchange pulpits on "Brotherhood Sunday"; the agencies which foster inter-racial summer camps and the groups which sponsor inter-racial teas. With the agencies that concentrate on situational factors, it is more apt to be regarded as a desirable by-product of such achievements as integration of minority workers into a factory. Much of the public relations output of inter-group agencies describes such inter-racial or inter-group activities, with the appeal that the example be emulated.

4. That public emphasis on inter-group relations is (a) desirable, or (b) undesirable.

Most inter-group organizations hold with (a) for most situations, though the degree of public emphasis considered desirable varies. The more activist or militant agencies are apt to seek public airing at all times on all issues. Agencies which rely heavily on general appeals aimed at modifying attitudes are apt to seek great public emphasis on such appeals, but to regard the airing of issues as "dangerous."

A few agencies operate almost exclusively by indirection, and these tend to be opposed to public emphasis on any aspect of inter-group relations they feel is likely to arouse controversy. Their public relations either concern small, behind-the-scenes, influential groups, or are conducted under the aegis of other organizations. Some of these agencies carry their point of view to its logical conclusion by conducting campaigns among the minorities with which they are concerned on "proper behavior in public," the avoidance of "too much" publicity, and so on.

HOW EFFECTIVE ARE INTER-GROUP PUBLIC RELATIONS?

The effectiveness of public relations based on the assumptions, content, and techniques thus far described cannot be measured reliably in terms of the betterment or worsening of the status of minorities. Certainly some advances in status have been achieved, but many of these have had little to do with the existence of inter-group agencies.

No agency, for example, would claim responsibility for the fact that a man-power shortage attracted an estimated 500,000 Negroes from the South to the North and West, thus raising, for the war years at least, their economic status. Organized pressure enhanced the gain by securing the federal fair employment order, by union guarantees of equal pay and upgrading, and the like. But the gain itself was primarily the result of a national labor shortage.

Effectiveness can only be measured reliably in terms of such authoritative and scientific knowledge as is thus far available, and in terms of the obvious gaps and inadequacies that appear when the public relations efforts of inter-group agencies are considered as a whole, as a combined effort to resolve a national problem.

A step toward such joint consideration of the total public relations problem was taken when some forty of the leading national organizations participated in a Public Relations Workshop initiated by the American Council on Race Relations and held in New York City in September, 1946. Here the public relations personnel of the organizations met for three days with social scientists, media experts, and professional public relations counsel to evaluate current programs, pool experience, and examine new ideas. Many of the authorities hereinafter quoted were among those who contributed to the Workshop's sessions.

To provide an inventory of relevant scientific knowledge both for its general value and as a basis for the Workshop discussions, Arnold Rose summarized all available studies up to 1945 which have bearing on the assumptions, contents, and techniques of inter-group public relations.

To date, these studies are so scattered, restricted in area, and varied in purpose as to do little more than point directions and corroborate hunches. Commenting on his summary, Rose has criticized such factors as the small size and lack of representativeness of samples, the emphasis on quantitative rather than interpretive analysis, and the use of outmoded techniques when new and more reliable methods were available.

Nevertheless, these studies and more recent research conducted by certain inter-group agencies themselves, do indicate that much of the inter-group public relations effort is misdirected.

For example, most findings relevant to the assumption that "facts will dispel prejudice" indicate that this is true only under certain conditions and within certain limits. Rose reports that many such studies have been carried on with a college or school audience, with testing of students' attitudes before and after a course of instruction on race differences, minority problems, or other aspects of inter-group relations. "These studies show that one must be cautious if one is to achieve results. The course which deliberately sets out to reduce bias achieves its aim better than one which merely seeks to bring facts to the student's attention and forces him to make his own interpretation without guidance."

"Another study showed that the attitude of the teacher was the important influence when factual material . . . was taught. . . . Still another study showed that there was no carryover effect from teaching about one minority group to attitudes toward another minority group."

"These studies carried on in a classroom situation should not be given too much weight, but they do teach us some ways in which we must pay attention to the *content* of propaganda and the *situation* under which it is communicated."

On another of the popular assumptions, "contact brings friendliness." Rose reports, "Some of the studies have led to negative results,
although an equal number have been most encouraging. Clearly,
one must pay attention to the *nature* of the contacts. One study, for
example, shows that the mere increase in the number of contacts
with Jews does not decrease anti-Semitism. Public opinion polls
show that there is more anti-Semitism in large cities, where Jews
are concentrated, than in the small towns. . . . It is not the *number*
of the contacts with members of a minority that is important: it is
the *intimacy* and the *equality* of contact that can cause a marked
decrease in prejudice. It is only when contact can lead to friendliness or to respect that it is significant."

Studies are now being conducted by the relatively new Department of Scientific Research of the American Jewish Committee
which have important implications for other of the popular assumptions, such as the view that public relations efforts should be directed
toward changing people's attitudes.

Samuel Flowerman, the Department's associate director, has described studies of specific items, such as a war-time cartoon showing
ghostly figures of Hitler, Hirohito and Mussolini riding a horse and
waving a banner painted with slogans damning minority groups.
The artist intended satire, but a study of comprehension showed
that only one-third of the sample understood the message, while
another one-third took the damning slogans on the banner literally
and thought the artist was attacking minority groups.

This and other studies have led Flowerman and his associates to
some preliminary conclusions. One of the most important for inter-
group public relations is that *prejudice acts as a screen to understanding,* i.e., the prejudiced person is more likely to misunderstand
(evade) the tolerance message than is the unprejudiced person.

Of the appeals designed to work on the public's "self-interest,"
Morris Janowitz, a University of Chicago specialist in inter-group
tensions, has this to say:

"Some of the contents of race relations propaganda today is based
on a superficial self-interest appeal; superficial in the sense that it
appeals to the apparent aspirations of the intolerant. Often these
appeals are in error in that they do not properly estimate what the
individual considers to be in his own self-interest."

In a statement which has relevance for most of the content and
assumptions we have discussed, Sol Ginsburg has said, "Anyone who
knows the struggle it is to rid oneself of his own prejudices, even
with the help of suitable psychotherapy, can understand the relative
superficiality of results obtained by ordinary propaganda and educational methods. There are experiences reported in the use of these

devices which would make one more hopeful . . . but always one must bear in mind the irrationality of prejudice and the fact that whatever other factors are involved, there are deep rooted psychological ones at work as well."

Thus, although the basic assumptions and public relations appeals of inter-group agencies have not yet been adequately tested, there are indications that many of them are not only ineffective but may be actively harmful, that is, may boomerang and actually increase prejudice and hostility toward minorities. Only the relative ineffectiveness of inter-group public relations techniques and the fact that these techniques reach a limited and already-sympathetic audience have thus far prevented possible boomerang effects from manifesting themselves in a manner so obvious as to cause the inter-group agencies to call a halt for self-analysis.

We have already noted the relative disregard of inter-group agencies for such media as films and radio, and the emphasis on printed materials and speakers. We have found that the most favored audiences were the already-converted—members, contributors, and the like—in the fields of religion and education.

Let us for a moment consider the audiences which receive too little attention, in terms of their strategic positions, or none at all.

Labor unions, one of the largest organized segments of the public, receive attention from only about one-third of the inter-group agencies. Only 18 per cent of the agencies make some effort to reach government officials (usually members of Congress). Only one organization reaches rural audiences, and only one the foreign-language press. Although several organizations have veterans' advisors on their staffs, none have reported any consistent public relations effort directed at veterans' organizations. No agency reported any effort directed at political organizations, either independent or partisan.

But perhaps the most startling omission is the ignoring of indigenous community and neighborhood groups—those small stable units which many a commercial enterprise has long ago learned are the core of its market.

Janowitz has stated as a premise, "To alter social attitudes, persistent and intimate persuasion is required. This is most likely to occur in face-to-face situations, in small stable groups, where the information specialist has direct, sustained and personalized contact with his audience." After citing several studies in documentation of his premise, he continues:

"But we need not limit ourselves to studies of race relations to prove this significant point. Totalitarian movements in Europe were built on mass propaganda efforts implemented by personalized appeals delivered directly to the smallest groups. For years propaganda analysts have been teaching us to fight totalitarian successes by carefully analyzing their arguments in order that they could be answered most effectively. This procedure, valid as it is, has shunted our attention from one of the most dynamic aspects of totalitarian propaganda—its organizational completeness. They saw that new attitudes could only be caused by persistent exposure of the audience to 'on the spot' propagandists who delivered their oral and printed propaganda via small, unit organizations."

In contrast to the proved effectiveness of the small-group method, a hierarchy of large national organizations pours out the bulk of the materials and conducts the major portion of public relations around inter-group problems. Local branches, with some exceptions, exist chiefly to implement the national program and distribute the nationally-produced materials. Very little planned effort goes into assistance for independent, unaffiliated local groups.

Moreover, this pattern constitutes one of the primary reasons for the inefficient and uncritical approach to use of mass media. The gulf between the national producer and the local audience is such that, in the absence of scientific testing, the producer has no reliable measure of the reactions of his ultimate audience. He must rely on the opinions of national colleagues or local constituents as his only index of his effectiveness.

In short, we have the paradox of the inter-group agencies, with one of the most difficult of all offerings to "sell," having failed to analyze their market, and directing appeals which have not been tested at limited and already receptive audiences.

NEW DIRECTIONS

This would be a discouraging picture were it not that a ferment of doubt, discussion, and self-criticism is bubbling among the inter-group agencies as, indeed, it is among all who are concerned with the communication media as a dynamic influence on our way of life. The growth of undemocratic attitudes, practices, and organizations both during and since a war ostensibly fought, along with other reasons, to discourage them has raised new questions about the assumptions, appeals, and techniques of organized effort for democracy.

The old simple explanations can't answer the new questions. For example, a recent study of attitudes among Negro and white members of a labor union, revealed (a) that the prejudice-quotient of the union members was insignificantly different from that of unorganized, racially segregated workers, and (b) that the union members accepted the no-discrimination policy of their union in much the same perfunctory spirit as other rules about dues payments or elections. A popular belief has held that workers in a non-discriminatory job and union situation would grow to be less prejudiced, and that their new understanding would carry over into other life situations.

Although the study is admittedly fragmentary, and therefore, inconclusive, it at least suggests several new questions: (a) why did the workers in this union *not* show *less* prejudice, especially since their union was one of those engaged in extensive race relations education; (b) to what extent does their behavior away from the job-union situation revert to the common social pattern of discrimination and hostility; and (c) what is required to significantly alter their racial attitudes and behavior?

To these new questions social science must help provide the answers, and its offspring, professional public relations, must help provide the skills. The inter-group agencies must either adapt their programs to such new insights as are developed, or become obstacles to the very goals they seek.

The use of such knowledge as is already available is the first step. Research aids exist, and are continually being perfected, which can remove from the realm of debate and opinion such questions as audience reaction to given appeals or specific items of propaganda; public attitudes or opinions on issues or situations, the effectiveness of a given technique; or the inter-group *content* of the commercial mass media.

Sociological data abound from which to ascertain the most strategic publics, in terms of geographic distribution, characteristics, and status or power. Equally available are the economic and other data describing the situational factors productive of prejudice and discrimination.

And, although exploration of the psychodynamics of prejudice is a new field, enough is known to warrant immediate abandonment of the endless repetition of factual or emotional platitudes noted as one of the most widely-used appeals of current inter-group public relations. The insight of the psychologist or psychiatrist also can be brought to bear upon other appeals and techniques, such as the use of sex symbols like a "Miss America" or a popular crooner to preach tolerance. (For example, with certain minority stereotypes serving as disapproved sex symbols in our culture, what is the effect of bringing an approved or permissible symbol into conflict with the stereotype?)

Additional research required. The clear need for additional research dictates its encouragement as the second necessary step toward more effective public relations. There are too many questions for which we have no answers. The main body of communications and socio-psychological research, oriented as it is toward other or purely methodological problems, can do little more than provide a base for research experimentally oriented toward the problems of inter-group relations.

Authoritative evaluation of the appeals in current use is urgent. Here there is little to borrow from existing research, for commercial public relations and advertising have not demanded it, relying mainly on the "trial-and-error" indices provided by sales, box office, and listener ratings.

Accurate measurement of the effect of mass media content and techniques on inter-group attitudes and behavior is another requisite. For from this point flow such related questions of strategy as whether inter-group agencies should attempt to inject their messages into the highly competitive mainstream of communications, or should attempt to modify the content of the stream itself.

Promising new developments need to be explored. The use of films and radio transcriptions in group psychotherapy for the rehabilitation of veterans suggests research on the adaptation of mass media techniques to emulate group therapy in tension situations.

The importance of cooperative effort. Finally, the inter-group agencies themselves must take such organizational steps as are required to put available knowledge to use and to encourage the discovery of new knowledge.

Just as the trade associations common to industry and commerce plan and carry out *cooperatively* their public relations on institutional or industry-wide problems, so the inter-group agencies must consider and act upon their public relations problems as a *whole*.

Such projects as a continuing content analysis of the mass media, public opinion polls, audience reaction testing, and the like, obviously cannot be carried on by single agencies independently, nor would it be desirable even if feasible. For example, it is just as important for agencies concerned with Negro-white relations to know how much anti-Semitism exists among Negroes as it is for agencies concerned with Jewish-gentile relations to know the trend of anti-Semitism in the general population. Or again, all agencies concerned with all ethnic minorities need to know the effect of a weekly radio program which continually get its laughs by means of ethnic stereotypes.

Two national agencies which have established their own research departments have already learned they must clear activities with each other to avoid wasting funds in duplication. A cooperative committee, representing all of the agencies as well as the social sciences, could not only avoid duplication but would serve to stimulate more research and more attention to its results throughout the field.

"Face-to-face" strategy needed. Lastly, at least a partial de-centralization of effort must be accomplished if emphasis on un-thinking enslavement to nationally-slanted appeals and techniques is to be shifted to the more promising level of small-group "face-to-face" contacts. That this must be accomplished democratically, with locally selected leadership, is self-evident. What the national organizations can provide are the resources and techniques to enable the local groups better to do their job.

The springing up in dozens of cities in recent years of volunteer citizens' committees, official mayors' commissions, and even some neighborhood groups is a hopeful sign. But these local groups are still too dependent on the general pamphlets written and printed in New York, or the speaker on a cross-country tour. And in some of the larger cities these groups are removed from the neighborhoods in the same way the national agencies are removed from many communities.

Materials designed for adaptation to local use are only part of the answer. There is need for trained information specialists to be assigned to local groups, where continuity of contact can be maintained, where the housewife can be taught how to discuss with her neighbor the admission of Negro mothers to the parent-teacher club.

Professionals in inter-group public relations often remind each other that "you can't sell race relations like soap." Certainly, if these comments have proved their point at all, they have verified the truth of that homily. But the fact remains that those who seek greater democracy for America's minorities have much to learn from the door-to-door salesman and the bridge club demonstrator.

▌ BUILDERS OF BROTHERHOOD [2]

THOMAS F. DOYLE

Tolerance seemed a good word in the dark heydays of the A.P.A. and the Ku-Klux Klan. But thoughtful citizens no longer pride themselves on mere tolerance of neighbors who happen to be Catholics, Protestants or Jews. Among all religious groups the emphasis is on active goodwill and cooperation for the common good without sacrifice of individual beliefs.

Much of the credit for this new spirit of friendship and understanding belongs to the National Conference of Christians and Jews,

2 Thomas F. Doyle, "Builders of Brotherhood," *The Marianist* (February, 1948). Used by permission of the Magazine.

rated by religious and secular leaders as one of the nation's foremost agencies in the fight to outlaw bigotry and to make America truly "one nation, indivisible."

The influence exerted by the NCCJ grows more apparent every day. In thousands of communities, it has become commonplace to see Catholics, Protestants and Jews gather under its auspices to talk over mutual problems and join hands to meet them. Millions of Americans reading recently written books with goodwill themes would be surprised to learn how many writers have been inspired by the "authors' conferences" initiated by the NCCJ five years ago. Many more millions listening to radio programs in which reference is made to intergroup harmony are unaware of the NCCJ inspiration behind the announcer's words. Meanwhile, through programs in schools, colleges, and all types of youth organizations, the National Conference has made young America the most brotherhood-conscious group in the world.

These accomplishments are only a fraction of the Conference's story. Now more and more Americans are asking such questions as "How, when and where was the NCCJ founded?" "How does it operate?" "How is it financed?" "Do Catholic authorities endorse the movement?" This article attempts to answer these and other queries which often arise, especially during Brotherhood Week, which occurs every February.

This annual observance was started by the Conference 15 years ago, and promises to become as much a part of the American calendar as Independence Day or Thanksgiving Day. First conceived by a priest—the late Rt. Rev. Hugh A. McMenamin, of Denver, Colorado—the Week was endorsed in successive years by President Roosevelt, and the custom of issuing a special White House message in connection with the event has been continued by President Truman.

A brief review of the National Conference's history and work is especially timely because of the formation of the International Council of Christians and Jews, a development for which the NCCJ is mainly responsible. Intended to apply NCCJ policies and techniques on a global scale, the ICCJ has been hailed by church leaders everywhere as representing one of the most notable advances in the social history of the present century.

The NCCJ was launched in New York in 1928 to meet the challenge of racial and religious intolerances which the Ku-Klux Klan had openly exploited to bring about the defeat of Alfred E. Smith, a Catholic, who was running for the Presidency that year. Leaders initiating the Conference were Charles Evans Hughes, afterwards Chief Justice of the U. S. Supreme Court, who first conceived the idea; Newton D. Baker, Secretary of War in President Wilson's

Cabinet, who wrote the by-laws; and Dr. S. Parkes Cadman, who signed the first letter inviting people to join the organization.

The two last-named co-founders, and many other leaders, Protestant, Catholic, and Jewish, who helped to organize the Conference, are dead; but its work is being constantly enlarged and perfected under the direction of the three present co-chairmen: Charles E. Wilson, president of General Electric Corporation, a Protestant; Roger W. Straus, industrialist and banker, a Jew; and Thomas E. Braniff, president of Braniff Air Lines, a Catholic. Mr. Braniff, a Knight of St. Gregory, succeeded Dr. Carlton J. H. Hayes, noted historian and former Ambassador to Spain, who resigned as Catholic co-chairman in 1946. The president of the National Conference since its inauguration has been Dr. Everett R. Clinchy, a former Presbyterian minister, who has won many citations for his leadership in the field of better human relations.

Among the early accomplishments of the NCCJ was the setting up of Religious News Service, now the world's leading interfaith news agency. Fifteen years old, this organization, which operates under independent management, has a paid subscriber list of 225 Protestant church papers, 60 Catholic publications, 155 secular newspapers and magazines, 75 church-centered organizations, and 90 radio stations which broadcast a specially-prepared weekly news script. RNS also has an extensive photo service—the only non-secular agency of its kind equipped to meet the demands of all types of publications for pictures of religious interest. Because it so often affords Catholic readers an insight into notable Protestant developments in social and humanitarian as well as religious fields, and vice versa, RNS ranks as one of the most important agencies contributing to inter-religious understanding.

Dependent entirely upon voluntary contributions, the National Conference has won support from an ever-growing number of well-wishers all over the nation. This is shown by the increase in donations from $13,000 in 1928 to $1,525,000 in the 12-month period up to October 1, 1947. Its 1947-48 budget calls for an income of $2,500,000.

NCCJ is controlled by a board of directors, comprising 200 Protestant, Catholic and Jewish leaders from every segment of America's religious, social and economic life. It has an executive committee of 35 members, also equally representative of the three faiths. Activities are channelled through nine national commissions and departments and 62 regional and area offices extending throughout the country. Each of the regional offices is headed by a director and a three-faith executive committee recruited from local community leaders. Through these offices, the NCCJ program radiates to more than 300 round tables in as many cities and to committees in more than 3,000 communities.

The regional offices carry on a more or less uniform program designed to spread the doctrine of goodwill inside the local community—in churches, schools, civic, professional, labor, and management groups. The offices maintain a speaker service, distribute books and pamphlets, study-action materials, and other literature, and provide consultant services to community groups. They also make available movies, film strips and recordings which are exhibited in theaters, schools, churches and clubs. The "visual-aid" program is sharply intensified during Brotherhood Week. Last year almost 10,000 movie theaters carried a Brotherhood news reel and about 7,000 churches, schools, and clubs showed NCCJ films.

Many important statements have been prepared and released by the Conference as means to mold public opinion on issues of vital concern to Americans of all faiths. In one recent statement, Dr. Clinchy warned against current Protestant-Catholic tensions over such issues as state-provided transportation for parochial school children, the retention of Myron C. Taylor as President Truman's personal envoy to the Vatican, and alleged Catholic attempts to "dominate" the United States. Subsequently, Willard Johnson, NCCJ program director, published a highly significant appeal to Protestants to look upon Catholics as Christian allies rather than as designing or scheming competitors. At the same time, Mr. Johnson urged leaders of both faiths to join in building "a society of respect for all men."

In 1933, when anti-Semitism was approaching a climax in Germany, the National Conference commissioned three speakers—Father John Elliot Ross, Rabbi Morris S. Lazaron, and Dr. Clinchy—to make a six-weeks', 9,000-mile goodwill "pilgrimage" of 38 western and southern cities. Everywhere the pilgrimage attracted popular attention and was given an extraordinary amount of newspaper publicity. A by-product of the tour was the formation of 25 additional local committees to foster interfaith fellowship and education.

Impressed by the success of the tour, NCCJ leaders decided to make the interfaith speaking trio a regular feature of the organization's work. In 1936, 25 trios were on the road, covering a total of 33,000 miles. Now almost every day of the year a three-faith trio may be found appearing before an audience anywhere from Maine to California. Trio teams speak before many kinds of groups—luncheon clubs, granges, church federations, business men's and women's groups, high school and college assemblies, and mass meetings organized by local NCCJ committees.

One interfaith team which still remains unique was the wartime group which barnstormed through a string of army camps from Arkansas through Oklahoma and Texas. The Catholic member of the trio was Archbishop Robert E. Lucey of San Antonio, the first member of the hierarchy to join an interfaith trio. His companions were the same minister and the same rabbi who made the first tour with Father Ross a decade or so before.

Through its interfaith tours and other programs, the NCCJ has done much to remove false and often slanderous notions about the Catholic Church. One of its most notable achievements in this respect was reported in 1942 when it persuaded the Haldemans-Julius Publishing Company to eliminate from its popular Blue Book series titles offensive to Catholics. The event was widely recorded in Catholic newspapers and the Conference's efforts praised in many editorials.

The NCCJ is strictly neutral in regard to the beliefs held by Catholics, Protestants and Jews, but it holds that the best Americans are those who try to live up to the high ideals of their respective faiths. This was the conviction which led the Conference to sponsor an annual Religious Book Week, intended to encourage the reading of books dealing with religion or human relations. Lists of books prepared by Catholic, Protestant and Jewish authorities and issued by the Conference are widely used in libraries, schools and churches. The success of the Week is shown by the increase in the number of lists distributed from 35,000 in 1943, the year the Week was first celebrated, to about 125,000 in 1947. Director of the Week is Mrs. Ellen O'Gorman Duffy, one of the Catholic members of the national staff.

Six years ago, the Conference inaugurated three commissions to promote projects for better human relations among educational, religious and community organizations. Catholic leader in the religious commission is the Rev. Allan P. Farrell, S.J., education editor of *America,* while the chairman of the community commission is former Assistant Secretary of State G. Howland Shaw, Laetare Medallist and Knight of St. Gregory. Three other commissions were also set up to enlist the press, radio, motion picture and other media in the cause of Brotherhood. Executive director of the media commissions is Edward J. Heffron, former executive secretary of the National Council of Catholic Men.

The accomplishments of these commissions are too numerous to be cited in detail. Some idea of the impact they have made on the nation during the past year may be gleaned from these isolated statistics: 3,500,000 items of goodwill literature distributed; 31,000 volunteer speakers supplied to community gatherings; 400,000,000 listened impressions made through radio programs; nearly 20,000 discussions arranged for schools, P.T.A. meetings, colleges, labor unions, women's and youth groups, and service and civic clubs; human relations material channelled to 2,000 newspapers and magazines, 600 religious journals, and thousands of churches and clubs.

A global spotlight was focussed on the National Conference in 1946 when it joined the National Council of Christians and Jews, its British counterpart, in sponsoring an international meeting of Christians and Jews at Oxford, England. Out of this conference emerged plans for the International Council of Christians and Jews which will link individuals throughout the world in making brotherhood a universally-accepted standard of the postwar social order. Dr. Clinchy has been named president of the ICCJ, and three co-chairmen appointed. The chairmen are: Dr. Jacques Maritain, French Ambassador to the Vatican, and an eminent Catholic philosopher; Lord Reading, former Viceroy of India, who is Jewish; and Dr. Henry Noble McCracken, former president of Vassar College, a Protestant.

First project of the ICCJ was the Emergency Conference to Combat Anti-Semitism held at Seelisberg, Switzerland, last August, and attended by 70 specially-invited persons from the United States, Britain, Australia, and 14 European countries. Out of the conference came a remarkable declaration on anti-Semitism recommending means by which churches and other groups should deal with what delegates described as "a sin against God and against humanity."

Returning last December from a ten-weeks' tour of Continental Europe, Dr. Clinchy disclosed that new councils of Christians and Jews have been organized in 17 cities in France, Switzerland, Italy, Holland, and Belgium. While in Italy, Dr. Clinchy had an audience with Pope Pius, who, he reported, showed a lively interest in the work of the NCCJ. The interfaith leader also spent some time in Britain, visiting leading cities and meeting religious leaders, including Bernard Cardinal Griffin, Archbishop of Westminster, who is one of the joint presidents of the British Council of Christians and Jews.

A sidelight of Dr. Clinchy's European tour was the announcement of J. Arthur Rank, Britain's top motion picture producer, that British film leaders would organize a permanent commission for the production of films aimed at promoting interfaith goodwill generally and the work of the ICCJ in particular. Another development was the promise given by Lord McGowan, chairman of Imperial Chemical Industries, Ltd., that British leaders would support the formation of an organization of industrialists to further the council's aims.

Meanwhile at home, the NCCJ envisions an ever-broadening program to unite all Americans in preserving the nation's spiritual heritages and upholding and strengthening the democratic way of life.

It is interesting to recall that in 1944 Archbishop Lucey and six bishops of Texas and Oklahoma issued a statement urging the necessity of Catholic collaboration with "all men of goodwill" in tasks for the common welfare, and declaring that "every thoughtful man, every good citizen should support the objectives of the National Conference of Christians and Jews."

More recently, Archbishop John Gregory Murray of St. Paul sent a letter to all priests in his diocese telling them that "all our people should not hesitate to unite with groups such as the Conference of Christians and Jews in their individual capacity as citizens for the good of all."

"Statements made by the sovereign Pontiffs in recent years," Archbishop Murray wrote, "call for concerted action of Catholics with all men of goodwill who believe in God and base their programs on mutual cooperation for the general welfare of mankind within the civic order under God."

Many other bishops have given cordial endorsement to the program of the NCCJ, and meanwhile hundreds of priests and thousands of Catholic laymen have taken an active part in its work. One of the charter members of the Conference is the Rev. Michael J. Ahern, S.J., of Weston College, Weston, Massachusetts, who was given a citation in 1946 for his lifelong efforts for interreligious understanding and cooperation.

A few years before his death, William Cardinal O'Connell, Archbishop of Boston, was quoted as hailing the development of "a better understanding among all races and creeds" in his community as the most important change he had noticed in the past 30 years. The development of the spirit of goodwill on a national rather than a local scale has been the aim of the NCCJ since its inception 20 years ago. It is due mainly to the Conference that Americans are more "interfaith-conscious" than ever before in their history. Increased support of its work by Catholices is clearly implied in numerous papal statements urging them to join with their "separated brethren" everywhere in securing what Pope Pius XII has termed "an economic and social order more in keeping with eternal law of God and the dignity of man."

❚ ADULT EDUCATION AND THE IMPROVEMENT OF RACE RELATIONS [3]

L. D. REDDICK

Any close student of democracy in America can scarcely fail to note the seeming reluctance with which the people use the available democratic processes to achieve the aims of the society. Surely, the American Creed is well known: eloquent lip service is paid to it wherever public speech occurs; little children recite passages from the Declaration of Independence, the Bill of Rights, and Lincoln's Gettysburg Address. Equally sure is the common knowledge that certain practices on both the local and national levels are direct violations of this creed. Yet when it comes to wiping out these practices and advancing the social order toward the ideal, the American people appear to become paralyzed.

The outstanding exception to this unfortunately true generalization is to be found in the field of politics. If something is wrong, the citizens, through their representatives, *will* pass a law about it. This does not mean that the whole political process is to be utilized, for often the enactment of a law or the election of a "reform" candidate to office is the final chapter of public thought on a particular issue.

The people constantly re-affirm their devotion to democracy; meanwhile when they observe persons or groups or institutions abusing it, they decline to take measures to curb these anti-democratic activities even when the means for curbing are immediately at hand.

ATTITUDE TOWARD EDUCATION

This whole point is illustrated by the general attitude toward education and the improvement of race relations. Everyone seems to be saying these days that the "Race Problem" is number one or number two on the list of national problems of the United States. There is more discussion of it now than at any other time in our history since the days of the Reconstruction period. The opinion polls show that from 34 to 50 per cent of the people of this country believe that extraordinary steps should be taken to "improve" race relations and insure social peace. "Revolution?" "Oh, no!" "New laws?" "Maybe." "Education?" "Yes, indeed!" This is it; almost everybody says that the most effective way of bettering these inter-group contacts is

[3] Reddick, L. D., "Adult Education and the Improvement of Race Relations," *The Journal of Negro Education*, Yearbook Number XIV (July, 1945), No. 3, pp. 488-493. Used by permission of the Journal.

"Education." Even the Commission upon whose recommendation the Ives-Quinn law of New York State was enacted made it clear that

we have already said, and it is self-evident, that the prejudices which cause discrimination cannot be removed by legislation alone.... The educational field is precisely the field in which the greatest opportunity and hence the greatest responsibility lie.

That responsibility daily becomes heavier as in this war-torn world the problems and difficulties of democracy become progressively complex and increase their demands upon the intelligence, unity, tolerance and civic duty of all our citizens. The close of the war will find our country confronted with vast unsettlements, tremendous economic pressures, and surging social and political tensions and conflicts which can easily expose our democracy to contagious demagogy, racism, bigotry, and class war. There is but one prophylactic, and that is to begin at once to immunize the body politic with more potent education in the American Creed of liberty, equality, justice and fair opportunity for everybody, and to vitalize through moral and religious precept the American sensitiveness to the ideals of human brotherhood and the Golden Rule.

The notion that education is a cogent lever for promoting unity appears to be vague and formless in the public mind. It is in some degree an easy "out," a simple faith in a peaceable settlement of a vexing question, an inexpensive, long-time, shock-proof procedure, a magical formula. The average person who says "Education" with so much relief and satisfaction does not take the time to consider what is involved in his decision. Education may well be a tremendous force in the struggle against prejudice (or any other social evil) *if it is directed toward that goal....*

The fact is that contrary to popular supposition the schools of the United States are now operating to increase rather than diminish sentiment against the Negro. Dr. Marie Carpenter, in summarizing most of the research done on the treatment of the Negro in school textbooks and adding to it her own work, has shown conclusively that the classroom materials of the average American school give an inaccurate and derogatory picture of the Negro and Negro-white relations. After considerable investigation, Dr. Edna Colson has come to a similar conclusion about the training which is provided for the teachers in American schools. Thus, actually, formal education in America when examined through either the textbook or the teachers is found to be worsening race relations. This may be amazing to many citizens.

When the definition of education is expanded to include all of the agencies and institutions of the society which transmit and re-create the culture, the picture becomes uglier. "The movie, radio, press and library all serve, in varying degrees, of course, to generate and reflect a harmfully stereotyped conception of the Negro. Their influence on the mind of the American people is overwhelming. This point, based upon hard labor, confirms the impressions of many alert readers and radio listeners.

Education, in this broad sense, of course, includes adult education. However, before these charges are to be finally written into the record a more direct examination should be made of the organized effort which goes by this name. As a result of a review of the journals, reports of the national conferences and virtually all of the meetings and sections of meetings on the Negro, it is plain that the movement for adult education in the United States has not only done little to improve race relations but has never conceived of this as an objective of its endeavor. The conclusion of the New York State Temporary Commission Against Discrimination is confirmed when it says that "the entire field of adult education as it relates to discrimination remains relatively under-developed, certainly so far as New York State is concerned." In this regard New York is in better shape than most places.

.   .   .   .

WHY NO PROGRAM?

What is the explanation for this failure of the adult education movement to embrace the improvement of race relations as a phase of its program? Three parts of a full answer immediately recommend themselves. First, the bulk of adult education among Negroes during the past decade was done through the WPA and related "relief" projects. The "red-tape" and terror imposed upon the personnel of these "jobs" are of recent and notorious memory. Ultimately, the persons and the projects which survived under these pressures were those that manifested not the slightest tendency toward social change. Courage and social intelligence found no welcome; caution and optimum loyalty were preferable. Many of the school men, who assisted in these endeavors, were likewise insecure or markedly conservative.

A second part of the explanation points to the American Association for Adult Education. Over $3,000,000 were poured into (or into projects through) this organization by the Carnegie Corporation. These resources, coupled with active leadership, gave the Association a decisive influence throughout the adult education realm. It initiated and financed the major conferences, research and publications in the field. Its prestige among the rank and file of adult educationalists has been immense. The Association has deliberately pursued a policy of emphasizing and encouraging the direct *self-*

improvement, strictly "cultural" side of adult education to the neglect of the direct *social*-improvement side.

Finally, part of the answer brings us back to the first sentence of this essay. For a long time the American people have not been very aware of the possibility and necessity of using the methods of the democratic process to advance the interests of their society. The fierce spirit of individualism—a carryover of the old frontier days—permitted and encouraged a person to get more education and thus help *himself* but it did not go beyond this to assume a social responsibility for the whole community. This is one of the characteristics of the so-called American Way which strikes the eyes of European visitors and travelers. Quite recently, a young countess from Sweden was amazed to find that "rich America" had such disgraceful slums— something almost unknown in her own "poor country." As Albert Einstein expressed it, the United States "is socially less advanced than many European countries. The sense of the democratic value of each person is stronger here; the feeling of their own value as individuals is stronger; but the social and political development is behind, here."

．　　．　　．　　．　　．　　．

Education, too, as has been implied all along, is a thoroughly legitimate function which contains vast possibilities for realizing a truly democratic culture. If the schools and out-of-school educational agencies would devote themselves to the "war" *against* racism and *for* equality, in a few years the minds of the American people could be cleansed of the monstrous misconceptions and stereotypes which are at once causes and functions of contempt, hatred, conflict and suffering.

SOCIAL RESPONSIBILITY

To expect education—particularly adult education—in a democratic culture to be concerned with the major problems of that culture does not seem to be an inordinate expectation. The tools for the job are readily at hand. The first phase of the Adult Education movement in our history, the phase which concentrated upon the self-improvement of the individual has been concluded. We should recognize this. As the New York Commission states in words that cannot be misunderstood: "Obviously, any educational system which would at heart be merely a mechanism for supplying information will not begin to meet the grave requirements of our democracy in the post-war world. Indeed, the implication from any such system that education is for the making of a living rather than a life, might well be anti-social and anti-democratic." There is no longer any excuse for Adult Education to shirk its role through real or simulated inertia. *It must either rise to the social necessity or cease to receive consideration as an important dynamic of the democratic process.* As E. C. Lindeman puts it, "... adult education is not merely education of adults; adult education is learning associated with social purposes ... The complete objective ... is to synchronize the democratic and learning process."

▌ INTERCULTURAL EDUCATION AND ACCULTURATION [4]

EMORY S. BOGARDUS

The recent extensive development of intercultural education in the United States has generally lacked a frame of reference. Its exponents have participated in it without fully realizing all of its possibilities. The intercultural workshop, as an aspect of intercultural education, has suffered for lack of a frame of reference. It is proposed here that such an identifying dynamism may be found in the acculturation process. This functional process appears in three types: (1) a speeded-up melting-pot procedure, (2) a hit-or-miss deterministic type, and (3) a democratic type involving cultural pluralism. Intercultural education takes on greatly enlarged and new functional meaning when seen as an aspect of democratic, pluralistic acculturation.

This third type of acculturation treats all culture patterns as meritorious until proved otherwise. It encourages the development of all culture patterns to their full stature and then judges them on their worth as agents for the growth and enrichment of human personality and of group life. It treats the human bearers of culture patterns fairly under all circumstances and ordinarily gives them agreeable working, housing, and living conditions, so that unaware to themselves, they gradually become integrated members of the group into which they have migrated and their full-grown culture patterns have contributed naturally to the making of an enlarged and well-functioning culture system.

Informal intercultural education takes place in daily experience. The average citizen, however, is likely to see an immigrant's culture in its more or less superficial aspects. He sees it in peculiar and unpleasant expressions. A disagreeable trait of an immigrant may becloud his excellent culture patterns. It is only when the native

[4] Emory S. Bogardus, "Intercultural Education and Acculturation," *Sociology and Social Research,* Vol. 34 (Jan., 1950), pp. 203-208. Used by permission of the Journal.

understands all the backgrounds of an immigrant culture that he enters into rapport with the given immigrant and his people. The native who possesses a measure of good will is likely to learn to understand the culture of an immigrant through daily contacts with him.

Travel, as well as daily experiences at home with immigrants, may afford natives real intercultural education. The traveler who goes to other lands with attitudes of trying to understand a people and their culture in their own environment usually experiences great strides in intercultural education. But the tourist who goes hurriedly and without a deep comprehension of culture differences and of the reasons for these differences is likely to magnify the unpleasant aspects of the living conditions of a people, to pity rather than to develop a fellow feeling, and to have his prejudices magnified.

A realistic interpretation of intercultural education has been given by Dr. Tanner G. Duckrey. He states that

intercultural education is an intentional effort, through education, to build in children and youth an understanding of the total cultural pattern of American life, its diversities, and common ideals. It attempts to increase the respect of people for one another and for the groups to which they belong. It attempts to set up, cooperatively, democratic living and working conditions among people of different faiths, racial strains, nationality backgrounds, and socio-economic conditions.

In the foregoing statement there will be noted an emphasis on the total cultural pattern and on each culture trait as affected by the whole culture, on building mutual and widespread respect for differences in culture systems within the total culture of the human race, and on a comprehensiveness which includes religion, ethnic nature, nationalities, social and economic systems—or, in short, an emphasis on many kinds of ideologies.

Planned intercultural education may take place on a large scale. An excellent procedure has been called the Springfield Plan, although Springfield Procedures would be a better name. In Springfield, Massachusetts, a city with a population of 160,000 and with many minority groups, Superintendent John Granrud and his associates a few years ago inaugurated "an all-out campaign against intolerance and prejudice." The idea was not the usual and formal one of teaching and lecturing pupils to be tolerant, but it centered in action. The teachers, principals, and other persons connected with the whole public school system became "living exponents of the democratic way." These leaders "act as examples" and thus teach, not simply by precept, but by daily behavior.

When children hear other children called opprobrious names, such as those frequently applied to the children of minority groups, they often repeat these obnoxious terms, and when they hear kindly names applied to these same children they do likewise. On the other hand, the Springfield Plan is a procedure not only of saying helpful things but doing thoughtful deeds. The children catch the spirit: A pupil complains that "some of the kids are calling names in the playground." "What do you think we ought to do about it?" asks the principal. "Well, maybe we can print a sign in the classroom, asking the kids not to call names in the playground." This was done, and as a result of many kindred activities the children learned to "accept each other for what they are worth, regardless of how they spell their names."

It is recognized in Springfield that the schools cannot go far in teaching democracy by example without the cooperation of the community. Hence, Dr. Granrud developed an adult education program as a complementary procedure to the school plan. Moreover, the teachers in the public schools work directly with the parents. When they find that a child's racial intolerance stems from his home, then the situation is explained to the parents and their cooperation with the school plan is earnestly encouraged. In the words of Dr. Granrud, "There is no place in America for racial or religious intolerance or for discriminatory practices, whether they be social, economic, or political."

A particular development in the field of intercultural education is the intercultural workshop. It is an institution for the training of teachers and other community leaders in practicing cultural democracy. It has as its antecedent the educational workshop, which came into operation about 1935 in the United States.

The intercultural workshop is a laboratory for studying what needs to be done to promote intercultural education. One of its basic problems is: What can be done to develop proper social attitudes and beliefs in the younger generation? It has a specific setting and equipment including a selected library of its own. The workshop room is equipped with tables and chairs, bulletin boards, audio-visual education devices, for informal meetings and discussion periods. It has its own staff and a corps of consultants who are community leaders.

The organization of the workshop includes a planning committee to provide the different kinds of experience needed by the members and to work out programs for meetings, which include shop conferences, lectures, exhibits, field trips, audio-visual programs, discussion group meetings. Each member has an individual project, or two or three persons join in a common project. These projects are interrelated; they are integrated into the total workshop plans. The members of the workshop eat together and if possible occupy the same general quarters and develop a unity of spirit as far as the methods of intercultural education are concerned.

The fundamental aim of the intercultural workshop is "the intercultural development of the personalities of youth." It devises educational procedures for establishing attitudes of fair play toward the members of all ethnic groups as individual beings, for building into human character the spirit of ethnic good will, for encouraging everyone to participate democratically in social situations as they arise.

In an experimental design carried out recently at the University of Southern California, it was found that an experimental group of graduate students who participated for a period of six weeks in an intercultural workshop experienced a definite change of attitudes in the direction of ethnic understanding, while a control group of graduate students who were matched with the experimental group on a number of points experienced no change. The amount of change on the part of the experimental group was found to exist without any decrease nine months after the workshop had closed.

Intercultural education must contend with ethnic enclavement. Culture systems naturally become enclaved, that is, enclosed by different, and by what are believed to be dangerous, culture patterns. In order to secure a degree of permanence for a group's culture its leaders work to prevent acculturation, for acceptance of what are considered "poor" or "lower" culture patterns will effect a deterioration in the given group's prized ways of doing and believing. In a city like Chicago, for instance, there are many culture "islands" where culture patterns are enclosed or enclaved by deprecated patterns of other ethnic groups. In a province such as Nova Scotia for example, the Catholic Scotch and the Presbyterian Scotch have lived side by side in adjoining counties for generations, but the differences in religious patterns prevent acculturation in other fields too.

Culture differences became imbedded in sentiments that are identified with what has been tried in the past and found effective. They are continued in the form of defense reactions against what appears to be undesirable and probable deteriorative effects. They are often maintained through ignorance and lack of techniques for participating in a larger cultural unity. When the members of different enclaved cultures get together in an intercultural workshop with its atmosphere of spontaneity and its lack of insecurity and of fear, then they come to appreciate the meaning of a larger cultural unity and of the acculturation process on its mutually helpful levels, and they perceive the advantages of stimulating their respective groups to move in such a general direction.

In studying cultures in Guatemala, Morris Siegel found a number of factors which prevent acculturation; these are probably characteristics of many regions in the world and indicate the nature of the problems that intercultural workshops face if they are to be developed widely. Outstanding in Guatemala (as well as elsewhere) is the practice of "white racial superiority" which hinders acculturation. In the second place, social mobility is blocked—politically, economically, educationally, and socially. Perhaps a better example today might be found in South Africa or even in certain parts of the United States. When social immobility is imposed on a minority group, it cannot demonstrate its worth. Moreover, the activities of an agency such as an intercultural workshop are unwelcome. Another way in which acculturation is artificially but effectively blocked is through the legal prevention of intermarriage. A legal procedure of this type is usually overcome when peoples of different cultures learn to respect the culture patterns of one another. In developing mutual respect for cultural systems, intercultural workshops are significant factors in bringing about changes in legal restrictions. To the extent that the members of intercultural workshops recognize the nature and origins of resistances to acculturation are they able to overcome these restrictions and to release the inhibitions that accompany them.

The members of an intercultural workshop are wise if they study carefully and seek to understand the nature of the factors that go into the making of different cultures. Stewart G. Cole has pointed out four such factors. These may be stated in modified form as follows: (1) ideas about race and how race becomes popularly fixated in culture patterns, (2) ideas about nationality and how these become involved in cultures, (3) ideas about religion and how religious beliefs and sentiments become ingrained in cultures, (4) ideas about socioeconomic status systems and how these become identified with cultures. Thus, in a consideration of factors and forces such as the aforementioned, an intercultural workshop has a large discussion field mapped out for its preliminary meetings.

The aim of the intercultural workshop is not to achieve complete acculturation. It does not seek to do away with cultural diversity. Its aim is to create and establish mutual respect and mutual understanding of diverse culture patterns. It would stimulate as much diversity as is consistent with unified effort based on mutual respect and understanding.

Perhaps the chief opportunity of the intercultural workshop as at present organized, is in the teaching profession. Its acculturation role is such as to justify the organization of enough intercultural workshops so that at least the majority of public school teachers can have the opportunity of becoming participants. The intercultural workshop may become a leading acculturation agency throughout the world. Its strength lies in its indirect, informal, even nondirective methods.

The essence of intercultural education which spells acculturation is found in the social relationships fostered between various participating groups. If the members of different culture groups can be stimulated to develop honest desires "to understand the other person" and "to face candidly the realities" of culture differences, then intercultural education will have performed its major function.

In countless ways intercultural education, largely informal, advances the process of democratic, pluralistic acculturation. Without such informal educational procedures it is doubtful whether acculturation can take place except in a compulsory or in a hit-or-miss-way. With it, acculturation becomes an effectively democratic process.

PROBLEMS FOR STUDY AND DISCUSSION

1. List the five organizations that you think are doing the most to improve ethnic relations in the United States, and give reasons for your selection of each group.

2. Select one of the organizations that is included in the reading by Blythe for intensive study. Explain, analyze, and criticize the program of the organization selected.

3. Outline and explain several of the techniques that have been used by the NCCJ in its attempt to improve intergroup relations in the United States.

4. Explain why adult education is important if ethnic relations are to be improved in the United States.

5. Give reasons why you agree or disagree with the statement quoted by Reddick from a speech by Lyman Bryson.

6. Outline and explain an educational program that you think would aid in the improvement of ethnic relations in the United States.

7. Point out and discuss the outstanding problems that are involved in the use of public relations techniques in attempting to improve ethnic relations.

SELECTED READINGS

ALLPORT, Gordon W., Editor, "Controlling Group Prejudices," *Annals of the American Academy of Political and Social Science,* Vol. 244 (March, 1946).

BROWN, F. J., and ROUCEK, J. S., *One America* (New York: Prentice-Hall, Inc., 1952), pp. 575-624.

BUNCHE, Ralph J., "Programs of Organizations Devoted to the Improvement of the Status of the American Negro," *Journal of Negro Education,* Vol. 8 (July, 1939), pp. 539-550.

CLINCHY, Everett R., "A New Concept for Human Relations in America," *Bulletin of the Bureau of Social Service* (College of Education, University of Kentucky, Vol. 14 (1947), pp. 488-493.

FINEBERG, Solomon A., *Overcoming Anti-Semitism* (New York: Harper and Brothers, 1943).

JOHNSON, Charles S., "National Organizations in the Field of Race Relations," *The Annals of the American Academy of Political and Social Science*, Vol. 244 (March, 1946), pp. 117-127.

MARDEN, Charles F., *Minorities in American Society* (New York: American Book Company, 1952), pp. 461-480.

President's Committee on Civil Rights. *To Secure These Rights* (Washington: Government Printing Office, 1947).

ROSE, Arnold M., "You Can't Legislate Against Prejudice, Or Can You," *Common Ground*, Vol. 9, No. 3 (1949), pp. 61-67.

WATSON, Goodwin, *Action for Unity* (New York: Harper and Brothers, 1947).

WILLIAMS, R. M., Jr., *The Reduction of Intergroup Tensions* (New York: Social Science Research Council, 1947).

XV
Trends in Ethnic Relations

SINCE THE termination of World War II, it has been possible to discern a number of significant changes in ethnic relations and legislation. Changes in legal interpretations often symbolize new landmarks in social attitudes. In retrospect the changes are of such great magnitude that a decade previous to 1945, few of the trends could have been anticipated. The high courts and action groups have stood for definite modifications of practices defined as undemocratic. Minority groups have accepted democracy in both its form and content; hence, practices that have fallen short of the ideal of democracy have been challenged. It may be worth noting that none of the radical or totalitarian ideologies have had any significant support from the minority groups discussed in this book. Minority groups want a free and open society where individuals may rise in the social order according to their particular gifts; hence, minority members want more democracy to make possible the reward of individual effort. Minority groups are likely to be aware of the fact that totalitarian governments have been very willing to make use of racism as a policy of expediency whenever necessary. In the United States, public opinion is committed to democratic practices among all members of society; however, there is some understandable disagreement as to the best methods for attaining the goals. This brief summary of ethnic trends is made to orient the reader to the pace at which old patterns are being challenged and, in some instances, supplemented by new ones.

1. Transportation

On June 3, 1946, in the *Morgan v. Virginia* case, the United States Supreme Court ruled in a 6 to 1 decision that segregation on interstate busses placed an undue burden on interstate commerce where uniformity is necessary for the smooth and unimpeded operation of bus carriers. In October, 1944, Mrs. Irene Morgan was convicted on a charge of disorderly conduct inasmuch as she did not accept a seat in the rear of the bus. In this southern state the usual pattern has been to seat Negroes and whites in separate sections of busses and trains. As a result interstate carriers had to segregate passengers if the route passed through a southern state. Drivers of busses could be prosecuted if they did not enforce the segregated seating of white and colored passengers.

On the matter of segregating passengers in the dining car the United States Supreme Court ruled on June 5, 1950, that the railroads on interstate travel could not segregate passengers because of race. The high court did not favor the policy of reserving a table for Negroes in dining cars. It pointed out that such a practice serves only to call attention to a social classification of passengers holding identical tickets and using a common public dining facility. Segregation of passengers violates Section 3, subsection 1 of the Interstate Commerce Act. Under the statute it is unlawful for any railroad to force persons to any undue or unreasonable prejudice or disadvantage. It appears that the United States Supreme Court is not favoring segregation where the matter involves federal regulation, i.e. interstate commerce.

In November, 1952, the United States Supreme Court ruled that "Jim Crow" railroad cars, which separate Negroes from white passengers, are unconstitutional. The decision was rendered in the case of *Atlantic Coast Line Railroad v. Chance*. Chance, a Negro school principal of North Carolina, was arrested for refusing to change from a white to a Negro coach in 1948. He filed a case in the lower court, which rendered a decision in his favor. The Atlantic Coast Line appealed the decision of the lower court to the United States Supreme Court.[1] Thus, it appears as if the segregation of passengers on railroad trains is in process of legal termination.

2. The White Primary

In the case of *Smith v. Allwright* the United States Supreme Court in 1944 ruled *that the white primary was an effort to deprive the Negro of his franchise to vote and a violation of the Fifteenth Amend-*

[1] *Chance v. Lambeth, et al.,* 186 F. 2nd 879; and *Atlantic Coast Line R.R. v. Chance,* U.S. Court of Appeals, 198 F. 2. 549.

ment.[2] The high court pointed out that the primary in Texas was an integral part of the machinery for choosing officials. It was not until the 1946 primaries that the southern states actually faced the implications of the *Smith v. Allwright* decision. Mississippi, South Carolina, and Alabama adopted various measures to preserve the principle of the white primary. South Carolina quickly repealed all state laws relating to the primary and therefore left the management of nominations to party authorities. However in the case of *Elmore v. Rice* in 1947, Judge J. W. Waring dismissed the idea that the Democratic party should be regarded as a private club.

Alabama attempted to circumvent the termination of the white primary with the intensification of the literacy test, the so-called Boswell amendment to the state constitution. The amendment carried by 89,163 to 76,843 and thus received the support of 53.7 per cent of those casting a vote on the measure. The voters of Alabama seemed pretty well divided on the matter. Counties with the highest percentage of Negro population were the most enthusiastic for the Boswell amendment. In January, 1949, a special three-judge federal district court composed of native sons of Alabama ruled that the amendment was unconstitutional. Needless to say the United States Supreme Court declined to overrule the lower court's decision on the matter.

Georgia's Governor, Herman Talmadge, has attempted to restore some aspect of the white primary, but to date has been unsuccessful. Arkansas attempted to devise two primaries, one for the election of state officials and the other one for the election of federal officials. The plan became so involved that several efforts have been made to repeal the dual primary. Mississippi's principal attempt has been to challenge the Negro applicant to read and interpret the constitution. However, the South for the most part has given up the white primary as a means of denying the vote to the Negro. The passing of the white primary marks the end of one form of political discrimination and thus an inferior legal status for the Negro.

3. Educational Facilities

Since the Gaines decision in 1938, which ruled that each state must provide equal educational facilities *within* the state, every state in

[2] For an adequate discussion of the white primary see V. O. Key, Jr., *Southern Politics* (New York: Alfred A. Knopf, Inc., 1949), chap. 29.

the South has been vulnerable to the criticism of "separate but not equal" education for Negroes and whites. The first genuine case brought to the United States Supreme Court to test this policy was made in the *Sipuel v. Oklahoma*. Miss Ada Sipuel in January of 1946 applied for entrance to the law school at the University of Oklahoma and was denied admission solely because of her race. She had a superior undergraduate record from Langston University. After two years of court battles through county, state, and, finally the United States Supreme Court, a decision was rendered on January 12, 1948 that ordered Oklahoma to admit Miss Ada Sipuel to the University of Oklahoma or provide equal educational facilities for her. It was thought, at first, that the court's decision had broken the segregation restrictions in Oklahoma, since less than three weeks remained before the Spring Semester registration period. However, on January 20, 1948, the State Regents of Oklahoma provided a "law school" for Negroes as a branch of Langston University, the Negro institution. The new school of law consisted of two rooms, three white professors, and the library in the state capitol. On January 27, 1948, Miss Ada Sipuel was refused admittance to the University of Oklahoma, since the new law school had been created for Negroes in the state capitol building. On January 29, 1948, six Negro candidates applied for admission in graduate and professional courses at the University of Oklahoma. They, of course, were refused admittance. It is especially significant to recall that at this time Langston University was not accredited by any recognized agency; hence the impossibility of building a graduate program of studies upon such a feeble foundation.

On January 31, 1948, two other state universities admitted Negroes to specialized courses. The University of Arkansas admitted Clifford Davis as the first Negro student in the law school. The Board of Trustees of the University of Delaware opened all divisions of the university to Negroes if instruction was not available in the Negro institution. The Sipuel case had broken the cultural fence of segregation in several southern states.

On October 7, 1948, the Attorney General of Oklahoma recommended that the Board of Regents of the State university "admit the Negro or close the Graduate School of Education." On October 12, George W. McLaurin, a retired professor from Langston University, entered the University of Oklahoma, as the first Negro to work toward a doctorate in the School of Education. His entrance paved the way for Miss Sipuel's entrance. McLaurin was admitted to the university on a segregated basis and many details of his life on the campus were unique and actually preferential. On December 4, 1948, the University of Missouri curators asked that legislation be enacted to admit Negroes to the institution in specialized areas of study.

Housing facilities have been planned for Negroes attending the University of Oklahoma. The Board of Regents of the University of Oklahoma directed its president to develop sufficient dormitory space for colored students. During the Spring Semester of 1952 more than one hundred Negroes attended the university. Blanket certification for Negro students who desire to do graduate work leading toward either a master's or a doctor's degree has been granted by the Oklahoma Regents of Higher Education. There is no question concerning the trend toward integrated education in the borderline states. Oklahoma a few years ago excluded all Negroes from its state university and at the present time accepts Negro candidates in a majority of the professional majors.

On June 5, 1950, the United States Supreme Court ruled in the Sweatt case that a law school cannot be created by legislation in haste and then assume that it "equals" an established law school. H. M. Sweatt had applied for admission to the law school of the University of Texas and was denied admission because he was a Negro. This denial of admission of Mr. Sweatt was tested in the courts. Chief Justice Fred M. Vinson noted that the law school at the University of Texas possessed certain qualities difficult to measure but important including: reputation of the faculty, influence of the alumni, prestige, and the experience of the administration in conducting a law school. In 1952 there were more than forty Negro students in attendance at the University of Texas. In addition, two other colleges and three junior colleges in Texas have opened their doors to qualified Negro students.

A most important issue was debated before the United States Supreme Court during the closing weeks of December, 1952. Is *segregation* of white and Negro pupils in the public schools *per se* unconstitutional? This question had been presented to the lower courts of the District of Columbia and in the states of Kansas, South Carolina, and Virginia. These four cases were aimed at the "separate but equal facilities" doctrine, which holds that segregation in itself is not discriminatory. Thurgood Marshall, representing the Negro side, through the National Association for the Advancement of Colored People, argued the state segregation laws violate the Fourteenth Amendment's promise of "equal protection of the law." He observed that if Ralph Bunche were assigned to South Carolina his children would have to go to a Jim Crow school. In defense of segregation John W. Davis argued that the Fourteenth Amendment has nothing to do with the right of a state to classify pupils in its public schools on the basis of sex or age or mental capacity or race.[3]

If the United States Supreme Court rules that racial segregation in the public schools is unconstitutional, a number of Southern leaders have threatened private action to perpetuate the principle of segregation. For instance, Governor James Byrnes remarked: "South Carolina will not, now nor for some years to come, mix white and colored children in our schools. If the court changes what is now the law of the land so that we cannot maintain segregation . . . we will abandon the public school system. To do that would be choosing the lesser of two great evils."[4] It is planned in South Carolina to turn the public schools over to churches and other private groups if segregation must be legally terminated in public education. Under Governor Herman Talmadge the Georgia legislature decided that any school district which did not provide separate schools would automatically lose its state funds. It appears that regardless of the decision of the high court there is considerable evidence to support the thesis that some of the states in the South will not give up racial segregation. Thurgood Marshall concedes that the blow to segregation might be lessened by redistricting so that most Negroes would attend one school and most whites another. Thus, the N.A.A.C.P. demands a basic change in the legal status of racial segregation, but favors an evolutionary acceptance of the termination of segregation. If the high court sustains racial segregation, the N.A.A.C.P. will probably demand a more "mathematic" definition of "equality" where separate facilities are provided for both ethnic groups. On this subject President Dwight D. Eisenhower has expressed, on numerous occasions, alarm concerning the generality of ethnic segregation. In fact, both Eisenhower and Truman have appointed commissions to study various aspects of segregation. One aspect of this question became the first matter of business in the 83rd Congress and almost upset the Congress into angry factions prior to President Eisenhower's inauguration.

3 *Time* (December 22, 1952), p. 12.
4 *Ibid.*, p. 12.

4. Regional Educational Proposals

Largely as a result of the Gaines and Sipuel cases the South has attempted to devise a way around the admittance of Negroes to white state universities and colleges. On February 7 and 8 (1948) at Wakulla Springs, Florida, the Southern Governors' Conference on Regional Education convened. Nine states signed a pact to consider the advisability of providing specialized and graduate education for colored and white students on a regional and segregated basis. The following states constituted the signers of this important document. Alabama, Arkansas, Georgia, Florida, Texas, Maryland, Mississippi, Tennessee, and South Carolina. Other states in the South have come into the plan as it has developed. The regional plan for segregated education envisions the support of selected professional schools including the following: medicine, dentistry, veterinary medicine, engineering, and perhaps law.

In June, 1949, the program was established on a permanent basis through the creation of a Board of Control. The Board serves as the contracting agency between the states on the one hand and the institution on the other. States pay $1,500 per year for medical and dental students and $1,000 for veterinary medical training. The money goes to the service institution. Each state acquires a quota of places at an institution, but the university selects the students from a list in accordance with its own standards. In the first year's operation of the plan, places for 388 students—181 Negroes and 207 whites— were provided under stipulated regional contracts. The academic year 1950-51 shows 545 places, 377 for whites and 168 for Negroes. Among the universities participating in the regional plan for medical, dental, and veterinary medicine are: Alabama Polytechnic, Duke University, Emory University, Louisiana State University, Medical College of Virginia, Meharry Medical College, Oklahoma A and M, Tuskegee Institute, University of Georgia, University of Maryland, University of Tennessee, Vanderbilt University, University of Alabama, and Texas A and M.[5]

The constitutionality of regional education has not been tested in the United States Supreme Court. It appears that regional education does not answer the requirement stated in the Gaines case, namely that equal educational opportunities must be provided

[5] For a careful examination of the implications of regional education see *The Crisis,* Vol. 57, No. 10 (Nov., 1950).

within the state. However, it is obvious that a state without a medical college may send ten of its residents to a state with a medical college for only $15,000 per year. The cost of a medical school whether segregated or not would run in the millions.[6]

5. Restrictive Covenants

On May 3, 1948, in the case of *Shelley v. Kraemer*, the United States Supreme Court handed down a decision that made headline copy from Maine to California. Chief Justice Vinson delivered the opinion of the court, which may be summarized in the following statement:

We conclude, therefore that the restrictive agreements standing alone cannot be regarded as a violation of any rights guaranteed to petitioners by the Fourteenth Amendment. So long as the purposes of those agreements are effectuated by voluntary adherence to their terms, it would appear clear there has been no action by the State and the provisions of the Amendment have not been violated. ... But here there was more. These are cases in which the purposes of the agreements were secured only by judicial enforcement by state courts of the restrictive terms of the agreements. The respondents urge that judicial enforcement of private agreements does not amount to state action; or, in any event, the participation of the State is so attenuated in character as not to amount to state action within the meaning of the Fourteenth Amendment.... These are cases in which the states have made available to such individuals the full coercive power of government to deny to petitioners on the grounds of race or color, the enjoyment of property rights in premises which petitioners are willing and financially able to acquire and which the granters are willing to sell. Hence, the states have denied petitioners the equal protection of the laws and the state action cannot stand.[7]

In other words, restrictive racial convenants are valid but not enforceable in state courts. The cultural fence surrounding ethnic neighborhoods has been lowered by this decision. Non-Caucasians may buy wherever a seller was willing, regardless of previous neighborhood agreements against selected ethnic groups. It might be observed that racial restrictive convenants are as effective as the property owner who believed least in them.[8]

[6] It might be of interest to realize that the State of California has appropriated a sum of $15,000,000 for a medical school on the Los Angeles campus. The cost of such medical schools is doubled if two "equal" medical schools are to be organized in every southern state. Segregation in professional schools is an economic luxury few southern states can afford, especially the small states.

[7] Quoted from *Supreme Court of the United States*, Nos. 72 and 87 (Oct. Term, 1947). Decision published May 3, 1948. Justices Reed, Jackson, and Rutledge took no part in the consideration or decision of this case.

[8] Other devices which have been suggested to circumvent the intent of the *Shelley v. Kraemer* decision are: (1) broker's agreements to sell to a selected ethnic group, (2) mortgage preference to particular ethnic groups, (3) leasehold system which restricts the use of the property for 99 years to designated ethnic groups, and (4) the "club membership" device.

6. Negro in Athletics

Signing Jackie Robinson on the team of the Dodgers a few years ago opened a new door of opportunity to deserving Negro athletes. Branch Rickey knew that the integration of Negroes in professional baseball would add competition to the game and perhaps increase the attendance at these contests. In boxing and track Negroes have had a conspicuous role, but certain sports were "off limits" to Negroes. Golf, tennis, and bowling were strictly "off limits" to Negroes and a few other non-Caucasian groups. However, the following are among the Negroes in professional baseball: Jackie Robinson, Brooklyn Dodgers; Don Newcombe, Brooklyn pitcher, Roy Campanella, Brooklyn catcher; Sam Jethroe, Boston Braves' outfielder; Larry Doby, Cleveland outfielder; Luke Easter, Cleveland Indians; The New York Giants have Monte Irvin, Willie Mays, and Henry Thompson. In professional football the names of George Taliaferro, Buddy Young, and Marion Motley are important. Althea Gibson has participated in a number of national tennis tournaments.[9] Tremendous changes have been occurring on the field of sport where persons of diverse ethnic background compete against each other. Recently, in the Texas Baseball League two Negroes have been added to the Dallas team, and in the Gulf Coast League the Galveston club secured a Negro player.

7. Civil Rights Program

November 2, 1948 will be remembered for a long time. Inasmuch as the political leaders from the deep South could not accept Mr. Truman's stand on civil rights, they formed their own party, the Dixiecrats. One of the popular magazines referred to the revolt in July as the gloomiest parallel since the South rebelled against Stephen Douglas in 1860. The President had fought a hard battle on specific criticisms of the 80th Congress, especially the Taft-Hartley legislation, high prices, and the need for compulsory health insurance. Yet, perhaps the most significant stand of the President was his complete endorsement without qualification of his civil-rights program including the following tenets: (1) safety and security, (2) citizenship, (3) freedom of conscience and expression, and (4) equality of opportunity. No other president had been so frank in speaking against ethnic prejudice.

[9] See the article "We're Winning the One that Counts," *Look* (Dec. 19, 1950).

It is worth observing that Truman's civil-rights program has not been enacted. In the general elections in the Fall of 1950 the Republicans and Democrats split about even in the Senate and there was a close margin in the House of Representatives. The Dixiecrat Democrats held the balance of power on matters of ethnic relations. The opposition to granting statehood to Hawaii was fought on the issue of ethnic relations. Hawaii with its freedom from ethnic conflict challenged some of the conservative Senators from the deep South.[10] In the Fall of 1950, ethnic relations became one of the major issues in spite of the Korean war and the gradual move toward national mobilization. The 1952 political platforms of both major political parties considered this important question as one of the paramount issues of the campaign. No doubt both parties attempted to win as many votes as possible by stressing particular aspects of this controversial problem. It appears that on the matter of civil rights both Republican and Democratic parties endorsed the idea of federal and state coöperation. It may be of some importance to note that neither party used the term FEPC. For comparative purposes the essentials of both platforms on civil rights are quoted:

Democratic. We favor Federal legislation effectively to secure these rights to everyone: (1) the right to equal opportunity for employment, (2) the right to security of persons, (3) the right to full and equal participation in the nation's political life. . . . We urge that action be taken at the beginning of the 83rd Congress to improve Congressional procedures so that majority rule prevails and decisions can be made after reasonable debate without being blocked by a minority in either house.

Republican. We believe that it is the primary responsibility of each State to order and control its own domestic institutions, and this power, reserved to the States, is essential to the maintenance of our Federal republic. However, we believe that the Federal government should take supplemental action within its constitutional jurisdiction to oppose discrimination against race, religion or national origin. . . . We will prove our good faith by . . . enacting Federal legislation to further just and equitable treatment in the area of discriminatory employment practices. Federal action should not duplicate State efforts to end such practices. . . .

President Dwight D. Eisenhower in his "State of the Union" message delivered on February 2, 1953 made several significant observations concerning ethnic relations in the United States. These words of the President of the United States have added meaning when it is realized that communist dominated governments of Europe have

[10] It is of interest to recall that a Gallup public opinion poll for December 10, 1950 indicated that 71 per cent of the respondents were for Hawaii's statehood. In 1941 only 48 per cent were for statehood for Hawaii.

apparently resumed the inclusive persecution of the Jews in almost the same manner as the Nazis. Briefly the President observed:

Our civil and social rights form a central part of the heritage we are striving to defend on all fronts and with all our strength.

I believe with all my heart that our vigilant guarding of these rights is a sacred obligation binding upon every citizen. To be true to one's own freedom is—in essence—to honor and respect the freedom of all others.

A cardinal ideal in this heritage we cherish is the equality of rights of all citizens of every race and color and creed.

We know that discrimination against minorities persists despite our allegiance to this ideal. Such discrimination—confined to no one section of the nation—is but the outward testimony to the persistence of distrust and of fear in the hearts of men.

This fact makes all the more vital the fighting of these wrongs by each individual, in every station of life, in his every deed.

Much of the answer lies in the power of fact, fully publicized; of persuasion, honestly pressed, and of conscience, justly aroused. These are methods familiar to our way of life, tested and proven wise.

I propose to use whatever authority exists in the Office of the President to end segregation in the District of Columbia, including the Federal government, and any segregation in the armed forces.

Here in the District of Columbia, serious attention should be given to the proposal to develop and authorize, through legislation, a system to provide an effective voice in local self-government. While consideration of this proceeds, I recommend an immediate increase of two in the number of District Commissioners to broaden representation of all elements of our population. This will be a first step toward insuring that this capital provide an honored example to all communities of our nation.

In this manner, and by the leadership of the Office of the President exercised through friendly conferences with those in authority in our States and cities, we expect to make true and rapid progress in civil rights and equality of employment opportunity.

There is one sphere in which civil rights are inevitably involved in Federal immigration.

It is a manifest right of our government to limit the number of immigrants our nation can absorb. It is also a manifest right of our government to set reasonable requirements on the character and the numbers of the people who come to share our land and our freedom.

It is well for us, however, to remind ourselves occasionally of an equally manifest fact: We are—one and all—immigrants or sons and daughters of immigrants.

Existing legislation contains injustices. It does, in fact, discriminate. I am informed by members of the Congress that it was realized at the time of its enactment that future study of the basis of determining quotas would be necessary.

I am therefore requesting the Congress to review this legislation and to enact a statute that will at one and the same time guard our legitimate national interests and be faithful to our basic ideas of freedom and fairness to all.

8. Prohibition of Interracial Marriages Rescinded in California

On October 1, 1948, California's law prohibiting the marriage of Caucasian persons to those of Negro, Mongolian, or Malayan origin was declared invalid by the State Supreme Court in a 4 to 3 decision in the Davis-Perez case. In August of 1947, Sylvester S. Davis, a Negro, and Andrea D. Perez, a Mexican, filed a petition for a *writ of mandamus* against the Los Angeles County officials in their effort to compel the County to issue the couple a marriage certificate. Both of the petitioners were Roman Catholics and the Church aided in fighting the case for them. Deputy Counsel Charles C. Stanley contended that interracial marriages are inimical to peace, good order, and the morals of society. However, Daniel G. Marshall, counsel for the plaintiffs, refuted most of the arguments of Mr. Stanley and cited numerous authorities in the field of anthropology. The California Supreme Court ruled that marriage is something more than a civil contract subject to regulation by the state, that it is definitely a fundamental right of free men.[11]

One of the senior author's students, Mr. Randall Risdon, made a careful study of the number of interracial marriages that took place in the metropolitan Los Angeles area during the first year after the State Supreme Court's decision in the Davis-Perez case. Upon a careful check of the marriage license applications he found that one hundred interracial marriages had taken place. He pointed out that the relative significance of the one hundred cases of interracial marriages in the Los Angeles metropolitan area became more evident when these marriages were compared with the total license applications issued. This latter figure was 21,060, and, for all practical purposes, it may be assumed that an application represented a marriage. This indicated interracial marriages to be .0047 per cent, or less than one in two hundred applications for marriage. Of all the interracial marriages, if the Mexican-American component were to be considered as a typical of "average" Caucasians, the figure would be further refined to 32 per cent of one per cent of the total, leaving a universe of 68 to contrast with the figure of 21,060. The ratio of interracial marriages to unclassified marriages thus becomes almost infinitesimally insignificant.

[11] Florence Murray, *The Negro Handbook of 1949* (New York: The Macmillan Company, 1949), pp. 78-79.

Risdon found upon interviewing the interracially married couples that the accommodation to society at large often rested, for the most part, on pseudo, rather than actual accommodation. From the evidence gathered it appeared to be almost a state of truce in which these people are living, not actually in a social atmosphere of acceptance. They seem to live with the feeling that social conflict in some form is always in the offing. He found that these couples are not readily welcomed as friends by most of their contacts in either race. Thus, despite frequent protestations to the contrary by interracial couples, their social contacts are most often relegated to other couples similarly married, to their more tolerant relatives, or to a few friends.[12]

9. Development of Fair Employment Legislation

President F. D. Roosevelt, on June 25, 1941, made public his Executive Order 8802 which created the Fair Employment Practice Committee as a method of reducing discrimination in defense industries. The President had been threatened with a march on Washington of some 50,000 Negroes if he did not make some concrete proposal to give defense jobs to qualified Negroes. The leader in the movement to demand the FEPC legislation was A. Philip Randolph, President of the Brotherhood of Sleeping Car Porters. Some definite progress was made in the employment of Negroes during the initial period of FEPC. However, in February, 1943, Mr. Roosevelt issued a new executive order (No. 9346) setting up a new committee with more power and authority to deal with violators. Any industry accepting a government contract was compelled to sign an agreement not to discriminate against minority members in the selection of employees.

Malcolm Ross, formerly director of the Fair Employment Practices Committee claims that the main function of the agency was to integrate all available manpower into war industry. He has written that the antidiscrimination feature was actually secondary to the need for manpower. Hence, when an industry refused to hire Negroes, it was rare that the government in a forceful way compelled conformity.[13] On the state level the fight is against discrimination and prejudice; whereas during the war period the need is the integration

[12] Randall Risdon, "Interracial Marriages in Los Angeles" (Los Angeles: University of Southern California, Aug., 1952), p. 103. Unpublished Master's Thesis.
[13] Malcolm Ross, *All Manner of Men* (New York: Reynal and Hitchcock, 1948), p. 50.

of all possible sources of manpower. War seems to be a catalyst in the process of upgrading ethnic groups in the military service and war industry.

As the war came to a close the demand to maintain a permanent FEPC failed. The Congress in April of 1946 refused to appropriate funds to maintain FEPC legislation. As a result the fight has shifted to individual states. At the present time, at least nine states have passed an enforceable fair employment practice measure. The states include: New York, New Jersey, Wisconsin, Oregon, Massachusetts, Connecticut, Washington, New Mexico, and Rhode Island. On the municipal level the following large communities may be cited: Chicago, Milwaukee, Minneapolis, Philadelphia, and Phoenix. Many of the large cities in the North have debated seriously the advisability of enacting fair employment legislation.

The state fair employment practice legislation varies from state to state in terms of punishment for violation, methods of enforcement, definitions of discrimination, and appropriations to make the legislation a functioning reality. A candid observation from some students of this innovation indicates that in some states the fair employment practice measure varies little from a resolution not to discriminate. For instance, in Milwaukee the fine does not exceed ten dollars for violating the FEPC ordinance. The task of a satisfactory fair employment practice measure involves at least the following: employment, dismissal, promotions, compensation, questions on application blanks, membership in unions, and practices of private employment services. The goals of FEPC are lofty, but the practical question centers on the success of such measures. In some instances ethnic prejudices may have been intensified by legislation designed to eliminate discrimination. Unfortunately, there are many ways around the best laws that public opinion can demand. Perhaps a campaign for fair employment in a state or city is the first step prior to the enacting of such legislation.

10. Ethnic Integration in the Armed Services

Prior to President Truman's order on integration in the armed forces, the Air Force and Navy had launched a program of integration and superior placement of men on merit rather than race. The United States Air Force has eliminated *all* segregated units and opened promotions for all personnel regardless of ethnic background. As a result the famous all-Negro fighter units have been disintegrated.

The Army Ground Force has featured a program of understanding the various minority groups through its orientation outlines and talks. The prospect of World War III brought home to the American people the importance of an integrated America and the desperate need for manpower regardless of ethnic ancestry. Since the Red Chinese and Russians threaten America with an almost unlimited manpower pool, integration of all ethnic groups in a common defense of the American democracy has become a reality. Survival is possible by the unification of the many facets of our way of life.

SUMMARY

These last several years give much promise for ethnic democracy. We can see "race" being discarded at the polls, on transportation facilities, the academic halls of learning, and in the armed forces. During the last decade with the constant aid of action groups the President of the United States and the United States Supreme Court have focused public sentiment in the direction of applied democracy, especially in matters of ethnic relations. We have made probably the greatest progress of any modern nation in testing the traditional assumptions that ethnic differences and social inequality are inherently linked. After completing a 6,000-mile trip of thirteen southern states in the Winter of 1951, Carl Rowan, reporter for the *Minneapolis Tribune*, concluded: "A dying generation of the Old South will not give [segregation] up without bitterness. A misled portion of the new generation will not relinquish segregation without a battle. . . . But it is evident that soon—very soon—segregation will vanish." [14]

PROBLEMS FOR STUDY AND DISCUSSION

1. Review ethnic relations as reported in *Time* or *Newsweek* for the past six weeks.
2. In the last year, what motion picture was devoted to the problem of race relations? What were the strong and weak features in this production?
3. What were some of the overtures made by Eisenhower and Stevenson to "win" support among minority members during the 1952 presidential campaign?

[14] *Time* (March 12, 1951), p. 51. It may be of some interest that Carl Rowan was one of the very few Negroes to be commissioned in the V12 program during World War II.

4. In what particular ways are democratic principles and ethnic relations closely related?
5. What is the most recent United States Supreme Court decision on some phase of ethnic relations? What are the implications of this decision to the American people?

SELECTED READINGS

BERRY, Brewton, *Race Relations* (Boston: Houghton Mifflin and Company, 1951).

BROWN, Francis J., and ROUCEK, Joseph S., *One America* (New York: Prentice-Hall, Inc., 1952).

MARDEN, Charles F., *Minorities in American Society* (New York: American Book Company, 1952).

SCHERMERHORN, R. A., *These Our People* (Boston: D. C. Heath and Company, 1949).

ROSE, Arnold and Caroline, *America Divided* (New York: Alfred A. Knopf, Inc., 1948).

WALTER, Paul A. F., Jr., *Race and Cultural Relations* (New York: McGraw-Hill Book Company, Inc., 1952).

INDEXES

Congressional Digest   *Reader's Guide*
International Index to Periodical Lit- *New York Times Index*
  erature

PERIODICALS

American Sociological Review   *Social Forces*
American Journal of Sociology   *Sociology and Social Research*

Glossary

Accommodation. A social process that permits the opposing groups to get along with each other in spite of differences and conflicts.

Alien. A foreign-born resident of a country in which he is *not* a citizen.

Amalgamation. A process in which somewhat diverse biological strains are fused, resulting in a new group. The terms miscegenation and interbreeding have similar connotations to the word amalgamation.

Anti-Semitism. Organized opposition to Jews and Jewish culture.

Attitude. A tendency to act in a particular way toward some person or value.

Caste. A group of persons who have *inherited* a common social status. This term is used generally to refer to the various endogamous groups of India.

Competition. The impersonal struggle for the symbols of high status.

Conflict. Personalized form of opposition or struggle. Neutralizing the opposition becomes the paramount issue rather than the attainment of the goal.

Denaturalization. The process or act of rescinding the rights of citizenship.

Endogamy. The practice of limiting or restricting marriage to members of a particular ethnic group, usually the in-group.

Ethnic group. A group of persons who because of a combination of physical or cultural characteristics is assigned a differential status from the majority group in a particular country. The term "ethnic" emphasizes the cultural aspects of a population group rather than the so-called biological differences.

Ethnocentrism. A common tendency to believe that one's own group is superior to other groups. In practice the standards of one's own group are used to judge other peoples and cultures.

Immigration. The voluntary movement of a population from one country to another. The refugee represents involuntary movement because of hostility. In practice the term *refugee* has been used to refer primarily to the Jews in flight from the adverse attitudes of the Nazis, whereas the term *displaced person* came into use after World War II to refer to the individual who had lost his country of residence because of the vicissitudes of modern war.

In-group. A group toward which the persons composing it have attitudes of loyalty and respect.

Invasion. The entrance into a neighborhood of a new ethnic group. Invasion usually implies that a group of lower social status enters the ecological area; however, exceptions to this statement may be observed.

Issei. Foreign-born Japanese in the United States or the *first* generation American-born Japanese.

Jews. A group of persons who identify themselves with a religious system known as Judaism. A most difficult term to use with precision. The late Professor Louis Wirth observed that a Jew was anyone who defined himself as such.

397

Kibei. American-born Japanese who have received a part of their education in Japan.

Marginal man. A person who has had the misfortune to be only partially socialized in two competing cultures. In most instances he is not completely accepted in either culture.

Miscegenation. The admixture resulting from the physical interbreeding of somewhat distinct "racial" stocks.

Nationality. A group of persons who maintain citizenship within or were born under the legal jurisdiction of a specific government.

Nisei. American-born Japanese, or the *second* generation of Japanese.

Out-group. All persons declared to be outside of one's own group. This term implies that members of the "out-group" are characterized by strangeness and inferiority.

Prejudice. Usually thought of as a negative judgment toward a group of persons based upon insufficient evidence and understanding.

Race. A large group of persons who are believed to have common *inherited* physical characteristics.

Racism. A belief system that ascribes cultural achievement to the inherent superiority of particular "races."

Restrictive Covenant. A written agreement of property owners not to sell or rent residential property to specific ethnic groups. These agreements cannot be enforced in the courts and thus represent private action of the property owners.

Sansei. American-born Japanese who represent the *third* generation.

Scapegoat. The tendency to single out a particular person or group as the cause of social maladjustment. Minority members are frequently selected as the "scapegoat" for many forms of social deviation.

Segregation. The legal separation of ethnic groups in the use of facilities that might otherwise be used in common.

Social assimilation. The absorption of persons or groups of a given culture into a larger group of somewhat different culture.

Social class. In its most elementary meaning it is a group of persons with the same status.

Social distance. The amount of sympathetic understanding existing between persons or groups of persons. The degrees of social distance range from intimacy (nearness) to exclusion (farness).

Social status. The position or rating that an individual or group receives from evaluators.

Social stereotypes. In a literal sense the term means "the pictures in our heads." In practice a stereotype is an image that is associated with a particular ethnic group. These images may be based on insufficient contact with representative members of the ethnic group. Examples from the movies might be: "the happy" Negro, "the cunning" Jew, "the intoxicated" Irishman, "the cruel" Indian, etc.

Social stratification. The arrangement of persons according to their degrees of superiority or inferiority. These degrees are usually depicted in horizontal levels.

Wetback. An illegal entrant to the United States from Mexico.

Note: More formal definitions for some of the terms defined may be found in *Dictionary of Sociology* by Henry P. Fairchild and *Handbook of Sociology* by Edward B. Reuter.

Name Index

Subject Index

Action programs, 347-380
Adult education,
  American Association for, 372
  and the improvement of race relations, 370-374
  attitude toward ethnic improvement, 370-372
  evaluation of program for improving ethnic relations, 372-373
  social responsibility of, 373-374
Alien Land Law in 1913, 278
Aliens,
  definition of, 289
  legal restrictions confronting, 307-308
American caste and class, 83-86
Americans, typical, defined, 18-19
Anti-Semitism, 154-159
  economic and religious factors and, 155-159
  emergency conference to combat, 368
Attitudes,
  development of, 35-38
  general, 34-35, 37
  of southern whites toward Negroes in the United States, 101, 109-110
  specific, 34, 35
Avoidance techniques in race relations, 129-130

Builders of Brotherhood, 363-369
  Brotherhood Week, 364
  National Conference of Christians and Jews and, 363-369
Bureau of Indian Affairs, 204, 210, 215-219

Caste,
  description of, 83
  in India, 21
  Negro, 83-86
Chinatowns, 263, 285-286
Chinese, Chap. XI
  admittance of, 265
  as laborers, 268
  assimilation of, 268-269
  attitudes toward, 266-269

Burlingame Treaty, 261, 278
  cities which show an increase in population of, 265
  classes admitted, 261-262, 267, 277
  denied naturalization rights, 276, 278
  early prejudices against, 268-269
  economic status of, 282-286
  educational status of, 280-281
  Exclusion Act, 261, 264, 277
  etiquette, 274
  immigration of, 260-261
  in California, 281
  legal status of, 276-279
  median school years completed, 280
  men as miners, 262-263
  occupational pattern of, 262, 282-284
  occupational restrictions, 284-285
  population in the United States, 260-266
  progress since the 1870's, 286
  property ownership, 278-279
  reaction to Chink or Chinaman, 272-273
  reaction to "Charlie", 273-275
  reasons for migration, 261, 267-268
  regional distribution of, 280
  repeal of Exclusion laws, 270, 279
  school attendance of, 182
  school years completed by, 252
  sex distribution of, 284
  social status of, 266-270
  types of crime, 162
  urbanization of, 263-265
Civil rights,
  Bill of 1875, 133
  program, 389-391
Commissioner of Indian Affairs, 204, 225
Court cases cited,
  Atlantic Coast Line R.R. v. Chance, U.S. Court of Appeals, 198 F.2. 549, 382
  Chance v. Lambeth, et al., 186 F.2nd 879, 382
  Davis-Perez Case, 392
  Dred Scott v. Sanford, U.S. 506 (1859), 99

403